Hurting Memories and Beneficial Forgetting

Hurting Memories and Beneficial Forgetting
Posttraumatic Stress Disorders, Biographical Developments, and Social Conflicts

Edited by

Michael Linden
*Charite University Medicine,
Berlin, Germany*

Krzysztof Rutkowski
*Jagiellonian University Medical College,
Kraków, Poland*

AMSTERDAM • BOSTON • HEIDELBERG • LONDON • NEW YORK • OXFORD
PARIS • SAN DIEGO • SAN FRANCISCO • SINGAPORE • SYDNEY • TOKYO

Elsevier
32 Jamestown Road London NW1 7BY
225 Wyman Street, Waltham, MA 02451, USA

First edition 2013

Copyright © 2013 Elsevier Inc. All rights reserved

No part of this publication may be reproduced or transmitted in any form or by any means, electronic or mechanical, including photocopying, recording, or any information storage and retrieval system, without permission in writing from the publisher. Details on how to seek permission, further information about the Publisher's permissions policies and our arrangement with organizations such as the Copyright Clearance Center and the Copyright Licensing Agency, can be found at our website: www.elsevier.com/permissions

This book and the individual contributions contained in it are protected under copyright by the Publisher (other than as may be noted herein).

Notices
Knowledge and best practice in this field are constantly changing. As new research and experience broaden our understanding, changes in research methods, professional practices, or medical treatment may become necessary.

Practitioners and researchers must always rely on their own experience and knowledge in evaluating and using any information, methods, compounds, or experiments described herein. In using such information or methods they should be mindful of their own safety and the safety of others, including parties for whom they have a professional responsibility.

To the fullest extent of the law, neither the Publisher nor the authors, contributors, or editors, assume any liability for any injury and/or damage to persons or property as a matter of products liability, negligence or otherwise, or from any use or operation of any methods, products, instructions, or ideas contained in the material herein.

British Library Cataloguing-in-Publication Data
A catalogue record for this book is available from the British Library

Library of Congress Cataloging-in-Publication Data
A catalog record for this book is available from the Library of Congress

ISBN: 978-0-12-398393-0

For information on all Elsevier publications
visit our website at store.elsevier.com

This book has been manufactured using Print On Demand technology. Each copy is produced to order and is limited to black ink. The online version of this book will show color figures where appropriate.

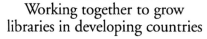

Contents

Preface		xi
List of Contributors		xv

Part One Basic Aspects — 1

1 Spectrum of Persisting Memories and Pseudomemories, Distortions, and Psychopathology — 3
Michael Linden
- 1.1 Memory Distortions and Beneficial Forgetting — 3
- 1.2 Spectrum of Psychopathological Memories, Thoughts, Images, Associations, and the Like — 4
  - 1.2.1 Intrusions — 4
  - 1.2.2 Flashbacks — 5
  - 1.2.3 Automatic Thoughts — 5
  - 1.2.4 Longing — 6
  - 1.2.5 Prejudice and Overvalued Ideas — 7
  - 1.2.6 Cognitive Rehearsal — 7
  - 1.2.7 Worrying — 8
  - 1.2.8 Hopelessness — 8
  - 1.2.9 Confabulation — 9
  - 1.2.10 Pseudologia and Wishful False Memories — 9
  - 1.2.11 Delusional Memories and Paramnesias — 10
  - 1.2.12 Obsessive Compulsive Thoughts — 10
  - 1.2.13 Thought Pressure — 11
  - 1.2.14 Rumination — 11
  - 1.2.15 Conditioned Reflex — 12
  - 1.2.16 Specific Monophobias — 12
  - 1.2.17 Explicitly or Implicitly Acquired Memories and Competencies — 13
  - 1.2.18 Developmental Learning — 13
- 1.3 Features and Development of Pathological Memories — 14
- 1.4 Conclusion — 16
- References — 17

2	**Electrophysiological Signature of Emotional Memories**	**21**
	Mathias Weymar and Alfons Hamm	
	2.1 Introduction	21
	2.2 Studying Emotional Memory in the Laboratory	21
	2.3 ERPs and Memory Retrieval	23
	2.4 Electrophysiological Correlates of Emotional Memory Retrieval	24
	2.5 ERPs of Emotional Memory After Long Retention Intervals	25
	2.6 Adrenergic Activation and the ERP Old/New Effect for Emotional Contents	27
	2.7 Neural Generators of the Parietal Old/New Effect for Emotional Pictures	30
	2.8 Conclusions	31
	References	31
3	**Pharmacological Approaches to Understand, Prevent, and Mitigate Hurting Memories. Lessons from Posttraumatic Stress Disorders**	**37**
	Hans-Peter Kapfhammer	
	3.1 Trauma and Psychological Models of Traumatic Memory	37
	3.2 Neurobiological Underpinnings of Trauma Memory Encoding, Consolidation, Retrieval, and Extinction	39
	3.3 Principal Pharmacological Strategies to Mitigate or Prevent Traumatic Memory: Results from Empirical Studies	40
	3.4 Conclusions	43
	References	44
4	**Memory and Social Meaning: The Impact of Society and Culture on Traumatic Memories**	**49**
	Nigel Hunt	
	4.1 Introduction	49
	4.2 Szechuan Earthquake	51
	4.3 World War II	52
	4.4 Spanish Civil War Memory	53
	4.5 Analysis	54
	References	56
5	**Retraumatization: The Vicious Circle of Intrusive Memory**	**59**
	Katrin Schock and Christine Knaevelsrud	
	5.1 Introduction	59
	5.2 Trauma and PTSD	59
	5.3 The Phenomenology of Traumatic Memory: Basic Principles of Psychobiology and the Fear Network	61
	5.3.1 Memory Systems	61
	5.3.2 Traumatic Memory	63
	5.3.3 Emotional Processing Theory: The Fear Network	63

	5.4	Empirical Studies on Retraumatization	64
		5.4.1 Effects of New Traumatic Events	65
		5.4.2 Effects of Trauma-Associated Stimuli	66
	5.5	Conclusions: Toward a Definition of Retraumatization	66
	References		67

6 Pathological Modes of Remembering: The PTSD Experience — 71
Michael Schönenberg

6.1	Introduction	71
6.2	Trauma Versus Life Event	71
6.3	Acute Stress Reactions	72
6.4	Posttraumatic Stress Disorder	73
6.5	General Risk Factors for PTSD	75
6.6	Cognitive Abnormalities and Memory Disturbances in PTSD	76
6.7	The Role of Metacognitive Appraisals	77
6.8	Dysfunctional Cognitive Strategies	77
6.9	Conclusions and Implications for Therapy	79
References		79

7 Hurting Memories and Intrusions in Posttraumatic Embitterment Disorders (PTED) as Compared to Posttraumatic Stress Disorders (PTSD) — 83
Michael Linden

7.1	Embitterment and Posttraumatic Embitterment Disorder	83
7.2	Revival of Events and Intrusions in the Context of Injustice and Embitterment	85
7.3	Differences Between Memories and Intrusions in PTED and PTSD	87
7.4	Conclusions	88
References		89

8 Symbolized Thinking as the Background of Toxic Memories — 93
Bohdan Wasilewski

8.1	Introduction	93
	8.1.1 Experimental Observations	97
References		102

9 False Memories — 105
Hans Stoffels

9.1	The Wilkomirski/Dössekker Case	105
9.2	Memory as Reconstruction	106
9.3	Personality and False Memories	107
9.4	Psychotherapy and Pseudomemory	108
9.5	Accusation and Recrimination	110
9.6	Criteria for Recognizing False Memories	112
References		113

10	**The Constitution of Narrative Identity**	**115**
	Theo Leydenbach	
	10.1 What Does Identity Mean?	115
	10.2 Collective Trauma and Narrative Identity	116
	10.3 Individual Narrative Identity	117
	10.4 The Case of Mrs. P	118
	10.5 The Case of Mrs. B	120
	10.6 Some General Remarks on Dreaming	121
	References	123

Part Two Clinical Aspects   125

11	**Implicit Memories and the Structure of the Values System After the Experience of Trauma in Childhood or Adulthood**	**127**
	Krzysztof Rutkowski and Edyta Dembińska	
	11.1 Introduction	127
	11.2 Aim of the Study	129
	11.3 Subjects	130
	11.4 Methods	131
	11.5 Results: Terminal Values	131
	11.6 Results: Instrumental Values	133
	11.7 Conclusions	135
	References	136
12	**Moving Beyond Childhood Adversity: Association Between Salutogenic Factors and Subjective Well-Being Among Adult Survivors of Trauma**	**139**
	Shanta R. Dube, Vincent J. Felitti and Shobhana Rishi	
	12.1 Introduction	139
	12.2 Trauma Survivors and Salutogenesis	140
	12.3 Methods	141
	12.3.1 Definitions of ACE and ACE Score	142
	12.3.2 Health-Promoting Factors	142
	12.3.3 Subjective Well-Being	144
	12.3.4 Depressed Affect	144
	12.3.5 Statistical Analyzes	144
	12.4 Results	144
	12.4.1 Demographics	144
	12.4.2 Health-Promoting Factors and Subjective Well-Being	145
	12.5 Discussion	145
	References	149
13	**Working with Unconscious and Explicit Memories in Psychodynamic Psychotherapy in Patients with Chronic Depression**	**153**
	Svenja Taubner	
	13.1 Introduction	153
	13.2 Representations of Early Attachment Experiences	154

13.3	Insecure Attachment, Loss, and Depression	155
13.4	Psychodynamic Treatment of Pathological Grief and Depression	156
13.5	Changes of Reflective Abilities and Attachment Disorganization in Depressed Patients After Long-Term Psychoanalytic Psychotherapy	157
13.6	Conclusions	160
References		160

14 Overcoming Hurting Memories by Wisdom and Wisdom Psychotherapy — 165
Barbara Lieberei and Michael Linden

14.1	Vulnerability and Resilience to Negative Life Events	165
14.2	Memories of Negative and Traumatic Life Events	166
14.3	Wisdom in Reconciliation with Hurting Memories	168
14.4	Wisdom Psychotherapy	170
	14.4.1 Initial Steps	170
	14.4.2 Wisdom Strategies to Cope with Hurting Memories and Emotions	171
	14.4.3 The Method of Unsolvable Problems	173
14.5	Conclusions	175
References		176

Part Three   Societal Aspects — 181

15 Healing of Psychological Trauma from Military Operations by Transformation of Memories — 183
Andreas Gewandt and Peter L. Zimmermann

15.1	Historical Background	183
15.2	Symptoms and Epidemiology of Military-Related Psychiatric Illnesses	184
	15.2.1 Military-Related PTSD	184
15.3	How Deployment-Related Mental Disorders Are Dealt With in the Bundeswehr	185
15.4	Case Report	187
	15.4.1 History	187
	15.4.2 Treatment	187
15.5	Discussion	188
References		190

16 The Creation and Development of Social Memories of Traumatic Events: The Oudewater Massacre in 1575 — 191
Erika Kuijpers

16.1	Culture and Memories	191
16.2	The Destruction and Massacre of Oudewater in 1575	193
16.3	The Production of Collective Memory	194
16.4	Time for Commemoration	197

	16.5 Conclusion	199
	References	200
17	**Conflict Avoidance, Forgetting, and Distorted Memories by Media Influence on Family Memories: Grandpa Was No Nazi and No Communist**	**203**
	Klaus Bachmann	
	17.1 Distorted Memories of the Political Activities of Family Members	203
	17.2 Study of Family Memories in Poland	204
	17.3 Intergenerational Conflict About the Past	206
	17.4 The Inclusiveness of Polish Family Memory	209
	17.5 The Impact of Media Frames	211
	17.6 Conclusions	215
	References	216
18	**Acting Out and Working Through Traumatic Memory: Confronting the Past in the South African Context**	**217**
	Pumla Gobodo-Madikizela	
	18.1 When Memory Kills: Acting Out Traumas	217
	18.2 Reenactment of Trauma	217
	18.2.1 Perspective from Social Psychology	217
	18.2.2 Psychoanalytic Perspective	218
	18.3 Transgenerational Transmission of Traumatic Memory	220
	18.4 Working Through the Past	221
	18.4.1 Provocations of Empathy: When Memory Heals	221
	18.4.2 Working Through Trauma, Working Through Shame and Guilt	221
	18.5 Conclusion	224
	References	224
19	**Empathy, Forgiveness, and Reconciliation: The Truth and Reconciliation Commission in South Africa**	**227**
	Melike M. Fourie, Pumla Gobodo-Madikizela and Dan J. Stein	
	19.1 Enduring Effects of Discrimination	228
	19.2 Survivors and Psychological Care	230
	19.3 Perpetrators of Evil	231
	19.4 The Role of Empathy	233
	19.5 Conclusion	236
	References	237

Preface

Every child in school knows that forgetting is a bad thing. And husbands have the same experience when they forget their wedding anniversaries. With increasing age, it becomes frightening to realize that one forgets names of persons to whom one has been introduced shortly ago. Finally, there is dementia, a terrible illness that causes memory impairment to the degree that it destroys the personality. To be able to remember and not to forget is extremely important to all human beings. Similarly, social groups try to keep memories alive. Families collect pictures or try to find traces of their ancestors, especially in so-called noble families. States take their identity from memories that often date back centuries, if not millennia.

In summary, memories are indispensable for individuals as well as for social groups. Forgetting can mean the loss of identity. Therefore it is not surprising that individuals keep pictures or write diaries. Societies publish history books, teach children about history, or erect monuments. An additional level of complexity is added when individual and societal memories interact. The importance or the self-definition and the behavior of a person can be dependent on memories of what ancestors have been or have done. Also, the interpretation of events, in the past or present, depends at least partly on what is seen as positive or negative on a societal level in the light of memories, be it the meaning of divorce or feelings about political actions.

But, as always in life, there is also a dark side to memories. They can be hurting and cause problems. With increasing research on posttraumatic stress disorders (PTSDs), it has become evident that memories can make a person sick. Memories can be intrusive. Because they are associated with emotions. Bad memories can elicit bad emotions and can result in problematic behavior. Memories and especially negative memories can escape the control of the individual. This is true for individuals as well as for social groups and even societies. Many political conflicts can be understood only when taking history and memories into account.

Acknowledging that some memories are hurting, cause pain, make persons sick, or even lead to societal or political conflicts, the question is why we do not erase such hurting memories and forget. First, it is difficult, if not impossible, to forget. Who can forget the name of one's spouse, especially if one no longer loves him or her? We tend to best remember negative events. Second, if one tries actively not to remember, memories become more and more vivid and more detailed. Third, it is not always clear whether afflicted persons want to forget, even when memories are hurting and not going anywhere. Remembering gives a feeling of control. Remembering can even be an aggressive act, especially if memories are associated with aggressive fantasies, as in posttraumatic embitterment disorders. How would one feel about a wife who wants a day to commemorate the infidelity of her spouse? Why do states erect monuments to remember their victories over neighbors? Fourth, there are memories of which persons are not aware themselves, that is, subconscious memories. There is motor learning, physiological learning, emotional learning, or attribution learning, and such memories are more important than explicit memories. This is why psychotherapy always deals with unconscious memories, whether they are persisting conditioned reflexes, memories of early bonding experiences, attributions, or cognitive schemata that have been learned long ago. Similarly, many political rules or societal values exert their influence unconsciously.

Remembering and forgetting are processes beyond conscious control. Individuals are frequently unable to remember what they would like to remember. On the other hand, even though they would consciously like to forget, they remember details of traumatic, painful experiences. The memories of traumatic experiences engage various psychological mechanisms. These mechanisms emerge as a complex structure that influences human thoughts, emotions, and behavior. It is plausible to consider that some mechanisms inherited from our distant ancestors are not beneficiary in today's world. The memory of traumatic experience that served in the distant past as a means to avoid the reoccurrence of trauma ensured purely biological survival. Today, the memory of traumatic experiences becomes more often the basis of pathological mechanisms. Many of the patients suffering from PTSD would like to forget, but complex psychological mechanisms keep those unwanted memories intact.

On the other hand, neurotic defense mechanisms (e.g., dissociation, repression) in some patients lead to false forgetting, which does not effectively lower the amount of suffering. These defense mechanisms can be observed in the pathology of symptoms. In summary, everything depends on the time of remembering and the time of forgetting. In an ideal reality, the memory of traumatic experience would always be *psychotherapeutically workable*, that is, susceptible to reformulation and attenuation; eventually, in the course of treatment, memories of trauma would be successfully forgotten. What usually remains in the memory of most past events that happened over 20 years ago are some general impressions, not much more. The memory of details fades away with the passage of time. Traumatic experiences are kept in memory in a different way: The details of experiences remain in memory as if the event had happened only recently. Repression and dissociation lead only to dysfunctional relief. On the basis of these defense mechanisms, new phenomena emerge in the unconscious. These lead to somatic symptoms, disturbance in thought processes (e.g., dysfunctional associations) and disturbance in behavior. The idea presented in this book is called *beneficial forgetting*—forgetting based on the reformulation of the memory of trauma into a psychologically integrated experience.

From a scientific point of view, many questions have to be answered: What is memory, and what is remembered? What is the interrelation between individual and collective memories? How can memories become hurting? What are the consequences for the individual and his or her social group? How can memories lose their negative consequences? Which therapeutic interventions are available and have been shown to be effective on the individual level? What can be done on a societal level to prevent conflicts because of memories? What would be a culture of helpful memories and beneficial forgetting?

In this volume, a comprehensive scientific overview is given on the development of hurting memories in individuals and societies. Consequences are described, from mental disorders in individuals, like PTSD or other neurotic disorders, to societal tensions and conflicts, from South Africa to Northern Europe. Additionally, beneficial forgetting is discussed, from treatments of individuals to reconciliation between social groups. There are promising new approaches on the individual and societal levels. This book on hurting memories and beneficial forgetting can help to solve neurotic memory-related disorders in individuals and conflicts of societies. The contrasting of hurting memories and beneficial forgetting can help in understanding that memories can have positive and negative results and that it is difficult to decide when to support memories and when to forget.

Michael Linden
Krzysztof Rutkowski

List of Contributors

Klaus Bachmann Warsaw School of Social Sciences and Humanities, Warsaw, Poland

Edyta Dembińska Department of Psychotherapy, Jagiellonian University Medical College, Kraków, Poland

Shanta R. Dube National Center for Chronic Disease Prevention and Health Promotion, Centers for Disease Control and Prevention, Atlanta, GA, USA

Vincent J. Felitti Department of Preventive Medicine, Southern California Permanente Medical Group (Kaiser Permanente), San Diego, CA, USA

Melike M. Fourie Department of Psychology, University of Cape Town, Cape Town, South Africa

Andreas Gewandt Center for Psychological Trauma of the Federal German Army, Berlin, Germany

Pumla Gobodo-Madikizela Postgraduate School, University of the Free State, Bloemfontein, South Africa

Alfons Hamm Department of Psychology, University of Greifswald, Greifswald, Germany

Nigel Hunt Institute of Work, Health and Organisations, University of Nottingham, Nottingham, UK

Hans-Peter Kapfhammer Department of Psychiatry, Medical University of Graz, Graz, Austria

Christine Knaevelsrud Center for the Treatment of Torture Victims, Berlin, and Department of Clinical Psychology and Psychotherapy at the Free University of Berlin, Berlin, Germany

Erika Kuijpers Institute for History, Leiden University, Leiden, The Netherlands

Theo Leydenbach Private Practice in Psychosomatics and Psychoanalysis, Paris, France

Barbara Lieberei Research Group Psychosomatic Rehabilitation at the Charité University Medicine Berlin and Department of Behavioral and Psychosomatic Medicine, Rehabilitation Center Seehof, Teltow/Berlin, Germany

Michael Linden Research Group Psychosomatic Rehabilitation at the Charité University Medicine Berlin and Department of Behavioral and Psychosomatic Medicine, Rehabilitation Center Seehof, Teltow/Berlin, Germany

Shobhana Rishi California Department of Education, Sacramento, CA, USA

Krzysztof Rutkowski Department of Psychotherapy, Jagiellonian University Medical College, Kraków, Poland

Katrin Schock Center for the Treatment of Torture Victims, Berlin, and Department of Clinical Psychology and Psychotherapy at the Free University of Berlin, Berlin, Germany

Michael Schönenberg Department of Clinical Psychology and Psychotherapy, University of Tübingen, Tübingen, Germany

Dan J. Stein Department of Psychiatry, University of Cape Town, Cape Town, South Africa

Hans Stoffels Department of Psychiatry, Hospital Sophie Charlotte, Berlin, Germany

Svenja Taubner Institute for Psychology, University of Kassel, Kassel and International Psychoanalytic University Berlin, Berlin, Germany

Bohdan Wasilewski Psychosomatic Institute, Warsaw, Poland

Mathias Weymar Department of Psychology, University of Greifswald, Greifswald, GermanyCenter for the Study of Emotion and Attention, University of Florida, Gainesville, FL, USA

Peter Zimmermann Center for Psychological Trauma of the Federal German Army, Berlin, Germany

Part One

Basic Aspects

1 Spectrum of Persisting Memories and Pseudomemories, Distortions, and Psychopathology

Michael Linden

Research Group Psychosomatic Rehabilitation at the Charité University Medicine Berlin and Department of Behavioral and Psychosomatic Medicine, Rehabilitation Center Seehof, Teltow/Berlin, Germany

1.1 Memory Distortions and Beneficial Forgetting

There is a large body of psychological theories and research on memory, encoding and retrieval of information, under a short-term and a long-term perspective (Dworetzky, 2001; Schacter & Tulving, 1994; Unsworth & Engle, 2007; Willingham & Goedert-Eschmann, 1999). Teachers and pupils have always sought about means of improving learning and making sure that information is not forgotten. Acquiring and remembering knowledge is a human capacity, on which personal development, the identity of persons, and culture are based. In clinical psychology and psychiatry, there is a long tradition of studying memory and especially memory disorders, with the focus of interest on difficulties with memory and forgetting. Problems with memory and enhancement of remembering have attracted much research, especially under the heading of dementia (Uzun, Kozumplik, & Folnegović-Smalc, 2011).

In contrast to the goal of improving remembering, there is almost no research on how to forget. It is only recently, with research on posttraumatic disorders and intrusions (Laposa & Rector, 2012; Michael, Ehlers, Halligan, & Clark, 2005; Molds & Holmes, 2011) that dysfunctional learning and forgetting also became a topic of interest.

It has been long known, not only to researchers but also to everybody, that memories are associated with emotions (Christianson, 1992; Weymar, Löw, Melzig, & Hamm, 2009). Emotional experiences are remembered best, and, when such memories are activated, they are associated with emotions similar to those that have been felt during the event itself. These can be memories with the association of longing and love, of a car accident and anxiety, of a situation where one has behaved in a ridiculous manner and shame, of events where one has been insulted and angered. Negative life events can cause enduring psychological problems because memories prevail, and whenever memories are activated, concomitant negative emotions are experienced. In some cases, such memories can even be haunting. They can be elicited by minor events or stimuli and cause repetitive psychological distress. This is typically the case in posttraumatic stress disorders (PTSD), which in essence must be understood as a memory disorder. The initial event must have been an exceptional life-threatening event that causes a severe anxiety reaction. Whenever this event is remembered, it is associated with a reexperience of severe anxiety. Because this is painful, the afflicted persons try to suppress these memories. This gives more emotional power to them and makes their reoccurrence even more frequent. This is then called *intrusion* (Laposa & Rector, 2012; Michael et al., 2005; Molds & Holmes, 2011). Recurring unwilling memories and psychologically inadequate attempts to suppress them, like dissociation, are the core of this lasting and disabling disorder.

Several lessons can be learned from PTSD:

1. Memory—and that is not only forgetting but also remembering—can play an important role in the development and understanding of distress and mental disorders.
2. Forgetting, or not learning from the beginning, can be beneficial and helpful. This general wisdom is summarized in the wonderful song from the operetta *Die Fledermaus* (The BAT) by Johann Strauss: "Glücklich ist, wer vergisst, was doch nicht zu ändern ist (Happy is he who forgets, what cannot not be altered anyway)." This insight dates back to Emperor Friedrich III, The placid (1415–1493).
3. The phenomenon of intrusions shows that it is not only explicit and willful memory that must be taken into account but that there are also more and different types of memory which are relevant in mental disorders.
4. The term *intrusions* has meanwhile widely been used but in a more and more unspecific manner. Some authors now talk about "transdiagnostic intrusions" (Bryant, O'Donnell, Creamer, McFarlane, & Silove, 2011; Moulds & Holmes, 2011). This assumes that intrusions can be found not only in PTSD but also in many other mental disorders such as social phobia in the form of reexperiencing of a humiliating social experience (Hackman, Suraway, & Clark, 1998), in obsessive-compulsive disorders (OCDs) such as seeing bacteria (de Silva, 1986), in unipolar or bipolar depression, or as memories of negative past or future events (Starr & Moulds, 2006; Williams & Moulds, 2007). Here, the term *intrusion*, by some authors, is no longer confined to unwilling, automatic, and anxiety-related memories of the past but includes thoughts about the future or willful memories. The question is whether this is appropriate. Mixing different phenomena impairs the validity and communicability of respective descriptions.

Descriptive psychopathology has differentiated and defined various phenomena that are similar to or related to memory and that should not be lumped together. Their discrimination is important in the delineation of different mental disorders. In the following section, a compilation and description will be given of different types of memory and of memory-related psychopathological signs and symptoms. It also presents an overview of different mental disorders in which memory distortions play a role.

1.2 Spectrum of Psychopathological Memories, Thoughts, Images, Associations, and the Like

1.2.1 Intrusions

Intrusions are memories of real events that have taken place in the past. Thoughts about some future event should therefore not be called intrusions. They are not only the remembering of the event but also the reactivation of emotions (Christianson, 1992; Laposa & Rector, 2012; Michael et al., 2005). Furthermore, more and more emotions can be associated with the memory depending on how often it has caused distress. Repeated memories can induce emotional learning. The memory of the event must also not be precise. We always remember in a selected and biased, or distorted, way. This is especially true when associated memories are strong, hurting, and unwanted. Finally, intrusions are automatic and unwanted. They can be elicited by some other stimulus, whether it is an external (view of a car) or internal (somatosenory stimuli) or only an associative stimulus (thinking about going to work and then being reminded of the need to take a car). Intrusions are seen in PTSD (Hathaway, Boals, & Banks, 2010; Michael et al., 2005), in posttraumatic embitterment disorder (PTED) (Linden, Rotter, Baumann, & Lieberei, 2007), or in pathological grief (Maercker & Lalor, 2012). See Box 1.1.

1.2.2 Flashbacks

Flashbacks are not memories of an event but rather reenactments of some earlier mental status (Abraham & Aldridge, 1993; Goldman, Galarneau, & Friedman, 2007; Halpern & Pope, 2003). There is no story to tell. They are short pseudohallucinations; the patient has some sensation without an external source of stimulation, which is similar to hallucinations. Still, the patient knows that he or she is the source of the experience, so that this is no real hallucination but a pseudohallucination. Flashbacks are typically visual impressions, like seeing blood running down the wall or dysmorphia, such as walls that are bending. Flashbacks typically occur in the aftermath of LSD intoxications. See Box 1.2.

1.2.3 Automatic Thoughts

Automatic thoughts are phenomena that play a central role in cognitive psychotherapy (Beck, Rush, Shaw, & Emery, 1979; Kopala-Sibley & Santor, 2009;

Box 1.1 Criteria for Intrusions

The memory refers to the past;
What is remembered is a real event, for example, an exceptional life-threatening experience;
Memory has mostly the form of gestalt-like memories, that is, pictures and impressions rather than elaborate stories;
Memories are imprecise and sometimes distorted;
They come up in milliseconds;
They are involuntary, intrusive, and automatic;
There is no subjective control;
They can be stimulated by external stimuli, somatosensory stimuli, or associations;
They evoke strong negative and hurting emotions;
Repetition of intrusions can induce sensitization processes, that is, further negative emotions.

> **Box 1.2 Criteria for Flashbacks**
>
> Not a memory but a revival;
> Involuntary;
> No subjective control;
> No story;
> Mostly a visual impression;
> Short duration;
> Reoccurring over and over;
> Subjective control in that there is no external stimulus.

> **Box 1.3 Criteria for Automatic Thoughts**
>
> Involuntary, automatic;
> No thinking as such but evaluative impression formation;
> No specific memory of some event but rather summarizing memories of repetitive experiences in life;
> Corresponding emotions;
> No subjective control in the first moment but possible voluntary secondary reappraisal;
> Normal psychological process.

Lamberton & Oei, 2008; Young, 2011). They are preconscious but can be made conscious by guided self-observation. Automatic thoughts are not thinking as such but rather evaluative impressions and feelings. They are gestalt-like. One sees "the kitchen is a mess ... it should be cleaned ... nobody is giving me a hand ... my husband is of no use ... maybe I will ask for a divorce." This is occurring in about 400 ms. It is automatic in that one does not think about the subject. The impression comes to one's mind. It is in essence an evaluation of the present situation. Memories are involved because the present evaluation depends on earlier experiences (they never helped to clean the kitchen, I have often asked for help in vain). There is no specific memory but rather an accumulative one. Automatic thoughts are associated with corresponding emotions, like, in our example, anger, reproach, and helplessness. Automatic thoughts occur in every person every second. They help us to make judgments of the present situation and to guide our behavior. See Box 1.3.

1.2.4 Longing

Longing is an emotion associated with memory, rather than a memory associated with emotion. The emotion of longing occurs if a person is separated from a loved one to whom there is or has been a strong bonding (Kotter-Grühn, Wiest, Zurek, & Scheibe, 2009; Maercker & Lalor, 2012; Scheibe, Freund, & Baltes, 2007). It is seen in lovesickness or in bereavement. The emotion then stimulates thoughts about the past and of events together with the separated persons. Afflicted persons have some addiction to

Box 1.4 Criteria for Longing

Consequence of separation;
Emotion;
Emotion stimulates memories;
Conscious thinking about the past;
Emotion and memories are hurting and consoling at the same time;
Emotion and memories come up again and again;
Partly under subjective control in that memories can actively be elicited and also stopped for short time.

Box 1.5 Criteria for Prejudice and Overvalued Ideas

Strong opinions;
No specific memory but "knowledge" about past events;
Strong emotional reactions to specific stimuli (persons, groups, situations);
Involuntary with no subjective control;
Resulting in adjustment problems and even ruthless behavior because of stubbornness and single-mindedness.

such thoughts and memories because they are hurting and consoling at the same time. Longing plays a role in Pathological Grief Disorders (PGD). See Box 1.4.

1.2.5 Prejudice and Overvalued Ideas

Prejudices and overvalued ideas are not memories but rather opinions about the world (Jones & Watson, 1997; Kozak & Foa, 1994; McKenna, 1984). But they refer to historical events similar to memories (people from that village have always looked down on us), not necessarily personal experiences. They result in respective automatic thoughts in relation to certain stimuli (women or black persons). Prejudices become overvalued ideas if they are associated with very strong emotions so that everything else has to stand back, if no compromises are possible any more, and if the specific opinion or value drives all behavior. This can result in ruthless behavior. See Box 1.5.

1.2.6 Cognitive Rehearsal

Cognitive rehearsal is the voluntary replay "in sensu" of an earlier or imagined event (Kirn, 2011; Lazarus, 1984). Everybody can do cognitive rehearsal whenever one wants to do it. One can go through what happened in a past specific situation. Memory details can be elicited by starting to think about details of the situation (time of the day, color of the carpet, position where one was standing). This allows the reliving of a situation in all details. One can go through events that happened very quickly in "slow motion". This is used as therapeutic technique in behavior

> **Box 1.6 Criteria for Cognitive Rehearsal**
>
> Voluntary;
> In reference to real events of the past or any newly created situation;
> Details of what is imagined can be modified in any direction;
> Accompanied by associated emotions;
> Possible for everybody.

> **Box 1.7 Criteria for Worrying**
>
> Related to the future;
> Mostly verbal and referring to a specific upcoming situation;
> Often unconscious and involuntary but can also be voluntary;
> Accompanied by emotions of anxiety;
> A way of anticipatory coping with pending dangers;
> There is a tendency to increase possible dangers and to catastrophize;
> If memories are involved, they are not related to a specific situation in the past but to what one has heard that can happen or experienced in general;
> Possible for everybody;
> Seen excessively in generalized anxiety.

therapy to make a behavioral analysis. Cognitive rehearsal can also be made with a situation that never happened. One can climb stairs or look out a high window in sensu. In any case, this imagining will elicit respective emotional reactions, so that one can do exposure training in sensu by using cognitive rehearsal. See Box 1.6.

1.2.7 Worrying

Worrying is a normal everyday mental process (Berenbaum, 2010; Davey, 1994; Kumar, 2009). It is like anticipatory cognitive rehearsal of upcoming situations in order to detect pending dangers early, so that it is possible to react in advance and prevent catastrophes. It is mostly unconscious. At any moment, it refers to some upcoming specific situations and extends to anything from minor matters to severe problems. If memories are involved, they are not related to a specific situation in the past but to what one has heard that can happen or experienced in general. It is the core symptom of generalized anxiety disorders (GADs) (Gladstone et al., 2005; Ruscio & Borkovec, 2004). See Box 1.7.

1.2.8 Hopelessness

Hopelessness is often presented as some reference to the past, that is, memory. Past events are given as a reason for hopelessness. But in essence hopelessness pertains to the future. It is a feeling that things will turn bad, and, in contrast to worrying, nothing can be done to prevent the outcome (Farran, Herth, & Popovich, 1995). It

> **Box 1.8 Criteria for Hopelessness**
>
> Related to the future;
> Primarily a state of mood;
> Memories can be used to justify the state of mood;
> Known to everybody.

> **Box 1.9 Criteria for Confabulation**
>
> Reports about past events that never happened;
> Filling of gaps in memory;
> Different answers given to the same question because patients neither know what really happened in the past nor what they answered last time;
> Typical for the Korsakoff syndrome in alcohol disorder.

is mostly a feeling. Memories are involved only in that they can be part of the argumentation why things will go bad. Hopelessness can be experienced by everybody; it is seen typically in depression. See Box 1.8.

1.2.9 Confabulation

Confabulations are reports about the past that look like memories but that do not refer to any real event and are made up in the moment to fill gaps in memory (AMDP, 1995; Guy, 1982; Moscovitch, 1995). Patients will answer the same question with respect to the past every time in different ways because they cannot remember either what has happened or what they answered the last time. This phenomenon is seen in Korsakoff dementia after long and severe alcohol intoxication (Zubaran, Fernandes, & Rodnight, 1997). See Box 1.9.

1.2.10 Pseudologia and Wishful False Memories

Pseudologias are stories that are made up in order to make the world look as it is desired. They are lines of argumentation, such as who is right or wrong or which political party is the best. They can also pertain to stories about the past, such as how big the fish was that one caught. In contrast to lies, such persons know that reality is a bit different as told, but in essence they wish their story to be true and in the end also believe by and large in their own storytelling. Another feature, in contrast to confabulation, is that the tellers remember what they said the last time. Once they came up with an argument or description of an event, they stick to it. Pseudologias can therefore become more and more elaborate. Everybody knows pseudologia. Whenever something is emotionally very important to a person, he or she will find arguments to defend it because it cannot be what shall not be. Pseudologias are seen in addiction disorders, where patients may be drunk and still insist that they did

> **Box 1.10 Criteria for Pseudologia and Wishful False Memories**
>
> Pertains to any argumentation;
> Can include descriptions of past events;
> Emotion driven in order to make the world look as it should look;
> Argumentations or descriptions of the past that have been made will be kept;
> New pseudologias will be created to make sure that one does not have to revoke what has been said before;
> Known to everybody;
> In severe forms, typically seen in addiction disorders or histrionic personality disorders.

> **Box 1.11 Criteria for Delusional Memories and Paramnesias**
>
> Wrong reports about the past;
> Patients repeat the identical memories when asked again;
> Patients are convinced that what they remember is right;
> In the case of delusional memories, patients can have at the same time a correct recollection of the past;
> Delusional memories are seen in schizophrenia.

not touch a drop of alcohol. It can be seen in personality disorders and especially histrionic personalities, who can tell dramatic and most impressive stories about the past, their parents, how they were raised or were sexually abused without anything true about the account. There is also a special disorder, pseudologia fantastica, which is characterized by hilarious but still concise stories (Newmark & Adityanjee, 1999). Pseudologia is also the core of wishful false memories, in which events are remembered that never took place because there is an emotional reason to remember (Loftus, 1997). See Box 1.10.

1.2.11 Delusional Memories and Paramnesias

Delusional memories and *paramnesias* are false memories embedded in delusions (AMDP, 1995; Guy, 1982; Markova & Berrios, 2000). Patients are convinced that things have happened as they remember them. Patients firmly believe in the rightness of their wrong memories, while sometimes knowing what really happened but not believing it. This can be seen in schizophrenia, where patients tell that they have been born as the child of a special person, while being able to correctly say who their father is. See Box 1.11.

1.2.12 Obsessive Compulsive Thoughts

Obsessive compulsive thoughts come to mind involuntarily and are in this sense sometimes mistaken for intrusions (Thomsen, 1999). Patients do not want to have

> **Box 1.12 Criteria for Obsessive Compulsive Thoughts**
>
> Experienced as coming from the patient's mind;
> Not willingly thought but forced to think, that is, ego-dystonic;
> Patients do not know what makes them think such thoughts;
> Often experienced as silly and witless;
> Repetitive, schematic, and simple in nature;
> Typical symptom of OCD.

> **Box 1.13 Criteria for Thought Pressure**
>
> Overflow of thoughts;
> Can refer to everything;
> Can include telling about stories of the past;
> Typically seen in mania.

them. Patients have the feeling that they cannot help thinking these thoughts. The patients feel that the thoughts come from their own mind, but they are ego-dystonic; that is, they do subjectively not belong to the person. The person does not willingly think these things, which are repetitive, schematic, and always the same in content and form. Often they are obscene. They can have any content but can also include some "forbidden memory," such as a repetitive thought like, "I have seen my mother naked." In contrast to intrusions, there is no eliciting traumatic event. OCD thoughts are a symptom of OCDs. See Box 1.12.

1.2.13 Thought Pressure

Patients with *thought pressure* show an overflow of ideas (AMDP, 1995; Guy, 1982). These are their own ideas. They agree with what comes to their mind; it may or may not look creative. Often thoughts are not brought to an end. This is a typical symptom of mania or schizophrenia (Klosterkötter, Schultze-Lutter, Bechdolf, & Ruhrmann, 2011; Simon et al., 2007). It can refer to everything, but also show up as storytelling about the past, where thousands of memories come up with millions of details. See Box 1.13.

1.2.14 Rumination

Ruminating patients have the feeling that they cannot "stop thinking" (AMDP 1995, Guy 1982, Kumar, 2009, Nolen-Hoeksema, Wisco, & Lyubomirsky, 2008). Still, they are convinced that they are thinking about important things. In contrast to worrying, this is not goal oriented. In contrast to obsessive compulsive thinking, ruminations are not schematic in content and experienced as ego-syntonic. It is rather a long

> **Box 1.14 Criteria for Rumination**
>
> Pervasive around some negative state of affairs;
> Experienced as one's own thoughts, that is, ego-syntonic;
> Feeling that one cannot stop thinking while feeling that thinking is important;
> Leading to no goal;
> Seen in depression or other states of hopelessness or despair.

> **Box 1.15 Criteria for Conditioned Reflexes**
>
> Memory of some conditioning process;
> Involuntary;
> Very quick, reflexive;
> Referring to physiological, motor, or emotional reactions, but not higher forms of thinking;
> Specific to a certain stimulus;
> Beyond subjective immediate control.

pervasive line of thoughts around some negative state of affairs. It often refers to past events or is even focused on the past and thereby sometimes looking like memories. But it can also refer to the present or future. It is typically seen in depressive disorders or other states of hopelessness or despair (Starr & Moulds, 2006; Williams & Moulds, 2007). See Box 1.14.

1.2.15 Conditioned Reflex

Conditioned reflexes are learned physiological, motor, or emotional answers when reexposed to the same stimulus (Miskovic & Keil, 2012). They require memories of earlier trials. They are stimulus related, involuntary, very quick, and beyond subjective immediate control. Conditioned reflexes can be learned by repetitive trials and also by one trial learning (Rachman, 1977; Seligman, 1971). See Box 1.15.

1.2.16 Specific Monophobias

A special form of phylogenetic memory consists of inborn reactions to selected stimuli like height, narrowness, spiders, or the gaze of other persons (Antony & Swinson, 2000; Merckelbach, de Jong, Muris, & van den Hout, 1996). It can be assumed that, in early times, those who always looked a second time—whether when going deep down or what is moving in the grass—are less likely to be our ancestors than those who responded with anxiety immediately and stayed away from the beginning. Almost all human beings react with more or less anxiety to such stimuli. Many persons rebound and scream when they see a spider even though they have never had

> **Box 1.16 Criteria for Specific Monophobias**
>
> Learned phylogenetically, not individually;
> Involuntary quick reaction, reflexive;
> Bound to selected stimuli that signaled danger millions of years ago.

> **Box 1.17 Criteria for Explicitly or Implicitly Acquired Memories and Competencies**
>
> Explicit and/or implicit learning;
> Acquisition can be very quick or take very long;
> Mostly in need of repetition;
> Refers to content and/or competence;
> High rate of forgetting/deterioration but sometimes also impossible to forget;
> Unstable about time and open to distortions.

any individual negative experience. Yet almost nobody will show the same reaction to electrical outlets, although most mothers scream at their children to prevent them from investigating what is in the holes. See Box 1.16.

1.2.17 Explicitly or Implicitly Acquired Memories and Competencies

What typically is associated with memory is *explicit* or in some cases also *implicit learning* (Lola, Tzetzis, & Zetou, 2012; Schacter & Tulving, 1994; Shanks & Berry, 2012; Willingham & Goedert-Eschmann, 1999). By means of reading, hearing, or explicit training, one acquires knowledge about facts in the world, from vocabulary to volleyball serves. Learning can sometimes be quick, like learning names or riding a bicycle, or take much practice, like learning a language or playing the piano. Similarly, forgetting can be quick or not, depending on the content, the complexity, and the mode of learning. Such memories are furthermore not stable and subject to errors. See Box 1.17.

1.2.18 Developmental Learning

A special type of learning, *developmental learning*, occurs during special sensitive developmental phases of the body and especially the brain. There are developmental periods with special neural plasticity for different tasks (Huttenlocher, 2002; Stiles, 2000). During this period of time, the brain is ready to learn in a special way and will then encode this learning and practice in a special neural structure. Examples are the development of the visual or speech system. Such learning processes occur in the time from prenatal development to the end of the twenties. There is meanwhile ample evidence that stimulation in such sensitive prenatal, perinatal, and postnatal

> **Box 1.18 Criteria for Developmental Learning**
>
> Specific stimulation (hormonal, visual, etc.) during fixed periods of brain development;
> Shaping the behavioral responses of persons for a lifetime;
> Mostly irrevocable.

developmental phases can even lead to special personality traits, like reaction to stressors (Davis & Sandman, 2012). See Box 1.18.

1.3 Features and Development of Pathological Memories

These examples of types of memories, intrusions, or pathological signs and symptoms show the variety of memory-related phenomena and distortions. When one wants to understand problems with dysfunctional memories, it is mandatory to discriminate among the many different features in order to understand what keeps memories alive and what makes them pathological.

Box 1.19 gives a summary of dimensions that have to be taken into account. They can come as images or abstract knowledge. Their emotional tone can be bad, neutral, or good. They can cause distress or not. They can be voluntary, stimulated, or involuntary. They can result in the wish to suppress them or keep them. They can be ego-syntonic or ego-dystonic. They can refer to a specific content or are rather a formal mode of thinking. They can refer to the past but include or not include thoughts about the present or future. They can be experienced based or induced by others. They can come once or be repetitive. They can refer to cognitions, motor behavior, emotional behavior, or physiological reactions. They can be acquired by one trial or by multiple repetitive learning. They can be associated with all types of emotions, from anxiety to feelings of love. They can be action related or action free. They can be true, distorted, or false.

When asking why unwanted memories do not disappear, several processes can play a role (Box 1.20). An important feature is that, whenever one wants to forget actively or suppress memories, the memories will become more frequent or vivid. Further mechanisms that hinder forgetting are negative appraisals of memories or metacognitions saying that one should not think this or that. Also the association with strong emotions keeps memories alive. This is especially so if emotions include a Zeigarnik effect (Savitsky, Medvec, & Gilovich, 1997; Zeigarnik, 1927; Zeigarnik, Louria, & Haigh, 1965), that is, an urge to end a problem, as is the case after experiences of humiliation and injustice. Certain subconscious reflexes can be activated by respective stimuli. Subconscious memories and preparedness reactions are especially persistent when acquired during sensitive developmental phases. Also, mental illness can activate pathological or dysfunctional memories, like negative memories of the past during depression. Most important for the persistence of memories is repetitive training. The more often a person remembers, the less he or she will forget.

Box 1.19 Features of Memories

- Vivid image (intrusions in PTSD) versus abstract knowledge (overvalued idea);
- Bad (intrusion in PTSD) versus neutral (remembering of what has to be done) versus good (happy with what happened);
- Distress (intrusion in PTSD) versus nondistress (overvalued idea);
- Urge to avoid thought (intrusion in PTSD) versus urge to continue (rumination in depression);
- Voluntarily (remembering the vacation) versus stimulated (reaction to a snake) versus involuntarily (intrusion in PTSD);
- Formal processing (rumination in depression) versus content (overvalued idea in personality disorder);
- Verbal (worrying in GAD) versus image (some intrusions in PTSD) versus color (flashback in substance abuse);
- Past (longing in PGD) versus presence (controlling in thought with reference to the past in OCD) versus future (worrying in GAD with reference to past events);
- Experience-based (intrusion in PTSD) versus injected memories (false memories of sexual trauma);
- Action related (problem-solving in GAD) versus free of action (rumination in depression);
- Single (delusional perception) versus repetitive (rumination);
- Ego-syntonic (worrying) versus ego-dystonic (OCD);
- Story (pseudologia) versus flash-like (automatic thought, flashback);
- Primary symptom (intrusion in PTSD) versus secondary symptom (hopelessness in depression);
- One topic (intrusion in PTSD) versus multiple topics (worrying in GAD);
- Anxiety (PTSD) versus embitterment (PTED) versus grief (PGD) versus joy (love) versus other emotions;
- Delusion (delusion of descent) versus others;
- Sequential processing of content (pseudologia) versus thought/argument (worrying in GAD) versus single automatic thought (depression);
- Event related (always, possibly, wrongly, not);
- Everybody (pseudologia) versus persons with special experiences (conditioned anxiety reaction) versus illness (delusion);
- Transdiagnostic (social phobia, bipolar, depression, OCD).

Therefore, all processes that make a person remember will inevitably keep memories and increase the problem if memories are hurting. This is a special problem in psychotherapy and psychotherapeutic techniques of working through past events. In the end, there is no active mode of forgetting. Forgetting happens only with time, indifference, disregard, ignoring, and stoic tolerance of possible concomitant emotions.

The question is which features make memories become pathological. Box 1.21 summarizes some important criteria. Memories are in any case pathological if they are part of an illness, as is the case with delusional memories in schizophrenia. It can also be that memories become pathological because they cause illness, although they may have no pathological character per se. This is the case in dysfunctional

> **Box 1.20 Mechanisms in the Development of Persisting Memories**
>
> - Negative appraisal of thought (metacognition in GAD);
> - Association of thought/imagery with emotion (intrusion in PTSD);
> - Humiliation or experience of injustice (intrusion in PTED);
> - Urge to act (OCD, worrying in GAD);
> - Urge to suppress (intrusion in PTSD);
> - Subconscious conditioned reflex (phobic anxiety);
> - Repetitive training (negative fluency in worrying);
> - Neural development (emotion regulation in persons who have been neglected in early childhood);
> - Illness processes (flashback after intoxication, delusions).

> **Box 1.21 Criteria for Pathology of Memories**
>
> - Symptom of an illness (rumination in depression, delusions in schizophrenia);
> - Part of an illness process (dysfunctional cognitions/schemata in depression or personality disorders);
> - Frequency and uncontrollability (rumination in depression, intrusions in PTSD);
> - Distortion of content (pseudologia);
> - Association with pathological emotions (intrusion in PTSD);
> - Intensity of reaction (phobic reaction in agoraphobia).

cognitions and depression (e.g., "My father wanted me to be successful" and depressive reaction after failure). Also the frequency and, by this, the uncontrollability of memories can be such that they lead to disability and must be called pathological, as is the case with rumination in depression. They can cause a problem because they are distorted, as is seen in pseudologia or in negative cognitive schemata. They can also be associated with emotions that make the problem, as in anxiety associated with intrusions in PTSD. Finally, they can result in dysfunctional or overintensive reactions, which cause problems like phobic conditioned reflexes and avoidance.

1.4 Conclusion

There is not one memory but many. To remember can be good but can also be a burden. Also, many memories cause disability and other problems. Keeping memories can be an essential part of mental illness. Memories are not reality but psychology and often psychopathology. Memories are more of an answer to the present than to the past. The truth of memories is always to be questioned.

If memories are dysfunctional, haunting, hurting, or causing problems, forgetting would be good. Forgetting is extremely difficult, especially in the case of problematic memories. In clinical practice, there are some approaches, such as pharmacotherapy for delusional memories, rescripting, reattribution, and other cognitive techniques, or exposure training, which aims at the mastery of negative emotions, and especially anxiety. These interventions show some success. Still, more and better interventions are needed. The topic of how to forget hurting memories is still a developing field and in need of much more scientific attention and research.

References

Abraham, H. D., & Aldridge, A. M. (1993). Adverse consequences of lysergic acid diethylamide. *Addiction, 88*, 1327–1334.

AMDP, Arbeitsgemeinschaft für Methoidik unbd documentation in der Psychiatrie, (1995). *Das AMDP-System. Manual zur dokumentation psychiatrischer befunde.* Göttingen: Hogrefe.

Antony, M. M., & Swinson, R. P. (2000). Specific phobia. In M. M. Antony & R. P. Swinson (Eds.), *Phobic disorders and panic in adults: A guide to assessment and treatment.* Washington, DC: American Psychological Association.

Beck, A. T., Rush, A. J., Shaw, B. F., & Emery, G. (1979). *Cognitive therapy of depression.* New York, NY: The Guilford Press.

Berenbaum, H. (2010). An initiation–termination two-phase model of worrying. *Clinical Psychology Review, 30*, 962–975.

Bryant, R. A., O'Donnell, M. L., Creamer, M., McFarlane, A. C., & Silove, D. (2011). Posttraumatic intrusive symptoms across psychiatric disorders. *Journal of Psychiatric Research, 45*, 842–847.

Christianson, S. A. (1992). *The handbook of emotion and memory: Research and theory.* Hillsdale, NJ: Lawrence Erlbaum.

Cummings, J. L. (1985). Amnesia paramnesia and confabulation. In J. L. Cummings (Ed.), *Clinical neuropsychiatry.* New York, NY: Grune & Stratton.

Davey, G. C. L. (1994). *Pathological worrying as exacerbated problem-solving.* Oxford: John Wiley & Sons.

Davis, E. P., & Sandman, C. A. (2012). Prenatal psychobiological predictors of anxiety risk in preadolescent children. *Psychoneuroendocrinology, 37*, 1224–1233.

de Silva, P. (1986). Obsessional-compulsive imagery. *Behaviour Research and Therapy, 24*, 333–350.

Dworetzky, B. A. (2001). The neurology of memory. *Seminars in Speech and Language, 22*, 97–108.

Farran, C. J., Herth, K. A., & Popovich, J. M. (1995). *Hope and hopelessness: Critical clinical constructs.* Thousand Oaks, CA: Sage Publications.

Gladstone, G. L., Parker, G. B., Mitchell, P. B., Malhi, G. S., Wilhelm, K. A., & Austin, M. P. (2005). A brief measure of worry severity (BMWS): Personality and clinical correlates of severe worriers. *Journal of Anxiety Disorders, 19*, 877–892.

Goldman, S., Galarneau, D., & Friedman, R. (2007). New onset LSD flashback syndrome triggered by the initiation of SSRIs. *Ochsner Journal Spring, 7*, 37–39.

Guy, W. (1982). *The AMDP-system: Manual for the assessment and documentation of psychopathology.* Berlin: Springer.

Hackman, A., Suraway, C., & Clark, D. C. (1998). Seeing yourself through others' eyes: A study of spontaneously occurring images in social phobia. *Behavioral and Cognitive Psychotherapy, 26*, 3–12.

Halpern, J. H., & Pope, H. G. (2003). Hallucinogen persisting perception disorder: What do we know after 50 years? *Drug and Alcohol Dependence, 69*, 109–119.

Hardie, T. J., & Reed, A. (1988). Pseudologia fantastica, factitious disorder and impostership: A deception syndrome. *Medicine, Science, and the Law, 38*, 198–201.

Hathaway, L. M., Boals, A., & Banks, J. B. (2010). PTSD symptoms and dominant emotional response to a traumatic event: An examination of DSM-IV criterion A2. *Anxiety, Stress & Coping, 23*(1), 119–126.

Hugdahl, K., & Johnsen, B. H. (1989). Preparedness and electrodermal fear-conditioning: Ontogenetic vs phylogenetic explanations. *Behaviour Research and Therapy, 27*, 269–278.

Huttenlocher, P. (2002). *Neural plasticity: The effects of environment on the development of the cerebral cortex*. Cambridge, MA: Harvard University Press.

Jones, E., & Watson, J. P. (1997). Delusion, the overvalued idea and religious beliefs: A comparative analysis of their characteristics. *The British Journal of Psychiatry, 170*, 381–386.

Kirn, T. (2011). Imagination und cognitive probe. In M. Linden & M. Hautzinger (Eds.), *Verhalgtenstherapiemanual*. Berlin: Springer.

Klosterkötter, J., Schultze-Lutter, F., Bechdolf, A., & Ruhrmann, S. (2011). Prediction and prevention of schizophrenia: What has been achieved and where to go next? *World Psychiatry, 10*, 165–174.

Kopala-Sibley, D. C., & Santor, D. A. (2009). The mediating role of automatic thoughts in the personality-event-affect relationship. *Cognitive Behaviour Therapy, 38*, 153–161.

Kotter-Grühn, D., Wiest, M., Zurek, P. P., & Scheibe, S. (2009). What is it we are longing for? Psychological and demographic factors influencing the contents of Sehnsucht (life longings). *Journal of Research in Personality, 43*, 428–437.

Kozak, M. J., & Foa, E. B. (1994). Obsessions, overvalued ideas, and delusions in obsessive-compulsive disorder. *Behaviour Research and Therapy, 32*, 343–353.

Kumar, S. M. (2009). *The mindful path through worry and rumination*. Oakland, CA: New Harbinger Publication.

Lamberton, A., & Oei, T. P. (2008). A test of the cognitive content specificity hypothesis in depression and anxiety. *Journal of Behavior Therapy and Experimental Psychiatry, 39*, 23–31.

Laposa, J. M., & Rector, N. A. (2012). The prediction of intrusions following an analogue traumatic event: Peritraumatic cognitive processes and anxiety-focused rumination versus rumination in response to intrusions. *Journal of Behavior Therapy and Experimental Psychiatry, 43*, 877–883.

Lazarus, A. (1984). *In the mind's eye: The power of imaginary therapy to give control over your life*. New York, NY: The Guilford Press.

Linden, M., Rotter, M., Baumann, K., & Lieberei, B. (2007). *The post-traumatic embitterment (PTED)*. Bern: Hogrefe & Huber.

Loftus, E. (1997). Creating false memories. *Scientific American, 277*, 70–75.

Lola, A. C., Tzetzis, G. C., & Zetou, H. (2012). The effect of implicit and explicit practice in the development of decision making in volleyball serving. *Perceptual and Motor Skills, 114*, 665–678.

Maercker, A., & Lalor, J. (2012). Diagnostic and clinical considerations in prolonged grief disorder. *Dialogues in Clinical Neuroscience, 14*, 167–176.

Markova, I. S., & Berrios, G. E. (2000). Paramnesias and delusions of memory. In G. E. Berrios & J. R. Hodges (Eds.), *Memory disorders in psychiatric practice*. Cambridge: Cambridge University Press.

McKenna, P. J. (1984). Disorders with overvalued ideas. *The British Journal of Psychiatry, 145*, 579–585.

Merckelbach, H., de Jong, P. J., Muris, P., & van den Hout, M. C. (1996). The etiology of specific phobias: A review. *Clinical Psychology Reviews, 16,* 337–361.

Michael, T., Ehlers, A., Halligan, S., & Clark, D. (2005). Unwanted memories of assault: What intrusion characteristics are associated with PTSD? *Behaviour Research and Therapy, 43,* 613–628.

Miskovic, V., & Keil, A. (2012). Acquired fears reflected in cortical sensory processing: A review of electrophysiological studies of human classical conditioning. *Psychophysiology, 49,* 1230–1241.

Moscovitch, M. (1995). Confabulation. In D. L. Schacter (Ed.), *Memory distortions: How minds, brains, and societies reconstruct the past.* Cambridge, MA: Harvard University Press.

Moulds, M. L., & Holmes, E. A. (2011). Intrusive imagery in psychopathology: A commentary. *International Journal of Cognitive Therapy, 4,* 197–207.

Newmark, N., & Adityanjee, K. J. (1999). Pseudologia fantastica and factitious disorder: Review of the literature and a case report. *Comprehensive Psychiatry, 40,* 89–95.

Nolen-Hoeksema, S., Wisco, B. E., & Lyubomirsky, S. (2008). Rethinking rumination. *Perspectives on Psychological Science, 3,* 400–424.

Rachman, S. (1977). The conditioning theory of fear acquisition: A critical examination. *Behaviour Research and Therapy, 15,* 375–387.

Ruscio, A. M., & Borkovec, T. D. (2004). Experience and appraisal of worry among high worriers with and without generalized anxiety disorder. *Behaviour Research and Therapy, 42,* 1469–1482.

Savitsky, K., Medvec, V. H., & Gilovich, T. (1997). Remembering and regretting: The Zeigarnik effect and the cognitive availability of regrettable actions and inactions. *Personality and Social Psychology Bulletin, 23,* 248–257.

Schacter, D. L., & Tulving, E. (1994). *Memory systems.* Cambridge, MA: MIT Press.

Scheibe, S., Freund, A. M., & Baltes, P. B. (2007). Toward a developmental psychology of Sehnsucht (life longings): The optimal (utopian) life. *Developmental Psychology, 43,* 778–795.

Seligman, M. (1971). Phobias and preparedness. *Behavior Therapy, 2,* 307–320.

Shanks, D. R., & Berry, C. J. (2012). Are there multiple memory systems? Tests of models of implicit and explicit memory. *The Quarterly Journal of Experimental Psychology, 65,* 1449–1474.

Simon, A. E., Cattapan-Ludewig, K., Zmilacher, S., Arbach, D., Gruber, K., Dvorsky, D. N., et al. (2007). Cognitive functioning in the schizophrenia prodrome. *Schizophrenia Bulletin, 33,* 761–771.

Starr, S., & Moulds, M. L. (2006). The role of negative interpretations of intrusive memories in depression. *Journal of Affective Disorders, 93,* 125–132.

Stiles, J. (2000). Neural plasticity and cognitive development. *Developmental Neuropsychology, 18,* 237–272.

Thomsen, P. H. (1999). *From thoughts to obsession.* London: Jessica Kingsley Publisher.

Unsworth, N., & Engle, R. W. (2007). The nature of individual differences in working memory capacity: Active maintenance in primary memory and controlled search from secondary memory. *Psychological Review, 114,* 104–132.

Uzun, S., Kozumplik, O., & Folnegović-Smalc, V. (2011). Alzheimer's dementia: Current data review. *Collegium Antropologicum, 35,* 1333–1337.

Weymar, M., Löw, A., Melzig, C. A., & Hamm, A. O. (2009). Enhanced long-term recollection for emotional pictures: Evidence from high-density ERPs. *Psychophysiology, 46,* 1200–1207.

Williams, A. D., & Moulds, M. L. (2007). Cognitive avoidance of intrusive memories: Recall vantage perspective and associations with depression. *Behaviour Research and Therapy, 45*, 1141–1153.

Willingham, D. B., & Goedert-Eschmann, K. (1999). The relationship between implicit and explicit learning: Evidence for parallel development. *Psychological Science, 10*, 531–534.

Young, J. (2011). Kognitionsevozierung. In M. Linden & M. Hautzinger (Eds.), *Verhaltenstherapiemanual*. Berlin: Springer.

Zeigarnik, B. (1927). Über das Behalten von erledigten und unerledigten Handlungen. *Psychologische Forschung, 9*, 1–85.

Zeigarnik, B. V., Louria, A. R., & Haigh, B. (1965). *The pathology of thinking*. New York, NY: Plenum Press.

Zubaran, C., Fernandes, J. G., & Rodnight, R. (1997). Wernicke–Korsakoff syndrome. *Postgraduate Medical Journal, 73*, 27–31.

2 Electrophysiological Signature of Emotional Memories

Mathias Weymar[1,2], Alfons Hamm[1]

[1]Department of Psychology, University of Greifswald, Greifswald, Germany
[2]Center for the Study of Emotion and Attention, University of Florida, Gainesville, FL, USA

2.1 Introduction

When remembering events from the past, it seems obvious that humans remember emotionally arousing events better than experiences without emotional relevance. These emotional memories are often extremely robust, long lasting, very detailed, and vivid. Therefore, it has been suggested that, like a camera's flash (Brown & Kulik, 1977), emotional memories vividly conserve an emotional incident as it happened at that moment (news of the death of a relative, the September 11 terrorist attacks, etc.). Moreover, individuals often feel that these emotional memories are very accurate; that is, they have higher confidence in these memories than in other memories of their lives. From an evolutionary perspective, robust, vivid memories for aversive and pleasant experiences are important for survival and should be consistent over time to facilitate avoidance and reproductive success when similar events are reencountered in the future (Dolan, 2002). Therefore, it is adaptive to enhance memory consolidation and storage for events that are emotionally engaging. However, such a survival system can become maladaptive; long lasting, hurting, emotional memories can cause anxiety disorders (e.g., posttraumatic stress disorder, PTSD) when experiences are extremely unpleasant or traumatic. In this case, traumatic memories can haunt the individual throughout the entire life span, lasting longer than any pleasant memories (Porter & Peace, 2007).

2.2 Studying Emotional Memory in the Laboratory

In laboratory settings, the effects of emotion on memory have been studied with a variety of stimuli, including words, sentences, pictures, and narrated slide shows (Bradley, Greenwald, Petry, & Lang, 1992; Cahill & McGaugh, 1995; Kensinger & Corkin, 2003). In these studies, free recall of emotional stimuli (unpleasant and pleasant) is enhanced compared to neutral stimuli. The same pattern holds in recognition memory tasks, but with less consistency (Christianson, 1992). Here, participants view emotional and neutral stimuli and later have to decide, when the same and novel stimuli are presented, which stimulus they have previously encoded (Dolcos, LaBar, & Cabeza, 2005; Ochsner, 2000; Weymar, Löw, Melzig, & Hamm, 2009). In some studies, emotions are not induced by different semantic contents of the stimuli; rather, an unpleasant stressful context is created during which learning tasks are presented and memory performance is then tested later (Cahill & van Stegeren, 2003; Weymar, Bradley, Hamm, & Lang, 2012).

Many emotion theorists assume that affective experiences can best be characterized by two orthogonal dimensions: arousal and valence, two factors that may capture the entire spectrum of emotions in a two-dimensional space (Lang, Greenwald, Bradley, & Hamm, 1993; Mehrabian & Russell, 1974). Arousal describes the intensity of activation varying from calm to excitement, whereas emotional valence varies from unpleasant, through neutral, to pleasant. Evidence indicates that primarily emotional arousal is critical for better encoding into episodic memory traces (Buchanan & Adolphs, 2002; Bradley et al., 1992, but for valence effects, see Kensinger & Schacter, 2008).

One influential neural hypothesis explaining the emotional memory effects is the modulation hypothesis, first proposed by McGaugh (2004). Based on data from extensive animal experimentation, this hypothesis posits that the better memory for emotional events is related to enhancing effects of the amygdala on medial temporal lobe (MTL) structures associated with episodic memory and other brain structures involved in memory storage that are engaged in sensory and cognitive processing at the time of amygdala activation. The crucial role of the amygdala in triggering the memory formation [also named emotional tagging (Richter-Levin & Akirav, 2003)] is mediated by adrenergic and glucocorticoid neuromodulation, hormonal changes that are activated during and after emotionally arousing experiences (McGaugh, 2000).

The modulation hypothesis has also been supported by findings in humans demonstrating that patients with amygdala lesions showed impaired memory advantage for emotionally arousing stimuli (Cahill, Babinsky, Markowitsch, & McGaugh, 1995; LaBar & Phelps, 1998). Moreover, administering adrenergic agonists prior to learning or encoding increases memory for emotional events, whereas administering adrenergic antagonists impairs facilitated memory performance for emotional events (Cahill et al., 1995; O'Carroll, Drysdale, Cahill, Shajahan, & Ebmeier, 1999). Finally, recent neuroimaging studies demonstrated that better memory for emotional events is related to enhanced amygdala and MTL memory region activation and stronger functional connectivity between these regions, substantiating the view that amygdala–MTL interactions might be important to promote emotional memory consolidation (Hamann, Ely, Grafton, & Kilts, 1999; Ritchey, Dolcos, & Cabeza, 2008).

In the following sections, we review recent findings from emotional memory retrieval studies using event-related potentials (ERPs), including major findings from our own laboratory. A key advantage of ERP methods compared to neuroimaging methods (e.g., functional magnetic resonance imaging (fMRI)) is that they provide measures of neural activity with extraordinary temporal resolution in real time. The time resolution of ERPs in milliseconds makes this methodology ideally suited to examine neural events responsible for human memory (Voss & Paller, 2008). Precisely, the methodology, even if it cannot compete with the spatial resolution of brain-imaging techniques, is most useful to unfold critical memory processes within the first second after the onset of stimulus and is probably more able to detect the brief cognitive events related to the effects that emotions may have on retrieval processes (Voss & Paller, 2008).

2.3 ERPs and Memory Retrieval

Electrophysiological responses to the retrieval of previously encoded items have been traditionally studied in recognition memory tasks. In a recognition task, ERPs are recorded while participants view a series of previously encoded and novel items in order to decide whether the presented item has been presented before (old) or not (new). It is a hallmark finding that ERPs elicited by correctly classified old items evoke an overall more positive-going ERP waveform than the ERP to the correctly classified new items (Rugg & Curran, 2007). This difference in ERP responses has been labeled as the *ERP old/new effect* (Figure 2.1). Distinct ERP old/new effects have been linked to different types of mnemonic processes, interpreted in the light of dual-process theories of recognition memory: remembering based on recollection and familiarity (reviewed in Yonelinas, 2002). *Recollection* involves the conscious experience of remembering the item, that is, the ability to recognize a past event with specific details such as spatial, temporal, or contextual features. In contrast, *familiarity* is more generally associated with the feeling of knowing the item without being able to recall specific details. There is broad consensus that conscious recollection is related to the later parietal old/new

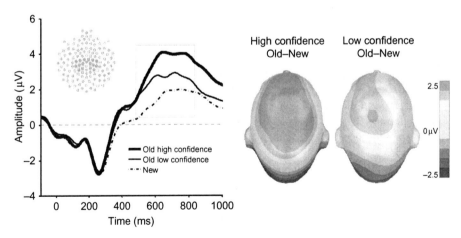

Figure 2.1 Representative late old/new effect during remembering of pictorial stimuli. Left panel: Grand-averaged ERP waveforms elicited by correctly classified old pictures receiving high- and low-confidence ratings and new pictures are displayed. The square represents the late (500–800 ms) time window used in the analyses. ERPs are averaged across channels within the parietal cluster used in the analyses (see inset: Geodesic Sensor net diagram). Right panel: Scalp potential differences (old minus new) for high-confidence and low-confidence responses for the 500- to 800-ms time interval (top view).

effect, a larger positive ERP deflection for old items than for new items, starting approximately 400 ms after the onset of stimulus and lasting until 800 ms over parietal electrode regions (Curran, Tepe, & Piatt, 2006; Friedman & Johnson, 2000; Mecklinger, 2000) (see inset of Figure 2.1). The parietal ERP old/new effect is known to be generated by hippocampus and parietal regions (Düzel, Vargha-Khadem, Heinze, & Mishkin, 2001; Vilberg & Rugg, 2009) and is sensitive to factors believed to affect recollection more than familiarity, such as depth of processing, correct source judgments, high-confidence ratings (Figure 2.1), or "remember" judgments (Rugg & Curran, 2007). In contrast, an early (lasting 300–500 ms after the onset of stimulus), more frontally distributed old/new effect (also known as FN400) is related to recognition based on familiarity, although recent evidence suggests that this frontal old/new effect might also index semantic/conceptual priming (see, for a current debate, Voss & Federmeier, 2011).

2.4 Electrophysiological Correlates of Emotional Memory Retrieval

ERP studies investigating the influence of emotion on explicit retrieval processing have produced mixed results. Some researchers found a clear potentiation of the ERP old/new effect for emotional relative to neutral stimuli when measuring recognition memory performance (Dietrich et al., 2001; Inaba, Nomura, & Ohira, 2005; Johansson, Mecklinger, & Treese 2004; Langeslag & Van Strien, 2008). For instance, Dietrich and colleagues found larger late (450–650 ms) parietal old/new effects for negative and positive words compared to neutral ones, indicating better conscious recollection-based remembering for this material. In another study, better memory performance and larger late parietal old/new effects were found only for unpleasant but not for pleasant words if compared to neutral stimuli (Inaba et al., 2005). Likewise, when words were embedded in unpleasant or neutral sentences (Maratos & Rugg, 2001; Exp I), greater recollection-sensitive ERP effects were found for neutral words encoded in unpleasant contexts. Similar findings were reported by Johannson, Mecklinger, and Treese (2004) using different facial expressions as emotional and neutral stimuli. Increased parietal memory effects for unpleasant faces were also shown by Righi et al. (2012). In this study, no emotion effects were observed for the early frontal old/new effect, supporting the view that facilitation of memory performance by emotion relies more on recollection-based memory.

In contrast, other studies found that the ERP old/new effect was not influenced by emotion (Koenig & Mecklinger, 2008; Maratos, Allan, & Rugg, 2000; Maratos & Rugg, 2001; Versace, Bradley, & Lang, 2006; Windmann & Kutas, 2001), suggesting that, during retrieval, the recognition of neutral and emotional materials may rely on the same neural processes. These inconsistent findings from ERP studies are still under debate (Weymar et al., 2009). One potential contributing factor for these discrepant findings might be that the arousal levels of the emotional materials often vary across the different experiments. For instance, arousal levels are lower for words and faces relative to affective pictures (Bradley, 2000; Keil, 2006; Lang, Bradley, & Cuthbert, 1998). In addition, discrepant findings could also be due to differences in the paradigms that were used to assess memory performance (continuous recognition versus study test; recognition versus source memory; intentional versus incidental encoding, etc.). Finally, one particularly critical factor to detect emotion effects in memory retrieval is the length of the retention interval. A number of recent studies have demonstrated that longer retention intervals can increase memory in part by facilitating consolidation processes (LaBar & Cabeza, 2006; Quevedo et al., 2003; Sharot & Phelps, 2004; Sharot & Yonelinas, 2008). Memory of emotionally arousing stimuli tested after long delay intervals have resulted in greater memory accuracy (Dolcos et al., 2005; Weymar et al., 2009) and stronger power of recollection (Schaefer, Pottage, & Rickart, 2011; Sharot & Yonelinas, 2008) compared to neutral events. These emotion modulation effects are much stronger than after short (immediate) testing. The large differences in the retention period might be a reason why some studies failed to find a memory advantage for emotional stimuli in behavior and electrical potentials when others do find such differences.

2.5 ERPs of Emotional Memory After Long Retention Intervals

Starting from these observations, we used a one-week retention interval and emotional and neutral pictures from the International Affective Picture System (Lang, Bradley, & Cuthbert, 2008) to measure behavioral and electrophysiological indices of recognition memory (Weymar et al., 2009). Especially when using emotional pictures in a recognition memory paradigm, long retention intervals should be used because, due to exceptionally good picture memory, immediate recognition can lead to ceiling effects (Bradley et al., 1992), distorting the emotional modulation of memory performance effects. To behaviorally dissociate familiarity from recollection, confidence ratings were assessed in this study following each recognition decision. High confidence should represent recollection-based retrieval processes, while low confidence in memory should be related to familiarity-based recognition. Previous studies have shown that emotion particularly increases recollection-based memory performance (Phelps & Sharot, 2008). Therefore, we hypothesized that better memory for emotional pictures is driven mainly by recollection in behavioral performance and brain potentials during recognition. As expected, the results showed enhanced memory performance for unpleasant and pleasant pictures relative to neutral pictures, substantiating previous long-term memory studies (Bradley et al., 1992; Dolcos et al., 2005). Moreover, we observed increased parietal old/new effects in the ERPs for emotionally arousing pictures relative to neutral pictures (500–800 ms), indicating that emotionally arousing contents facilitate the electrophysiological correlates of recognition memory (Figure 2.2). In this study, old/new effects were largest over posterior sites but also present over frontal sensors, probably suggesting an overlap in time of early frontal and later parietal effects elicited during the memory task. Interestingly, the parietal ERP old/new effect increased with increasing recognition confidence, supporting the idea that the late parietal old/new effect indexes recollection rather than familiarity (Curran,

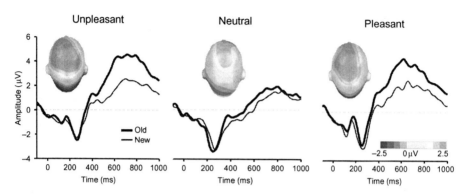

Figure 2.2 The old/new effect is modulated by emotional contents. Grand-averaged ERPs elicited by correctly judged old and new items depicted separately for unpleasant, neutral, and pleasant pictures. Top view: Display of scalp potential differences (old minus new) separately for the three picture categories.

2004; Düzel, Yonelinas, Mangun, Heinze, & Tulving, 1997). In contrast, the early frontal old/new difference (300–500 ms) was driven mainly by low-confidence judgments and was not modulated by emotional contents. This is consistent with recent behavioral evidence showing that recollection is specifically modulated by emotion (Dolcos et al., 2005; Ochsner, 2000).

In a similar ERP study (Weymar, Löw, Schwabe, & Hamm, 2010), we used the remember/know paradigm (Tulving, 1985), which is another procedure to tap recollection and familiarity differentially. In this study, participants rated a series of unpleasant and neutral pictures and 24 h later returned for a surprise recognition test, in which the participants introspectively indicated whether their recognition was based on conscious recollection (remembered) or familiarity (known). As expected, emotional pictures received higher rates of remember judgments than neutral pictures. In accordance with the behavioral data, the enhanced recollection of emotional contents was related to larger ERP amplitudes in the parietal old/new effect in the time range of 500–800 ms. These data suggest that emotion enhances not only memory accuracy (Weymar et al., 2009) but also the power of recollection. A recent long-term memory ERP study by Schaefer et al. (2011) confirmed these results, showing that enhanced memory for emotional pictures is driven by remember responses, accompanied by enhanced old/new differences (500–700 ms) largest over parietal sensors for emotional contents.

To investigate whether the enhanced memory performance and the underlying electrophysiological signature for emotional pictures could also be observed for longer retention intervals (up to 1 year), we tested participants after one week and also after 1 year (Weymar, Löw, & Hamm, 2011). The results showed robust emotional memory effects. Although overall memory performance declined over time, emotional pictures were still better remembered than neutral pictures even 1 year after encoding (cf. Bradley et al., 1992; Dolcos et al., 2005). On the neural side, we could replicate our previous findings (Weymar et al., 2009) that enhanced memory for emotional content was related to an enhanced parietal ERP old/new effect after a week. Surprisingly, when measuring ERPs 1 year later, only unpleasant (but not pleasant)

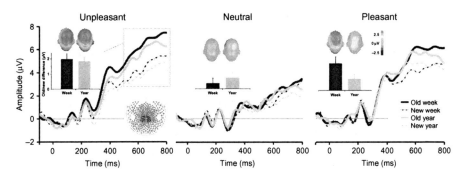

Figure 2.3 Effects of time on the old/new effect for emotional pictures. Recognition-test ERPs averaged across the parietal channel cluster are shown for correctly judged old and new items depicted separately for unpleasant, neutral, and pleasant pictures and retention interval (week versus year). The square represents the late (500–800 ms) time window used in the analyses. ERPs are averaged across channels within the specific parietal cluster used in the analyses. The upper bar graphs illustrate the old/new effect (old minus new) of the mean amplitudes recorded over the centroparietal cluster during the 500–800 ms time window separately for the three picture categories and two retention intervals (week versus year).

pictures showed augmented old/new differences in comparison to the neutral picture category (Figure 2.3). As in our previous studies, the memory advantage for emotional stimuli was based on high-confidence responses, supporting the role of recollection in emotional memory. Following these results, it seems that particularly unpleasant experiences are remarkably persistent in long-term memory. These data suggest that unpleasant materials are even more persistent in emotional memory than pleasant ones of the same arousal level when longer retention periods are taken into account (for a detailed discussion of the special characteristics of unpleasant memories, see Mickley Steinmetz, Addis, & Kensinger, 2010; Ochsner, 2000; Porter & Peace, 2007). In our sample, however, participants rated the unpleasant pictures also as more arousing than pleasant pictures, making it possible that the higher arousal levels evoked by the unpleasant stimuli may have led to enhanced long-term memory storage in the brain via enhanced noradrenergic transmission in the brain (McGaugh, 2004).

2.6 Adrenergic Activation and the ERP Old/New Effect for Emotional Contents

As described earlier in this chapter, animal data suggest that the adrenergic stress hormone system is essentially involved in the storage of emotional experiences (McGaugh, 2004). Recent pharmacological studies in humans indicate that administration of a non-selective β-antagonists (propranolol) during learning abolishes the emotional enhancement of memory (Cahill et al., 1995; Maheu, Joober, Beaulieu, & Lupien 2004; O'Carroll et al., 1999; van Stegeren, Everaerd, Cahill, McGaugh, & Gooren, 1998) targeting this finding as a potential treatment concept for humans suffering from traumatic life events as is the case in patients with PTSD.

To address whether the neural signature of emotional memories during recognition depends on such adrenergic mechanism, we investigated whether the old/new effect for emotional events would be impaired or blocked by systemic administration of propranolol prior to incidental encoding (Weymar, Löw, Modess, et al., 2010). In addition to autonomic measures (heart rate and blood pressure), we also collected saliva samples to assess the secretion of salivary alpha-amylase (sAA), which is a biomarker for noradrenergic activity and more reflective of central noradrenergic release than measures of the cardiovascular system (Ehlert, Erni, Hebisch, & Nater, 2006). Thus, we expected an association between sAA changes during encoding and the parietal old/new effect for emotional stimuli.

In a double-blind, placebo-controlled clinical trial, we examined 46 healthy male participants who watched a series of pictures and one week later returned for a recognition memory test. Half of the participants received either propranolol (80 mg) or a placebo capsule during picture viewing (encoding). We found that the placebo group showed larger old/new effects during recognition of pictures with emotional contents, replicating our previous findings (Weymar et al., 2009; Weymar, Löw, Schwabe, et al., 2010). Most interestingly, administration of the non-selective β-adrenoreceptor blocker propranolol prior to encoding selectively reduced this enhanced old/new effect during remembering of unpleasant pictures but not for pleasant and neutral pictures (Figure 2.4). Analysis of the sAA activity revealed that the neural signature of retrieving unpleasant memories was clearly related to endogenous noradrenergic activation during encoding, but not for the other picture categories. Based on these findings, the question is whether different mechanisms might contribute to the enhanced old/new effect for unpleasant and pleasant contents. Animal and human research on the noradrenergic modulation effects on emotional long-term memory processes (Chamberlain, Müller, Robbins, & Sahakian, 2006) has mainly focused on unpleasant experiences (e.g., inhibitory avoidance learning, unpleasant stimuli), not on pleasant experiences, thus making it difficult to evaluate the present findings. One reason might be that the pictorial stimuli evoked different individual arousal levels. Subjective ratings of the stimuli collected at the end of the experiment indicated that unpleasant pictures were rated as more arousing than pleasant pictures, possibly resulting in increased noradrenergic activation during encoding. Other data (Talmi, Schimmack, Paterson, & Moscovitch, 2007) suggest that enhanced memory for unpleasant and pleasant stimuli may rely on different mechanisms, suggesting that unpleasant memories are mediated more by emotional arousal, whereas pleasant memories are mediated by attention. Recent fMRI findings also point to a special role of valence, reporting that emotional arousal has an impact on neural connectivity within emotional memory networks that is greater when stimuli were unpleasant than when they were pleasant (Mickley Steinmetz et al., 2010). Our findings of a better long-term memory for unpleasant compared to pleasant stimuli would also support this conception.

In addition to our ERP findings, brain-imaging studies showed that propranolol, given during either encoding or memory retrieval, can alter the activity in structures recruited during memory reactivation of emotional stimuli (e.g., amygdala and hippocampus; Schwabe, Nader, Wolf, Beaudry, & Pruessner, 2012; Strange &

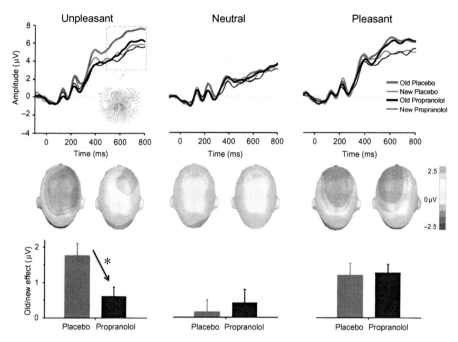

Figure 2.4 Propranolol blocks the neural signature of memory retrieval for unpleasant pictures. Recognition-test ERPs, averaged across the parietal channel cluster, are shown for correctly judged old and new items depicted separately for unpleasant, neutral, and pleasant pictures. Upper panel: ERP waveforms for the placebo group (Blue in online version) and the group receiving ß-blockers (Black). The squares mark the time intervals (500–800 ms) used in the analyses. The middle section displays the corresponding scalp potential differences (old minus new) separately for the three picture categories (top view) and group. The lower section shows the old/new effect (old minus new) of the mean amplitudes recorded over the centroparietal cluster during the 500–800 ms time window for each group (placebo versus propranolol). Error bars represent standard errors of the mean. Asterisks indicate significant differences, $p<0.05$.

Dolan, 2004), substantiating the opportunity that affecting the β-adrenergic transmission in the brain could change the neural signature of emotional (unwanted) memories. Thus, administering propranolol after traumatic experiences might reduce consolidation of trauma memories and thus reduce PTSD symptoms. First promising findings from Vaiva et al. (2003) show that propranolol given on the intensive care ward immediately after experiencing a traumatic event (car accident or experience of violence) indeed reduces the incidence for developing a PTSD. As a caveat, it has to be mentioned that the sample in this study was very small. Moreover, this treatment does not help patients who have already developed a PTSD. Brunet et al. (2008) therefore, for the first time, started a clinical trial to test the effect of propranolol for the treatment of chronic PTSD. Narrative scripts were used to activate the traumatic memory and propranolol was administered to interfere with the reconsolidation of the traumatic memories. After one week the traumatic scripts were presented again and emotional reactivity to these scripts was assessed. Patients who were treated with propranolol showed decreased autonomic responses to the trauma-related scripts compared to patients who received placebo treatment. Although these results are encouraging, it is still an open question whether these differences in emotional responding in an experimental paradigm are predictive for clinical outcome and prognosis. A possible problem of this form of treatment, however, could be that the β-blockers impair not only the reconsolidation of traumatic memories but also the consolidation of extinction memory. Therefore, it is important to get more information about the neural generators that are involved in both forms of memory formation.

2.7 Neural Generators of the Parietal Old/New Effect for Emotional Pictures

To estimate the cortical distribution of the current source density that accounts for emotional memory retrieval-related ERPs, we used the sLORETA algorithm (Pasqual-Marqui, 2002) in addition to the ERP analysis. In two studies (Weymar, Löw, Modess, et al., 2010; Weymar et al., 2011), we found maximal activity in parietal voxels (Figure 2.5) that contributed to enhanced retrieval of emotionally arousing stimuli. Source analysis revealed that parietal voxel activation was greater when old pictures were correctly identified as old, compared to when new pictures were correctly categorized as new. This parietal old/new activation is enhanced during retrieval of emotionally arousing stimuli (Weymar, Löw, Schwabe, et al., 2010; Weymar et al., 2011) and is sensitive to β-adrenergic activation during learning (Weymar, Löw, Modess, et al., 2010), suggesting that structures within the posterior parietal cortex are involved during reactivation of emotional memory traces. The centroparietal distribution of the old/new effect and the identification of the underlying brain sources within the

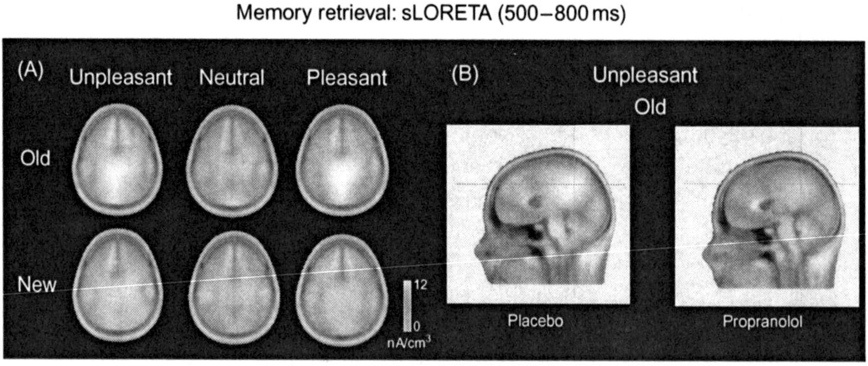

Figure 2.5 (A) Source activity associated with correctly judged old and new pictures are plotted for pleasant, neutral, and unpleasant pictures after a one-week interval, showing the parietal distribution of source activity in the 500–800 ms time interval. (B) Propranolol reduces source activity during memory retrieval in the parietal cortex. Source activity associated with correctly judged old unpleasant pictures are plotted for the placebo and propranolol group, showing the distribution of source activity in the time interval 500–800 ms.

parietal cortex are in agreement with recent fMRI studies (Cabeza, Ciaramelli, Olson, & Moscovitch, 2008; Vilberg & Rugg, 2009), showing convergent recollection effects in the precuneus and the lateral posterior parietal cortex. Functionally, parietal lobe activity may serve in guiding attention to internal representation as an episodic working memory buffer or as a gauge for the vividness of individuals' experience (Olson & Berryhill, 2009). Taken together, parietal lobe activation seems to be a part of the memory retrieval network, helping the individual to recollect highly vivid emotional experiences. Whether these networks are also involved during recollection of traumatic episodic memory needs to be investigated.

2.8 Conclusions

In the present review on emotional memory retrieval, we focused on recent electrophysiological findings, addressing the influence of emotion on the ERP old/new effect. Based on the available ERP work, we conclude that memory for emotional contents is better compared to neutral contents, especially after longer retention intervals. In accordance with better behavioral performances for emotional stimuli, ERP memory differences related to old rather than new items are already visible at the scalp 500ms after a stimulus's appearance originating in the parietal cortex. This neural signature is controlled by adrenergic transmission in the brain during encoding. Memory for emotional (unpleasant) experiences and the underlying electrophysiological correlates are remarkably stable and long lasting and are associated with higher confidence and a larger recollection power than for neutral stimuli. Future research has to transfer these findings obtained from normal student populations to the clinic and also needs to study in more detail the role of different steps and mechanisms involved during memory formation, consolidation, retrieval, and reconsolidation. Particularly, interactions with hormonal changes in these processes are very important avenues for future research. In a recent paper, we demonstrated that acute stress increases encoding and later memory performance for unpleasant events occurring immediately after stress induction (Weymar, Schwabe, Löw, & Hamm, 2012). The same effects seem to hold true after chronic stress. Unfolding the neural mechanisms for such effects might help to develop treatments for patients who suffer from their hurting memories for years.

References

Bradley, M. M. (2000). Emotion and motivation. In J. T. Cacioppo, L. G. Tassinary, & G. Berntson (Eds.), *Handbook of psychophysiology (pp. 602–642)*. New York, NY: Cambridge University Press.
Bradley, M. M., Greenwald, M. K., Petry, M. C., & Lang, P. J. (1992). Remembering pictures: pleasure and arousal in memory. *Journal of Experimental Psychology: Learning, Memory and Cognition, 18*, 379–390.
Brown, R., & Kulik, J. (1977). Flashbulb memories. *Cognition, 5*, 73–99.

Brunet, A., Orr, S. P., Tremblay, J., Robertson, K., Nader, K., & Pitman, R. K. (2008). Effect of post-retrieval propranolol on psychophysiologic responding during subsequent script-driven traumatic imagery in post-traumatic stress disorder. *Journal of Psychiatry Research, 42*, 503–506.

Buchanan, T. W., & Adolphs, R. (2002). The role of the human amygdala in emotional modulation of long-term declarative memory. In S. Moore & M. Oaksford (Eds.), *Emotional cognition: From brain to behavior (pp. 9–34)*. Amsterdam: John Benjamins Publishing.

Cabeza, R., Ciaramelli, E., Olson, I. R., & Moscovitch, M. (2008). The parietal cortex and episodic memory: An attentional account. *Nature Reviews Neuroscience, 9*, 613–625.

Cahill, L., Babinsky, R., Markowitsch, H. J., & McGaugh, J. (1995). Involvement of the amygdaloid complex in emotional memory. *Nature, 377*, 295–296.

Cahill, L., & McGaugh, J. L. (1995). A novel demonstration of enhanced memory associated with emotional arousal. *Consciousness and Cognition, 4*, 410–421.

Cahill, L., & van Stegeren, A. (2003). Sex-related impairment of memory for emotional events with β-adrenergic blockade. *Neurobiology of Learning and Memory, 79*, 81–88.

Chamberlain, S. R., Müller, U., Robbins, T. W., & Sahakian, B. J. (2006). Noradrenergic modulation of working memory and emotional memory in humans. *Psychopharmacology, 188*, 397–407.

Christianson, S. A. (1992). Emotional stress and eyewitness testimony: A critical review. *Psychological Bulletin, 112*, 284–309.

Curran, T. (2004). Effects of attention and confidence on the hypothesized ERP correlates of recollection and familiarity. *Neuropsychologia, 42*, 1088–1106.

Curran, T., Tepe, K. L., & Piatt, C. (2006). ERP explorations of dual processes in recognition memory. In H. D. Zimmer, A. Mecklinger, & U. Lindenberger (Eds.), *Binding in human memory: A neurocognitive approach (pp. 467–492)*. Oxford: Oxford University Press.

Dietrich, D. E., Waller, C., Johannes, S., Wieringa, B., Emrich, H. M., & Münte, T. F. (2001). Differential effects of emotional content on event-related potentials in word recognition memory. *Neuropsychobiology, 43*, 96–101.

Dolan, R. J. (2002). Emotion, cognition, and behavior. *Science, 298*, 1191–1194.

Dolcos, F., LaBar, K. S., & Cabeza, R. (2005). Remembering one year later: Role of the amygdala and medial temporal lobe memory system in retrieving emotional memories. *Proceedings of the national academy of sciences of the United States of America, 102*, 2626–2631.

Düzel, E., Vargha-Khadem, F., Heinze, H. J., & Mishkin, M. (2001). Brain activity evidence for recognition without recollection after early hippocampal damage. *Proceedings of the national academy of sciences of the United States of America, 98*, 8101–8106.

Düzel, E., Yonelinas, A. P., Mangun, G. R., Heinze, H. J., & Tulving, E. (1997). Event-related brain potential correlates of two states of conscious awareness in memory. *Proceedings of the national academy of sciences of the United States of America, 94*, 5973–5978.

Ehlert, U., Erni, K., Hebisch, G., & Nater, U. (2006). Salivary alpha-amylase levels after yohimbine challenge in healthy men. *Journal of Clinical Endocrinology and Metabolism, 91*, 5130–5133.

Friedman, D., & Johnson, R. J. (2000). Event-related potential (ERP) studies of memory encoding and retrieval: A selective review. *Microscopy Research and Technique, 51*, 6–28.

Hamann, S. B., Ely, T. D., Grafton, S. T., & Kilts, C. D. (1999). Amygdala activity related to enhanced memory for pleasant and aversive stimuli. *Nature Neuroscience, 2*, 289–293.

Inaba, M., Nomura, M., & Ohira, H. (2005). Neural evidence of effects of emotional valence on word recognition. *International Journal of Psychophysiology, 57*, 165–173.

Johansson, M., Mecklinger, A., & Treese, A. C. (2004). Recognition memory for emotional and neutral faces: An event-related potential study. *Journal of Cognitive Neuroscience, 16,* 1840–1853.
Keil, A. (2006). Macroscopic brain dynamics during verbal and pictorial processing of affective stimuli. *Progress in Brain Research, 156,* 217–232.
Kensinger, E. A., & Corkin, S. (2003). Memory enhancement for emotional words: Are emotional words more vividly remembered than neutral words? *Memory and Cognition, 31,* 1169–1180.
Kensinger, E. A., & Schacter, D. L. (2008). Memory and emotion. In M. Lewis, J. M. Haviland-Jones, & L. F. Barrett (Eds.), *The handbook of emotion* (3rd ed.). New York, NY: Guilford.
Koenig, S., & Mecklinger, A. (2008). Electrophysiological correlates of encoding and retrieving emotional events. *Emotion, 8,* 162–173.
LaBar, K. S., & Cabeza, R. (2006). Cognitive neuroscience of emotional memory. *Nature Neuroscience Reviews, 7,* 54–64.
LaBar, K. S., & Phelps, E. A. (1998). Arousal-mediated memory consolidation: Role of medial temporal lobe in humans. *Psychological Science, 9,* 490–493.
Lang, P. J., Bradley, M. M., & Cuthbert, B. N. (1998). Emotion, motivation, and anxiety: Brain mechanisms and psychophysiology. *Biological Psychiatry, 44,* 1248–1263.
Lang, P. J., Bradley, M. M., & Cuthbert, B. N. (2008). International affective picture system (IAPS): Affective ratings of pictures and instruction manual. *Technical Report A-8.* Gainesville, FL: University of Florida.
Lang, P. J., Greenwald, M., Bradley, M. M., & Hamm, A. O. (1993). Looking at pictures: Evaluative, facial, visceral, and behavioral responses. *Psychophysiology, 30,* 261–273.
Langeslag, S. J. E., & van Strien, J. W. (2008). Age differences in the emotional modulation of ERP old/new effects. *International Journal of Psychophysiology, 70,* 105–114.
Maheu, F. S., Joober, R., Beaulieu, S., & Lupien, S. J. (2004). Differential effects of adrenergic and corticosteroid hormonal systems on human short- and long-term declarative memory for emotionally arousing material. *Behavioral Neuroscience, 118,* 420–428.
Maratos, E. J., Allan, K., & Rugg, M. D. (2000). Recognition memory for emotionally negative and neutral words: An ERP study. *Neuropsychologia, 38,* 1452–1465.
Maratos, E. J., & Rugg, M. D. (2001). Electrophysiological correlates of the retrieval of emotional and non-emotional context. *Journal of Cognitive Neuroscience, 13*(7), 877–891.
McGaugh, J. L. (2000). Memory—a century of consolidation. *Science, 287,* 248–251.
McGaugh, J. L. (2004). The amygdala modulates the consolidation of memories of emotionally arousing experiences. *Annual Review of Neuroscience, 27,* 1–28.
Mecklinger, A. (2000). Interfacing mind and brain: A neurocognitive model of recognition memory. *Psychophysiology, 37,* 565–582.
Mehrabian, A., & Russell, J. (1974). *An approach to environmental psychology.* Cambridge, MA: Massachusetts Institute of Technology Press.
Mickley Steinmetz, K. R., Addis, D. R., & Kensinger, E. A. (2010). The effect of arousal on the emotional memory network depends on valence. *Neuroimage, 53,* 318–324.
Ochsner, K. N. (2000). Are affective events richly recollected or simply familiar? The experience and process of recognizing feelings past. *Journal of Experimental Psychology General, 129,* 242–261.
Olson, I. R., & Berryhill, M. E. (2009). Some surprising findings on the involvement of the parietal lobe in human memory. *Neurobiology of Learning and Memory, 91,* 155–165.
O'Carroll, R. E., Drysdale, E., Cahill, L., Shajahan, P., & Ebmeier, K. P. (1999). Stimulation of the noradrenergic system enhances and blockade reduces memory for emotional material in man. *Psychological Medicine, 29,* 1083–1088.

Pascual-Marqui, R. D. (2002). Standardized low resolution brain electromagnetic tomography (sLORETA): Technical details. *Methods and Findings in Experimental and Clinical Pharmacology, 24D*, 5–12.

Phelps, E. A., & Sharot, T. (2008). How (and why) emotion enhances the subjective sense of recollection. *Current Directions in Psychological Science, 17*, 147–152.

Porter, S., & Peace, K. (2007). The scars of memory: A prospective, longitudinal investigation of the consistency of traumatic and positive emotional memories in adulthood. *Psychological Science, 18*, 435–441.

Quevedo, J., Sant' Anna, M. K., Madruga, M., Lovato, I., de-Paris, F., Kapczinski, F., Izquierdo, I., & Cahill, L. (2003). Differential effects of emotional arousal in short- and long-term memory in healthy adults. *Neurobiology of Learning and Memory, 79*, 132–135.

Richter-Levin, G., & Akirav, I. (2003). Emotional tagging of memory formation—in the search for neural mechanisms. *Brain Research Reviews, 43*, 247–256.

Righi, S., Marzi, T., Toscani, M., Baldassi, S., Ottonello, S., & Viggiano, M. P. (2012). Fearful expressions enhance recognition memory: Electrophysiological evidence. *Acta Psychologica, 139*, 7–18.

Ritchey, M., Dolcos, F., & Cabeza, R. (2008). Role of amygdala connectivity in the persistence of emotional memories over time: An event-related fMRI investigation. *Cerebral Cortex, 18*, 2494–2504.

Rugg, M. D., & Curran, T. (2007). Event-related potentials and recognition memory. *Trends in Cognitive Sciences, 11*, 251–257.

Schaefer, A., Pottage, C. L., & Rickart, A. J. (2011). Electrophysiological correlates of remembering emotional pictures. *Neuroimage, 54*, 714–724.

Schwabe, L., Nader, K., Wolf, O. T., Beaudry, T., & Pruessner, J. C. (2012). Neural signature of reconsolidation impairments by propranolol in humans. *Biological Psychiatry, 71*, 380–386.

Sharot, T., & Phelps, E. A. (2004). How arousal modulates memory: Disentangling the effects of attention and retention. *Cognitive Affective Behavioral Neuroscience, 3*, 294–306.

Sharot, T., & Yonelinas, A. P. (2008). Differential time-dependent effects of emotion on the recollective experience and memory for contextual information. *Cognition, 106*, 538–547.

Strange, B. A., & Dolan, R. J. (2004). Beta-adrenergic modulation of emotional memory-evoked human amygdala and hippocampal responses. *Proceedings of the national academy of sciences of the United States of America, 101*, 11454–11458.

Talmi, D., Schimmack, U., Paterson, T., & Moscovitch, M. (2007). The role of attention in emotional memory enhancement. *Emotion, 7*, 89–102.

Tulving, E. (1985). Memory and consciousness. *Canadian Psychology, 26*, 1–12.

Vaiva, G., Ducrocq, F., Jezequel, K., Averland, B., Lestavel, P., Brunet, A., & Marmar, C. R. (2003). Immediate treatment with propranolol decreases posttraumatic stress disorder two months after trauma. *Biological Psychiatry, 54*, 947–949.

van Stegeren, A. H., Everaerd, W., Cahill, L., McGaugh, J. L., & Gooren, L. J. G. (1998). Memory for emotional events: Differential effects of centrally versus peripherally acting beta-blocking agents. *Psychopharmacology, 138*, 305–310.

Versace, F., Bradley, M. M., & Lang, P. J. (2006). Recognition memory for emotional pictures presented at slow and fast rates. *Psychophysiology*, S7.

Vilberg, K. L., & Rugg, M. D. (2009). Functional significance of retrieval-related activity in lateral parietal cortex: evidence from fMRI and ERPs. *Human Brain Mapping, 30*, 1490–1501.

Voss, J. L., & Federmeier, K. D. (2011). FN400 potentials are functionally identical to N400 potentials and reflect semantic processing during recognition testing. *Psychophysiology, 48*, 532–546.

Voss, J. L. & Paller, K. A. (2008). Neural substrates of remembering: Electroencephalographic studies. In H. Eichenbaum (Ed.), *Memory systems* (pp. 79–98), *Vol. 3 of Learning and memory: A comprehensive reference, 4 Vols.* (J. Byrne, Ed.). Oxford: Elsevier.

Weymar, M., Bradley, M. M., Hamm, A. O., & Lang, P. J. (2012). When fear forms memories: Threat of shock and brain potentials during encoding and retrieval. *Cortex.* 2012 Mar 8. [Epub ahead of print], http://dx.doi.org/10.1016/j.cortex.2012.02.012.

Weymar, M., Löw, A., & Hamm, A. O. (2011). Emotional memories are resilient to time: Evidence from the parietal ERP old/new effect. *Human Brain Mapping, 32,* 632–640.

Weymar, M., Löw, A., Melzig, C. A., & Hamm, A. O. (2009). Enhanced long-term recollection for emotional pictures: Evidence from high-density ERPs. *Psychophysiology, 46,* 1200–1207.

Weymar, M., Löw, A., Modess, C., Engel, G., Gründling, M., Petersmann, A., Siegmund, W., & Hamm, A. O. (2010). Propranolol selectively blocks the enhanced parietal old/new effect during long-term recollection of unpleasant pictures: A high density ERP study. *Neuroimage, 49,* 2800–2806.

Weymar, M., Löw, A., Schwabe, L., & Hamm, A. O. (2010). Brain dynamics associated with recollective experiences of emotional events. *NeuroReport, 21,* 827–831.

Weymar, M., Schwabe, L., Löw, A., & Hamm, A. O. (2012). Stress sensitizes the brain: Increased processing of unpleasant pictures after exposure to acute stress. *Journal of Cognitive Neuroscience, 24,* 1511–1518.

Windmann, S., & Kutas, M. (2001). Electrophysiological correlates of emotion-induced recognition bias. *Journal of Cognitive Neuroscience, 13,* 577–592.

Yonelinas, A. P. (2002). The nature of recollection and familiarity: A review of 30 years of research. *Journal of Memory and Language, 46,* 441–517.

3 Pharmacological Approaches to Understand, Prevent, and Mitigate Hurting Memories. Lessons from Posttraumatic Stress Disorders

Hans-Peter Kapfhammer
Department of Psychiatry, Medical University of Graz, Graz, Austria

3.1 Trauma and Psychological Models of Traumatic Memory

Traumatic memory in its distinctive and often pervasive form plays a central role in the diagnostic criteria of posttraumatic stress disorder (PTSD). Classical conditioning seems to explain some of the symptomatic peculiarities. Unspecific stimuli that are in spatial and temporal contingency to the traumatic scene will gain the quality of conditioned stimuli and trigger the unconditional reactions of fear, panic, and helplessness experienced during the initial trauma. Often lifelong persisting traumatic memories and associated stress symptoms, with their possible tendency to generalize even to neutral stimuli of daily life situations and to escalate in its intensity, underline arrested processes of normal extinction on the one hand and of additional nonassociative learning processes, such as sensitization, on the other (Pitman, Shalev, & Orr, 2000). Some of the memory disturbances prevailing in PTSD seem to be rather specific; some other mnestic features are shared by several other psychological disorders as well (Brewin, Gregory, Lipton, & Burgess, 2010). Memory capacity, contents of memory, and memory processes may be variably affected by traumatic events and may mediate a differential causal risk in the transition to PTSD (Brewin, 2011).

With respect to *memory capacity*, empirical studies inconsistently report on an increased general state of conditionability in patients with PTSD and find medium effect sizes at most (Lissek, Powers, & McClure, 2005). Compared with control persons, however, PTSD patients show more signs of second-order conditioning. Affective, cognitive, and physiological stimuli out of the original trauma scene seem to take on the quality of unconditional traumatic stimuli contributing to conditioned stress reactions even in the absence of trauma, thereby underlining the arrest of normal extinction processes (Wessa & Flor, 2007) or failure of extinction memory when required in defined situations (Milad, Pitman, & Ellis, 2009). Reduced extinction learning already existing before any traumatic exposition may contribute to a higher and more persistent symptom load subsequent to posttraumatic stress (Guthrie & Bryant, 2006).

Significant deficits both in verbal learning and in working memory often detected in PTSD patients are considered as predisposing risk factors rather than as consequences of trauma exposition or PTSD (Gilbertson, Paulus, & Williston, 2006). The capacity to suppress either intrusive memories of negative affective valence or irrelevant cognitions in completing important executive tasks seems to be significantly impaired and to characterize a personality trait (Brewin & Smart, 2005).

With respect to *memory content*, the highest level of autobiographical memory may be profoundly affected when trauma alters core aspects of personal identity. Identity refers to a self-related conceptual knowledge that allows us to consistently and congruently structure our personal goals according to biographical stage, present life situation, and required psychosocial role performance (Conway, 2005). The vast majority of PTSD patients restructure their life narratives according to a period before and a period after a drastic traumatic event. Despite its significance of trauma as central point of reference in subjective biography, it seems paradoxical that relevant features of trauma itself may be only partially integrated in autobiographical memory (Rubin, Berntsen, & Bohni, 2008). Indeed, many patients suffering from acute stress disorder or PTSD may face great difficulties in reporting coherent autobiographical memories of the traumatic event (Evans, Ehlers, Mezey, & Clark, 2007; Jones, Harvey, & Brewin, 2007). The proportion of disorganization and fragmentation in voluntary remembrance is significantly correlated with the extent of dissociation during and after trauma exposition. It is still open whether these deficits in declarative memory of trauma episodes are due to an original disturbance of verbal representation of trauma or due to intrusive, highly emotional, and sensation-based trauma memories that impair the actual process of retrieval (Brewin, 2007). These traumatic memories, particularly in the form of intrusive visual flashbacks, significantly differ from other types of autobiographical memories. They are beyond voluntary control and are automatically triggered by external or internal stimuli related to the original trauma context. They are characterized by a strong visualization and are associated with fierce somatic reactions. They may be only poorly accessible to verbalization, accompanied by a distorted sense of time often presenting as actual experience rather than as self-reflective memory. This type of trauma memories seems to be highly specific of PTSD, as has been outlined by Brewin (2011). His theoretical model of dual representation accounts for verbally structured autobiographical memories on the one hand and for a dissociation-related, situation-dependent, and sensation-based storage of traumatic memories without further cognitive and linguistic processing subsequent initial conditioning on the other. A subgroup of patients, however, report on a delayed onset of their PTSD symptoms (Andrews, Brewin, & Stewart, 2009; Bonanno, Brewin, & Kaniasty, 2010). This empirical observation makes classical conditioning as a generally sufficient basis of explanation unlikely, instead focusing on additional processes of cognitive and emotional reappraisal of the earlier trauma and ongoing neurobiological sensitization in the further course of posttraumatic development (Yehuda & LeDoux, 2007).

With respect to additional *memory processes* that may mediate or even potentiate the risk of PTSD subsequent to initial trauma exposition, several actual cognitive processes may be stressed. For example, memory bias, overgeneral memory, emotion-based strategies of reassessing the personal significance of trauma, increasing trauma-related avoidance behavior, false recognition and negative appraisal of intrusive memories may all strategically contribute to the onset, delayed onset, and maintenance of PTSD symptoms (Brewin, 2011).

3.2 Neurobiological Underpinnings of Trauma Memory Encoding, Consolidation, Retrieval, and Extinction

Storage and processing of traumatic memories and mode of recall refer to a neuronal circuit that allows direct communication between thalamus and amygdala and that mediates rapid sensory-perceptive-affective processing (Metcalfe & Jacobs, 1998; Shin & Liberzon, 2010). This system guarantees basic emotional evaluation in states of threat and initiates a pattern of adaptive motor, visceral, and neurohumoral reactions. Processes of classical conditioning may be started in the basolateral nuclei of the amygdala as the center of emotional memory (LeDoux, 2007). Under the impact of high stress, these conditioned emotional experiences very often remain cognitively unelaborated in further processing. Already at thalamic level, information may have become fragmented and disorganized when the field of perception is focused on central details of a threatening situation, excluding, however, peripheral contextual aspects. This state of early thalamic processing may be correlated with an altered sense of time and changed polymodal perception (color, size, temporal and spatial relations, posture, and analgesia) and may stress the basic processes of dissociative compartmentalization (Bremner, Elzinga, Schmahl, & Vermetten, 2008; Holmes, Brown, & Mansell, 2005). The representation of social reality by necessity becomes less structured and distorted by dissociative processes and defines what may finally be conditioned in the basolateral nuclei of the amygdala. There above all perceptive and affective details of the original traumatic scene are conditioned without proper temporal, spatial, and self-referential contextualization because hippocampal functioning may be hampered under impact of high distress. Transfer of both to higher cortical systems of language, episodic, and autobiographical memory may be disturbed, thus also determining a special mode of recall (Kapfhammer, 2011).

Several *neurochemical* and *neurohumoral* factors show a major impact on the various stages in the processing of traumatic memories. *Norepinephrine* decisively regulates any associative emotional learning according to classical and operant conditioning (McGaugh, 2004). The noradrenergic system of locus coeruleus seems to be highly vulnerable to sensitization in states of prolonged and uncontrollable stress, thus contributing to a persisting autonomous hyperarousal (Krystal & Neumeister, 2009). The overconsolidation of traumatic memories in the amygdala is thereby facilitated on the one hand, and adequate processing of information in the hippocampal and prefrontal areas may be severely hampered on the other (Southwick, Davis, & Aikins, 2007). Noradrenergic hyperactivity also facilitates the special mode of intrusive sensation-based memories and simultaneously impairs processes of natural extinction learning (Roozendaal, McEwen, & Chattarji, 2009). *Glutamate* plays a basic and central role in regulating consciousness and learning. It carries on the process of emotional conditioning that is under primary control of norepinephrine, induces long-term potentiation by stimulation of glutamatergic NMDA-receptors and determines consolidation. A dysfunctional glutamatergic system, in alliance with a disturbed interaction of GABA and serotonin system, may participate in dissociative processes (D' Souza, Gil, & Zuzarte, 2006) and seems to be correlated with dysfunctional performance or even structural deficits of the hippocampus (Bremner et al., 2008). Glutamate also contributes to extinction learning, which must be considered as active and new learning of modulating conditioned emotional patterns. In general, extinction learning is regulated by a complex interplay of excitatory glutamatergic and inhibitory GABAergic, endocannabinoid, and other neurotransmitter effects (Garakani, Murrough, Charney, & Bremner, 2009). The endogenous *opioid* system again is significantly engaged in a dissociative counterregulation of noradrenergic hyperactivity and mediates psychomotor freezing, emotional numbness, and states of analgesia. Endogenous opioids contribute to a functional disconnection of amygdala and hippocampus and may impair control of reality and active coping (Schmahl & Bohus, 2007).

HPA axis is regularly involved in any initiated stress reactions. Its main function appears to be in the regulation and containment of sympathetic (and parasympathetic) responses to stress. Multiple effects of glucocorticoids must be considered within different stages of memory processes. Short and minor traumatic episodes trigger an upsurge of cortisol that strengthens initial memory consolidation in accordance with norepinephrine. However, prolonged high levels of cortisol seem to counteract this synergism (Joëls, Fernandez, & Roozendaal, 2011). On the other hand, cortisol impairs both memory retrieval and working memory (De Quervain, Aerni, Schelling, & Roozendaal, 2009). If only insufficient levels of cortisol are available in states of acute or chronic stress that characterizes a major subgroup of traumatized persons (Yehuda & LeDoux, 2007), then a predominantly noradrenergic mode of remembrance prevails, which is paradigmatically indicated by intrusive sensation-based memories, such as flashbacks (Roozendaal et al., 2009). Cortisol mediates its differential effects by both genomic and nongenomic mechanisms. Rapidly acting nongenomic mechanisms may be involved when the endocannabinoid system seems to mediate glucocorticoid effects on memory consolidation via a modulation of GABAergic activity. Effects of this complex neuromodulatory interplay on memory retrieval and working memory have still to be investigated (Atsak, Roozendaal, & Campolongo, 2012).

3.3 Principal Pharmacological Strategies to Mitigate or Prevent Traumatic Memory: Results from Empirical Studies

Because *norepinephrine* plays a central role in emotional memory encoding and consolidation from the very beginning of any traumatic exposition, and because noradrenergic hyperarousal may lead both to basic impairments of cognitive control and effective modulation of emotional excitement normally mediated by prefrontal systems, counteracting noradrenergic hyperactive might be a promising first step to prevent a risky transition to PTSD subsequent to traumatic stress. Noradrenergic hyperactivity may be reduced both by postsynaptic β- and α_1-adrenergic antagonism and by presynaptic α_2-adrenergic agonism (Schwabe, Nader, Wolf, Beaudry, & Pruessner, 2012). Several pharmacological tools are available and have been investigated in empirical studies. So far, the results have been inconsistent.

Pitman, Sanders, and Zusman (2002) did a first pilot study. They recruited 41 persons who presented with DSM-IV criteria A1 and A2 and signs of increased autonomous activity (resting pulse >80/min) in an emergency room immediately after a traumatic event (mostly severe motor vehicle accidents). Patients were enrolled in a randomized, double-blind, and placebo-controlled trial, receiving either 4×40mg *propranolol*/day or placebo over 10 days. After one month, two patients of the propranolol group fulfilled the diagnostic criteria of PTSD according to the Clinician-Administered PTSD Scale, however six patients of the placebo group ($p=0.19$). At 3-month follow up, one patient of the propranolol group and three patients of the placebo group had PTSD ($p=0.35$). This positive but statistically nonsignificant trend (due to much too low a power) was underlined in an additional, trauma script-driven psychophysiological investigation, indicating autonomous hyperarousal in none of the patients of the propranolol group and in eight patients of the placebo group ($p=0.004$). Other controlled but nonblinded and nonrandomized trials also spoke in favor of a β-adrenergic blockade in this indication (Taylor et al., 2002; Vaiva, Ducrocq, & Jezequel, 2003). A randomized, double-blind, and placebo- or gabapentin-controlled trial with patients after traumatic injuries could not confirm any advantage of propranolol (Stein, Kerridge, Dimsdale, & Hoyt, 2007). There are negative results from a prophylactic use of propranolol in patients after severe burns regarding the incidence of later PTSD (McGhee, Maani, & Garza, 2009; Sharp, Thomas, & Rosenberg, 2010).

Open studies with α_2-agonistic substances as *clonidine* or *guanfacine* that both reduce the release of norepinephrine from presynaptic vesicles into the synaptic cleft promise a preventive potential (Morgan, Krystal, & Southwick, 2003). So far, however, no prospective controlled trials have investigated any preventive use of these substances. Controlled trials in the treatment of veterans with chronic PTSD found negative results of guanfacine (Davis et al., 2008; Neylan, Lenoci, & Samuelson, 2006). The α_1-antagonist *prazosine*, whose positive effects on PTSD-related sleep disturbances and nightmares have been well established in several randomized controlled trials (Germain, Richardson, & Moul, 2012; Raskind, Peskind, & Hoff, 2007; Raskind, Peskind, & Kanter, 2003; Taylor, Martin, & Thompson, 2008), might be another promising candidate in possibly preventing the transition to PTSD after trauma exposition. This indication, however, requires proper pharmacological investigation.

In general, counteracting noradrenergic hyperactivity subsequent to traumatic stress seems to be still an interesting option for early trials to prevent or to reduce the risk of transition to PTSD. Randomized placebo-controlled studies carried out so far are rare and as a rule have included only small samples of patients. The results of the trials are inclusive (Hoge, Worthington, & Nagurney, 2012). Any intervention, such as with a β-adrenergic blockade, has to assess clinical signs of autonomous hyperarousal very carefully and to appreciate overall pathophysiology that may be rather complicated in states of bodily injuries (e.g., burns) or associated somatic diseases (Schelling, 2008).

There is overwhelming evidence for dysfunctional HPA axis in PTSD, indicating low levels of cortisol as possible personality-bound predisposing factor and probable risk factor of PTSD after traumatic exposition (Yehuda, 2009). Glucocorticoids are crucially involved in the regulation of memory and have differential impact on memory consolidation, memory retrieval, and working memory. Its suppressive effect on recurrent intrusive sensation-based trauma memories might be considered as one decisive step to restrain any overconsolidation of traumatic memory. Therefore, substituting stress-related doses of *hydrocortisone* has to be investigated as a prophylactic strategy. There are confirming results from some randomized, double-blind, and placebo-controlled trials with patients treated on ICU for reasons of acute respiratory distress syndrome, septic shock, or cardiac surgery (Schelling, Briegel, & Roozendaal, 2001; Schelling, Kilger, & Roozendaal, 2004; Weis, Kilger, & Roozendaal, 2006). These severe medical conditions are associated with a relative insufficiency of cortisol and a subsequent high risk of PTSD (Kapfhammer, Rothenhäusler, & Schelling, 2004). Substituting hydrocortisone in these narrowly defined pathophysiological states delivers a statistically significant and clinically relevant reduction of PTSD risk. There are first clinical data that the early use of hydrocortisone might be a promising preventive strategy even in persons affected by severe civil traumata, as Zohar, Juven-Wetzler, et al. (2011) showed in a recent randomized, controlled trial. The authors stressed the importance of cortisol administration in the early "golden hours" after trauma exposition and discussed a remarkably reduced or even absent effect of cortisol given later on. Regarding this delicate time schedule of intervention, they referred to some experimental data in animal experiments. On the other hand, however, there are controlled clinical observations that the administration of hydrocortisone might still be helpful in patients suffering from chronic PTSD symptoms, particularly from intrusive trauma recollections, via suppressing the mode of intrusive remembrance on the one hand and enhancing adequate extinction learning on the other (Aerni, Traber, & Hock, 2004). Following the same theoretical rational, there are also well controlled data derived from several studies that glucocorticoids may mediate positive effects in phobic disorders (De Quervain & Margraf, 2008).

GABAergic inhibitory control seems to be crucially involved in any precise regulation of consolidation, expression, and extinction of emotional, that is, traumatic conditioning (Mahan & Ressler, 2012; Roozendaal et al., 2009). Deriving from clinical and experimental studies that established a profound disruptive effect of benzodiazepines (BDZs) on fear memory consolidation (Bustos, Maldonado, & Molina, 2006; Savić, Obradovic, Ugresic, & Bokonjic, 2005), one might consider the use of BDZs in early states of posttraumatic processing. The story with BDZs, however, seems to be complex. Although BDZ mediates strong anxiolytic effects in states of any emotional upheaval, they induce typical anterograde amnesia that might be counterproductive in further processing. BDZ may facilitate retrieval of trauma-related memories, simultaneously suppressing neutral information, being detrimental to the restoration of trauma memories after reactivation and negatively interfering with the formation of newly acquired extinction memories (Makkar, Zhang, & Cranney, 2010). Zohar, Yahalom, et al. (2011) stress that BDZ abolish the normative adaptive HPA-axis response that seems to be vital for any posttraumatic recovery and discuss that, after trauma exposition, BDZ might increase the long-term risk of later PTSD via this mechanism. Indeed, early systematic use of BDZ for preventive reasons might not be a good clinical idea, as some randomized controlled trials showed, underlining no superiority of BDZ to placebo on the one hand (Mellman, Bustamante, & David, 2002) and, on the other hand, stressing a statistically significant increase of both PTSD and depression compared to placebo (Gelpin, Bonne, & Peri, 1996).

It is well established that the *endogenous opiate* system participates in the regulation of emotional learning and memory and thereby plays a central role during and after trauma exposition (Garakani et al., 2009). Based on clinical reports, early use of *opiates* in patients with severe traumatic burns seems be correlated with a lower incidence of later PTSD (Saxe, Stoddard, & Courtney, 2001; Stoddard, Sorrentino, & Ceranoglu, 2009). Military medical experiences with soldiers severely wounded during combat also strengthen a strategy of early use of opiates (Holbrook, Galarneau, & Dye, 2010). Persisting and uncontrollable pain may be considered a proper risk factor for later PTSD (Norman, Stein, Dimsdale, & Hoyt, 2008; Schelling, 2008). It has still to be established, however, whether opiates deliver a genuine general effect of reducing PTSD risk beyond a special analgesic effect (Bryant, Creamer, O'Donnell, Silove, & McFarlane, 2009).

Serotonin modulates noradrenergic reactivity and autonomous arousal. It has an impact on HPA-axis functioning. It generally mediates inhibitory effects both on neuronal activity and on plasticity. A well-balanced serotonergic neurotransmission is a basic precondition to flexible reality orientation and adequate reaction. Any prolonged and uncontrollable stress, as in traumatic situations, may lead to serotonergic dysfunction (Krystal & Neumeister, 2009). Serotonergic antidepressants play a paramount role in the pharmacological treatment of established PTSD. There have been, however, only very few attempts to empirically prove any preventive potential of serotonergic substances shortly after trauma exposition (Zohar, Sonnino, Juven-Wetzler, & Cohen, 2009). A randomized, double-blind, and placebo-controlled trial could not establish a superior effect of escitalopram in this indication with adults after various traumata (Shalev et al., 2012). With children suffering from severe burns, however, sertraline demonstrated a statistically significant preventive effect that had to be considered, in clinical terms, as medium at most (Stoddard, Luthra, & Sorrentino, 2011).

3.4 Conclusions

There exists a vast empirical literature on evidence-based pharmacological strategies in the treatment of diagnostically established PTSD, whereas research on pharmacological approaches to prevent the development of posttraumatic disorders is still only just beginning (Fletcher, Creamer, & Forbes, 2010; Friedman, 2008; Pitman & Delahanty, 2005). The modulation of the process of traumatic memory seems to be at the center of any such preventive approach. Inasmuch as the transfer of traumatic experience into a chronically cemented trauma memory with a persisting suffering refers to a complex process that is determined by many biopsychosocial factors, it seems to be quite unlikely that one psychopharmacological tool will overcome this clinical challenge once. However, some promising avenues are worth further research activities in the future. Apart from pharmacological endeavors to mitigate or prevent traumatic memories, any clinician or researcher has to deal with ethical and societal skepticism. This discussion should not be led solely on an abstract philosophical level but has to be clinically well-informed and especially focused on the severe and potentially lasting suffering many people are going to face after trauma exposition (Donovan, 2010).

References

Aerni, A., Traber, R., Hock, C., Roozendaal, B., Schelling, G., Papassotiropoulos, A., et al. (2004). Low-dose cortisol for symptoms of posttraumatic stress disorder. *The American Journal of Psychiatry, 161*, 1488–1490.

Andrews, B., Brewin, C. R., Stewart, L., Philpott, R., & Hejdenberg, J. (2009). Comparison of immediate-onset and delayed-onset posttraumatic stress disorder in military veterans. *Journal of Abnormal Psychology, 118*, 767–777.

Atsak, P., Roozendaal, B., & Campolongo, P. (2012). Role of the endocannabinoid system in regulating glucocorticoid effects on memory for emotional experiences. *Neuroscience, 204*, 104–116.

Bonanno, G. A., Brewin, C. R., Kaniasty, K., et al. (2010). Weighing the costs of disaster: Consequences, risks, and resilience in individuals, families, and communities. *Psychological Science and Public Interest, 11*, 1–49.

Bremner, J. D., Elzinga, B., Schmahl, C., & Vermetten, E. (2008). Structural and functional plasticity of the human brain in posttraumatic stress disorder. *Progress in Brain Research, 167*, 171–186.

Brewin, C. R. (2007). Autobiographical memory for trauma: Update on four controversies. *Memory, 15*, 227–248.

Brewin, C. R. (2011). The nature and significance of memory disturbance in posttraumatic stress disorder. *Annual Review of Clinical Psychology, 7*, 203–227.

Brewin, C. R., Gregory, J. D., Lipton, M., & Burgess, N. (2010). Intrusive images in psychological disorders: Characteristics, neural mechanisms, and treatment implications. *Psychological Review, 117*, 210–232.

Brewin, C. R., & Smart, L. (2005). Working memory capacity and suppression of intrusive thoughts. *Journal of Behavioral Therapy and Experimental Psychiatry, 36*, 61–68.

Bryant, R. A., Creamer, M., O'Donnell, M., Silove, D., & McFarlane, A. C. (2009). A study of the protective function of acute morphine administration on subsequent posttraumatic stress disorder. *Biological Psychiatry, 65*, 438–440.

Bustos, S. G., Maldonado, H., & Molina, V. A. (2006). Midazolam disrupts fear memory reconsolidation. *Neuroscience, 139*, 831–842.

Conway, M. A. (2005). Memory and the self. *Journal of Memory and Language, 53*, 594–628.

Davis, L. L., Ward, C., Rasmusson, A., Newell, J. M., Frazier, E., & Southwick, S. M. (2008). A placebo-controlled trial of guanfacine for the treatment of posttraumatic stress disorder in veterans. *Psychopharmacology Bulletin, 41*, 8–18.

De Quervain, D. J. F., Aerni, A., Schelling, G., & Roozendaal, B. (2009). Glucocorticoids and the regulation of memory in health and disease. *Frontiers in Neuroendocrinology, 30*, 358–370.

De Quervain, D. J. F., & Margraf, J. (2008). Glucocorticoids for the treatment of post-traumatic stress disorder and phobias: A novel therapeutic approach. *European Journal of Pharmacology, 583*, 365–371.

Donovan, E. (2010). Propranolol use in the prevention and treatment of posttraumatic stress disorder in military veterans: Forgetting therapy revisited. *Perspectives in Biology and Medicine, 53*, 61–74.

D'Souza, D. C., Gil, R. B., Zuzarte, E., MacDougall, L. M., Donahue, L., Ebersole, J. S., et al. (2006). γ-Aminobutyric acid-serotonin interactions in healthy men: Implications for network models of psychosis and dissociation. *Biological Psychiatry, 59*, 128–137.

Evans, C., Ehlers, A., Mezey, G., & Clark, D. M. (2007). Intrusive memories in perpetrators of violent crimes: Emotions and cognitions. *Journal of Consulting and Clinical Psychology, 75*, 134–144.

Fletcher, S., Creamer, M., & Forbes, D. (2010). Preventing post traumatic stress disorder: Are drugs the answer? *The Australian and New Zealand Journal of Psychiatry, 4*, 1064–1071.

Friedman, M. J. (2008). The role of pharmacotherapy in early intervention. In M. Blumenfield & R. J. Ursano (Eds.), *Intervention and resilience after mass trauma* (pp. 107–125). Cambridge: Cambridge University Press.

Garakani, A., Murrough, J. W., Charney, D. S., & Bremner, D. (2009). The neurobiology of anxiety disorders. In D. S. Charney & E. J. Nestler (Eds.), *Neurobiology of mental illness* (pp. 655–690) (3rd ed.). Oxford, NY: Oxford University Press.

Gelpin, E., Bonne, O., Peri, T., Brandes, D., & Shalev, A. Y. (1996). Treatment of recent trauma survivors with benzodiazepines: A prospective study. *The Journal of Clinical Psychiatry, 57*, 390–394.

Germain, A., Richardson, R., Moul, D. E., Mammen, O., Haas, G., Forman, S. D., et al. (2012). Placebo-controlled comparison of prazosin and cognitive-behavioral treatments for sleep disturbances in US military veterans. *Journal of Psychosomatic Research, 72*, 89–96.

Gilbertson, M. W., Paulus, L. A., Williston, S. K., Gurvits, T. V., Lasko, N. B., Pitman, R. K., & Orr, S. P. (2006). Neurocognitive function in monozygotic twins discordant for combat exposure: Relationship to posttraumatic disorder. *Journal of Abnormal Psychology, 115*, 484–495.

Guthrie, R. M., & Bryant, R. A. (2006). Extinction learning before trauma and subsequent posttraumatic stress. *Psychosomatic Medicine, 68*, 307–311.

Hoge, E. A., Worthington, J. J., Nagurney, J. T., Chang, Y., Kay, E. B., Feterowski, C. M., et al. (2012). Effect of acute posttrauma propranolol on PTSD outcome and physiological responses during script-driven imagery. *CNS Neuroscience & Therapeutics, 18*, 21–27.

Holbrook, T. L., Galarneau, M. R., Dye, J. L., Quinn, K., & Dougherty, A. L. (2010). Morphine use after combat injury in Iraq and posttraumatic stress disorder. *The New England Journal of Medicine, 362*, 110–117.

Holmes, E. A., Brown, R. J., Mansell, W., Fearon, R. P., Hunter, E. C., Frasquilho, F., & Oakley, D. A. (2005). Are there two qualitatively distinct forms of dissociation? A review and some clinical implications. *Clinical Psychology Review, 25*, 1–23.

Joëls, M., Fernandez, G., & Roozendaal, B. (2011). Stress and emotional memory: A matter of timing. *Trends in Cognitive Sciences, 15*, 280–288.

Jones, C., Harvey, A. G., & Brewin, C. R. (2007). The organisation and content of trauma memories in survivors of road traffic accidents. *Behaviour Research and Therapy, 45*, 151–162.

Kapfhammer, H. P. (2011). Psychologische Störungen des autobiografischen Gedächtnisses— Einflüsse von Trauma, Dissoziation und PTSD. *Psychiatrie & Psychotherapie, 7*, 43–55.

Kapfhammer, H. P., Rothenhäusler, H. B., Krauseneck, T., Stoll, C., & Schelling, G. (2004). Posttraumatic stress disorder in survivors of ARDS. Results of a follow up study in a university C/L service. *The American Journal of Psychiatry, 161*, 45–52.

Krystal, J. H., & Neumeister, A. (2009). Noradrenergic and serotonergic mechanisms in the neurobiology of posttraumatic stress disorder and resilience. *Brain Research, 1293*, 13–23.

LeDoux, J. (2007). The amygdala. *Current Biology, 17*, R868–R874.
Lissek, S., Powers, A. S., McClure, E. B., Phelps, E. A., Woldehawariat, G., Grillon, C., & Pine, D. S. (2005). Classical fear conditioning in the anxiety disorders: A meta-analysis. *Behaviour Research and Therapy, 43*, 1391–1424.
Mahan, A. L., & Ressler, K. J. (2012). Fear conditioning, synaptic plasticity and the amygdala: Implications for posttraumatic stress disorder. *Trends in Neurosciences, 35*, 24–35.
Makkar, S. R., Zhang, S. Q., & Cranney, J. (2010). Behavioral and neural analysis of GABA in the acquisition, consolidation, reconsolidation, and extinction of fear memory. *Neuropsychopharmacology, 35*, 1625–1652.
McGaugh, J. L. (2004). The amygdala modulates the consolidation of memories of emotionally arousing experiences. *Annual Review of Neuroscience, 27*, 1–28.
McGhee, L. L., Maani, C. V., Garza, T. H., Desocio, P. A., Gaylord, K. M., & Black, I. H. (2009). The effect of propranolol on posttraumatic stress disorder in burned service members. *Journal of Burn Care and Research, 30*, 92–97.
Mellman, T. A., Bustamante, V., David, D., & Fins, A. I. (2002). Hypnotic medication in the aftermath of trauma. *The Journal of Clinical Psychiatry, 63*, 1183–1184.
Metcalfe, J., & Jacobs, W. J. (1998). Emotional memory: The effects of stress on "cool" and "hot" memory systems. In G. (1998). Bowers (Ed.), *The psychology of learning and motivation* (Vol. 38, pp. 187–222). New York, NY: Academic Press.
Milad, M. R., Pitman, R. K., Ellis, C. B., Gold, A. L., Shin, L. M., Lasko, N. B., et al. (2009). Neurobiological basis of failure to recall extinction memory in posttraumatic stress disorder. *Biological Psychiatry, 66*, 1075–1082.
Morgan, C. A., 3rd, Krystal, J. H., & Southwick, S. M. (2003). Towards early pharmacological posttraumatic intervention. *Biological Psychiatry, 53*, 834–843.
Neylan, T. C., Lenoci, M., Samuelson, K. W., Metzler, T. J., Henn-Haase, C., Hierholzer, R. W., et al. (2006). No improvement of posttraumatic stress disorder symptoms with guanfacine treatment. *The American Journal of Psychiatry, 163*, 2186–2188.
Norman, S. B., Stein, M. B., Dimsdale, J. E., & Hoyt, D. B. (2008). Pain in the aftermath of trauma is a risk factor for post-traumatic stress disorder. *Psychological Medicine, 38*, 533–542.
Pitman, R. K., & Delahanty, D. L. (2005). Conceptually driven pharmacologic approaches to acute trauma. *CNS Spectrums, 10*, 99–106.
Pitman, R. K., Sanders, K. M., Zusman, R. M., Healy, A. R., Cheema, F., Lasko, N. B., et al. (2002). Pilot study of secondary prevention of posttraumatic stress disorder with propranolol. *Biological Psychiatry, 51*, 189–192.
Pitman, R. K., Shalev, A. Y., & Orr, S. P. (2000). Posttraumatic stress disorder: Emotion, conditioning, and memory. In M. S. Gazzaniga (Ed.), *The new cognitive neurosciences* (pp. 1133–1147) (2nd ed.). Cambridge, MA: MIT Press.
Raskind, M. A., Peskind, E. R., Hoff, D. J., Hart, K. L., Holmes, H. A., Warren, D., et al. (2007). A parallel group placebo controlled study of prazosin for trauma nightmares and sleep disturbance in combat veterans with post-traumatic stress disorder. *Biological Psychiatry, 61*, 928–934.
Raskind, M. A., Peskind, E. R., Kanter, E. D., Petrie, E. C., Radant, A., Thompson, C. E., et al. (2003). Reduction of nightmares and other PTSD symptoms in combat veterans by prazosin: A placebo-controlled study. *The American Journal of Psychiatry, 160*, 371–373.
Roozendaal, B., McEwen, B. S., & Chattarji, S. (2009). Stress, memory and the amygdala. *Nature Reviews Neuroscience, 10*, 423–433.
Rubin, D. C., Berntsen, D., & Bohni, M. K. (2008). A memory based model of posttraumatic stress disorder: Evaluating basic assumptions underlying the PTSD diagnosis. *Psychological Review, 115*, 985–1011.

Savić, M. M., Obradovic, D. I., Ugresic, N. D., & Bokonjic, D. R. (2005). Memory effects of benzodiazepines: Memory stages and types versus binding-site subtypes. *Neural Plasticity, 12,* 289–298.

Saxe, G., Stoddard, F., Courtney, D., Cunningham, K., Chawla, N., Sheridan, R., et al. (2001). Relationship between acute morphine and the course of PTSD in children with burns. *Journal of the American Academy of Child and Adolescent Psychiatry, 40,* 915–921.

Schelling, G. (2008). Post-traumatic stress disorder in somatic disease: Lessons from critically ill patients. *Progress in Brain Research, 167,* 229–237.

Schelling, G., Briegel, J., Roozendaal, B., Stoll, C., Rothenhäusler, H. B., & Kapfhammer, H. P. (2001). The effect of serum cortisol levels and the norepinephrine dosage-cortisol ratio during septic shock on traumatic memories and post-traumatic stress disorder in survivors. *Biological Psychiatry, 50,* 978–985.

Schelling, G., Kilger, E., Roozendaal, B., de Quervain, D. J., Briegel, J., Dagge, A., et al. (2004). Stress doses of hydrocortisone, traumatic stress, and symptoms of posttraumatic stress disorder in patients after cardiac surgery: A randomized trial. *Biological Psychiatry, 55,* 627–633.

Schmahl, C., & Bohus, M. (2007). Translational research issues in dissociation. In E. Vermetten, M. J. Dorahy, & D. Spiegel (Eds.), *Traumatic dissociation. Neurobiology and treatment* (pp. 121–138). London: American Psychiatric Publishing.

Schwabe, L., Nader, K., Wolf, O. T., Beaudry, T., & Pruessner, J. C. (2012). Neural signature of reconsolidation impairments by propranolol in humans. *Biological Psychiatry, 71,* 380–386.

Shalev, A. Y., Ankri, Y., Israeli-Shalev, Y., Peleg, T., Adessky, R., & Freedman, S. (2012). Prevention of posttraumatic stress disorder by early treatment: Results from the Jerusalem trauma outreach and prevention study. *Archives of General Psychiatry, 69,* 166–176.

Sharp, S., Thomas, C., Rosenberg, L., Rosenberg, M., & Meyer, W., 3rd (2010). Propranolol does not reduce risk for acute stress disorder in pediatric burn trauma. *The Journal of Trauma, 68,* 193–197.

Shin, L. M., & Liberzon, I. (2010). The neurocircuitry of fear, stress, and anxiety disorders. *Neuropsychopharmacology, 35,* 169–191.

Southwick, S. M., Davis, L. L., Aikins, D. E., Rasmusson, A., Barron, J., & Morgan, C. A., III. (2007). Neurobiological alterations associated with PTS. In M. J. Friedman, T. M. Keane, & P. A. Resick (Eds.), *Handbook of PTSD. Science and practice* (pp. 166–189). London: Guilford Press.

Stein, M. B., Kerridge, C., Dimsdale, J. E., & Hoyt, D. B. (2007). Pharmacotherapy to prevent PTSD: Results from a randomized controlled proof-of-concept trial in physically injured patients. *Journal of Traumatic Stress, 20,* 923–932.

Stoddard, F. J., Jr, Luthra, R., Sorrentino, E. A., Saxe, G. N., Drake, J., Chang, Y., et al. (2011). A randomized controlled trial of sertraline to prevent posttraumatic stress disorder in burned children. *Journal of Child and Adolescent Psychopharmacology, 21,* 469–477.

Stoddard, F. J., Jr, Sorrentino, E. A., Ceranoglu, T. A., Saxe, G., Murphy, J. M., Drake, J. E., et al. (2009). Preliminary evidence for the effects of morphine on posttraumatic stress disorder symptoms in one- to four-year-olds with burn. *Journal of Burn Care and Research, 30,* 836–843.

Taylor, F., & Cahill, L. (2002). Propranolol for reemergent posttraumatic stress disorder following an event of retraumatization: A case study. *Journal of Traumatic Stress, 15,* 433–437.

Taylor, F. B., Martin, P., Thompson, C., Williams, J., Mellman, T. A., Gross, C., et al. (2008). Prazosin effects on objective sleep measures and clinical symptoms in civilian trauma posttraumatic stress disorder: A placebo-controlled study. *Biological Psychiatry, 63,* 629–632.

Vaiva, G., Ducrocq, F., Jezequel, K., Averland, B., Lestavel, P., Brunet, A., & Marmar, C. R. (2003). Immediate treatment with propranolol decreases posttraumatic stress disorder two months after trauma. *Biological Psychiatry, 54*, 947–949.

Weis, F., Kilger, E., Roozendaal, B., de Quervain, D. J., Lamm, P., Schmidt, M., et al. (2006). Stress doses of hydrocortisone reduce chronic stress symptoms and improve health-related quality of life in high-risk patients after cardiac surgery: A randomized study. *The Journal of Thoracic and Cardiovascular Surgery, 131*, 277–282.

Wessa, M., & Flor, H. (2007). Failure of extinction of fear responses in posttraumatic stress disorder: Evidence from second-order conditioning. *The American Journal of Psychiatry, 164*, 1684–1692.

Yehuda, R. (2009). Status of glucocorticoid alterations in post-traumatic stress disorder. Glucocorticoids and mood. *Annals of the New York Academy of Sciences, 1179*, 56–69.

Yehuda, R., & LeDoux, J. (2007). Response variation following trauma: A translational neuroscience approach to understanding PTSD. *Neuron, 56*, 19–32.

Zohar, J., Juven-Wetzler, A., Sonnino, R., Cwikel-Hamzany, S., Balaban, E., & Cohen, H. (2011). New insights into secondary prevention in post-traumatic stress disorder. *Dialogues in Clinical Neuroscience, 13*, 301–309.

Zohar, J., Sonnino, R., Juven-Wetzler, A., & Cohen, H. (2009). Can posttraumatic stress disorder prevented? *CNS Spectrums, 14*(Suppl. 1), 44–51.

Zohar, J., Yahalom, H., Kozlovsky, N., Cwikel-Hamzany, S., Matar, M. A., Kaplan, Z., et al. (2011). High dose hydrocortisone immediately after trauma may alter the trajectory of PTSD: Interplay between clinical and animal studies. *European Neuropsychopharmacology, 21*, 796–809.

4 Memory and Social Meaning: The Impact of Society and Culture on Traumatic Memories

Nigel Hunt

Institute of Work, Health and Organisations, University of Nottingham, Nottingham, UK

4.1 Introduction

The majority of psychological work on memory has focused on it being a series of phenomena relating to the individual. The focus has been on individual short-term and long-term memory, working memory, and the like, and in the cognitive tradition any sense of meaning (whether individual or social) has been deliberately downplayed in order to try and understand the basic individual cognitive memory processes. This research has serious limitations because it omits the key foci of memory, that of enhancing and understanding the internal and social worlds. There are two ways in which memory should not be seen in isolation. First, with regard to individual memory processes, the sense of meaningfulness is important. We are not concerned about remembering things unless they mean something to us. Second, memories are not uploaded, stored, and recalled without regard to the outside world. The environment and the people in the environment matters. They determine, at least to some extent, what goes into memory, what is stored, and how it is stored, interpreted, and changed, and what is recalled and when. In other words, social context and meaning are essential if we are to understand how memory works (Hunt & McHale, 2008; Park, 2010). This is particularly important when we are trying to understand and treat traumatic memories. We know that social support is an important factor in determining whether someone is traumatized. Social support should, as we will see, be considered in relation to not only individual people but also the society in which the traumatized person lives. Support can be provided by community, culture, and society, as well as friends and family.

A number of researchers stand out from the crowd of the first 100 years of memory researchers. The two in particular are Pierre Janet and Frederick Bartlett. Pierre Janet was not a memory researcher as such, but in the field of traumatic stress, he highlighted the importance of the distinction between the traumatic memory and the narrative memory, as well as that traumatized people have memory problems that are resolved through making sense of them by developing a narrative approach (Janet, 1925). Frederick

Bartlett explored the nature of normal memory and noted how memories in the real world are transformed by what we already know and what we expect, that memories are not accurate depictions of past events but rather our interpretations of those events. Memories are essentially narratives of the past (Bartlett, 1932).

If memories are narratives of the past, then it is clear that several levels are important. The focus here is on the development of the individual narrative and on the importance of social discourse. Both are key to determining what will be remembered and how it will be remembered.

In the field of traumatic stress, it is widely recognized that resolving problems relating to traumatic memories usually involves making sense of the traumatic event (Crossley, 2000), that is, developing a narrative so that the event is understood in its context in relation to the person who had the experience and the environment—the social context. Treatment for traumatic stress involves two stages. The first stage is the development of behavioral control, that is, the ability to relax, to not be constantly emotionally controlled by the memory of the trauma, the fixation with the past. It is basically about being able to live in the world, though, still troubled by the traumatic memory.

The second stage involves the development of the narrative, enabling the traumatic memory to be placed in its context as part of the past rather than as part of the present. It is placing the traumatic event in the context of life, as something that happened in the past. It is finding a way of recognizing that, although terrible things happen and some people do awful things, these ideas should not be extended to the rest of life. It does not matter how this narrative develops, but if a person is to live a successful life it is important that it does. Many people learn to live with trauma; they learn the first, behavioral, element, so that they can lead their lives, but life will not be fulfilling unless they also develop the narrative. They are not going to forget the traumatic event, but they can put the event in a context.

In recent years, much has been said about the concept of posttraumatic growth (PTG), how many people can eventually make sense out of their traumatic experiences and somehow change for the better, where life might have more meaning, or friendships might become important, or the meaning of death might become clearer (Joseph, 2012). These are often fundamental changes to the person and may represent a growth in wisdom as a result of the traumatic experience.

Evidence shows that though PTSD and growth may coexist, the levels of PTSD reduces overtime as growth increases (Linley & Joseph, 2004). What may be important is the relationship between PTG and narrative. Is PTG just another way of saying that the coherence of the narrative, the making sense of the experience, is growing?

Whatever one's perspective, trauma resolution is in the end about forming a narrative, with the social world having a variable importance in relation to the traumatic memory. Three examples from different areas illustrate this. These are all research projects that I am or have been involved with. The traumatic events are very different, the populations are different, and the aims of the projects are different. In the end, however, they are all concerned with individual narration, the social world, and hurting memories, in the broadest sense of the term, and each example varies in the extent to which the social world or culture has an impact on the memory.

The first example—one that is largely individual but using a technique developed in other populations—focuses on illiterate people traumatized by the 2008 Szechuan earthquake. We administered narrative exposure therapy (NET; McPherson, 2011; Schauer, Neuner, & Elbert, 2012), which helped reduce traumatic symptoms. The second example, which demonstrates the importance of both the individual narrative and the social narratives, is a study conducted a few years ago with British World War II veterans who were in retirement but who were troubled by their wartime memories (Hunt & Robbins, 2001a, 2001b). The final example is broader, with the focus largely on the social, and concerns how memories of the Spanish Civil War are interpreted in Spain in the present day (Hunt, 2011). The examples vary across the individual/social dimension, but they all relate to psychological damage impacted on by the social world and the need for restorative social narratives to help the people come to terms with their experiences.

4.2 Szechuan Earthquake

In 2008, a major earthquake destroyed cities in several parts of Szechuan province, causing perhaps 20,000 deaths and many more physical injuries. About a year after the event, we introduced two forms of psychological assistance to help those still suffering from the psychological consequences of the earthquake. The first part is NET, an approach initially designed to help refugees and others who have suffered the effects of war. It is an approach that can be used by people who have received only basic training in the technique, and it has been proved to be effective in several studies (McPherson, 2011; Robjant & Fazel, 2010). The sample for this study was illiterate, and so the work was conducted one on one. The second part of this study involved a group exercise with children based on Pennebaker's expressive writing task (Baikie & Wilhelm, 2005; Pennebaker & Beall, 1986).

The China study arose out of some initial research involving questionnaires. We asked 120 people to complete a questionnaire that contained a series of standardized measures relating to traumatic experience, symptoms, and coping strategies. What we found was that participants wanted to talk in more detail about their experiences, with this being their first opportunity to do so. In the end, 80 of the 120 participants provided detailed narrative accounts of their experiences. This led to the decision to use NET with those who had high levels of trauma symptoms. A waiting list controlled study was used, and a shortened form of NET (four sessions) was administered to 22 people. The results showed a clear benefit of NET compared to the control. NET led to significant reductions in posttraumatic stress symptoms and in levels of anxiety and depression (Zang, Hunt, & Cox, 2012).

Because the children were literate, it was possible to use a group writing task in order to explore their narratives. Two classes of 30 children were given an expressive writing task with instructions about what to write. There were three sessions. In the first session, they were asked to write about the earthquake. In the second, they were asked to write about any negative emotions or feelings that they had with respect to the earthquake. In the third, they were asked to write about anything positive that might have come out of the earthquake experience. The children were aged between 9 and 12 years. The older children managed to do the task successfully, but many of the younger ones had difficulty in writing about the earthquake three times in three days, so many defaulted to creating drawings about their experiences. The overall task was successful in reducing symptoms of traumatic stress, though not so dramatic as for the NET adult group. This may be because all the children in each class were included in the study (the teachers insisted on this), and perhaps also, because writing is less effective than talking directly to an individual. This needs further exploration. In terms of hurting memories, the study does show the importance of narrative development, particularly for the people in the NET study and those who spontaneously produced their accounts.

4.3 World War II

World War II was the most devastating war in history. Although we are unclear on how many people were killed, it is in the order of 50 million, with many times more both physically and psychologically damaged. Our study concerned one small group of veterans, British men who had fought in the war against either the Germans or the Japanese. The study took place 40 years after the war was over, so it would be reasonable to assume that any psychological issues would have been dealt with. At the time of the research, there was very little information published on the long-term effects of war.

Over 700 veterans completed a detailed questionnaire about their experiences and memories of war, and a smaller number were interviewed in depth about the impact of the war. People were chosen for interview because they (1) had experienced severe traumatic events during the war and (2) had either significant current psychological problems or had no apparent problems. Detailed analyses are presented elsewhere (Hunt, 1997; Hunt & Robbins, 2001a, 2001b); here is just a brief summary in relation to the importance of social and personal narratives for determining the psychological outcome.

Perhaps the most important finding was that up to 20% of the veterans had psychological problems as a result of their war experiences. Most of them had lived their lives symptom-free for most of their lives, but they started to experience problems after retirement. Many of them described how retirement itself was part of the problem. When they had finished work, when the children had grown up and left, there was lot of free time that started to reflect on their lives, and for many of them the war was the most important period. Memories would start to reemerge, events they had not thought about for many years, and they would begin to be troubled. This is not to say that they all experienced full symptoms of PTSD; for most of them, it caused occasional temporary distress. The exceptions were those who had been prisoners of the Japanese. Most of these had significant problems that they said had been with them since the war. Many of them reported to have both physical and psychological symptoms due to their experiences, and their lives had been significantly affected.

In many cases, the veterans reported that their problems were associated not only with personal memories of traumatic events but also with the social world around them. Their hurting memories arose partly as a result of society. Many reported that they had fought not only to rid the world of fascism, but to build a better future; and that this was why many of them voted Labor in 1945, they wanted a good health service, good education, and good pensions. This is the society, which they saw themselves, building in the postwar years. Unfortunately, as they saw it, this society was steadily destroyed, particularly during the Thatcher years. In the end, just at the time they needed a good pension and a decent health service, these were being significantly eroded. Many reported that the bitterness and anger they felt about this was a direct cause of the symptoms they were experiencing. In this way, society can affect memory.

We extended this research and examined the role of social support and narrative coherence (Burnell, Coleman, & Hunt, 2010). The criticality of the narrative was clearly demonstrated. By using a novel technique of analysis, we could determine the degree to which a transcript of an interview could demonstrate the degree of coherence of the narrative. There was a very close relationship between narrative coherence and the effectiveness of social support. This research not only demonstrated that it is possible to quantify the narrative to some extent and to make decisions regarding the degree of coherence, but it also showed how we rely on the social world to help reduce symptoms. Again, this shows how important the social world is in determining what effects our memories may have on us.

4.4 Spanish Civil War Memory

This example is associated more closely with the sociocultural aspects of hurting memories rather than individual memory as such. It demonstrates again how our personal memories and how they are displayed in public are constrained by the social world. The Spanish Civil War tore apart the Spanish nation between 1936 and 1939 and, with Franco's fascist victory, the nation remained torn asunder, with those on the losing side permanently exiled, imprisoned, or just unable to discuss the war or politics. This lasted, with some softening of the regime, until Franco's death in 1975, but it was not until two decades later that people started to publicly address the trauma memories of the war and its aftermath. Discussion of that period is still controversial and still damaging to individuals and communities. These are genuine hurting memories.

The Spaniards are now starting to come to terms with their memories of the Civil War, and the reinterpretation of memories plays a critical role in this. During and after the Franco era, people were compelled, either explicitly through law or implicitly through community pressure, to forget (or to not explicitly recall) how people from the same village fought on opposite sides or where atrocities took place (including mass burials). It is only since the participants have died, or are at least very old, that the younger, post-Franco generations are interested in recalling the war back to memory. In the last few years, a growing number of museums dedicated to the war have started up, the mass graves are starting to be opened, memorials are being erected, and, after a long period when the British produced the best books about the war, the Spaniards are starting to feel free enough to write about it.

The Battle of the Ebro took place during the summer of 1938, which led to the destruction of the Cataluñan army, and hastened the end of the war. The key battlefield was a bend in the River Ebro, around the towns of Gandesa and Corbera del Ebro. The republicans crossed the river and took these towns, holding on to them for three months before being pushed back by the rebels under Franco. There were an estimated 100,000 casualties.

Until recently, there were only a few old memorials to the battle, which had been placed by the fascists in the years afterward. The only other reminder was the town of Corbera del Ebro, which was left in the same devastated state, as it was, after the fascists overran it. The townspeople rebuilt the town at the bottom of the hill, leaving the ruins for posterity.

In the last few years, a number of memorials have appeared, including a museum in Corbera, a series of marked battlefield routes, and the reconstruction of some of the trenches and dugouts of the battle. These resulted from the establishment of consorci memorial dels espais de la batalla de l'ebre (COMEBE) in 2002, which was founded to help people find their missing relatives from the Battle of the Ebro.

In 2007, a law named Ley de Memoria Historica (historical memory law) was passed that recognized the rights of citizens to personal and family memory in relation to the Spanish Civil War and the Franco era. This is an unusual law in that it explicitly attempts to enable social and cultural memories of a past generation to be regenerated. There is currently little discussion within Spain on the potential disadvantages of the reopening of old wounds. The exception is the contentious burial site of Garcia Lorca, over which there is an argument between the relatives of Lorca and those of another person buried in the same spot about whether the bodies should be exhumed.

The interesting thing about this Spanish example is that psychologists have largely ignored its psychological significance in relation to the traumatic memories of individuals and how those traumatic memories are, in some way, passed down through the generations. Even if the participants' traumatic memories are not resolved, there appears to remain a need in future generations to achieve closure, to develop the narrative, and to make sense of these memories.

4.5 Analysis

If we are to understand recovery from traumatic memories, we need to examine not only the memories problems at the individual level—the level that is usually the focus of therapy—but also the sociocultural factors that are just as important for understanding memory. The brief examples given, that of providing therapy to survivors of the Szechuan earthquake, interviewing World War II veterans, and examining Spanish memories of the Civil War, all in their way, show the importance of narrative development and the importance of social factors. The Chinese example is perhaps the most individualistic, but even here there was a demonstrable need for the people to talk, to make sense of their experiences. Given the opportunity to talk about what happened with a stranger (the researcher), opened up a powerful sense of narrative. The World War II example overtly draws on both the individual experience and how outcomes are affected by the social world. The World War II veterans made explicit reference to the way they wanted to build the new, fairer world in the 1940s and their despair when that world was pulled apart in the 1980s. The example of the Spanish Civil War is most explicitly social. The analysis of the Spanish Civil War is still largely at the level of the media, politics, and heritage. At these levels, the debate is very heated, but the personal impact of opening up the wounds of the war has not been fully explored. This is a psychologically interesting example because the debate is occurring between descendants of those who actually fought. The nature of the civil war means that families and villages are still divided. This is an example of societal hurting memories.

What these examples demonstrate is the complexity of the relationship between the individual narrative and the social world. Hurting memories, especially traumatic memories, though they may sometimes be largely personal, in many cases they are not; they are intimately interlinked with the workings of the society in which people live. This is often missed by clinicians, who often make the assumption that if a person is troubled by traumatic memories, then an entirely individualistic approach can be taken to deal with them. Unfortunately, where there is an interaction with the social world—and at the basic level most people do interact with friends and family—then the social world needs to be taken into account during treatment. When assisting a person to develop a narrative, the clinician should be bringing in these social elements as necessary and should assume that these social elements are important.

The next question is why some people are effective at developing their trauma narratives while others are not. Individual factors such as personality, resilience, intelligence, coping styles, and the like have all been studied in detail, and they do play an important role; but future research should take more account of the social world in which the person lives. What impact does the social world have on their ability to develop a narrative? One example of the importance of society in helping to develop narratives is memorialization. After wars, particularly in the twentieth century, it is very common to construct memorials to those who have died or to specific battles or events. Currently, there is little research about why we memorialize, but it clearly plays a role in helping us to develop the story about what happened during the war, to remind and help society (and individuals) to tell the story in the way they want it to be told, to help participants remember, and to help those who did not participate remember, whether they are civilians at home or the next generations of people. This is why memorials to the Spanish Civil War are springing up around the country; there is a perceived need to tell the story of the war in a way that is very different from the traditional Franco perspective.

Society can help people recover from trauma in other ways. It is common to acknowledge people's experiences not only through memorialization and commemorative activities, but also through the media, providing a space for people to speak, acknowledging what has happened, and providing a supportive environment. It remains to be seen whether the plethora of web sites that are available for this will serve the intended purpose and will continue to do so.

One problem that we face in our research group is that it is difficult to study and interpret narratives across language boundaries. Toward the end of 2011, I was working with 10 PhD students from seven different language groups. Methodologically, it is difficult to study narratives across languages because the nuances are often lost in translation. This creates some difficulties when trying to analyze the narratives, particularly in languages that are structured in a very different way from English.

Psychological growth is closely associated with narrative development, and the relationship between growth, narrative, and symptoms needs further exploration, as does how the concept of growth itself functions in different societies. Narratives are constantly changing throughout life irrespective of traumatic experiences (the change is just more dramatic and sudden, and it possibly has permanent effects when it is traumatic), so it may be that growth simply reflects whether a person has a positive outlook on life, one where the person gains from novel experiences, interactions, and events.

There is general agreement that the experience of trauma is concerned with three main phases: (1) pretrauma coherent narrative/biography, (2) trauma disruption/destruction of narrative/biography, and (3) posttrauma development of new meaningful narrative/biography that acknowledges the traumatic event through narrative development (thinking, writing, and talking therapy). What this chapter has tried to show is the importance of the social world in helping to develop the individual narrative. With severe traumatic experiences such as war, it can be argued that the society itself is traumatized (as in the case of Spain), and working through the process of developing the new narrative, can take generations. Within this, we should not lose sight of those individuals who have been traumatized by their experiences, and we should ensure that everyone receives appropriate help, including the acknowledgment of the societal levels of support and damage.

References

Baikie, K. A., & Wilhelm, K. (2005). Emotional and physical health benefits of expressive writing. *Advances in Psychiatric Treatment, 11*, 338–346.
Bartlett, F. (1932). *Remembering: A study in experimental and social psychology*. Cambridge: Cambridge University Press.
Burnell, K. J., Coleman, P., & Hunt, N. (2010). Coping with traumatic war memories: Second World War veteran's experiences of social support in relation to the narrative coherence of war memories. *Ageing and Society, 30*, 57–78.
Crossley, M. (2000). Narrative psychology, trauma and the study of self/identity. *Theory & Psychology, 10*(4), 527–546.
Hunt, N. (1997). The long term psychological consequences of war experience. *The Psychologist, 10*(8), 357–360.
Hunt, N. (2011). Recuerdo la Guerra Civil España: Turning forgotten history into current memory. In M. Andrews, C. Bagot-Jewitt, & N. Hunt (Eds.), *Lest we forget*. London: The History Press.
Hunt, N., & McHale, S. (2008). Memory and meaning: Individual and social aspects of memory narratives. *Journal of Loss and Trauma, 13*, 42–58.

Hunt, N., & Robbins, I. (2001a). The long term consequences of war: The experience of World War Two. *Aging and Mental Health, 5(2)*, 184–191.

Hunt, N., & Robbins, I. (2001b). World War Two veterans, social support and veterans' associations. *Aging and Mental Health, 5(2)*, 176–183.

Janet, P. (1925). *Psychological healing* (2 vol.). New York, NY: Macmillan. Reprint: Amo Press, New York, NY, 1976.

Joseph, S. (2012). *What doesn't kill us: The new psychology of posttraumatic growth.* London: Piatkus.

Linley, P. A., & Joseph, S. (2004). Positive change following trauma and adversity: A review. *Journal of Traumatic Stress, 17*, 11–21.

McPherson, J. (2011). Does narrative exposure therapy reduce PTSD in survivors of mass violence? *Research on Social Work Practice, 22(1)*, 29–42.

Park, C. L. (2010). Making sense of the meaning literature: An integrative review of meaning making and its effects on adjustment to stressful life events. *Psychological Bulletin, 136(2)*, 257–301.

Pennebaker, J. W., & Beall, S. K. (1986). Confronting a traumatic event. Toward an understanding of inhibition and disease. *Journal of Abnormal Psychology, 95*, 274–281.

Robjant, K., & Fazel, M. (2010). The emerging evidence for narrative exposure therapy: A review. *Clinical Psychology Review, 30(8)*, 1030–1039.

Schauer, M., Neuner, F., & Elbert, T. (2012). *Narrative exposure therapy: A short term treatment for traumatic stress disorders.* Gottingen: Hogrefe.

Zang, Y., Hunt, N., & Cox, T. (2012). The effects of a guided narrative technique among children traumatized by an earthquake. In D. Mortimer, B. Haylock, & C. Barette (Eds.), *Trauma: Theory and practice.* Oxford: Inter-Disciplinary Press.

5 Retraumatization: The Vicious Circle of Intrusive Memory

Katrin Schock, Christine Knaevelsrud

Center for the Treatment of Torture Victims, Berlin, and Department of Clinical Psychology and Psychotherapy at the Free University of Berlin, Berlin, Germany

5.1 Introduction

Two case vignettes (Cases 5.1 and 5.2) can illustrate what is commonly described as *retraumatization*. The mechanisms and trigger that cause reactivation of earlier trauma and posttraumatic stress disorder (PTSD) symptoms are different in both cases. Case 5.1 reacted heavily on a trauma-associated stimulus. Case 5.2 experienced a new traumatizing event, which resulted in a new, full-blown PTSD but also reactivated intrusions of the initial traumatic event.

Although we encounter the phenomenon of retraumatization repeatedly in the clinical context, its conceptual base is hardly empirically investigated and theoretically poorly understood. This chapter provides an introduction to the phenomenon of retraumatization. First, a short overview of the definition of trauma and PTSD is given. An overview on characteristic memory phenomena and their psychophysiological base in traumatized individuals is then provided. A summary of current empirical findings on retraumatization is given, and open questions that need to be studied in order to reach a uniform definition of retraumatization are outlined.

5.2 Trauma and PTSD

The term *retraumatization* is used in the juristic and psychotherapeutic context to refer to the increase of posttraumatic symptoms after a distressing event or situation. However, there is a lack of consensus regarding what represents retraumatization. The literature is inconsistent about the nature of the trigger and the intensity and duration of the increase of PTSD symptoms.

To understand retraumatization, it is important to comprehend the course of trauma and PTSD. The term *trauma* (Greek for "wound" or "injury") is more and more popularly used for a wide range of stressful life events. In psychological/psychiatric classification systems, however, the term describes a tightly defined event: An event is designated as a trauma when it is associated with a potential or real threat of

Case 5.1 Trauma Reactivation After Confrontation by Trauma-Associated Stimuli

The young Mr. A fled from Iran to Germany. He had been politically active, had taken part in demonstrations, and had been arrested several times. During his last arrest, he had been detained for two months, daily hearing the screams of other prisoners and being picked up by the guards who tortured him with bandaged eyes. When he came out of prison, his family managed to help him flee to Germany. For nearly two years, he has been in Germany. Six months after his arrival in Germany, he started psychotherapy. In the beginning, the full picture of PTSD was diagnosed. During therapy the symptoms decreased, and after two years at the end of therapy, he showed no more PTSD symptomatology.

A few weeks later, a police officer asked him in a harsh way for his documents. Suddenly, the images from Iran were back. Mr. A felt set back to the time of his arrest, reexposed to the mercy of the guards. From that moment, he again could hardly sleep and had nightmares about his traumatic experience in prison; also, during the day, the images of torture came back into his mind. The PTSD symptoms increased again. He signed up again with his therapist. Half a year later, the PTSD symptoms were again reduced.

Case 5.2 Trauma Reactivation After Experiencing a New Traumatic Event

Mrs. M, a Kurd from Turkey, fled to Germany in 2007. Several times, security forces had broken into her house, threatening and abusing her in order to find out where her husband was hiding. When the men had come to her the last time, they had raped her. She then fled to Germany. Six months after her flight, she went into psychotherapy. She was diagnosed with PTSD and depression. After one and a half years in therapy, the PTSD and depression symptoms diminished to the extent that one could no longer speak of a PTSD. She had no more nightmares, had become calmer, and was able to concentrate well in the German language course. Then she was involved in a car accident. The full picture of PTSD was present again; also the depressive symptoms rose to the level of a major depression. When asked about the content of the intrusions, she replied that it is a mixture of nightmares about both the assault in Germany and the rape in her home country, as well as flashbacks in which she relives the rape and assault. One year later, the patient still showed symptoms of a severe PTSD and depression. She had the feeling that she could not be safe anywhere in the world.

death, serious injury, or threat to physical integrity. This event can be experienced or observed happening to others. To define an event as trauma, the subjective reaction of the person must be included: The person must respond to the event with immediate intense fear, helplessness, or horror [American Psychiatric Association (APA), 2000].

PTSD is the most frequent disorder to develop in the aftermath of a traumatic event (Galea, Nandi, & Vlahov, 2005; Steel et al., 2011). PTSD is characterized by intrusions, avoidance, and hyperarousal (APA, 2000). Dysfunctional beliefs about one's own integrity and safety, about the unpredictability of the world, and about the self underlie the PTSD symptoms and intensify each other in a vicious circle (Foa & Rothbaum, 1998).

Intrusions are unwanted memories or memory fragments of the traumatic event, which can occur as thoughts or sensory (re)experiences. They could be triggered by external recollections of the trauma (*triggers*), such as sensory impressions, stories, or thoughts of the traumatic experience. The intensity ranges from single memories to overwhelming memories (i.e., flashbacks). A flashback usually appears suddenly and creates in the victim the threatening impression that the trauma is experienced again with all the sensations in the here-and-now (APA, 2000).

Avoidance, in contrast, is the deliberate effort to avoid stressful memories. Individuals with PTSD seek to avoid activities, people, or feelings associated with the traumatic experience in order to avoid triggering intrusive memories of the trauma. Cognitive and behavioral avoidance strategies maintain the PTSD symptoms in preventing the exposure to corrective information into the structure (Riggs, Cahill, & Foa, 2006). Avoiding memories of the trauma may eventually lead to dissociative states and amnesia (of parts of or the whole traumatic memory).

The third symptom cluster, *hyperarousal*, includes symptoms associated with the increase of the excitation levels of the autonomic nervous system. Stressful situations are earlier and more intensively experienced. This becomes evident in sleep and concentration problems, increased vigilance, or increased startle response (APA, 2000).

In an American representative sample, lifetime prevalence of experiencing a traumatic event is reported in 51.2% of women and 60.7% of men. The prevalence for the development of PTSD is 10.4% in women and 5.0% in men (Kessler, Sonnega, Bromet, Hughes, & Nelson, 1995). A German epidemiological study revealed a notably lower trauma prevalence of 28.0% for women and 20.3% for men, as well as a lower lifetime prevalence for the development of PTSD, which is 2.5% in women and 2.1% in men (Maercker, Forstmeier, Wagner, Glaesmer, & Brähler, 2008).

Confrontation with trauma-associated stimuli, critical life events, or so-called threshold situations (e.g., retirement) can lead to an increase of the symptoms even after decades (Paratz & Katz, 2011; Wenk-Ansohn & Schock, 2008).

5.3 The Phenomenology of Traumatic Memory: Basic Principles of Psychobiology and the Fear Network

For a better understanding of the underlying mechanisms of retraumatization, it is important to take a look at the specific nature of traumatic memory.

5.3.1 Memory Systems

The human long-term memory can be roughly divided into an explicit (or declarative, cold) and implicit (or nondeclarative, hot) memory. *Explicit memories* can be

Table 5.1 Differences in the Nondeclarative and Declarative Memory

Nondeclarative Memory (Hot Memory)	**Declarative Memory (Cold Memory)**
– Event-specific emotional/sensoric network – Automatically triggered by certain indicative stimuli – Sensory, emotional, and physiological perceptions – Fragmented content – Here-and-now feeling	– Knowledge about stages of life, specific and general events – Intentionally accessible – Knowledge about the event in the context of life, time, and space – Chronological report

retrieved consciously. Their contents are deliberately available and can easily be verbalized. They involve explicit knowledge of many different aspects of a situation. Not only is information about an event recalled but also the contextual information about the location, the time, and the people who were present is stored.

Implicit memories are nonconscious. They are sometimes characterized as nondeclarative because the individual is unable to verbally declare these memories. The implicit memory stores sensory-perceptual and emotional information about an event. The contents of this information are linked to each other in an associative network. Within the associative network, the activation of a single element can therefore entail the activation of other elements.

The elements of the explicit memory are also linked in an associative network. Single information can be retrieved from the memory system and classified in the spatial and temporal context of one's own life story. A disconnection of the explicit context memory, termed *cold memory* (Metcalfe & Jacobs, 1996) and the implicit memory, *hot memory* system, is supposed to underlie the core symptoms of PTSD (Elbert, Rockstroh, Kolassa, Schauer, & Neuner, 2006). Table 5.1 summarizes the most important features of the different memory systems.

For memory consolidation—that is, the transfer of contents from the short-term to long-term memory—the hippocampus is of crucial importance. The hippocampus is one of the evolutionarily ancient structures of the brain. It is located in the temporal lobe and can be understood as central control station of the limbic system. In the hippocampus, the information of different sensory systems merge, are processed, and are then returned to the cortex. Therefore, individuals whose hippocampus has been removed or destroyed cannot produce new memories and thus have anterograde amnesia. However, most old memories remain preserved. The hippocampus is conceived as a structure that generates memories, whereas the memories are stored in various other places in the cerebral cortex (Bremner, 1999; Stein, Koverola, Hanna, Torchia, & McClarty, 1997). In the amygdala, emotional memories are stored in fragments in the form of sensations, feelings, and emotions without space–time reference. They are activated by triggers and are barely controllable. Therefore, the amygdala is also known as emotional memory. Since no spatial and temporal connections are stored in the amygdala, it is hardly possible during activation to distinguish whether a threat is happening now or has happened in the past (Brewin, 2001; Claas & Schulze, 2002; Resick, 2003).

5.3.2 Traumatic Memory

PTSD may lead to changes in the central memory functioning. Cognitive processes (such as peritraumatic dissociation) during the trauma may disturb and impair the encoding and integrating of the traumatic content in the autobiographical memory (Van der Kolk & Fisler, 1995). There is evidence that individuals with PTSD show problems with voluntary and involuntary memory recall. Specific memories of the trauma may be retrieved easily, unintentionally and uncontrollably (Brewin, Dalgleish, & Joseph, 1996; Ehlers & Clark, 2000). Individuals with PTSD have fragmented memories and are suffering from unintentional intrusions of memory fragments of elements of the traumatic event. At the same time, intentional and controlled retrieval of other aspects of the traumatic memory may be difficult because memories are disorganized and fragmented (see review of McNally, 2003). Thus, although individuals can hardly control intrusive memories, they have problems in intentionally revealing the traumatic experiences in a coherent way and to verbalize them (Bremner, 1999; Brewin, 2001, 2007; Van der Kolk, 2000).

5.3.3 Emotional Processing Theory: The Fear Network

Cognitive models focus on the cognitive processing of the traumatic event, that is, how the traumatized individual interprets the meaning of the traumatic event for himself- or herself and makes sense of it (Zayfert, 2012). Based on cognitive models of PTSD, it is assumed that processing during the trauma was incomplete and that therefore inaccurate or distorted memories and meaning of the event are produced (Zayfert, 2012).

Empirically validated cognitive models provide an explanation for the development and maintenance of dysfunctional traumatic memories of PTSD patients (emotional processing theory, Foa & Kozak, 1986; dual representation model, Brewin, 2003; integrative cognitive disorder model, Ehlers & Clark, 2000). Without going into the detail of each model, crucial elements of the emotional processing theory by Foa and Kozak (1986) are presented to explain the processing during retraumatization.

Based on knowledge about the different effects of stress, particularly on the functioning of hippocampus and amygdala, Foa and Kozak (1986) proposed that the experience of a traumatic event results in the formation of a fear structure in memory. They assume that it is a fear network in which memories, emotions, behaviors, and physiological responses are closely interconnected (Foa & Kozak, 1996; Foa & Rothbaum, 1998). Fear structures contain emotional experiences, which are encoded in organized semantic networks. In these networks, sensory information about the stimulus (e.g., smells and sound), physiological reactions (e.g., sweating and rapid heartbeat), cognitive responses, and emotional meanings (e.g., own vulnerability and being near death) (Lang et al., 1998) are enclosed. In response to every new traumatic event that violates basal assumptions about one's own safety and integrity, the fear network is strengthened and extended. The intensity of psychophysiological arousal during the traumatic event is decisive for the extent in which stimuli are integrated into the fear network and how they are activated subsequently. The more intensely the initial trauma is experienced, the more comprehensively the fear structure is formed (McNally, 2007). The fear network can easily be activated by cognitive elements, physiological responses, and emotional meanings (Foa & Kozak, 1986). Traumatized individuals with PTSD have an increased sensitivity toward anxiety-causing, trauma-associated stimuli (Foa & Kozak, 1986). Foa and Rothbaum (1998) have shown that individuals with PTSD perceive stimuli violating their own safety assumptions as more threatening than traumatized individuals without PTSD and nontraumatized individuals. This goes in line with the findings of McNally, Kaspi, Riemann, and Zeitlin (1990), who reported increased awareness of trauma-associated stimuli in PTSD patients.

It is assumed that the more traumatic memories a fear network contains, the more rigid it will become and the less probable will be a spontaneous dissolution of the fear network, leading to spontaneous remission of PTSD. According to Perkonigg and colleagues (2005) in a longitudinal study on traumatized adolescents, the experience of new traumatic events has been the most robust predictor of a chronic course of PTSD. In the moment of a new confrontation with a situation of helplessness, the affected individual experiences a strong feeling of fear, which results in a sustainable activation of the fear network. The duration of activation seems to depend on the intensity of the experienced confrontation to a new traumatic event or trauma-associated stimuli and on whether the individual has already developed a PTSD in the aftermath of the initial trauma.

Findings of neuroimaging studies seem to support theories of impaired memory consolidation. Individuals who experienced traumatic events show a significantly reduced volume of the hippocampus compared to the ones not exposed to traumatic events. This difference becomes even more evident when the latter are compared with those who were suffering from PTSD (Karl et al., 2006; Smith, 2005; Woon, Sood, & Hedges, 2010). Reduced hippocampal activity has also been associated with more severe PTSD symptoms (Astur et al., 2006). There is evidence that, during a traumatic event, the hippocampus temporarily reduces its activity by the action of glucocorticoids, whereas the amygdala is activated (Ruegg, 2010). The amygdala has direct connections to the sensory cortex and, in contrast to the hippocampus, no direct connection to the language center. This may explain the fragmentation of the sensory-perceptual memories of the traumatic event.

As described, traumatic memory is supposed to be strongly connected to the subcortical motivation circuit due to the high emotional intensity at the time of encoding. Even simple cues can easily gate the access to this stored information. However, it is not yet clear whether traumatized individuals are equally vulnerable to a new trauma or to trauma-associated stimuli.

5.4 Empirical Studies on Retraumatization

In general, the term *retraumatization* (or *reactivation*) is used to describe traumatic stress reactions occurring in the aftermath of subsequent traumatic events after an initial experienced trauma (Duckworth and Follette, 2012). In the literature, the terms *retraumatization* and *reactivation* are often used simultaneously (Bramsen,

Van der Ploeg, & Boers, 2006; Heir & Weisaeth, 2006; Nashoni & Singer, 2006). Studies on the symptom course of PTSD after confrontation with new stressors can be assigned to the different triggering situations: trauma-associated stimuli on the one hand and experience of a new trauma on the other hand.

5.4.1 Effects of New Traumatic Events

Previous studies investigated the effects of a new traumatic event on the symptom course of PTSD in already traumatized individuals. Bramsen et al. (2006) examined the impact of a fireworks explosion in Enschede. The authors reported an increase in PTSD symptoms in the persons who were already identified as traumatized survivors of World War II. Asked about the content of the intrusions, they stated that it did not refer to the fireworks explosion but to memories of the traumatic experience during World War II. The duration of the symptom increase was not assessed in this study.

This goes in line with the findings of Robinson et al. (1994), who studied the impact of SCUD missile attacks in Israel on traumatized Holocaust survivors. The content of the intrusions, described by the traumatized individuals, referred to the initial trauma of the Holocaust as well as to the new trauma of SCUD missile attacks. However, in this study it is unclear whether, after the initial trauma, a posttraumatic stress reaction had already occurred earlier.

Furthermore, Hantman and Solomon (2007) found a significantly higher PTSD symptom severity in a group of Holocaust survivors affected by cancer than in a control group also suffering from cancer but not traumatized initially. However, it is also unclear in this study whether the group of Holocaust survivors suffered already from PTSD after the initial trauma of the Holocaust. In contrast to the study conducted by Robinson et al. (1994), there is no information about the content of the intrusions in this study.

In a prospective epidemiological study, Breslau, Borges, Hagar, Tancredi, and Gilman (2009) observed the influence of a new traumatic event on the symptom course of PTSD. They examined traumatized adults with and without PTSD after experiencing a new traumatic event approximately 10 years later. Individuals who had already developed PTSD in the aftermath of the initial trauma showed a significantly more frequent increase in symptoms after the new trauma. The authors conclude that, for the increase of PTSD, the characteristic of the new trauma is not of importance, but the presence of PTSD after the initial trauma is.

An indication of the duration of the symptom increase is given in the study results of Kinzie, Boehnlein, Riley, and Sparr (2002). They examined the effects of a new traumatic event (September 11) on traumatized refugees from different backgrounds, with and without preexisting PTSD. Two months after the attacks, a posttraumatic stress reaction and an increase in comorbid disorder were seen in all the refugees. Regardless of their origin, the highest increase in PTSD could be observed in refugees with an already existing PTSD. Five months after the attacks, the symptoms decreased again to the baseline level (symptoms before September 11). However, this study did not examine the content of the intrusions, so it is unclear whether the initial trauma has been updated by the new trauma (the attacks).

In summary, it can be concluded that traumatized individuals who already developed PTSD in the aftermath of the initial trauma are vulnerable for the increase in PTSD symptoms after a new traumatic event. Thus, they show stronger psychopathological reactions as direct response to repeated traumatic events, but the reactions decrease in time.

5.4.2 Effects of Trauma-Associated Stimuli

The confrontation with trauma-associated stimuli may induce a partial activation of the fear network and may subsequently lead to an increase in PTSD symptoms. The impact of trauma-associated stimuli on the course of PTSD has not been clarified conclusively. In a study on the impact of an asylum interview on the course of PTSD, a significant increase in intrusions is found (Schock, Rosner, & Knaevelsrud, submitted). According to the respondents, the content of the intrusions referred to the trauma experienced in their home countries. These results emphasize the importance of considering the content of the intrusions in the context of retraumatization. However, the results of previous studies did not show an impact of trauma-associated stimuli. Orth and Maercker (2004) investigated whether legal proceedings lead to an increase of PTSD symptoms. Victims of rape and sexual violence were studied before and after trial. The results showed that hearing their own detailed reports about the traumatic experience had no significant effect on the intensity of the PTSD symptoms. To investigate the effects of foreign reports on the traumatic event, about one group of the victims was reported in the media. Maercker and Mehr (2006) examined the trauma victims 5 and 11 months after the trauma. There were no differences with respect to the severity of PTSD symptoms between the two groups. However, due to the small number of results available concerning the impact of trauma-associated stimuli, the need for more studies is evident in order to make valid statements and to testify whether trauma-associated stimuli can also lead to a retraumatization.

5.5 Conclusions: Toward a Definition of Retraumatization

Traumatized individuals with PTSD have an increased sensitivity to anxiety-causing, trauma-associated stimuli. They remain vulnerable for life for an increase of the symptoms. The increase of the symptoms is characterized as retraumatization. The theory of the fear network can be used as an explanation for the underlying mechanisms of the processing during retraumatization. The traumatic memory is supposed to be strongly connected to the subcortical motivation circuit due to the high emotional intensity at the time of encoding. Even simple cues can easily gate the access to this stored information. However, there is uncertainty about what triggers lead to a retraumatization. Discussed are both new trauma and trauma-associated stimuli or threshold situations.

Existing studies show an inconclusive picture of the phenomenon of retraumatization, partly due to the lack of a common definition. Trigger situations have not yet been consistently identified or defined, and they include trauma-associated stimuli as well as newly traumatic events or threshold situations. There also is a lack of clarity about the duration of the symptom increase and the intensity of the increase in PTSD symptoms or eventually other comorbid symptomatology.

Previous studies provide first information of the crucial aspects with respect to an operationally precise and universally used definition of retraumatization:

- *Trauma-associated stimuli and new traumatic events:* In the clinical context, we encounter the phenomenon of retraumatization rather often, either after a confrontation with trauma-associated stimuli or after the experience of a new traumatizing event. The existing studies indicate that, after both (a confrontation with trauma-associated stimuli and the experience of a new trauma), there can be an increase in PTSD symptoms. However, the impact of trauma-associated stimuli has not yet been explored sufficiently to be able to draw final conclusions concerning the possibility of being retraumatized by trauma-associated stimuli.
- *Development of PTSD in the aftermath of the initial trauma:* There is evidence that, for an increase in PTSD symptoms after the new traumatic event (retraumatization), the individual had to have PTSD in the aftermath of the initial trauma (Breslau et al., 2009). The results of a prospective epidemiological study on the influence of a new traumatic event on PTSD symptoms showed that people who had already developed PTSD after the initial traumatic situation are more vulnerable and showed significantly more frequent an increase of PTSD symptoms after being confronted with a new traumatic event.
- *Duration of the symptom increase:* With respect to the duration symptom increase, there is too little evidence so far to be able to make decisive statements for the definition of retraumatization.

Based on these aspects, the following questions have to be answered in order to come to a general definition of retraumatization:

- Is a retraumatization caused by both trauma-associated stimuli and renewed traumatic events?
- Has the traumatized individual already developed a PTSD in the aftermath of the initial trauma?
- Would it be helpful to refer also to the score of comorbid disorders and not only to the PTSD symptoms?
- How is the duration of the symptom increase?
- Would it be helpful to differentiate an acute reaction on a potentially retraumatizing event, acute retraumatization, and long-term retraumatization?

The open aspects should be clarified in order to establish an operationally precise and universally used definition of retraumatization, to ensure adequate intervention, and to avoid a vicious circle of traumatic memory in individuals suffering from PTSD and other disorders occurring in the aftermath of a traumatization. To settle these questions, further research is urgently needed.

References

American Psychiatric Association (APA), (2000). *Diagnostic and statistical manual of mental disorders* (4th ed.). Washington, DC: American Psychiatric Association. *text revised.*

Astur, R. S., St Germain, S. A., Tolin, D., Ford, J., Russell, D., & Stevens, M. (2006). Hippocampus function predicts severity of post-traumatic stress disorder. *Cyberpsychology & Behavior, 9*, 234–240.

Bramsen, I., van der Ploeg, H. M., & Boers, M. (2006). Posttraumatic stress in aging World War II survivors after a firework disaster—a controlled perspective study. *Journal of Traumatic Stress, 19*, 291–300.

Bremner, J. D. (1999). Does stress damage the brain? *Biological Psychiatry, 45*, 797–805.

Breslau, J., Borges, G., Hagar, Y., Tancredi, D., & Gilman, S. (2009). Immigration to the USA and risk for mood and anxiety disorders: Variation by origin and age at immigration. *Psychological Medicine, 39*, 1117–1127.

Brewin, C. R. (2001). Memory processes in post-traumatic stress disorder. *International Review of Psychiatry, 13*, 159–163.

Brewin, C. R. (2003). *Posttraumatic stress disorder: Malady or myth?* New Haven, CT: Yale University Press.

Brewin, C. R. (2007). Autobiographical memory for trauma: Update on four controversies. *Memory, 15*(3), 227–248.

Brewin, C. R., Dalgleish, T., & Joseph, S. (1996). A dual representation theory of post traumatic stress disorder. *Psychological Review, 103*(4), 670–686.

Claas, P., & Schulze, C. (2002). *Prozessorientierte psychotherapie bei der traumaverarbeitung*. Tübingen: DGVT-Verlag.

Duckworth, M. P., & Follette, M. V. (2012). Conclusions and future directions in the assessment, treatment, and prevention of retraumatization. In M. P. Duckworth & V. M. Follette (Eds.), *Retraumatization—assessment, treatment, and prevention (pp. 9–31)*. New York, NY: Routledge.

Ehlers, A., & Clark, D. M. (2000). A cognitive model of posttraumatic stress disorder. *Behaviour Research and Therapy, 38*(4), 319–345.

Elbert, T., Rockstroh, B., Kolassa, I. T., Schauer, M., & Neuner, F. (2006). The influence of organized violence and terror on brain and mind—a co-constructive perspective. In P. Baltes, P. Reuter-Lorenz, & F. Rösler (Eds.), *Lifespan development and the brain: The perspective of biocultural co-constructivism*. Cambridge, UK: Cambridge University Press.

Foa, E. B., & Kozak, M. J. (1986). Emotional processing of fear: Exposure to correcting information. *Psychological Bulletin, 99*, 20–35.

Foa, E. B., & Rothbaum, B. O. (1998). *Treating the trauma of rape: Cognitive-behavioral therapy for PTSD*. New York, NY: The Guilford Press.

Galea, S., Nandi, A., & Vlahov, D. (2005). The epidemiology of post-traumatic stress disorder after disasters. *Epidemiologic Reviews, 28*, 78–91.

Hantman, S., & Solomon, Z. (2007). Recurrent trauma: Holocaust survivors cope with aging and cancer. *Social Psychiatry and Psychiatric Epidemiology, 45*, 396–402.

Heir, T., & Weisaeth, L. (2006). Back to where it happened: Self-reported symptom improvement of tsunami survivors who returned to the disaster area. *Prehospital and Disaster Medicine, 23*, 225–230.

Karl, A., Schaefer, M., Malta, L. S., Dörfel, D., Rohleder, N., & Werner, A. (2006). A meta-analysis of structural brain abnormalities in PTSD. *Neuroscience and Biobehavioral Reviews, 30*, 1004–1031.

Kessler, R. C., Sonnega, A., Bromet, E., Hughes, M., & Nelson, C. B. (1995). Posttraumatic stress disorder in the national comorbidity survey. *Archives of General Psychiatry, 52*, 1048–1060.

Kinzie, J. D., Boehnlein, J. K., Riley, C., & Sparr, L. (2002). The effects of September 11 on traumatized refugees: Reactivation of posttraumatic stress disorder. *The Journal of Nervous and Mental Disease, 190*, 437–441.

Lang, P. J., Bradley, M. M., Fitzsimmons, J. R., Cuthbert, B. N., Scott, J. D., Moulder, B., et al. (1998). Emotional arousal and activation of the visual cortex: An fMRI analysis. *Psychophysiology, 35,* 199–210.

Maercker, A., Forstmeier, S., Wagner, B., Glaesmer, H., & Brähler, E. (2008). Posttraumatische belastungsstörungen in Deutschland: Ergebnisse einer gesamtdeutsche epidemiologischen untersuchung. *Der Nervenarzt, 5,* 577–586.

Maercker, A., & Mehr, A. (2006). What if victims read a newspaper report about their victimization? *European Psychologist, 11,* 137–142.

McNally, R. J. (2003). Remembering trauma: *Cambridge, MA.* Harvard University Press.

McNally, R. J. (2007). Mechanisms of exposure therapy: How neuroscience can improve psychological treatments for anxiety disorders. *Clinical Psychology Review, 27,* 750–759.

McNally, R. J., Kaspi, S. P., Riemann, B. C., & Zeitlin, S. B. (1990). Selective processing of threat cues in posttraumatic stress disorder. *Journal of Abnormal Psychology, 99,* 398–402.

Metcalfe, J., & Jacobs, W. (1996). A "hot-system/cool-system" view of memory under stress. *PTSD Research Quarterly, 7,* 1–3.

Nachshoni, T., & Singer, Y. (2006). Reactivation of combat stress after a family member's enlistment. *Military Medicine, 171,* 1211–1214.

Orth, U., & Maercker, A. (2004). Do trials of perpetrators retraumatize crime victims? *Journal of Interpersonal Violence, 19,* 212–227.

Paratz, E. D., & Katz, B. (2011). Ageing holocaust survivors in Australia. *The Medical Journal of Australia, 16,* 194–197.

Perkonigg, A., Pfister, H., Stein, M. B., Hofler, M., Lieb, R., Maercker, A., et al. (2005). Longitudinal course of posttraumatic stress disorder and posttraumatic stress disorder symptoms in a community sample of adolescents and young adults. *The American Journal of Psychiatry, 162,* 1320–1327.

Resick, P. A. (2003). *Stress und trauma.* Bern: Verlag Hans Huber.

Riggs, D. S., Cahill, S. P., & Foa, E. B. (2006). Exposure treatment of posttraumatic stress disorder. In V. Follette & J. Ruzek (Eds.), *Cognitive-behavioral therapies for trauma.* New York, NY: The Guilford Press.

Robinson, S., Hemmendinger, J., Netanel, R., Rapaport, M., Zilberman, L., & Gal, A. (1994). Retraumatization of holocaust survivors during the Gulf War and SCUD missile attacks on Israel. *The British Journal of Medical Psychology, 67,* 353–362.

Rüegg, J. C. (2010). *Gehirn, psyche und körper. Neurobiologie von psychosomatik und psychotherapie.* Stuttgart: Schattauer.

Schock, K., Rosner, R., & Knaevelsrud, C. *Impact of asylum hearings on the mental health of traumatized asylum seekers.* Manuscript submitted for publication.

Smith, M. E. (2005). Bilateral hippocampal volume reduction in adults with post traumatic stress disorder: A meta-analysis of structural studies. *Hippocampus, 15,* 798–807.

Steel, Z., Momartin, S., Silove, D., Coello, M., Aroche, J., & Tay, K. W. (2011). Two year psychosocial and mental health outcomes for refugees subjected to restrictive or supportive immigration policies. *Social Science & Medicine, 72,* 1149–1156.

Stein, M. B., Koverola, C., Hanna, C., Torchia, M. G., & McClarty, B. (1997). Hippocampal volume in women victimized by childhood sexual abuse. *Psychological Medicine, 27,* 951–960.

Van der Kolk, B. A., & Fisler, R. (1995). Dissociation and the fragmentary nature of traumatic memories: Overview and exploratory study. *Journal of Traumatic Stress, 8*(4), 505–525.

Van der Kolk, B. A., Van der Hart, O., & Marmar, C. M. (2000). Dissoziation und informationsverarbeitung beim posttraumatischen belastungssyndrom. In B. A. Van der Kolk, A. C. McFarlane & L. Weisaeth (Hrsg.), *Traumatic stress* (S241–S261). Paderborn: Junfermann.

Wenk-Ansohn, M., & Schock, K. (2008). Verlauf chronischer traumafolgen—zum Begriff "retraumatisierung". *ZPPM, 4*

Woon, F. L., Sood, S., & Hedges, D. W. (2010). Hippocampal volume deficits associated with exposure to psychological trauma and posttraumatic stress disorder in adults: A meta-analysis. *Progress in Neuropsychopharmacology & Biological Psychiatry, 34*, 1181–1188.

Zayfert, C. (2012). Cognitive behavioral conceptualization of retraumatization. In M. P. Duckworth & V. M. Follette (Eds.), *Retraumatization—assessment, treatment, and prevention (pp. 931)*. New York, NY: Routledge.

6 Pathological Modes of Remembering: The PTSD Experience

Michael Schönenberg

Department of Clinical Psychology and Psychotherapy, University of Tübingen, Tübingen, Germany

6.1 Introduction

The ability to remember is a prerequisite for effective functioning in everyday life. Due to restricted memory capacity, forgetting information that is no longer needed is critical for new learning. Sometimes it is even beneficial to forget certain moments in life, as in the case of an embarrassing or sad experience. However, extremely stressful events are capable of exerting enormous psychological impact on the individual and lead to recurrent recollections of the aversive experience in some cases. Whereas these symptoms decline over the following weeks in most individuals, a small but significant proportion develops a chronic posttraumatic stress disorder (PTSD), as well as secondary symptoms that lead to enduring distress and substantial impairments in daily life. This chapter is an attempt to outline the types of events resistant to forgetting, the differences between normal and a pathological stress responses, and risk factors that can be related to an onset of the disorder. Furthermore, the influence of negative appraisals and dysfunctional cognitive strategies on the exacerbation and maintenance of unwanted traumatic memories are considered.

6.2 Trauma Versus Life Event

Although the term *trauma*, in its psychological sense, is commonly used as a synonym for a broad variety of more or less ordinary stressful life events in everyday language, it technically refers to a serious, horrific stressor that has a potential to cause long-lasting mental disorders. When the phrase *psychological trauma* was first introduced in the psychiatric diagnostic and statistical manual (DSM III, American Psychiatric Association, 1980), it was conceptualized as a stressor that was "outside the range of usual human experience and would be markedly stressing to almost anyone." The idea behind this definition was that the trauma concept should be limited to catastrophic events such as war experiences, torture, rape, and natural disasters and thus can be reliably differentiated from ordinary stressful live events (e.g., chronic illness, divorce, unemployment), which occur more frequently and are considered to be associated with less severe (and predominantly nonpathological), emotional, and psychological adjustment problems. Hence, persisting symptoms of distress, depression, and anxiety were referred to as an *exclusive shock-reaction syndrome*, a normal reaction to an abnormal event that has the potential to exert distinctive psychological impact on the individual. This conceptualization stimulated an emerging field of research on trauma responses and, due to the findings of some influential epidemiological studies (Breslau, 1998; Creamer, Burgess, & McFarlane, 2001; Kessler, Sonnega, Bromet, Hughes, & Nelson, 1995), it became evident that, although the majority of individuals reported at least one lifetime trauma that is sufficient to fall within this imprecise definition, only a minority of subjects went on to develop long-lasting posttraumatic psychiatric morbidity. As a consequence, the trauma criterion was revised to include two aspects: (1) the experience of an objective and serious threat ("The person experienced, witnessed or was confronted with an event or events that involved actual or threatened death or serious injury, or a threat to the physical integrity of self or others"), and (2) the subjective response of the individual to the stressor ("The person's response involved intense fear, helplessness, or horror"). Most of the recent studies confirmed the importance of the objective aspect of this definition and demonstrated the highest prevalence rates for chronic mental disorders as a sequel to protracted interpersonal and complex traumatization (e.g., sexual abuse, torture, military combat), whereas single impersonal and nonlife-threatening events (e.g., moderate accidents) were rarely associated with long-lasting psychopathology. Research, however, also indicated that the subjective reaction to the traumatic experience should be expanded to include intense individual reactions such as disgust and anger that were shown to predict the development and maintenance of posttraumatic stress symptomatology (Dalgleish & Power, 2004; Hathaway, Boals, & Banks, 2010). Thus, the current definition of psychological trauma requires the experience of a single threat or a series of them that overwhelms the individual's ability to cope with the experience and its sequels.

6.3 Acute Stress Reactions

The immediate psychological response to a traumatic stressor may include symptoms such as shock, agitation, anxiety, depression, and withdrawal. Some of these reactions emerge in almost every affected individual. These early phenomena are usually considered as transient and normal adjustment problems that naturally decrease and that are not indicative of an emerging mental disorder. Shalev (2002) postulates three successive response phases after the confrontation with a potentially life-threatening stressor: During the *impact phase*, the organism is engaged in survival-driven behavior, subject to strong emotions and an intense endocrinological stress response. Under these exceptional circumstances, sensory impressions of the event and the way the individual responded to it (behavioral reactions, cognitions, emotions) can frequently provoke early intrusive ruminations. In the *rescue phase*, immediately postevent, the individual is faced with injuries, losses, additional stressors, and the unexpected intensity of his own behavioral and emotional reactions. First attempts to cope with the new situation might end in confusion and bewilderment. During the *early recovery phase*, the subject will then seek to assimilate the traumatic experience, which is the point where "concrete events become mental events" (Shalev, 2002). Within this posttraumatic stage, the involuntary recall of the stressful event through thoughts, flashbacks, and nightmares may be repeatedly experienced by the majority of traumatized subjects. Consistently, a large body of research indicated that these acute reactions are common during the initial days and weeks after the experience of a traumatic stressor but that they will usually abate in most individuals, leaving a relatively small but significant number of survivors who suffer from ongoing and stable symptomatology (Bryant, 2003). For instance, one early and influential study (Rothbaum, Foa, Riggs, Murdock, & Walsh, 1992) employed a prospective weekly assessment of the severity of posttraumatic distress in recently traumatized rape victims and found that over 90% reported clinically significant posttraumatic distress approximately 12 days postevent. One month after the assault, the incidence of severe psychological impairment dropped to 65%, and 3 months postevent, around 40% of the survivors reported to suffer from ongoing posttraumatic psychopathology. Another study conducted telephone surveys to determine trends in the prevalence of posttraumatic stress reactions in the population of New York after the September 11 terrorist attacks (Galea et al., 2003). More than one-fourth of the residents who were directly affected (i.e., who were in the World Trade Center during the attacks, were injured, lost friends, relatives, possessions, or property) exhibited substantial psychological symptoms 1 month postevent. However, 4 months postevent, approximately 8% reported stable symptomatology. Hence, it appears that transient intrusive ruminations and flashbacks are most commonly experienced in trauma victims, whereas long-lasting severe impairments signal an abnormal response to an abnormal experience.

6.4 Posttraumatic Stress Disorder

To meet criteria for a diagnosis of PTSD following the experience of a traumatic event, the individual has to suffer from symptoms corresponding to three distinctive dimensions: reexperiencing, avoidance, and hyperarousal. To nonpathologize these normal reactions to extreme stress, which often involve transient symptoms that may fall into each of these symptom clusters, PTSD criteria explicitly require the symptomatology to cause a clinically relevant impairment in everyday functioning that must be present for a least 1 month after the traumatic experience. Thus, normal stress phenomena and clinical significant PTSD symptoms may be similar in phenomenological aspects, but they are distinguishable with respect to the persistence and severity of impairments (O'Donnell, Elliott, Lau, & Creamer, 2007).

The *reexperiencing* symptom cluster encompasses recurrent and involuntary recollections of the event (intrusions), which usually involve vivid sensory impressions and/or perseverative distressing nightmares during which the experience is relived. Interestingly, although intrusive memories are often referred to as thoughts, most trauma victims report that they are usually experienced as short visual fragments and, to a lesser extent, as bodily sensations (i.e., pain), sounds, smells, or tastes and only rarely described as thoughts (Michael, Ehlers, Halligan, & Clark, 2005). Intrusive memories are typically perceived to come out of the blue, and individuals are often unaware of external or internal cues that might trigger such unwanted memories (Brewin, 2001). These sensory impressions of the traumatic event are accompanied by a strong feeling of "nowness," which means that the person actually believes to be in the traumatic situation (Ehlers, Hackmann, & Michael, 2004). Episodes of intrusive reliving can last from seconds up to several minutes or even hours and can involve a complete loss of the awareness of present surroundings (dissociation). The experiencing of such sensory fragments as well as the confrontation with trigger stimuli that resemble or symbolize aspects of the traumatic event (e.g., the sound of a fire truck siren, a person with a physical resemblance to the perpetrator) is usually accompanied by intense emotions and psychological distress. Hence, intrusive reexperiencing is regarded to be the core symptom of PTSD that is phenomenologically distinguishable from thoughts and ruminations with regard to the notion that intrusions are sensory impressions that occur spontaneously and involuntarily and lack a clear association to a triggering stimulus, as well as the mental awareness that these impressions are tied to the past and have nothing to do with the present reality.

The *avoidance* cluster refers to any effort made by the individual to avoid thoughts and potential reminders of the trauma (situations, places, and people). Symptoms include behavioral, cognitive, and emotional avoidance strategies that are frequently used by trauma victims to protect themselves from being overwhelmed by intense emotional reactions triggered by traumatic cues. In addition, the avoidance cluster includes numbing symptoms (i.e., a sense of foreshortened future, diminished interests in previously enjoyed activities, a feeling of being detached from others) and a restricted range of affect (i.e., a reduced ability to feel and express emotions). Symptoms of the avoidance/numbing cluster are some of the least frequently reported symptoms and may be more likely to emerge later in the course of PTSD than the other criteria (North, Smith, & Spitznagel, 1997). Accordingly, a longitudinal study in trauma survivors demonstrated that intrusions tend to decrease over time, whereas initially very mild avoidance symptoms intensified in subjects who subsequently developed PTSD. Moreover, it was shown that survivors who exhibited increased avoidance symptoms reported a greater deal of harm, more severe impairments in daily life, and more psychiatric comorbidities or secondary disorders (McMillen, North, & Smith, 2000; North et al., 1999).

The *hyperarousal* cluster includes symptoms such as concentration deficits, irritability, sleep disturbances, or difficulties staying asleep that may result from recurrent nightmares. In addition, this symptom dimension covers symptoms of generally increased anxiety and tonic arousal, as well as an attentional hypervigilance to signals of potential threat and an exaggerated startle response. Numerous studies have shown that traumatized subjects suffering from chronic PTSD exhibit strongly increased physiological arousal (Orr, Metzger, & Pitman, 2002), when compared to trauma victims without PTSD, both during basal assessment and during exposure to traumatic reminders (Elzinga, Schmahl, Vermetten, Van Dyck, & Bremner, 2003; Sack, Hopper, & Lamprecht, 2004). Moreover, there is some evidence to suggest that hyperarousal symptoms appear early after a traumatic experience and thus may be indicative of a higher risk of developing and maintaining PTSD.

The diagnostic criteria for PTSD distinguish several courses of posttraumatic reactions. An acute PTSD is diagnosed when symptoms persist for fewer than 3 months and a chronic PTSD requires symptom maintenance for 3 or more months. A delayed-onset PTSD is diagnosed if symptomatology develops at least 6 months postevent. The existence and prevalence of the latter phenomenon, however, is controversially discussed because prior subsyndromal impairment was demonstrated to be present in the majority of such cases (Andrews, Brewin, Philpott, & Stewart, 2007).

PTSD is essentially considered to be associated with a strong fear response to traumatic recollections, which leads to the development and maintenance of avoidance behavior. Hence, it is diagnostically referred to as an anxiety disorder and therefore has to be differentiated from other posttraumatic conditions such as posttraumatic embitterment disorder or complicated grief where other psychopathological symptoms and emotions predominate the clinical picture (Linden, 2011).

Over the past years, a growing body of evidence has suggested that some severe posttraumatic reactions are not adequately covered by a PTSD diagnosis and that there may be a need for an additional diagnostic category (referred to as complex PTSD) that better accounts for the profound alterations in personality characteristics frequently observed in victims of repeated physical, emotional, or sexual abuse (Cloitre et al., 2010; van der Kolk, Roth, Pelcovitz, Sunday, & Spinazzola, 2005).

PTSD often co-occurs with other mental disorders that bear additional impact on the individual's quality of life. Depression, substance abuse, other anxiety, and psychosomatic disorders, as well as personality disorders, were frequently observed in trauma victims with chronic PTSD. Several epidemiological studies found that up to 70% of PTSD patients fulfill diagnostic criteria for another psychiatric disorder (Calabrese et al., 2011; North et al., 1999), which strongly suggests that a PTSD diagnosis increases the vulnerability to develop other disorders and impairments. Notably, it was documented that the presence of depression and/or alcohol abuse secondary to a PTSD diagnosis increases the risk of suicidality more than seven-fold (Calabrese et al., 2011).

6.5 General Risk Factors for PTSD

The notion that trauma exposure is more common than expected, but that only a minority of individuals suffer full-blown and long-lasting psychopathology after an early transient phase of adjustment, has led to attempts to elucidate which sociodemographic/environmental, physiological, and psychological factors might determine a higher susceptibility to the development and maintenance of PTSD symptomatology. Pretraumatic risk factors, such as female gender (Gavranidou & Rosner, 2003), lower education (Schnurr, Lunney, & Sengupta, 2004), a (family and/or personal) psychiatric history (Ozer, Best, Lipsey, & Weiss, 2003), as well as previous traumatization that has led to a prior diagnosis (Breslau, Peterson, & Schultz, 2008), were repeatedly linked to PTSD development. In addition, several peritraumatic or early posttraumatic risk factors, including event characteristics [e.g., severe physical injury (Koren, Norman, Cohen, Berman, & Klein, 2005), early, complex, and repetitive traumatization (Kessler et al., 1995)] and subjective responses [e.g., the experience of being "threatened to life"

(Holbrook, Hoyt, Stein, & Sieber, 2001), mental defeat (Dunmore, Clark, & Ehlers, 2001), dissociative symptoms (Ozer et al., 2003), as well as severe intrusions, avoidance, and hyperarousal (Schönenberg, Jusyte, Hautzinger, & Badke, 2011)] were associated with enhanced vulnerability. Subsequent posttraumatic or maintaining factors that have been associated with a poor prognosis are low social support (Kilpatrick et al., 2007) and negative appraisal of early stress symptoms (Dunmore et al., 2001). According to some recent studies, preexisting psychological problems and specific characteristics of early severe intrusive symptoms (nowness, distress, lack of context), as well as an avoidant coping style, were the best predictors of PTSD (Armour, Shevlin, Elklit, & Mroczek, 2011; Kleim, Ehlers, & Glucksman, 2007; Michael et al., 2005; Schönenberg et al., 2011).

6.6 Cognitive Abnormalities and Memory Disturbances in PTSD

PTSD is basically a disorder of memory, where sensory fragments of the traumatic experience with its original emotional intensity are involuntarily relived in the present, thereby causing high levels of distress, anxiety, and profound impairments in everyday functioning. Much as in other anxiety disorders, the development of PTSD is considered a consequence of classical and operant conditioning processes (Grillon & Morgan, 1999). However, it is the uncontrollability of these intrusive recollections that distinguishes PTSD from other disorders (e.g., phobias), where a confrontation with the phobic stimulus can be successfully avoided.

Research indicates that deficits in basal cognitive functions, such as attention, working memory, verbal and visual memory, executive functions, and alterations in related brain regions, can be related to chronic PTSD (Vasterling et al., 2002). Most importantly, the analyses of laboratory-collected trauma narratives and nontraumatic autobiographical material demonstrated that memories of the traumatic event were profoundly disorganized in PTSD patients but not in trauma survivors without subsequent PTSD, even when basal memory dysfunctions were controlled for (Jelinek, Randjbar, Seifert, Kellner, & Moritz, 2009; Jones, Harvey, & Brewin, 2007). This finding fits well with basic assumptions of etiological illness models positing that extreme stress might impact the encoding of details of the event and lead to a fragmented traumatic memory that may be characterized by a poor elaboration and a lack of context in time, place, and reference to other autobiographical memories (Brewin, Dalgleish, & Joseph, 1996; Ehlers & Clark, 2000). Such disintegrated memory traces were assumed to account for the persistent intrusive sensory impressions in PTSD. However, it remains unclear whether memory disorganization is caused by encoding difficulties during the traumatic experience or develops later as a consequence of the disorder. Moreover, it is difficult to determine whether (voluntarily retrieved) trauma narratives reflect disorganized memory or the emergence of spontaneous high emotive images might have caused the disorganized recall (Brewin, 2011). There is evidence suggesting that impairments in trauma memory are not stable and change over time, thereby predicting the development and severity of posttraumatic stress reactions (Halligan, Michael, Clark, & Ehlers, 2003; Jones et al., 2007). Importantly, these studies failed to show the development of a more coherent memory after recovery. Thus, fragmented memory may be present in trauma victims and may predict the onset of PTSD symptoms, but it cannot explain why some individuals develop the disorder whereas others do not or why some recover more quickly. Hence, influential cognitive approaches to PTSD propose that negative appraisals of the event and its sequelae as well as the development of dysfunctional automatic or strategic response styles prevent trauma memories from being updated and integrated, thereby exacerbating or preserving PTSD symptomatology (Ehlers & Clark, 2000; Foa & Rothbaum, 2001).

6.7 The Role of Metacognitive Appraisals

Some evidence suggests that the amount of distress caused by early intrusive memories of the traumatic event is more predictive of persistent PTSD than their frequency (Michael et al., 2005). The experience of distress and anxiety largely depends on the negative appraisal of such symptoms and the individual's perception of incompetence to cope with trauma sequels. For instance, intrusive flashbacks may be interpreted as signs of impending mental illness (e.g., "My reactions since the event mean I'm going crazy"). More generally, trauma-related negative cognitions of the self (e.g., "Nothing good can happen to me anymore"), self-blame (e.g., "There is something about me that made the event happen"), as well as negative cognitions about the world (e.g., "I have to be on guard all the time") might foster a sense of continuous threat that perpetuates PTSD symptoms (Ehlers & Clark, 2000). Recent studies demonstrated that negative self-appraisal relative to other posttraumatic appraisals played the most influential role in determining subsequent psychopathology (Hatcher, Whitaker, & Karl, 2009; Schönenberg et al., 2012). Specifically, these inadequate cognitions about the self were also found to increase over time in individuals diagnosed with PTSD (O'Donnell, Elliott, Wolfgang, & Creamer, 2007). Therefore, subjects who appraise themselves as unable to cope with the traumatic experience are likely to develop an internally driven sense of threat that may also elicit other beliefs (e.g., "The world is dangerous", "People can't be trusted") and thus contribute to the exacerbation of PTSD symptoms. In some individuals, however, these threat appraisals intensify over time, thereby strengthening anxiety symptoms and the severity of the disorder. Apparently, the existence of general risk factors, such as specific event characteristics, pretraumatic psychopathology, and personality traits, may further influence the occurrence and aggravation of dysfunctional traumatic cognitions.

6.8 Dysfunctional Cognitive Strategies

As a consequence of increasing anxiety, the individual may adopt behavioral and cognitive coping styles to avoid thoughts, memories, and unpleasant emotions that are related to the traumatic experience. Although these strategies are effective to decrease the occurrence of aversive symptoms in the short term, they interfere with the extinction of trauma-related fear responses, resulting in the increased frequency and severity of PTSD symptomatology in the long term (Kumpula, Orcutt, Bardeen, & Varkovitzky, 2011). Thought suppression is an important dysfunctional coping style that was suggested to be critically involved in maintaining symptoms (Brewin, 2011; Ehlers & Clark, 2000). To assess thought suppression in traumatized populations via an experimental task, participants are usually instructed to write down whatever comes to mind (including their traumatic experience) within a defined time slot. The task is then repeated with the instruction that they are not allowed to think about their traumatic experience but that, if they do, they should write these thoughts down. In a third step, the task is repeated again with the instruction that it is now permitted to think about the traumatic event. It was shown that subjects with PTSD exhibited a rebound effect after they had suppressed their thoughts, that is, thoughts about the event dramatically increased after suppression instructions were removed (Shipherd & Beck, 1999, 2005).

Traumatized victims without PTSD did not show such pattern. Remarkably, when the instruction was to suppress thoughts about a neutral daily activity, there was no subsequent rebound effect in trauma victims without, and in trauma victims with, PTSD. Hence, when transferring these findings to naturally occurring PTSD symptoms, one can speculate that individuals suffering from chronic PTSD may suppress trauma-related thoughts in daily life and thus are most likely to experience naturally occurring rebound effects, that is, intrusive traumatic memories (Shipherd & Beck, 2005).

Interestingly, there is some evidence suggesting that individuals prone to PTSD development have a tendency to (automatically) avoid intense aversive aspects of the trauma in the early aftermath of the event. Several studies indicated that peritraumatic dissociation (i.e., symptoms of depersonalization, altered sense of time, confusion at the time of or shortly after the traumatic experience) may reflect early attempts of avoidance that allow the individual to cope with the experience. However, the occurrence of these symptoms increases the risk for subsequent PTSD (Birmes et al., 2003; Marmar, Weiss, Schlenger, & Fairbank, 1994). In addition, two studies found that traumatic stress can lead to an attentional shift away from threat-related information in anxious individuals and that this attentional bias contributes to the development of psychopathology (Bar-Haim et al., 2010; Wald, Lubin, et al., 2011). Consistently, patients with severe acute stress symptoms performed significantly better than trauma-exposed controls when asked to intentionally forget trauma-associated words (Moulds & Bryant, 2002).

Existing research implies that early avoidance can be related to the development of PTSD but has little independent predictive value for psychopathology beyond the acute trauma phase (Schönenberg et al., 2011; van der Velden & Wittmann, 2008; Wald, Shechner, et al., 2011). However, results of a recently published prospective study suggest that the pretraumatic tendency to suppress or avoid unwanted internal experiences (e.g., "I am afraid of my feelings," "I worry about not being able to control my feelings") predicts the occurrence of peritraumatic dissociation and the use of postevent avoidance strategies that, in turn, are strongly related to the severity and maintenance of PTSD symptoms (Kumpula et al., 2011). Hence, the appearance of early (automatic) and subsequent (strategic) cognitive avoidance might be affected by preexisting personality traits, beliefs, and experiences, as well as by appraisals and cognitions related to details of the stressful experience and its symptomatic consequences.

6.9 Conclusions and Implications for Therapy

The exposure to a traumatic stressor during the course of a lifetime is a common experience. The majority of affected individuals report acute stress symptoms that naturally decline in the following weeks and months. Only a small subgroup of traumatized individuals go on to develop a chronic PTSD with persistent intrusive recollections of the trauma, symptoms of hyperarousal, and an intensifying avoidance behavior that cause significant distress and impairments in everyday functioning. Research has indicated that fragmented memory traces might account for the intrusions and that recovery is facilitated when the individual allows these spontaneous sensory impressions to occur. In contrast, it was emphasized that negative appraisals of symptoms, as well as the experience of distress and anxiety, induce dysfunctional coping styles, such as thought suppression, that may prevent reexperiencing symptoms from remitting.

These factors, which have been shown to play a role in the amplification and maintenance of posttraumatic symptomatology after an initial phase of psychological adjustment, may help to focus research on the prevention of the disorder. In order not to overemphasize initial stress reactions but rather to prevent the development of long-lasting psychopathology, it is useful to consider a period of watchful waiting after a traumatic event. In addition, it may be a promising strategy to routinely assess early cognitive avoidance (e.g., an attentional bias away from threatening information) in trauma survivors putatively at risk for the development of chronic PTSD (e.g., after severe and/or repetitive interpersonal trauma, in subjects with preexisting psychological problems). Recent research indicates that attentional bias modification treatments are successful in reducing symptomatology in other anxiety disorders and therefore might also be effective in the treatment of PTSD (Hakamata et al., 2010).

References

American Psychiatric Association, (1980). *Diagnostic and statistical manual of mental disorders* (3th ed.). Washington, DC: American Psychiatric Association.

Andrews, B., Brewin, C., Philpott, R., & Stewart, L. (2007). Delayed-onset posttraumatic stress disorder: A systematic review of the evidence. *American Journal of Psychiatry, 164*(9), 1319–1326.

Armour, C., Shevlin, M., Elklit, A., & Mroczek, D. (2011). A latent growth mixture modeling approach to PTSD symptoms in rape victims. *Traumatology, 18*(1), 20–28.

Bar-Haim, Y., Holoshitz, Y., Eldar, S., Frenkel, T. I., Muller, D., Charney, D. S., et al. (2010). Life-threatening danger and suppression of attention bias to threat. *American Journal of Psychiatry, 167*(6), 694–698.

Birmes, P., Brunet, A., Carreras, D., Ducassé, J. L., Charlet, J. P., Lauque, D., et al. (2003). The predictive power of peritraumatic dissociation and acute stress symptoms for posttraumatic stress symptoms: A three-month prospective study. *American Journal of Psychiatry, 160*(7), 1337–1339.

Breslau, N. (1998). Epidemiology of trauma and posttraumatic stress disorder. *Psychological Trauma, 17,* 1–29.

Breslau, N., Peterson, E. L., & Schultz, L. R. (2008). A second look at prior trauma and the posttraumatic stress disorder effects of subsequent trauma: A prospective epidemiological study. *Archives of General Psychiatry, 65*(4), 431–437.

Brewin, C. R. (2001). Memory processes in post-traumatic stress disorder. *International Review of Psychiatry, 13*(3), 159–163.

Brewin, C. R. (2011). The nature and significance of memory disturbance in posttraumatic stress disorder. *Annual Review of Clinical Psychology, 7,* 203–227.

Brewin, C. R., Dalgleish, T., & Joseph, S. (1996). A dual representation theory of posttraumatic stress disorder. *Psychological Review, 103*(4), 670–686.

Bryant, R. A. (2003). Acute stress reactions: Can biological responses predict posttraumatic stress disorder? *CNS Spectrums, 8,* 668–674.

Calabrese, J. R., Prescott, M., Tamburrino, M., Liberzon, I., Slembarski, R., Goldmann, E., et al. (2011). PTSD comorbidity and suicidal ideation associated with PTSD within the Ohio Army National Guard. *Journal of Clinical Psychiatry, 72*(8), 1072–1078.

Cloitre, M., Stovall-McClough, K. C., Nooner, K., Zorbas, P., Cherry, S., Jackson, C. L., et al. (2010). Treatment for PTSD related to childhood abuse: A randomized controlled trial. *American Journal of Psychiatry, 167*(8), 915–924.

Creamer, M. C., Burgess, P., & McFarlane, A. C. (2001). Post-traumatic stress disorder: Findings from the Australian national survey of mental health and well-being. *Psychological Medicine, 31*(7), 1237–1247.

Dalgleish, T., & Power, M. J. (2004). Emotion-specific and emotion-non-specific components of posttraumatic stress disorder (PTSD): Implications for a taxonomy of related psychopathology. *Behaviour Research and Therapy, 42*(9), 1069–1088.

Dunmore, E., Clark, D. M., & Ehlers, A. (2001). A prospective investigation of the role of cognitive factors in persistent posttraumatic stress disorder (PTSD) after physical or sexual assault. *Behaviour Research and Therapy, 39*(9), 1063–1084.

Ehlers, A., & Clark, D. M. (2000). A cognitive model of posttraumatic stress disorder. *Behaviour Research and Therapy, 38*(4), 319–345.

Ehlers, A., Hackmann, A., & Michael, T. (2004). Intrusive re-experiencing in post-traumatic stress disorder: Phenomenology, theory, and therapy. *Memory, 12*(4), 403–415.

Elzinga, B. M., Schmahl, C. G., Vermetten, E., Van Dyck, R., & Bremner, J. D. (2003). Higher cortisol levels following exposure to traumatic reminders in abuse-related PTSD. *Neuropsychopharmacology, 28*(9), 1656–1665.

Foa, E. B., & Rothbaum, B. O. (2001). *Treating the trauma of rape: Cognitive-behavioral therapy for PTSD.* New York, NY: The Guilford Press.

Galea, S., Vlahov, D., Resnick, H., Ahern, J., Susser, E., Gold, J., et al. (2003). Trends of probable post-traumatic stress disorder in New York City after the September 11 terrorist attacks. *American Journal of Epidemiology, 158*(6), 514–524.

Gavranidou, M., & Rosner, R. (2003). The weaker sex? Gender and post-traumatic stress disorder. *Depression and Anxiety, 17*(3), 130–139.

Grillon, C., & Morgan, C. A. (1999). Fear-potentiated startle conditioning to explicit and contextual cues in Gulf War veterans with posttraumatic stress disorder. *Journal of Abnormal Psychology, 108*(1), 134–142.

Hakamata, Y., Lissek, S., Bar-Haim, Y., Britton, J. C., Fox, N. A., Leibenluft, E., et al. (2010). Attention bias modification treatment: A meta-analysis toward the establishment of novel treatment for anxiety. *Biological Psychiatry*, *68*(11), 982–990.

Halligan, S. L., Michael, T., Clark, D. M., & Ehlers, A. (2003). Posttraumatic stress disorder following assault: The role of cognitive processing, trauma memory, and appraisals. *Journal of Consulting and Clinical Psychology*, *71*(3), 419–431.

Hatcher, M. B., Whitaker, C., & Karl, A. (2009). What predicts post-traumatic stress following spinal cord injury. *British Journal of Health Psychology*, *14*(3), 541–561.

Hathaway, L. M., Boals, A., & Banks, J. B. (2010). PTSD symptoms and dominant emotional response to a traumatic event: An examination of DSM-IV Criterion A2. *Anxiety, Stress & Coping*, *23*(1), 119–126.

Holbrook, T. L., Hoyt, D. B., Stein, M. B., & Sieber, W. J. (2001). Perceived threat to life predicts posttraumatic stress disorder after major trauma: Risk factors and functional outcome. *The Journal of Trauma*, *51*(2), 287–292.

Jelinek, L., Randjbar, S., Seifert, D., Kellner, M., & Moritz, S. (2009). The organization of autobiographical and nonautobiographical memory in posttraumatic stress disorder (PTSD). *Journal of Abnormal Psychology*, *118*(2), 288–298.

Jones, C., Harvey, A. G., & Brewin, C. R. (2007). The organisation and content of trauma memories in survivors of road traffic accidents. *Behaviour Research and Therapy*, *45*(1), 151–162.

Kessler, R. C., Sonnega, A., Bromet, E., Hughes, M., & Nelson, C. B. (1995). Posttraumatic stress disorder in the national comorbidity survey. *Archives of General Psychiatry*, *52*(12), 1048–1060.

Kilpatrick, D., Koenen, K., Ruggiero, K., Acierno, R., Galea, S., Resnick, H., et al. (2007). The serotonin transporter genotype and social support and moderation of posttraumatic stress disorder and depression in hurricane-exposed adults. *American Journal of Psychiatry*, *164*(11), 1693–1699.

Kleim, B., Ehlers, A., & Glucksman, E. (2007). Early predictors of chronic post-traumatic stress disorder in assault survivors. *Psychological Medicine*, *37*(10), 1457–1467.

Koren, D., Norman, D., Cohen, A., Berman, J., & Klein, E. M. (2005). Increased PTSD risk with combat-related injury: A matched comparison study of injured and uninjured soldiers experiencing the same combat events. *American Journal of Psychiatry*, *162*(2), 228–276.

Kumpula, M. J., Orcutt, H. K., Bardeen, J. R., & Varkovitzky, R. L. (2011). Peritraumatic dissociation and experiential avoidance as prospective predictors of posttraumatic stress symptoms. *Journal of Abnormal Psychology*, *120*(3), 617.

Linden, M. (2011). Posttraumatic embitterment disorder, PTED. In M. Linden & A. Maercker (Eds.), *Embitterment (pp. 255–273).* Wien: Springer.

Marmar, C. R., Weiss, D. S., Schlenger, W. E., & Fairbank, J. A. (1994). Peritraumatic dissociation and posttraumatic stress in male Vietnam theater veterans. *American Journal of Psychiatry*, *151*(6), 902–907.

McMillen, J. C., North, C. S., & Smith, E. M. (2000). What parts of PTSD are normal: Intrusion, avoidance, or arousal? Data from the Northridge, California, earthquake. *Journal of Traumatic Stress*, *13*(1), 57–75.

Michael, T., Ehlers, A., Halligan, S., & Clark, D. (2005). Unwanted memories of assault: What intrusion characteristics are associated with PTSD? *Behaviour Research and Therapy*, *43*(5), 613–628.

Moulds, M. L., & Bryant, R. A. (2002). Directed forgetting in acute stress disorder. *Journal of Abnormal Psychology*, *111*(1), 175–179.

North, C. S., Nixon, S. J., Shariat, S., Mallonee, S., McMillen, J. C., Spitznagel, E. L., et al. (1999). Psychiatric disorders among survivors of the Oklahoma City bombing. *Journal of the American Medical Association*, *282*(8), 755–762.

North, C. S., Smith, E. M., & Spitznagel, E. L. (1997). One-year follow-up of survivors of a mass shooting. *American Journal of Psychiatry*, *154*(12), 1696–1702.

Orr, S. P., Metzger, L. J., & Pitman, R. K. (2002). Psychophysiology of post-traumatic stress disorder. *Psychiatric Clinics of North America*, *25*(2), 271–293.

Ozer, E. J., Best, S. R., Lipsey, T. L., & Weiss, D. S. (2003). Predictors of posttraumatic stress disorder and symptoms in adults: a meta-analysis. *Psychological Bulletin*, *129*(1), 52–73.

O'Donnell, M. L., Elliott, P., Lau, W., & Creamer, M. (2007). PTSD symptom trajectories: From early to chronic response. *Behaviour Research and Therapy*, *45*(3), 601–606.

O'Donnell, M. L., Elliott, P., Wolfgang, B. J., & Creamer, M. (2007). Posttraumatic appraisals in the development and persistence of posttraumatic stress symptoms. *Journal of Traumatic Stress*, *20*(2), 173–182.

Rothbaum, B. O., Foa, E. B., Riggs, D. S., Murdock, T., & Walsh, W. (1992). A prospective examination of post-traumatic stress disorder in rape victims. *Journal of Traumatic Stress*, *5*(3), 455–475.

Sack, M., Hopper, J. W., & Lamprecht, F. (2004). Low respiratory sinus arrhythmia and prolonged psychophysiological arousal in posttraumatic stress disorder: Heart rate dynamics and individual differences in arousal regulation. *Biological Psychiatry*, *55*(3), 284–290.

Schnurr, P. P., Lunney, C. A., & Sengupta, A. (2004). Risk factors for the development versus maintenance of posttraumatic stress disorder. *Journal of Traumatic Stress*, *17*(2), 85–95.

Schönenberg, M., Jusyte, A., Hautzinger, M., & Badke, A. (2011). Early predictors of posttraumatic stress in accident victims. *Psychiatry Research*, *190*(1), 152–155.

Schönenberg, M., Reimitz, M., Jusyte, A., Maier, D., Badke, A., & Hautzinger, M. (2012). Depression, posttraumatic stress and risk factors following spinal cord injury. *International Journal of Behavioral Medicine*, 10.1007/s12529-012-9284-8 [Epub ahead of print].

Shalev, A. Y. (2002). Acute stress reactions in adults. *Biological Psychiatry*, *51*(7), 532–543.

Shipherd, J. C., & Beck, J. G. (1999). The effects of suppressing trauma-related thoughts on women with rape-related posttraumatic stress disorder. *Behaviour Research and Therapy*, *37*(2), 99–112.

Shipherd, J. C., & Beck, J. G. (2005). The role of thought suppression in posttraumatic stress disorder. *Behavior Therapy*, *36*(3), 277–287.

van der Kolk, B. A., Roth, S., Pelcovitz, D., Sunday, S., & Spinazzola, J. (2005). Disorders of extreme stress: The empirical foundation of a complex adaptation to trauma. *Journal of Traumatic Stress*, *18*(5), 389–399.

van der Velden, P. G., & Wittmann, L. (2008). The independent predictive value of peritraumatic dissociation for PTSD symptomatology after type I trauma: A systematic review of prospective studies. *Clinical Psychology Review*, *28*(6), 1009–1020.

Vasterling, J. J., Duke, L. M., Brailey, K., Constans, J. I., Allain, A. N., & Sutker, P. B. (2002). Attention, learning, and memory performances and intellectual resources in Vietnam veterans: PTSD and no disorder comparisons. *Neuropsychology*, *16*(1), 5–14.

Wald, I., Lubin, G., Holoshitz, Y., Muller, D., Fruchter, E., Pine, D., et al. (2011). Battlefield-like stress following simulated combat and suppression of attention bias to threat. *Psychological Medicine*, *41*(4), 699–707.

Wald, I., Shechner, T., Bitton, S., Holoshitz, Y., Charney, D., Muller, D., et al. (2011). Attention bias away from threat during life threatening danger predicts PTSD symptoms at one-year follow-up. *Depression and Anxiety*, *28*(5), 406–411.

7 Hurting Memories and Intrusions in Posttraumatic Embitterment Disorders (PTED) as Compared to Posttraumatic Stress Disorders (PTSD)

Michael Linden

Research Group Psychosomatic Rehabilitation at the Charité University Medicine Berlin and Department of Behavioral and Psychosomatic Medicine, Rehabilitation Center Seehof, Teltow/Berlin, Germany

7.1 Embitterment and Posttraumatic Embitterment Disorder

Embitterment is an emotional state known to everybody (Linden & Maercker, 2011). Aristotle gave a description as:

> *Embittered are those who can not be reconciled, who keep their rancor, they hold their arousal in themselves, not coming to rest unless revenge has come. Revenge reduces arousal and changes pain into contentment. Does this not happen, then the pressure grows. As the internal turmoil does not open itself to others, nobody can counsel and help. It needs time to overcome internal arousal. Those persons are a burden to themselves and their dearest friends.*
>
> Susemihl (1912)

The terms *bitterness* and *embitterment* are also frequently used in colloquial language. According to Znoj (2008, 2011), embitterment is a complex emotion accompanied, among others, by mistrust, despair, anger, aggression, grief, pessimism, weariness, hopelessness, dissatisfaction, disappointment, obsessiveness, or fanatism—a spectrum of very diverse and even contradictory emotions. Embitterment is, by its very nature, a reactive emotion after having been let down or humiliated and includes the drive to fight back. It has been described as reaction to injustice, to protracted unemployment, or to traumatic experiences (Baures, 1996; Linden, Baumann, Lieberei, Lorenz, & Rotter, 2011; Linden, Rotter, Baumann, & Lieberei, 2007; Muschalla & Linden, 2011; Pirhacova, 1997; Zemperl & Frese, 1997). Coming from psychoanalysis, Alexander (1960) interpreted embitterment as aggression by self-destruction. This type of reaction can already be seen in children who have dreams of dying because they want to punish the mother. Embittered persons can attack regardless of the consequences, start useless legal fights, do ridiculous actions like keying somebody's car, or even running amok (Felber, Lammel, Sutarski, & Lau, 2010).

Embitterment is different from depression because emotional modulation is unimpaired. Embittered persons can smile when distracted or reminded of revenge. It is also different from hopelessness because such persons cling to the idea that something may happen or be done in order to make the critical event undone. It is also different from anger because it has the additional quality of self-blame and feelings of injustice. One can be angry at somebody without being embittered. In contrast to depression, it can be understood as the final step in a row of experiences of helplessness:

- When things do not go as expected, it comes to frustration.
- If things could have gone otherwise, it additionally comes to disappointment.
- If somebody could have done something about it, it additionally comes to anger.
- If some other person is seen as guilty, it additionally comes to aggression.
- If one has to admit that oneself should have done something, it additionally comes to shame.
- If one is disparaged by others, it additionally comes to humiliation.
- If repeated trials to do something turned things even worse, it additionally comes to despair.
- If one can do nothing more to react, it additionally comes to hopelessness, depression, and giving up.
- If injustice, infidelity, or feelings of having been let down are involved, it additionally comes to embitterment.
- If this involves the violation of central basic beliefs, it additionally comes to severe embitterment.
- If the state of embitterment is unbearable, it additionally comes to rampage.

The complex emotion of embitterment can be measured with the Posttraumatic Embitterment Disorder (PTED) Self-Rating Scale, PTED Scale (Linden, Rotter, Baumann, & Schippan, 2009) or the Bern Embitterment Inventory (BEI) (Znoj, 2008, 2011). Similar to anxiety, embitterment is a widespread emotion. About half of the persons in the normal population report that they harbor feelings of embitterment in relation to recent experiences (Linden et al., 2007). In about 5% of the population, this emotion is so strong and lasting that daily activities are impaired. Although there is no conclusive research so far, it can be assumed that, similar to anxious personalities, there are also so-called embitterment prone personalities, that is, easily offended and misanthropic persons. Also, embitterment can occur in the context of other mental disorders, such as personality disorders, either as part of their primary emotional spectrum or because persons with personality disorders are often treated unfairly by others (Rotter, 2011). Finally, there is also a specific embitterment disorder, PTED (Linden, 2003; Linden et al., 2007, 2011), which can be seen as parallel to the anxiety disorder, posttraumatic stress disorder (PTSD). PTED is characterized by embitterment, by feelings of humiliation or of having been let down, by helplessness and hopelessness, by aggression against oneself and others, by reduction in drive, by multiple somatoform symptoms, by phobic avoidance of selected places and persons, or by retraction from social activities. The diagnostic criteria for PTED are summarized in Box 7.1. (Linden, Baumann, Rotter, & Schippan, 2008).

The disorder is called posttraumatic not because the eliciting event has been by its very nature extraordinary, as required in PTSD (Smith, Bem, & Nolen-Hoeksema, 2001)

Hurting Memories and Intrusions in Posttraumatic Embitterment Disorders (PTED) 85

> **Box 7.1 Diagnostic Criteria of PTED**
>
> **A.** Core criteria
>   1. A single exceptional negative life event precipitates the onset of the illness.
>   2. Patients know about this life event and see their present negative state as a direct and lasting consequence of it.
>   3. Patients experience the negative life event as unjust and respond with embitterment and emotional arousal when reminded of the event.
>   4. No obvious mental disorder in the year before the critical event. The present state is no recurrence of a preexisting mental disorder.
> **B.** Additional signs and symptoms
>   1. Patients see themselves as victims and as helpless to cope with the event or the cause.
>   2. Patients blame themselves for the event, for not having prevented it, or for not being able to cope with it.
>   3. Patients report repeated intrusive memories of the critical event. They even think that some part is important not to forget.
>   4. Patients express thoughts that it no longer matters how they are doing and are even uncertain whether they want the wounds to heal.
>   5. Patients can express suicidal ideation.
>   6. Additional emotions are dysphoria, aggression, downheartedness, which can resemble melancholic depressive states with somatic syndromes.
>   7. Patients show a variety of unspecific somatic complaints such as loss of appetite, sleep disturbances, pain.
>   8. Patients can report phobic symptoms in respect to the place or to persons related to the event.
>   9. Drive is reduced and blocked. Patients experience themselves not so much as drive inhibited but rather as drive unwilling.
>   10. Emotional modulation is not impaired, and patients can show normal affect when they are distracted or can even smile when engaged in thoughts of revenge.
> **C.** Duration: Longer than three months
> **D.** Impairment: Performance in daily activities and roles is impaired.

but because the course of illness is such that patients fall, in a second, from full health to a severe, lasting, and impairing state of mental illness in a direct causal relationship to an external event. Furthermore, humiliation or severe injustice can rightfully also be called a severe event.

7.2 Revival of Events and Intrusions in the Context of Injustice and Embitterment

A regular feature and diagnostic criterion of PTED is that "patients report repeated intrusive memories of the critical event and that for some part they even think that it is important not to forget." Embittered persons recall the insulting or humiliating event over and over again, comparable to intrusive thoughts in PTSD (McFarlane, 1992).

In PTED there is initially an insult, humiliation, or injustice, which leaves the person helpless and causes embitterment. To understand why injustice can have such dire consequences, one has to understand the psychology of "belief in a just world" (Dalbert, 1999, 2011; Lerner, 1980; Rubin & Peplau, 1975). From childhood on, we are given as firm belief that positive behavior will be rewarded and negative behavior will be punished. That belief is the prerequisite for social behavior because it gives the security that one can influence others by what one does oneself. The willful infliction of injustice means that the offender wants to be aggressive and at the same time believes that he can do so because the victim cannot defend himself or herself. In modern societies, where physical aggression is forbidden, injustice is a frequent substitute. A first reaction to injustice therefore is counteraggression (Willebrand, Kildal, Andersson, & Ekselius, 2002).

This type of aggression has especially negative consequences when injustice puts into question important values in life, that is, when basic beliefs are violated. Basic beliefs of a person or personal theories of reality or internal world models are, similar to language, learned in childhood from 5 to 20 (Beck, Rush, Shaw, & Emery, 1979; Bolby, 1969; Collins, Taylor, & Skokan, 1990; Epstein, 1991; Hautzinger, 2008; Janoff-Bulman, 1985, 1992; Janoff-Bulman & Frieze, 1983; Parkes, 1975; Schwartz, 1997; Schwartzberg & Janoff-Bulman, 1991; Taylor, 1983). They allow coherent behavior across the life span of an individual (e.g., "money must be saved, not wasted," which results in thriftiness in many situations over the life span), define large groups of persons (e.g., "belief in Mohamed" defines muslims), and are passed on from generation to generation, i.e., define culture or nations (e.g., French versus British). They therefore also define what is correct or incorrect, just or injust. Given this important role, it is evident that basic beliefs are by and large resistant to environmental changes. Persons will still feel that they are German, even after living most years of their lives in the United States. Because basic beliefs are learned, different persons will react differently to the same event. Persons for whom the highest value in life is their professional career will react severely if they are not promoted, even though they had given everything to their company. At the same time, they will show no serious reaction when they are left by their wife but instead just look for another one who fits better with their present professional position. In the same situation, a person who has the basic belief that the most important thing in life is the family will react in an opposite way.

When life events challenge the basic beliefs of persons, they touch on the security of who one is and the assumption that the world is predictable and controllable (Rini et al., 2004). There must be intense feelings, if basic beliefs are put into question by events or persons (i.e., their social status, nation, religion, or assumptions about justice). Persons go to war, if basic beliefs are endangered, and the defense of basic beliefs makes martyrs. The violation of basic beliefs without remedy will cause breakdowns of individuals and societies (Janoff-Bulman, 1985, 1989, 1992, 1998; Janoff-Bulman & Frieze, 1983). One reaction is embitterment and aggression and rampage against everybody else and oneself.

Violation of basic beliefs by injustice or humiliation can explain the occurrence of repetitive intrusive memories of what happened. There is a double side. First, the event and memories of the event are associated with hurting feelings of being blamed, disappointed, shamed, guilty, and so on. These are very negative feelings, and there is an urge to suppress such emotions and memories. But the more one tries to suppress and avoid the thoughts, the more emotionally intense they become, and the more frequent they pop up (Weymar, Bradley, Hamm, & Lang, 2012; Weymar, Löw, & Hamm, 2011; Weymar, Löw, Melzig, & Hamm, 2009; Weymar, Schwabe, Löw, & Hamm, 2012). Also, many stimuli in the world can remind the person of what has happened. After divorce, all families, all women and children, all shops for child clothing, and other stimuli will evoke memories of the breakup of the family. This also results in frequent hurting reexperiences.

Although persons try on one hand to suppress memories, they at the other hand nevertheless want to remember. Embitterment includes the urge to make events undone, to turn around what happened, or to get revenge and come even. Therefore, thinking about what happened and reenactment of the negative event in all details is not only hurting but at the same time necessary and to some degree even rewarding. There is something addictive to memories of the trigger event. Memories of what happened come along with memories of what should or could have happened or what will happen in the future, and how the person could have reacted in the past or will react in the future. In their fantasy, patients engage in vivid scenes of how they could have reacted in a superior manner, how they could have brought the offender down, and, even more, how justice will be brought about. Some persons hope in justice from God. It is to some degree consoling to dream about their former company going bankrupt and the former boss sitting on the street. Persons who suffer from embitterment can, in a second, turn from despair to smiling when thoughts of revenge are stimulated. They think about how to key the car of the former boss or to set fire to the company. And some patients do exactly what they were thinking about, up to the point of murder and suicide.

7.3 Differences Between Memories and Intrusions in PTED and PTSD

Although PTED patients suffer from intrusions similar to those of PTSD, there are still important differences. To explain this, we first summarize some characteristic features of intrusions in PTSD and then compare them with those in PTED.

The criteria for PTSD require that there must have been an "exceptional, severe, and life threatening situation to which almost everybody reacts with panic" (American Psychiatric Association, 1980). But epidemiological data show that this does not predict that later on there will be PTSD (Breslau, 1998). Furthermore, it is of interest to note that patients with agoraphobia also regularly report that their illness started after some panic-producing initial event, without the development of PTSD. In both illnesses, there is at the beginning an anxiety- or panic-producing situation. It is in the nature of anxiety that it keeps persons from going twice where danger is waiting. The "unconditioned initial anxiety-provoking stimulus (UCS)" is accompanied by anxiety-provoking "conditioned stimuli (CS)." Not only the car crash per se (UCS) but the street corner (CS) will from now on cause anxiety. The natural reaction is avoidance, which will lead to a generalization of anxiety-provoking stimuli by *negative reinforcement* (not only the corner but the street or traffic in general will provoke anxiety). The characteristic of agoraphobia is that these patients feel perfectly well, as long as they can avoid the confrontation with the anxiety-provoking stimuli (e.g., stay at home), whereas they react with panic when confronted with or exposed to the anxiety-provoking stimulus. Of importance is that this confrontation can be in reality or "in sensu" by *cognitive rehearsal* (Kirn, de Jong-Meyer, & Engberding, 2009). One can provoke anxiety in every person by making him or her vividly think, for example, about standing on a very high point. Images and cognitive ideas of anxiety-provoking stimuli can cause the same reaction as confrontation with the real event.

It is now only one step further to PTSD. When cognitive rehearsal and memories of the event come up unwillingly and patients try to suppress them and try not to think about what has happened, cognitive rehearsal develops into intrusions. The more persons try to suppress upcoming images, the stronger the associated emotions become and the more intrusive they will be. In the end, there is a vicious circle (Ehlers, Hackmann, & Michael, 2004; Hathaway, Boals, & Banks, 2010; McMillen, North, & Smith, 2000; Michael, Ehlers, Halligan, & Clark, 2005; Moulds & Bryant, 2002; van der Velden & Wittmann, 2008; Wald et al., 2011).

In agoraphobia, avoidance of real situations decreases feelings of acute anxiety, while at the same time it increases generalization. In PTSD, avoidance of cognitive rehearsal and memories leads to the increase of acute anxiety by intensification of the unwilling memories or cognitive images that are associated to anxiety. In contrast to agoraphobia, PTSD patients do not have the possibility of successful avoiding of anxiety-provoking stimuli. In this respect, PTSD can be called a memory disorder. In agoraphobia and in PTSD, the problem is not the threatening event but the successive avoidance behavior. And therefore in both disorders the treatment aims at overcoming avoidance by exposure.

When comparing PTSD and PTED, the common feature is that in both conditions vivid images come to mind involuntarily and with high frequency. The core psychology in PTSD is the urge to flee anxiety-provoking situations and/or images, that is, anxiety-driven avoidance behavior. In embitterment, the situation is more complex. Embitterment is nagging, and something is unsolved. There is a Zeigarnik effect (Savitsky, Medvec, & Gilovich, 1997; Zeigarnik, 1927; Zeigarnik, Louria, & Haigh, 1965); unfinished tasks keep psychological processing alive. Patients cannot be done with what happened. Memories are intrusive and hurting but at the same time welcome. Thinking about what happened can even have for short moments a consoling effect. Cognitive rehearsal of what happened or could happen is some kind of coping. Whereas intrusive memories in PTSD are driven by avoidance and negative reinforcement, in PTED they are driven by the urge to fight, cope, and positively reinforce.

7.4 Conclusions

PTSD and PTED are frequent and disabling illnesses. Although they have many similarities, there are also distinct differences. It is important to see both disorders as separate entities because they have different etiologies, psychologies, and are in need of different treatments. It can even be assumed that many cases of PTSD and especially complex PTSD are in essence cases of PTED. This is especially true in cases where the symptomatology does not appear directly after the intitial event but only later on (Dunmore, Clark, & Ehlers, 2001; Andrews, Brewin, Philpott, & Stewart, 2007). Often, experiences of injustice and embitterment because of unfair treatment in spite of what has endured are the core problem.

The comparison of PTSD and PTED allows us to keep PTSD as a well-defined limited disorder, which is part of the anxiety-disorder spectrum, while PTED is reserved for cases in which embitterment is the leading emotion. Furthermore, the comparison of PTSD and PTED supports the concept of descriptive classification instead of etiological concepts. Neither PTSD nor PTED can be predicted because of some event, but the prevailing emotion, anxiety versus embitterment, is the leading diagnostic feature. Finally, the comparison of symptoms shows that it is important to have a close look at the phenomenology of mental disorders. Seemingly similar phenomena—intrusions in this case—can be very different once one takes a closer look.

References

Alexander, J. (1960). The psychology of bitterness. *International Journal of Psychoanalysis, 41*, 514–520.
American Psychiatric Association, (1980). *Diagnostic and statistical manual of mental disorders* (3th ed.). Washington, DC: American Psychiatric Association.
Andrews, B., Brewin, C., Philpott, R., & Stewart, L. (2007). Delayed-onset posttraumatic stress disorder: A systematic review of the evidence. *American Journal of Psychiatry, 164*(9), 1319–1326.
Baures, M. M. (1996). Letting go bitterness and hate. *Journal of Humanistic Psychology, 36*, 75–90.
Beck, A. T., Rush, A. J., Shaw, B. F., & Emery, G. (1979). *Cognitive therapy of depression*. New York, NY: The Guilford Press.
Bolby, J. (1969). *Attachment and loss: Vol. 1—Attachment*. New York, NY: Basic Books.
Breslau, N. (1998). Epidemiology of trauma and posttraumatic stress disorder. *Psychological Trauma, 17*, 1–29.
Collins, R. l., Taylor, S. E., & Skokan, L. A. (1990). A better world or a shattered vision?: Changes in life perspectives following victimization. *Social Cognition, 8*, 263–285.
Dalbert, C. (1999). The world is more just for me than generally: About the personal belief in a just world scale's validity. *Social Justice Research, 12*, 79–98.
Dalbert, C. (2011). Embitterment—from the perspective of justice psychology. In M. Linden & A. Maercker (Eds.), *Embitterment*. Wien: Springer.
Dunmore, E., Clark, D. M., & Ehlers, A. (2001). A prospective investigation of the role of cognitive factors in persistent posttraumatic stress disorder (PTSD) after physical or sexual assault. *Behaviour Research and Therapy, 39*(9), 1063–1084.
Ehlers, A., Hackmann, A., & Michael, T. (2004). Intrusive re-experiencing in post-traumatic stress disorder: Phenomenology, theory, and therapy. *Memory, 12*(4), 403–415.
Epstein, S. (1991). The self-concept, the traumatic neurosis, and the structure of personality. In D. Ozer, J. M. Healy, & A. J. Steward (Eds.), *Perspectives on personality* (Vol. 3). London: Jessica Kingsley.

Felber, W., Lammel, M., Sutarski, S., Lau, S. (Hrsg.). (2010). *Plurale suizide*. Berlin: MWV Wissenschaftliche Verlagsgesellschaft.

Hathaway, L. M., Boals, A., & Banks, J. B. (2010). PTSD symptoms and dominant emotional response to a traumatic event: An examination of DSM-IV criterion A2. *Anxiety, Stress & Coping, 23*(1), 119–126.

Hautzinger, M. (2008). Grundüberzeugungen ändern. In M. Linden & M. Hautzinger (Hrsg.), *Verhaltenstherapiemanual*. Berlin: Springer-Verlag.

Janoff-Bulman, R. (1985). The aftermath of victimization: Rebuilding shattered assumptions Figley (Ed.), *Trauma and its wake* (Vol. 1). New York, NY: Bruner/Mazel.

Janoff-Bulman, R. (1989). Assumptive world and the stress of traumatic events: Applications of the schema construct. *Social Cognition, 7*, 113–136.

Janoff-Bulman, R. (1992). *Shattered assumptions: Towards a new psychology of trauma*. New York, NY: Free Press.

Janoff-Bulman, R. (1998). From terror to appreciation: Confronting chance after extreme misfortune. *Psychological Inquiry, 9*, 99–101.

Janoff-Bulman, R., & Frieze, I. H. (1983). A theoretical perspective for understanding reactions to victimization. *Journal of Social Issues, 39*, 1–17.

Kirn, T., de Jong-Meyer, R., & Engberding, M. (2009). *Imagination in der Verhaltenstherapie*. Heidelberg: Springer.

Lerner, M. J. (1980). *The belief in a just world: A fundamental delusion*. New York, NY: Plenum Press.

Linden, M. (2003). The posttraumatic embitterment disorder. *Psychotherapy and Psychosomatics, 72*, 195–202.

Linden, M., Baumann, K., Lieberei, B., Lorenz, C., & Rotter, M. (2011). Treatment of posttraumatic embitterment disorder with cognitive behaviour therapy based on wisdom psychology and hedonia strategies. *Psychotherapy and Psychosomatics, 80*, 199–205.

Linden, M., Baumann, K., Rotter, M., & Schippan, B. (2008). Diagnostic criteria and the standardized diagnostic interview for posttraumatic embitterment disorder (PTED). *International Journal of Psychiatry in Clinical Practice, 12*, 93–96.

Linden, M., & Maercker, A. (Eds.). (2011). *Embitterment. Societal, psychological, and clinical perspectives*. Wien: Springer.

Linden, M., Rotter, M., Baumann, K., & Lieberei, B. (2007). *The post-traumatic embitterment (PTED)*. Bern: Hogrefe & Huber.

Linden, M., Rotter, M., Baumann, K., & Schippan, B. (2009). The posttraumatic embitterment disorder self-rating scale (PTED scale). *Clinical Psychology and Psychotherapy, 16*, 139–147.

McFarlane, A. C. (1992). Avoidance and intrusion in posttraumatic stress disorder. *Journal of Nervous & Mental Disease, 180*, 439–445.

McMillen, J. C., North, C. S., & Smith, E. M. (2000). What parts of PTSD are normal: Intrusion, avoidance, or arousal? Data from the Northridge, California, earthquake. *Journal of Traumatic Stress, 13*(1), 57–75.

Michael, T., Ehlers, A., Halligan, S., & Clark, D. (2005). Unwanted memories of assault: What intrusion characteristics are associated with PTSD? *Behaviour Research and Therapy, 43*(5), 613–628.

Moulds, M. L., & Bryant, R. A. (2002). Directed forgetting in acute stress disorder. *Journal of Abnormal Psychology, 111*(1), 175–179.

Muschalla, B., & Linden, M. (2011). Embitterment and the workplace. In M. Linden & A. Maercker (Eds.), *Embitterment. Societal, psychological, and clinical perspectives*. Wien: Springer.

Norris, F. H., Perris, J. L., Ibañez, G. E., & Murphy, A. D. (2001). Sex differences in symptoms of posttraumatic stress: Does culture play a role? *Journal of Traumatic Stress, 14*, 7–28.

Parkes, C. M. (1975). What becomes of redundant world models? A contribution to the study of adaptation to change. *British Journal of Medical Psychology, 48*, 131–137.

Pirhacova, I. (1997). Perceived social injustice and negative affective states. *Studia Psychologica, 39*, 133–136.

Rini, C., Manne, S., DuHamel, K. N., Austin, J., Ostroff, J., Boulad, F., et al. (2004). Changes in mother's basic beliefs following a child's bone marrow transplantation: The role of prior trauma and negative life events. *Journal of Traumatic Stress, 17*, 325–333.

Rotter, M. (2011). Embitterment and personality disorder. In M. Linden & A. Maercker (Eds.), *Embitterment. Societal, psychological, and clinical perspectives*. Wien: Springer.

Rubin, Z., & Peplau, L. A. (1975). Who believes in a just world? *Journal of Social Issues, 31*, 65–89.

Savitsky, K., Medvec, V. H., & Gilovich, T. (1997). Remembering and regretting: The Zeigarnik effect and the cognitive availability of regrettable actions and inactions. *Personality and Social Psychology Bulletin, 23*, 248–257.

Schwartz, S. H. (1997). Values and culture. In D. Munro, J. F. Schumaker, & S. C. Carr (Hrsg.), *Motivation and culture* (S69–S84). New York, NY: Routledge.

Schwartzberg, S. S., & Janoff-Bulman, R. (1991). Grief and the search for meaning: Exploring the assumptive worlds of bereaved college students. *Journal of Social and Clinical Psychology, 10*, 270–288.

Smith, E. E., Bem, D. J., & Nolen-Hoeksema, S. (2001). *Fundamentals of Psychology*. Orlando, FL: Harcourt College Publishers.

Susemihl, F. (Ed.). (1912). *Aristotelis Ethica Nicomachea*. Leipzig: Apelt.

Taylor, S. E. (1983). Adjustment to threatening events: A theory of cognitive adaptation. *American Psychologist, 38*, 1161–1173.

van der Velden, P. G., & Wittmann, L. (2008). The independent predictive value of peritraumatic dissociation for PTSD symptomatology after type I trauma: A systematic review of prospective studies. *Clinical Psychology Review, 28*(6), 1009–1020.

Wald, I., Shechner, T., Bitton, S., Holoshitz, Y., Charney, D., Muller, D., et al. (2011). Attention bias away from threat during life threatening danger predicts PTSD symptoms at one-year follow-up. *Depression and Anxiety, 28*(5), 406–411.

Weymar, M., Bradley, M. M., Hamm, A. O., & Lang, P. J. (2012). When fear forms memories: Threat of shock and brain potentials during encoding and retrieval. *Cortex* Mar 8. [Epub ahead of print].

Weymar, M., Löw, A., & Hamm, A. O. (2011). Emotional memories are resilient to time: Evidence from the parietal ERP old/new effect. *Human Brain Mapping, 32*, 632–640.

Weymar, M., Löw, A., Melzig, C. A., & Hamm, A. O. (2009). Enhanced long-term recollection for emotional pictures: Evidence from high-density ERPs. *Psychophysiology, 46*, 1200–1207.

Weymar, M., Schwabe, L., Löw, A., & Hamm, A. O. (2012). Stress sensitizes the brain: Increased processing of unpleasant pictures after exposure to acute stress. *Journal of Cognitive Neuroscience, 24*, 1511–1518.

Willebrand, M., Kildal, M., Andersson, G., & Ekselius, L. (2002). Long-term assessment of personality after burn trauma in adults. *Journal of Nervous and Mental Disease, 190*, 53–56.

Zeigarnik, B. (1927). Über das Behalten von erledigten und unerledigten Handlungen. *Psychologische Forschung, 9*, 1–85.

Zeigarnik, B., Louria, A. R., & Haigh, B. (1965). *The pathology of thinking*. New York, NY: Plenum Press.

Zemperl, J., & Frese, M. (1997). Arbeitslose: Selbstverwaltung überwindet die Lethargie. *Psychologie Heute, 24*, 36–41.

Znoj, H. (2008). *BVI. Berner Verbitterungs Inventar. Manual.* Bern, Goettingen: Hogrefe & Huber.

Znoj, H. (2011). Embitterment—a larger perspective on a forgotten emotion. In M. Linden & A. Maercker (Eds.), *Embitterment. Societal, psychological, and clinical perspectives.* Wien: Springer.

8 Symbolized Thinking as the Background of Toxic Memories

Bohdan Wasilewski

Psychosomatic Institute, Warsaw, Poland

8.1 Introduction

In technology, *biocybernetics* and *physiology memory* as terms are reduced mainly to the functions of memorization and reproduction of information (a scan and print-out model). In this chapter, a broader understanding of memory is adopted. Memory entries, which are beyond the scope of information acquired from visual, auditory, olfactory, and tactile receptors and from the monitoring of internal organs and body posture, are related to emotions in a particular situation. They also refer to the sequence of time and to current structure of values, dominating judgments and attitudes. This reference is made with regard to currently experienced situations as well as analogies to previous personal and borrowed sensations, associated with stories told by important people from the surrounding environment, as well as virtual messages, transmitted by films, television, or Internet media.

I shall use the term *dynamic memory* and differentiate it from the static memory. It emphasizes the dynamic and complex nature of the phenomenon of memorizing and processing sensations, with which an individual is confronted. The dynamic memory is a multidimensional phenomenon. It changes and is closely linked to other elements of the psyche. It is especially visible in the case of memory traces with a strong emotional load, related to sensitive regions of personality structure. Toxic memory is constituted of memory entries that, when manifested, can destabilize the psychic structure of its bearer or, through his or her actions, the structure of other people.

According to Piaget (1950), symbolized thinking is manifested in the early stages of child development. Children who begin to label observed objects of everyday life are largely susceptible to internalize stereotypes from the adults. Related elements of the dynamic memory can exist in an emotional buffer zone. They sometimes remain in disharmony with convictions of a conscious part of the personality. The liveliness and strength of the buffer zone depend on the location of particular information in the personality structure. The deeper it is positioned, the less often exposed, and the more it is distant from an actively cultivated self-image, the bigger toxic potential it has.

Symbolized thinking is an archaic form of thinking in a simplified pattern. It occurs fully in nonpathological situations related to a strong emotional arousal or persisting disorders of logical thinking. Human memory has a social reference that is stronger proportionally to its social and emotional context. This reference can be made in relations with close people who are internalized, that is, identified with themselves. They can be real, physically existing people like a father, mother, husband, wife, or any other object of an emotional relation, but they can also exist virtually and be known only indirectly, such as gods, heroes, or other significant persons. It is, however, difficult to make a distinction between the physical and virtual existence of a person because the image of such a person is constantly processed and adapted to the individual needs and psychic structure of the bearer who remembers it. Memory traces that do not match the image of the person become emotionally blocked, blurred, and relativized; others become idealized and exaggerated. An image of a person can mix and unite with other images of people, both existing and fictional. Most of the discussed identification processes take place in the sphere of convictions and expressed social attitudes, reinforced in the circle of one's close friends who are selected in the perspective of having similar opinions.

The preferred model of social functioning and associated convictions and lifestyle define models of sociopolitical and religious identification in a given period. The acceptance of a particular model gives access to a related group of people and to structures of support at their disposal. The dynamics of historical and sociological changes support or eliminate particular socioideological structures and involve changes in the identification of individuals. It is especially visible in the present period of intensive social and economical changes, which destabilize the mechanisms of social reference. They increase the loneliness of individuals confronted with the demands of life that they are not able to meet. This destabilization is transferred onto the structure of personality, including the structure of memory images, and fosters the expression of toxic resources of memory. Authoritarianism is a factor that facilitates the creation and activation of symbolized thinking and the related stereotypes and prejudices, which will be discussed in more detail later in this chapter.

As mentioned, the resources of dynamic memory are not static; they are constantly modified, valuated, and updated with regard to the current dimension of our identity and the image of the surrounding world. This process is located in both the conscious and unconscious layers of our psyche. Memory adapts the individuals to a constantly changing environment. Studies of memory reactivation show that states of plasticity can be induced in representations that were supposedly stable. The mechanisms that induce plasticity, update some memories, and protect others from modifications are scientifically proven but still poorly explored (Nadel & Hardt, 2011).

Memory entries that do not harmonize with a current, autoaccepted dimension of our identity (those dissonant ones) are subject to various adaptation mechanisms. These include value judgments, which deactivate or reduce the importance or timeliness of the entries. The liveliness (distinctness) of memory traces depends on the force of the emotional component at the entry of the particular trace and on the degree of emotional support accompanying its maintenance (Berntsen & Rubin, 2002). Memory entries that are not emotionally supported gradually become weaker and relativized under a considerable influence of environmental factors, including culture forming ones. Emotional maintenance can happen through contacts with an object, a person, or a literary fiction that refers to a memory trace located in the emotional buffer zone.

These relations shall be discussed in more detail later in the chapter describing experimental situations.

Memory traces can undergo a process of personalization and become an autobiographic memory (Conway & Pleydell-Pearce, 2000). The autobiographic memory is influenced especially by emotional factors at the stages of both memorization and reproduction, as documented in the scientific observations (Holland & Kensinger, 2010). Personalized memories are in permanent process of transformation. The recreation of verbalized personal information does not make a direct reference to the recollection of particular experiences. It is mainly subordinated to sensations, convictions, and similarities. Every recollection of a past sensation causes it to be experienced again, and the chronology of particular events is rearranged (Wheeler, Stuss, & Tulving, 1997). Recollected information is integrated with many subsystems: sensory, linguistic, emotional, narrative, and other (Rubin, 2006).

They are integrated into the rest of the personality in a partly conscious process. It involves different levels: individual, familiar, national, and global. Personalized memories constitute an integral part of continuous process of sustainable development. When a certain memory stays in a conflict with the main core of our personality, it must be changed or relativized. Prejudices, stereotypes, and symbolized thinking are the methods used to simplify the current psychological integration. They modify some categories of memories that are difficult to integrate with the current image of oneself. To a large extent, prejudices and stereotypes observed in adulthood are related to the memory learned in childhood. In his classic book, *The Nature of Prejudice*, the psychologist Allport (1954) concluded that children are more likely to grow up tolerant if they live in supportive and loving families. "They feel welcome, accepted, loved, no matter what they do. In such an environment, different views are welcomed; punishment is not harsh or capricious. Children generally think of people positively and carry a sense of goodwill and even affection." The atmosphere of the family house has therefore a dominating influence on the formation of stereotypes and nonlogical judgments in the future of children. The convictions of parents and the atmosphere at home depend on the social and cultural situation in which the family functions. A child can become distanced in the period of revolt and disagreement toward convictions cultivated by the family. The memory traces remain in their psyche deeply imprinted by strong affective priming. It is especially relevant in cases of social groups involved in long-lasting, multigenerational conflicts that result in persecution and discrimination.

We carry stereotypes, attitudes, and instinctive forms of reactions, which create only partially, and the majority of which we inherit, together with our culture and family tradition, closely linked with national, class, religious, and tribal identity. They are often an integral element of our own identity. While having a permissive attitude toward the tradition as a whole, we unconsciously practice stereotypes despite our declarative individual detachment from these stereotypes or other particular elements of the tradition. It is fully and clearly expressed in critical situations of a high emotional load or in the crowd psychology. It is also expressed while talking about people with whom one identifies but who differ in terms of declared opinions. Various psychological mechanisms are then used to avoid taking a stance on their behaviors. One rationalizes them, or, if all else fails, one admits that in a given situation they would behave in the same way. It is especially visible in conflicts that last many years or centuries and cover several generations, who are brought up in a culture of fight and confrontation. Stereotypes of enemy become the basic element of keeping the group identity, and the stereotype of warrior becomes a way of realizing one's life vocation. In a situation of an existing conflict, attempts undertaken by individuals to break these stereotypes are treated as a treason or collaboration and are punished with ostracism, persecution, or physical elimination.

Nations or ethnic and religious groups in a long-lasting open or hidden confrontation associated with violence using military or police methods, terrorism, repression, or various forms of persecutions and discrimination adapt by using a mainly authoritarian model of thinking. They implement it by creating authoritarian family relations and social structures. An authoritarian style of social interactions is adapted to the functioning of militarized institutions of these societies. It is a fertile soil for the development of authoritarian forms of political and religious movements, countries, or international organizations. Authoritarian thinking is adapted to a situation of fight, where quick and strong decisions are required. They are facilitated by the use of stereotypes and intentional thinking, in which arguments are subordinated to one's needs and serve the determined goal. This strengthens stereotypes and prejudices and fosters the consolidation of the group in the fight. After the end of a direct conflict, stereotypes and prejudices constitute a significant inhibitor for subsequent generations, despite a gradual evolution of attitudes. Strong mechanisms from the period of an aggravated confrontation remain in insular forms. This issue will be further discussed later in this chapter using the example of Yugoslavia.

Large-scale studies were initiated by renowned scientific centers (Harvard University, the University of Virginia, and the University of Washington) as part of the project Implicit (Andersen, Moskowitz, Blair, & Nosek, 2007), which covered 34 countries and over 500,000 people. The project proved that, despite declarations of egalitarian opinions, nonlogical judgments and prejudices with regard to sex, race, religion, or mental illness are still common. These studies have demonstrated that biases considered to be absent or extinguished persist as "mental residue" in most examined individuals. It has been demonstrated that people can reconcile conscious commitment to egalitarianism and deliberate attempts to behave without prejudice with hidden negative prejudices or stereotypes. Implicit Association Tests (IATs) are examples of the tests used in the studies. They elicit hidden, or automatic, stereotypes and prejudices that evade conscious control.

Psychiatry examines thinking disorders occurring in psychotic states, especially in schizophrenic ones. They are usually accompanied by emotional disorders and can be largely helpful in the analysis of thinking disorders related to strong emotional states in healthy individuals. Very intensive emotional states can lead to the domination of an atavistic thinking based on instincts and drives, with symbolized thinking, assumptions, prejudices, and stereotypes as constant elements. The collision of instinct-based thinking with rational cause-and-effect thinking is reduced by the suppression of neocortical activity, manifested in a narrowing or sometimes even temporary disconnection of the consciousness despite the continuation of complex motor functions and the maintenance of verbal contact. Apparently, analogical mechanisms function not only in special life-threatening situations but also in everyday life to less of a degree. The mechanism of emotional narrowing of the scope of analyzed associated memory traces processed in different degree facilitates their easier relocation in autoidentification structure. It also gives access to sensitive entries, protected by emotions. Personalized memory traces, including those constituting autobiographic memory, are especially influenced by emotional factors at the stages of both memorization and reproduction, as documented in the scientific observations (Holland & Kensinger, 2010). This goal can also be achieved through dream experiences and products of culture such as films, computer games, literature, music, and the like. Both the contents and the frames (emotional, social, cultural, and volitional) of an induced memory trace are partially modified. The Auschwitz experiment, reported on later in this chapter, was based on these grounds.

We carry stereotypes, attitudes, and instinctive forms of reactions, which we create only partially. Mostly, we inherit them, together with our culture and family tradition, closely linked with national, class, religious, and tribal identity. They are an integral element of our own identity. Despite an individual adaptation to the requirements of our culture, which rejects some stereotypes, we often reproduce them unconsciously, regardless of our declarative denial. It is fully and clearly expressed in critical situations of a high emotional load or in the crowd psychology.

8.1.1 Experimental Observations

In the European perspective, we are stigmatized by a global confrontation and cruelties of the World War II, after which it seemed that the logic of hatred and cruelty would not be reborn.

However, the symbolized thinking that cultivates the stereotype of enemy survives in many places on our continent. The nations of former Yugoslavia have become a sad example of this, despite 50 years of their peaceful coexistence and joint successes in the development of the country.

When the organization of International Physicians for the Prevention of Nuclear War (IPPNW) was awarded a Nobel Peace prize, I was elected by the VII World Congress of IPPNW In Moscow in 1987, as its active member of the board, to represent this organization as a Nobel Prize Laureate with rights to use prize funds to finance meetings and lectures dedicated to the psychological and medical consequences of stress in life associated with social factors. Consequently, I went on a round of lectures to popularize the Official Statement of the Nobel Committee upon awarding the 1985 Nobel Peace Prize to IPPNW across Europe, the United States, Canada, Asia, Australia, and Japan.

As a continuation of my tasks, I was entrusted by IPPNW with a "mission of last resort" in Yugoslavia, which was threatened by dissolution and civil war. In an attempt to enable the renewal of peace negotiations aimed at ending the conflict, I visited most of the successor republics of the former Yugoslavia and had conversations with significant representatives of administrations, medical doctors, and politicians. While analyzing conversations, especially with doctors and scientists of a high personal culture and both professional and personal experience, I observed manifestations of symbolized thinking, resistant to rational arguments. The dissolution of the previous state structures and social relations generated a sensation of threat, fear of others, distrust, and hidden or openly expressed hostility. Friendly, neighborly, or professional relations, which had existed for 50 years, were replaced by clan-tribal logic, by which friendly and peaceful people were attributed cruelty and ruthlessness observed in their nations in the Middle Ages or marginally in the times of World War II. When the subject of Serbs was brought up with Croats or inversely, conversations that started in a conciliatory atmosphere and a friendly emotional attitude became negatively emotional and aggressive to an extent of being a threat to the interlocutor. It happened despite the fact that the interlocutor was neutral in the conflict and had initially declared a lack of prejudices toward the other party, as well as a readiness to look for ways of agreement. Almost none of my interlocutors had personal traumatizing experiences associated with the other party of the conflict. During the conversation, however, they identified themselves with even remote past situations of their far relatives to document their convictions about the cruelty, ruthlessness, and deceitfulness of the other party.

Authoritarianism was a common feature of my interlocutors regardless of their nationality, religion, or liberal or radical opinions. It was expressed in the conversations in which they stated their opinions and defended their beliefs, even to the extent of making threats of physical violence. It was also conveyed by an authoritarian personal style of functioning, probably affecting their professional and family relations. The authoritarianism of the authority, based on the personality cult of Marshal Josip Broz Tito and the single political party, created a favorable background for this scheme. The motive of a constant fight with an external and internal enemy was the main issue that consolidated the country. When the leader and the central authority involved in internal fights were gone, the existing mechanisms reinforced the nationalism and religious radicalism with their whole potential, leading to a conflict, in which humanitarian and positivist arguments lost their significance.

In such circumstances, I was forced to end my peace mission and prepare a report concluding the failure of the mission and expecting an armed conflict. A few months later, it actually started with all of its cruelty.

Observations in Yugoslavia supported my previous analogical conclusions from studies related to prejudices and stereotypes in Polish-German, Polish-Jewish, and Jewish-German relations. The framework of this chapter does not allow a broader development of this topic; I will, however, refer to its most important elements. First, I will discuss in more detail the issue of the authoritarianism as a mechanism that paves the way for the manifestation of stereotypes of enemy, using nonrational opinions and creating a philosophy of hate or revenge.

In the 1970s, when a Soviet model of so-called real socialism was used as an intermediary form in the implementation of the communist regime, the Polish Academy of Sciences (PAN) used its special status to conduct a large-scale research. The research exploited results achieved by the Institute of Social Research in Frankfurt, whose employees looked for reasons of a mass support to the then emerging fascism in Germany. When the fascists came to power, this research was interrupted, and the scientists were forced to emigrate. They started a cooperation with researchers from the Berkley University, where they continued the interrupted work. The book entitled *The Authoritarian Personality*, published in 1950, was the product of this cooperation. The authors—Adorno, Frenkel-Brunswik, Levison, and Sanford (1950)—included in it some basic assumptions of their authoritarian personality theory and presented a tool for measuring it. In the studies carried out in the Institute of Psychology of the PAN, authoritarianism was defined as "orientation based on conviction of a hierarchical organisation of human relations and on the necessity to surrender one's subjectivity" (Korzeniowski, 1999). The studies conducted in 1978–1980 showed a high level of authoritarianism in Polish society. They also comprised intercultural comparisons of the authoritarianism level, which demonstrated a significant disproportion between capitalist and socialist countries showing a low level of authoritarianism in the former and the high level in the latter.

The same team of sociologists from PAN conducted comparative studies in 1993, after 4 years of functioning of a new sociopolitical framework, adopted from the West. They showed a statistically significant reduction of the level of authoritarianism of Polish society and the level of manifestation of stereotypes and nonlogical opinions, as compared to the results of 1978–1980 studies.

A positive trend of the democratization of the Polish population's social awareness, noted after an increasing democratization of the state institutions, was unfortunately inhibited in the 1990s and then changed into an opposite tendency. This phenomenon worried the researchers working on the issue of authoritarianism so much that it resulted in the publishing of an intellectuals' appeal related to an increasingly authoritarian style of government in Poland and subsequent increase of authoritarianism of the Polish society.

Thanks to the support of the international organization of IPPNW and institutions such as the Auschwitz Committee, the Polish Medical Association, the Psychiatric Department and Clinic of the Medical Academy in Cracow, and important people such as Professors K. Bonhoffer, J. Groen, J. Bogusz, and A. Szymusik, I conducted in 1989 an experiment at the location of the Auschwitz–Birkenau camp.

The experiment was organized as a 6-day working meeting of Polish and German students—10 in each group—and students from the Czech Republic and the Netherlands. They stayed together in the camp or in buildings directly attached to it. They communicated in English, which was the language of the majority of the meetings. I was a tutor of the group, observer, and interpreter of former prisoners' testimonies. The experiment preceded directly the celebration of the 50th Anniversary of the World War II, organized in Auschwitz. After the experiment was finished, its participants took part in a scientific conference related to the anniversary and in the celebration in the camp, including an assembly at night and meditation at the place where the ashes of the cremated prisoners were damped.

The experiment reconstructed the course of life in the camp and involved daily participation of two former prisoners of the camp who had spent 5–6 years in it, where they were imprisoned as children but treated like adults. Every day before midday, the participants in a joint group recreated subsequent stages of the life in the camp, starting at the Selection Ramp. Reconstruction included listening to personal stories told by the former prisoners in the setting arranged with elements of the camp equipment in the background, supported by the photographic and material documentation, all based on the exhibitions of the Museum in Auschwitz. After a meal and a short break, the participants took part in discussion sessions about the reality of camp life, including the motivations and behaviors of prisoners, as well as of the supervising and administrative staff of the camp. They had exhibits of the museum in Auschwitz at their disposal with a rich collection of memoirs and diaries of prisoners, SS soldiers, officers, and other camp staff members.

The group had formal and informal discussions that took place both in scheduled sessions and in spontaneous meetings—during meals, free time (which the participants spent together). Camp documents and diaries were read and thoughts exchanged in organized morning and afternoon meetings and during conversations before going to sleep (the participants stayed in rooms divided according to nationality). To maintain spontaneity, the meetings were not recorded, and the notes were not taken during the sessions. The notes were taken by the observer in his room, after the sessions were finished.

The contents of the experiment involved strong emotional reactions, especially in Polish and German participants. All of them had some basic knowledge about how the death camps functioned and about the history of the World War II. The majority of them were personally or indirectly (through their parents or close friends) related to organizations of antimilitary, ecological, or protest movements in Poland or Germany. The political and social opinions of the participants were not examined; however, the discussions revealed mostly liberal opinions. Part of the group emphasized their relations with the Evangelic Church Community. German members of the group came from both the German Democratic Republic and the Federal Republic of Germany. Students of medicine, participants of the IPPNW movement, constituted a large part of the group.

As the participants learned more about the functioning of the death camp, the reality of the fascist state, and the period of the occupation of Europe, they identified themselves more with characters from the period of camp's existence. The first, two-day phase of the project was dominated by the shock resulting from the confrontation with the brutality and the immensity of the crimes committed in the camp. Most opinions expressed in that phase were general, condemned the crimes, and were often related to official declarations and speeches of important people. Participants avoided expressing personal opinions and commenting on dramatic situations reported by the former prisoners. They rather chose a detailed analysis of the general situation and knowledge about the particularities of the everyday life in the camp. None of the participants was psychically decompensated. Many of them, however, were in the state of a strong emotional tension and a lowered mood. It was more the case of German, rather than the Polish, members of the group. The dynamics of establishing closer relations in the group was initially impeded by linguistic and national differences, as well as by an emotional load of the place and reported facts. In the first days of the project, the participants declared condemnation of the Auschwitz crime, the criminal activity of its organizers, and the fascist ideology that they professed; often the opinions contained expressions borrowed from press releases, official speeches, and literature.

Detailed discussion about prisoners' direct relations, reading diaries of prisoners and staff members, and getting used to the ruthless rules of everyday life in the death camp allowed the participants a more direct and deeper involvement in the sessions. They started expressing opinions referring to personal conclusions and family-related facts from the times of war. Opinions involving family members and close friends were no longer presented in the black-and-white perspective but contained reflections about the motivation that inclined them either to take part in activities organized under the totalitarian regime of Hitler or to participate in illegal actions against the Germans. The language clearly changed from impersonal declarations to personal stories. Friendly relations appeared among participants from Poland, Germany, and other European countries. The dominating subject evolved from the issue of the camp routines seen from the perspective of two young prisoners and the analyses of drastic scenes from their lives, to a more personal angle, including facts from private life of the participants and their relatives and their personal opinions. More attention was dedicated to the motivations of people on the both sides of the camp fence, their driving forces, and the meaning of particular events from prisoners' and administrators' perspectives. Despite its terror, a more complete picture of the camp life showed a surprising ability of people to adapt and to recreate elementary social mechanisms. The prisoners' constant fight for survival and dignity, which was taken away from them, was contrasted with the haughtiness of the master race members in immaculate uniforms, spending their evenings with a glass of champagne and classical music as exemplary family men. The world of SS officers differed from the reality of regular soldiers living in barracks. A constant mutual observation and denunciations fomented fear in staff members. Their doubts were dispelled by provoking situations that were supposed to prove the moral and physical degeneration of the prisoners and their inability to live in a civilized society. This aim was achieved by provoking scenes of abuse and cruelty of kapos toward the prisoners, forcing woman to have public intercourse with the dogs used to patrol the camp or savoring scenes of humiliating and intimidating prisoners, making them beg for mercy and ordering many hours of penal roll calls, during which people died from exhaustion. Deeper knowledge of the camp life revealed the dominating fear and the sense of threat to the physical existence, most clearly visible in prisoners, but also present in camp staff, who lived in constant fear of being relocated to the Eastern Front, which would have meant a deadly danger in the final phase of the war. The characters of prisoners and staff members seemed more realistic, which incited an emotional dissonance in the members of the experiment and coexisted with the change of reactions within the group. The meetings held in the final phase of the experiment included increasingly emotional arguments, full of symbolized thinking. Opinions became more personal, and the group was gradually divided again into the Polish and German subgroups, in which most conversations were held in the rooms. The participants from other countries presented more neutral attitudes, and their opinions were less emotional. Some thinking patterns, absent in the first phase of the experiment, appeared then: "The Germans may have done wrong things but their intention was to change the world into a better place" or "The Poles were the martyrs for their and others' freedom," ignoring the fact that Auschwitz was mainly the place of extermination of Jews. Increasingly, these young people, who came to seek conciliation, regained a deep sense of unredressed wrong and blame, and they looked for support within the nationality circles. In the political context of that time, the discussion was very straightforward, what was sometimes treated as breaking of the convention of the meeting and threatening, especially for the participants from the German Democratic Republic.

The scientific conference related to the 50th anniversary of the outbreak of World War II, held in Cracow and Auschwitz, took place directly after the meeting and was an interlude that relieved the increasing tension. In the conference, I presented a plenary paper, discussing the significance of authoritative attitudes and violence-oriented thinking as a possible threat of military confrontation and emphasized the fact that the indicators of authoritarianism were high in Poland and the Soviet Union (Wasilewski, 1991).

The conference and the anniversary celebrations were closed by a meditation session, which was organized at night, by candlelight, at the place where the ashes of cremated prisoners were damped. It played a special role in reuniting the participants through a strong experience, during which, in the darkness and silence, their imagination recalled the tragic characters about whom they had read and heard in the meetings.

The Auschwitz experiment showed the potential of the symbolized thinking and related stereotypes and prejudices. It led to the manifestation of the deeper contents of memory with associated emotions and created conditions for their further processing. Whether it contributed to a change in the participants' attitudes, especially modifications of thinking patterns based on symbolized thinking, can be stated only after repeated observations of the experimental group.

References

Adorno, T. W., Frenkel-Brunswik, E., Levinson, D. J., & Sanford, R. N. (1950). *The authoritarian personality*. New York, NY: Norton.
Allport, G. W. (1954). *The nature of prejudice*. Cambridge, MA: Addison-Wesley.
Andersen, S. M., Moskowitz, G. B., Blair, I. V., & Nosek, B. A. (2007). Automatic thought. In E. T. Higgins & A. W. Kruglanski (Eds.), *Social psychology: Handbook of basic principles (pp. 138–175)*. New York, NY: The Guilford Press.
Berntsen, D., & Rubin, D. C. (2002). Emotionally charged autobiographical memories across the life span: the recall of happy, sad, traumatic, and involuntary memories. *Psychology and Aging, 17*(4), 636–652.
Conway, M. A., & Pleydell-Pearce, C. W. (2000). The construction of autobiographical memories in the self-memory system. *Psychological Review, 107*(2), 261–288.
Holland, A. C., & Kensinger, E. A. (2010). Emotion and autobiographical memory. *Physics of Life Reviews, 7*(1), 88–131.
Korzeniowski, K. (1999). Autorytaryzm i jego psychologiczne konsekwencje. In K. Skarżyńska (Ed.), *Psychologia polityki*. Poznań: Zysk i S-ka.

Nadel, L., & Hardt, O. (2011). Update on memory systems and processes. *Neuropsychopharmacology, 36*(1), 251–273.

Piaget, J. (1950). Introduction à l'épistémologie génétique: *Tome III: La pensée biologique, la pensée psychologique et la pensée sociale*. Paris: Presses Universitaires de France.

Rubin, D. C. (2006). The basic-systems model of episodic memory. *Perspectives on Psychological Science, 1*, 277–311.

Wasilewski, B. W. (1991). Ideologien der gewalt—erinerung aus der vergangenheit oder problem der gegenwart? In: *Die manung der vergangenheit—ein hinweis fur das Europa des friedens. Internationales symposiumzum 50 jahrestag des ausbruchs des II weltkrieges. Auschwitz, 31.08.1989–1.09.1989* (pp. 57–61). Państwowe Zakłady Graficzne, Kraków.

Wheeler, M. A., Stuss, D. T., & Tulving, E. (1997). Toward a theory of episodic memory: the frontal lobes and autonoetic consciousness. *Psychological Bulletin, 121*(3), 331–354.

9 False Memories

Hans Stoffels
Park-Klinik Sophie Charlotte, Heubnerweg 2a, Berlin

9.1 The Wilkomirski/Dössekker Case

In 1999, there was a psychotherapy congress in Vienna on the occasion of the 59th centenary of the Reichsprogromnacht. The conference was entitled "Survival of the Shoa—and Beyond. Late Impact of Prosecution from an Academic Point of View." It was organized by a group of physicians of the Viennese Jewish community. International academics met to discuss the topic of extreme traumatization.

There was a speaker named Binjamin Wilkomirski. Together with the Israeli psychotherapist Elitsur Bernstein, he spoke about "Problems of Identification of Children Surviving the Holocaust." They presented a new form of psychotherapy that they claimed was able to bring back lost memories. It was said that this therapy could reconstruct early childhood memories, even decades later. According to Wilkomirski and Bernstein, the soul keeps an exact picture of traumatic experiences. The thesis of Wilkomirski and Bernstein received great interest and positive feedback by the audience. In the evening, a ceremonial act was held for all conference participants and in the presence of represantatives of the city and the state, actors performed two texts originating from a book called *Fragments. A Childhood from 1939 Until 1948*, written by Wilkomirski (1995). The book deals with the successful reconstruction of his own traumatized childhood by the then 55-year-old clarinetist and instrument maker. It was said that he was born in Riga, Latvia, into a Jewish family, was the only one of his family surviving the Holocaust, and was given to insensitive Swiss adoptive parents after the war. In search of his own past, Wilkomirski traveled to the places of prosecution, discovered his parent's house in Riga, and foung the barrack in which he lived in the concentration camp Majdanek, Poland (Wilkomirski, 1995). This rediscovery of his memory was possible in the course of an intensive psychotherapy. After the sessions with his psychotherapist, he used to write down what came to his mind and sent it to her by fax to continue the work in the next session.

The book by Wilkomirski (1995) received high awards for literature, was translated into 12 languages, and was seen as a classic piece of Holocaust literature. Temporarily, it was the best-selling book in Switzerland. Even the well-known author Elfriede Jelinek—among others, such as Elie Wiesel and Paul Celan—recited his texts at the Salzburg Festspiele. Historians like Wolfgang Benz, head of the Berlin Institute for Anti-Semitism Studies at the Freie Universität, Berlin, recommended the reading of Wilkomirski because he had "made an amazing effort to reveal his past, his identity. "His search" leads to a presentation that almost like no other document communicates insights to the complex tragedy of Holocaust." The historian Benz declared that Wilkomirski's book impresses by its authenticity and deals directly with the Holocaust itself, differently from the book by Anne Frank, which only "saves the real" (Benz, 1998). Wilkomirski gave a lot of speeches, worked on three films for the Spielberg foundation, and traveled on behalf of the Holocaust museum in Washington to collect donations. There were three television documentaries on him. Innumerable recensions praised the work. He traveled to the United States and even met a person who recognized him and confirmed that she had been with him in the concentration camp.

About 1 year later, it became evident that Wilkomirski had fully invented his childhood memories and that there was not one true word (Blake, 2002). He was neither born in Riga, nor was he the child of Jewish parents. He was born in 1941 in Biel, Switzerland, under the name of Bruno Grosjean as the child of a Swiss seasonal worker, who gave him to a children's home and later put him up for adoption under the name of Bruno Dössekker. He had never been in any concentration camp nor even been at that time anywhere outside of Switzerland. Similarly, the person who had recognized him as coinmate from the concentration camp had herself never left Great Britain during the war.

This case is an internationally discussed example of false memories. It is only one example among many others. Such cases raise numerous questions for historians, psychologists, and psychotherapists. Did Wilkomirski/Dössekker believe his story, at least at times? Why did he choose the identity of a child surviving the Holocaust? Are there certain advantages in being a victim? What role did the psychotherapist play? Why did so many people believe him and were unable to distinguish between reality and fantasized memory?

9.2 Memory as Reconstruction

It is evident that the human memory is susceptible to faults. Memory changes over the years, which is why in criminal justice the lapse of time causes problems. The longer an event dates back, the more difficult it is to reconstruct it, and the more legal certainty declines. However, even events that do not date back years or decades can in testimonies be reported very differently from reality. The unreliability of memory, its high selectivity, and its relation to situations are the reasons for the saying that, if in court four witnesses are asked, five different versions of the event are reported.

Selection, modulation, forgetting, and conversion are inherent processes of remembering. Our memory stores our experiences not like pieces in a museum, but it is rather constantly in motion. Because memory is part of our debate with the present, past facts are permanently recomposed. There is not one memory because memory is related to the moment (Fried, 2004). That is why memory has no archive-like character like digital data media. Memory is rather working like a theater ensemble, playing scenes over and over again. It is creative and realizes new interpretations. Memory is reconstruction (Schacter, 1996; Stoffels, 2005).

Neurobiological research supports that the brain is no data pool that collects and encodes information. The model of a cerebral photo album or a videotape is wrong. The brain is not a data pool from which scenes can be easily replayed (Loftus & Pickrell, 1995). This is especially true for traumatic memories that are supposed to be stored in brain regions that are not easily accessible to subjective influence but are related to emotions. This is the biological background of flashbacks, which repeat traumatic events in a modified version. Memory is a process; it is ductile, subject to conversion and configuration, always a product of interaction and always an expression of our accomplishment with the present. Our memory eclipses what is important and repels what is dispensable. It is always active, eliminates, discards, and appreciates. The book, *Searching for Memory. The Brain, the Mind and the Past*, by Daniel L. Schacter (Schacter, 1996) gives a comprehensive overview on the subjectivity of memory.

This is also the reason why memories can be induced by the person himself or herself or by others and why pseudomemory exists. It is quite easy to induce false memories, especially when social expectations are high. Elisabeth Loftus, a researcher on the malleability and reliability of repressed memories, has proven this in numerous experiments (Loftus & Pickerell, 1995). These kinds of experiments are not harmless. Loftus reports the example of a colleague who conducted an experiment with his younger brother; 14-year-old Chris was asked to remember five childhood incidents related to some key words he had been given. He was then asked to write down every day all new facts and details he remembered. One of the incidents was made up. First Chris did not remember the invented occasion but was asked to try to remember how he at the age of five got lost in a department store, screamed, and finally was brought back by an old man. Indeed, over the ensuing days, Chris recalled more and more details of the traumatic event, such as what the man looked like. Some weeks later, Chris was interviewed again, and at that time he remembered even more details, such as how desperate he had been, that the man wore a flannel shirt, had glasses, and so on. Chris then was informed that this event had never happened, but he could not believe that the department store story was fictitious. He even had problems because the pseudomemory did not stop haunting his mind (Loftus & Pickrell, 1995).

9.3 Personality and False Memories

It is well known that children in particular may develop false memories when social expectations are high. Children learn easily how to answer in a way that is anticipated. It is astonishing how realistic and detailed descriptions may be and how difficult it may be to detect them as pseudomemory. In his book *Green Heinrich* (*Der grüne Henrich*), the poet Gottfried Keller gives a perfect depiction of a 7-year-old boy involved into a fictitious narration.

But adults are also susceptible to the induction of false memories. Persons are suggestible in different degrees (Brenneis, 1998). About 5% of the population show a high imaginative ability. These people have the competence of actualization and are able to add emotional appeal to memory. They can present previous events in a way that they appear real and actual. They evoke all forms of emotions and experience them again so that the listener feels like a direct witness of the event. People highly gifted with fantasy also have the ability to mix real and imaginative cognitions. Instructions used in some forms of psychotherapy (e.g., to relax or let one's mind wonder) induce this kind of thinking, which works as if in a trance condition (Brenneis, 1998). Those people have difficulties discriminating inside and outside, reality and fantasy.

Especially prone for false memories are patients with borderline personality disorders. Such patients are characterized by an insecure perception of reality, abrupt changes of mood, impulsive actions, and disturbed social interaction with high ambivalence and "hostile dependency" (Herpertz & Saß, 2003). They are highly vulnerable to pseudomemory, especially if talented with fantasy. When such persons are exposed to distress, the line between inside and outside and between subject and object becomes indistinct. When borderline personalities report traumatic memories, clinicians face a special challenge. Many studies have shown that borderline patients have experienced high levels of stress and burdens in their life. In particular, sexual abuse is said to have happened in up to 90% of all borderline patients and is a reason for the development of this disorder. But prospective studies are missing, and some researchers suggest that many of these reports are false memories because such patients have such difficulty differentiating between inner and outer experiences and their high level of suggestibillity. All clinicians and researchers who deal with previous events depend on the report of the patient.

9.4 Psychotherapy and Pseudomemory

A special problem in this respect is given in psychotherapy. Here the interaction between spontaneous and indiced false memories is almost inextricable. There can be a vicious circle because presumptions of clinicians have an impact on what patients report. So it is possible that it isn't sexual trauma that causes the borderline disorder, but rather the belief of patients and therapists in the sexual trauma that results from theoretical concepts about borderline disorders (Böhm et al., 2002). For methodological reasons, it is difficult to come to reliable scientific evidence. Questionnaires are definitely not suitable. Solid research needs information from more persons than only the patient, and in the end some cases cannot be clarified.

Independent of the special problem with borderline disorders, every psychotherapeutic situation, independent of the kind of intervention and intentions of the therapist, has a certain suggestive character. In the process of psychotherapy, it is indispensible to change attributions and induce new explanations of the world. This mixes new insights with memories. The longer a psychotherapeutic treatment lasts, the more sensitive a patient gets to conscious or unconscious assumptions of the psychotherapist. The patient recognizes more and more what the psychotherapist is interested in, when he inquires in more detail, or when he remains unaffected. If the psychotherapist is convinced that sexual traumata regularly causes mental suffering, he presumably will convey this to the patient directly or implicitly. The patient aims to achieve accordance between the assumptions of the psychotherapist and his own experiences. To endure nonaccordance would require a high mental stability and independence of judgement, which is exactly what patients are lacking. Patients typically seek to please the psychotherapist. Therefore, therapeutic assumptions that mental disorders are caused by traumatic childhood experience, especially sexual abuse, can cause severe problems. It leads to a search for the trauma supported by therapeutic expectations. Patients amenable to suggestion tend to generate pseudomemory while trying to achieve compliance with their psychotherapist views. Brainerd and Reyna (2005) have demonstrated several cases related to different psychotherapy techniques.

In summary, even if psychotherapists try to be neutral, it is impossible to avoid suggestions (Stoffels, 2003; Weizsäcker, 1926). Therefore, psychotherapists must always be aware that memory is not a reliable data pool from which past events can be recalled, comparable to playing and replaying a videotape, but that it is always related to a context, which needs to be taken into account, especially in the understanding of a trauma narrative (Fried, 2004; Schacter, 1996).

But there is so far no consensus among psychotherapists with respect to the occurrence and meaning of false memories in the context of psychotherapy. This especially is true for traumatic childhood memories of sexual abuse. The German research association (Deutsche Forschungsgemeinschaft) comissioned a book entitled *Trauma and Truth, Resurfacing Memory from a Psychotherapeutic Point of View* (Kirsch, 2001), which is introduced by two opposing prefaces. The first is written by Ullrich Sachsse, a leading trauma expert. He states that he questioned himself more than once on the validity of traumatic experiences as reported by patients. "Is it really true what I hear? Did it really happen?" In the past, the doubtful validity of such reports has not been taken serious. He admitted that he himself took part in trivialization of the validity question by arguing: "It is irrelevant for psychotherapy, what is true and what is phantasy. We work with pictures. We are only interested in subjective reality" (Kirsch, 2001). In the second preface, Rainer Krause, chairman of the Department of Clinical Psychology and Psychotherapy at Saarbrücken University, speaks of multiple possibilities of "unrecognized self-delusion." If a psychotherapist refers to the validity of patient's memories as irrelevant, he is just lying to himself because he obviously thinks he knows the truth about what happened or not.

The book by Kirsch (2001) demonstrates that psychotherapists highly disagree with respect to the correct approach toward patients' memories. Thirty-five percent believe that the question of truth is rather irrelevant for the understanding of their patients. Forty percent hold a contrary conception. About one-half of the surveyed psychotherapists think that the suggestive effect of an assumed sexual trauma is minor if openly expressed. The other half contradicts this opinion. Kirsch (2001) assumes "more or less unconscious assumptions," which control the psychotherapist's attitude toward those questions. A psychotherapist who is aware of his own presumptions is able to question them and has the ability to detach himself from the constraint of certain psychotherapy techniques. The therapist is thus less likely to expose patients to his own expectations and will develop a concept for the real problems together with the patient.

Apart from the psychotherapeutic concepts per se, psychotherapeutic approaches are also subject to societal influences. One is that elderly people who come to psychotherapy look back at their biography and search for possible explanations for their development in life. This includes questions on possible trauma in childhood or later on in life. Given this perspective, present conflicts take a backseat. The present seems to be pushed away in favor of a distant past. For the elderly person, this has the immediate advantage that he or she does not have to deal with present problems, be it the process of aging itself or collateral restrictions. The search for former traumata includes an element of unlimitedness. A history-oriented or even psychotraumatological perspective moves away from what is important for survival now.

Apart from individual lay concepts on "reasons" for mental disorders, there are also fashions in the public that exert their influence on psychotherapy. An example is the film *The Celebration* (originally entitled *Vesten*) from the Danish director Thomas Vinterberg. It won the jury prize at the Cannes Film Festival and was honored by international film critics. The central event of the film is the gathering of family and friends marking the 60th birthday of the family patriarch. At dinner, the eldest son accuses his father of having sexually abused both him and his recently deceased twin sister and blames him for her suicide. Guests, as well as the cinema audience, witness the moral demolition of the father and later on the mother too, who is accused to have known of the sexual abuse. The drama of disclosure ends the next morning. The father concedes his inexcusable behavior, and the son asks him to leave the house. Irene Berkel (2006) has analyzed Vinterberg's film and discovered many incoherences. She comes to the conclusion that Vinterberg is not interested in the characters' psychology but only in the confrontation of generations and that this explains the success of the movie. According to Berkel (2006), this underscores that during recent years the relationship between generations and gender has changed, most notably seen in a dramatic downfall of traditional family structures. Such societal trends will also influence the understanding of mental illness by patients and therapist, and such mutual corresponding assumptions and worldviews will then induce compliant interpretations of events and in the end pseudomemories of event.

Psychotherapy-induced pseudomemory is not harmless. Despite the morbid gain, they imply a heavy burden for the patient. They might strain the social context, lead to deep desperation and bitterness within the family, exceed the therapeutic situation, and challenge judiciary. The debate over psychotherapy-induced pseudomemory is not closed.

9.5 Accusation and Recrimination

In 2007, the court journalist Rückert (2007) revealed a case in Northern Germany. A young woman in psychiatric treatment blamed two men of sexual abuse and rape over many years during her childhood. The men, the father and the uncle of the woman, were accused and finally sentenced to four and a half and seven years in prison. A journalist investigated the case and found contradictions. Finally, the case was reopened, and the two men were discharged because of proven innocence. Also, two major criminal proceedings in Germany (the so-called Montessori trial and the Wormser sexual abuse trial) dealing with childhood sexual abuse ended in a debacle. After years of hearings, all defendants had to be discharged. The second expert witness referred to suggestive interrogations, which had led to pseudomemory of the children (Schulz-Hardt & Köhnken, 2000).

The disastrous course of these trials resulted in a question that is still not answered sufficiently (Schulz-Hardt & Köhnken, 2000): How could ordinary men, facing no extraordinary problems and being generally open-minded—such as parents, detectives, and state attorneys, as well as psychological expert witnesses—come to such an unrealistic conclusion and not recognize the pseudocharacter of memory?

Twenty years ago, the False-Memory-Syndrome Foundation (FMS-Foundation) was founded in Philadelphia, Pennsylvania, as a nonprofit organization. The initiators were Pamela and Peter Freyd, a teacher and a professor of mathematics. Peter Freyd was accused by his own daugther Jennifer of having sexually abused her between her 3rd and 16th birthdays. She successively remembered the episodes during psychotherapeutic treatment. The father denied the reproaches. He and his wife were convinced that the traumatic memories were not real and had been produced in psychotherapy by intrinsic or extrinsic suggestion (Brown et al., 1998).

Mr. and Mrs. Freyd released a press statement and faced an overwhelming feedback. A charitable trust was founded in 1992 and since then has about 3,000 paying members and maintains contact with approximately 18,000 affected families. The FMS-Foundation publishes a monthly newsletter with book recommendations, congress tips, and case reports. It offers workshops for concerned families and organizes training and informational events. The foundation has an independent advisory board, as well as a network of cooperating lawyers, who advise accused parents on their rights.

The typical case is a grown-up daughter who is in psychotherapeutic treatment due to eating or anxiety disorders, depression, or other mental problems. Together with the psychotherapists, she "discovers" that she has sexually been abused in childhood, in most cases by her father. Many of the women cut all ties with their families, sometimes even encouraged by their therapists, because parents and also siblings often reject the accusations. In 7% of all cases, it comes to a trial in court. The percentage of mothers, and not only father or other male relatives, being charged as a perpetrator has also steadily increased to 30% (Merskey, 1996).

Meanwhile, the struggle about memory is taking a new turn. There are a growing number of cases in which former patients now accuse their therapists of having brought up false memories about sexual abuse. False memories have caused many problems and ruined whole families. In at least one case in the United States, the patient was granted a recompensation of several million dollars because of the induction of false memories in psychotherapy. In Germany, the case of Elisabeth Reuter, an illustratror of childrens' books, got much attention. She was one of the first women who spoke in public about having been sexually abused by her own father. The documentary called *Gap in the Head* (1994) was used in high-ranking congresses for trauma therapy to demonstrate a dissociative identity disorder because Elisabeth Reuter claimed to suffer from those dissociative conditions. In a television broadcast titled "The Delusion of Psychotherapists," she explained how she thought she had been sexually abused by her father while being in psychotherapeutic treatment. Later on, she brought her psychotherapist to trial, alleging that he had induced the memory of sexual abuse by her father and that she had adopted it under the influence of psychotherapy and its special atmosphere. Her father, a protestant pastor, indeed had been cruel but had never abused her sexually (Kuballa, 2003). In court, her claim was rejected because in the early 1990s there had not been enough scientific background on the subject of false and suggested memories so that the therapist could not know what he did and what was going on.

9.6 Criteria for Recognizing False Memories

Four different forms of subjective recollection can be distinguished: (1) mostly exact memory, (2) composition of real event and fantasy, (3) pure fantasy, and (4) mostly exact memory of fantasy (Box 9.1). Correct memory is rather the exception than the rule. The task is therefore always to disentangle what has happened on one hand and what is interpretation or pure wishes on the other.

Box 9.1 Types of Resurfacing Memories

1. Mostly exact memory
2. Composition of real event and fantasy
3. Pure product of fantasy
4. Mostly exact memory of fantasy.

Among clinicians and scientists, it is generally accepted that differentiating these forms of correct and false memories is very difficult. Many persons are fully convinced of what they think is their history. Inner conceptions can replace real memory without any substitution. In particular, the fourth form of recollections can be difficult to recognize because it concerns a "real memory," but not to a real event but rather to a "real fantasy." There are no reliable criteria or no guidelines on how to discriminate false from correct tales. The fantastic may be real, and the obvious can emerge as an illusion.

One approach is the comparison of repeated reports. Changes of content or emotional experience over the course of time are indicators of false memories. According to Brenneis, several criteria can help to differentiate between memories and pseudomemories (Box 9.2). First is the context of remembering. The more there are social expectations, the more careful one has to be. Second is the quality

> **Box 9.2 Criteria to Differentiate Between Memory and Pseudomemory**
>
> 1. Context of remembering: Skepticism if social expectation is high and appropriate searching preceded
> 2. Quality of remembering: Skepticism if there are diffuse feelings, visions, and bodily sensations, followed by richness of visual details
> 3. Plausibility of remembering: Skepticism if, for example, the displaced sexual abuse lasts till late childhood or adolescence
> 4. Plausibility of neglect: Skepticism if, for example, events in later life cannot be recalled.

of remembering. The more there are diffuse feelings, visions, and bodily sensations, followed by richness of visual details, the more skepticism is warranted. Third is the plausibility of remembering. If, for example, the sexual abuse lasts till late childhood or adolescence, or if memories date back in memory before the age of three, doubt is justified. Fourth is the plausibility of neglect. Skepticism is justified if events in later life cannot be recalled.

References

Benz, W. (1998). Deutscher mythos. *Die zeit* 37/1998.
Berkel, I. (2006). *Missbrauch als phantasma. Zur krise der genealogie.* München: Wilhelm Fink Verlag.
Blake, E. (2002). *A life in pieces: The making and unmaking of Binjamin Wilkomirski.* London: Norton Professional Books.
Böhm, H., Meuren, R., & Storm-Wahlich, M. (2002). Die Borderlinestörung als quelle (nicht)-intentionaler falschaussagen. *Praxis der rechtspsychologie, 12,* 1–15.
Brainerd, C. J., & Reyna, V. F. (2005). *The science of false memory.* New York, NY: Oxford University Press.
Brenneis, C. B. (1998). Gedächtnissysteme und der psychoanalytische Abruf von Trauma-Erinnerungen. *Psyche, 52,* 801–823.
Brown, V. D., Hammond, C., & Scheflin, A. W. (1998). *Memory, trauma treatment and the law.* New York, NY: Norton Professional Books.
Fried, J. (2004). Der schleier der erinnerung: *Grundzüge einer historischen memorik.* München: Beck.
Herpertz, S. C., & Saß, H. (2003). *Persönlichkeitsstörungen.* Stuttgart: Georg Thieme Verlag. 84ff.
Kirsch, A. (2001). Trauma und wirklichkeit: *Wiederauftauchende erinnerungen aus psychotherapeutischer sicht.* Stuttgart: Kohlhammer.
Kuballa, F. (2003). Der wahn der therapeuten. ARD-Fernsehsendung vom 27.08.2003, Köln.
Loftus, E. F., & Pickrell, J. E. (1995). The formation of false memories. *Psychiatric Annals, 25,* 720–725.
Merskey, H. (1996). Ethical issues in the search for repressed memories. *American Journal of Psychotherapy, 50,* 323–335.
Rückert, S. (2007). Unrecht im namen des volkes: *Ein justizirrtum und seine folgen.* Hamburg: Hoffmann und Campe.

Schacter, D. L. (1996). *Searching for memory: The brain, the mind, and the past.* Reinbek: Rowohlt Verlag.

Schulz-Hardt, S., & Köhnken, G. (2000). Wie ein verdacht sich selbst bestätigen kann: Konfirmatorisches hypothesentesten als ursache von falschbeschuldigungen wegen sexuellen kindesmissbrauchs. *Praxis der Rechtspsychologie,* 10(Special issue), 60–88.

Stoffels, H. (2003). Grundfragen anthropologischer Psychotherapie. Viktor von Weizsäckers Konzeption der "Seelenbehandlung". In J. Hainz (Ed.), *Heilung aus der begegnung.* Eppenhain: Selbstverlag.

Stoffels, H. (2005). Kunst und trauma. In E. Böhlke, A. Heinz, & M. P. Heuser (Eds.), *Über fiktive realitäten.* Berlin: Über Gott und die Welt.

Weizsäcker, V. V. (1926). Seelenbehandlung und Seelenführung. Nach ihren biologischen und metaphysischen grundlagen behandelt. In P. Achilles, D. Janz, M. Schrenck, & C. F. V. Weizsäcker (Eds.), *Gesammelte schriften band* (5, pp. 67–142). Frankfurt: Suhrkamp. 1987.

Wilkomirski, Binjamin (1995). *Bruchstücke. Aus einer kindheit 1939–1948.* Frankfurt: Jüdischer Verlag.

10 The Constitution of Narrative Identity

Theo Leydenbach

Psychoanalyst, Department of Medical Psychology, Psychosomatic Medicine, University Paris XII, France

10.1 What Does Identity Mean?

Narrative comes from the Latin verb *narrare*, "to tell"; a narrative is a "story" that describes a sequence of nonfictional or fictional events. The concept of narrative identity, fundamental to the notion of selfhood and self-understanding, is progressively elaborated by the French philosopher Paul Ricoeur (1913–2005) in his last philosophical writings; it finds its highest achievements in *Time and narrative*, *From text to action: Essays in hermeneutics II*, and *Oneself as another*. For Paul Ricoeur, narrative identity is "the sort of identity to which a human being has access thanks to the mediation of the narrative function" (Ricoeur, 1991, p. 73).

Of two or more separate things that agree in every detail, we say that they are identical. In logic, it designates a proposition whose terms express an identity or denote the same thing, as "a man is a man." To the question of what is a circle, we could look up the word in a dictionary and come to the univocal definition of the circle as "[t]he line enclosing a perfectly round plane figure whose circumference is everywhere equidistant from its centre." In the philosophy of Immanuel Kant, this type of proposition corresponds to an analytic judgment. Analytic judgments are those whose predicates are wholly contained in their subjects, adding nothing to their concept. For instance, the circle is round: Nothing is added from the outside because its roundness is wholly contained in the definition of the circle itself. If asked about my house, the answer would certainly be more circumstantiated, but in giving a detailed account of its construction, I could give an almost univocal description of the type of house I am living in.

But what about the answer to the question of who am I? How can I characterize the person that I am? Because there is no access to myself from the outside, I cannot define myself as I could define any other object in the world. Does that mean that I mustn't say anything about myself? Of course, I have a lot to *tell* about myself, but this is a discourse fundamentally different in nature and brings us to the notion of narrative identity.

10.2 Collective Trauma and Narrative Identity

The title *Hurting memories and beneficial forgetting* brings me back to a recent visit to Japan in September 2011, 6 months after the earthquake of March 11 and the subsequent tsunami and nuclear catastrophe in Fukushima. As a group of three medical doctors from Europe, we had a meeting with the Psychosomatic Society of the University of Sendai. The next day, we were taken north of the city and visited the zone where the earthquake and the tsunami had hit the hardest. The coast was devastated, with broken houses, broken bridges everywhere. When we arrived at a cleared space, the shock set in. Everything was destroyed. The only sign of what had once been were a few metallic structures on the horizon. For as far as we could see, there was only destruction. We drove down a few cleared streets and stopped in a small parking lot, close to the metal frame of what had been a house. Blackbirds were circling all around; the scene was like something out of a Hitchcock film—no sign of life anywhere, the end of the world. Six months after the catastrophe, the smell of mud and trash was still in the air. The few roads opened to traffic were surrounded by huge piles of debris from destroyed buildings and broken cars. One of these buildings was a nursery school, where only a few of the children had survived. In the distance were the remains of a newly built hospital. Some half-ruined houses had moved from their original sites. Wherever we went, we smelled a persistent and obsessive odor of mud and rot. A small bus stopped not far from where we were standing, and a dozen people got out. Standing in front was a man giving them instructions. They seemed to be rescue workers, and we wondered what is left to save? Some police vehicles circled in this no-man's land, like robots left behind in a forgotten time, and again we wondered what mission could they have in this hallucinatory landscape? There was something delusional about it all, something beyond reality.

In this apocalyptic no-man's, I had the surreal perception of an overall and insistent smell of radioactivity. It was pure delusion because radioactivity doesn't smell and furthermore Fukushima was a 100 km south of the place we were at. Yet, I felt as if I were in a nightmare, where death, devastation, and nuclear anxiety collided in a total confusion. Hiroshima, Fukushima, Nagasaki, and Chernobyl flashed through my mind and were all mixed together. It was as if time had stopped, and we stood next to each other, looking at the destruction. No one spoke or moved, glued to the ground. The five of us, two Japanese doctors from Sendai and three Europeans, shared a common silence, confronted by disaster and death. However different our cultural references might be, when facing the extreme, we shared the same human experience.

This book focuses on traumatic memories. The question that came to me was fundamentally: How will the Japanese cope with this trauma not only individually but also collectively? Different we may be, how we overcome trauma in various cultures, yet, despite all the differences, I would make the hypothesis that the more severe the trauma, the deeper we must go into ourselves to draw on the vital energies. I felt it strongly when we were standing silently together. However, finding the point of resilience in ourselves is not sufficient. We are equally supported by collective energies, being part of a community, sharing common values and a common collective narrative.

Standing silently together, the five of us had the same intense experience, but five different stories would be told. However common earthquakes may be in Japan, even of this magnitude, the March 11 tsunami, with its subsequent nuclear disaster, is a historical turning point. Fukushima, after Hiroshima, represents for Japan a kind of existential paradigm shift, a profound refiguration of its collective narrative. Later that evening, while we were having a beer, one of my German colleagues told me for the first time of the bombing of Dresden, something deeply fixed in his childhood memory: *Hurting memories*, deposited however deeply in the archives of the past, forgotten and not forgotten at the same time, are *transfigured* into the universal narrative of tragedy. When facing the incommensurable, the created narrative exceeds by far any possible objective description and permeates our very being; it becomes, in a sense, consubstantial to our being-in-the-world, reframing thus the experience of selfhood itself.

This means, as M.R. Somers puts it, a "shift from a focus on *representational* to *ontological* narrativity" (Somers, 1994, p. 613). Somers also explains:

> *The expressions of this narrative reframing are broad and diverse ... Before this shift, philosophers of history had argued that narrative modes of representing knowledge (telling historical stories) were representational forms imposed by historians on the chaos of lived experience. Recently, however, scholars are postulating something much more substantive about narrative: namely, that social life is itself* storied *and that narrative is an ontological condition of social life. Their research is showing us... that people construct identities (however multiple and changing)...; that "experience" is constituted through narratives; that people make sense of what has happened and is happening to them by attempting to assemble or in some way to integrate these happenings within one or more narratives; and that people are guided... on the basis of the projections, expectations, and memories derived from a multiplicity but ultimately limited repertoire of available social, public, and cultural narratives.*
>
> Somers (1994, pp. 613–614)

We were quite aware that the "experience" of our Japanese colleagues was mediated by a cultural background different from ours, each of us processing with the same intensity but through the different founding myths of their own culture.

10.3 Individual Narrative Identity

Humans are storytellers. Ricoeur asks:

> *After all, do not human lives become more readable (lisibles) when they are interpreted in function of the stories people tell about themselves? And these "life stories," are they not rendered more intelligible when they are applied to narrative models—plots—borrowed from history and fiction (drama or novels)?... It is therefore plausible to affirm the following assertions: a) knowledge of the self is an interpretation; b) the interpretation of the self, in turn, finds narrative, among other signs and symbols, to be a privileged mediation; c) this mediation borrows from history as much as [from] fiction[,] making the life story a fictive history or, if you prefer, an historical fiction, comparable to those biographies of great men where both history and fiction are found blended together.*
>
> Ricoeur (1991, p. 73)

If for literature is of essential importance, it's because texts allow us to understand ourselves. They can function as *plot templates*, so to speak, on which we may draw and which may help us to *figure*, as well as to *refigure*, our own storytelling, even beyond the time period that is knowable to us. Indeed:

> [T]here is nothing in real life that serves as a narrative beginning; memory is lost in the hazes of early childhood; my birth and, with greater reason, the act through which I was conceived belong more to the history of others—in this case, to my parents—than to me. As for my death, it will finally be recounted only in the stories of those who survive me. I am always moving toward my death, and this prevents me from ever grasping it as a narrative end.
>
> Ricoeur (1992, pp. 160–161)

This is why Ricoeur proposes "to make a detour through the literary forms of narrative and more precisely through those of fictional narratives. The problematic ... of identity, finds itself raised to a level of lucidity and also perplexity in fictional narratives that is not achieved by stories immersed in the course of life" (Ricoeur, 1991, p. 77).

One aim of this essay is to argue that dreams constitute fictional stories and can, in the same way, intervene in the dynamic construction of narrative identity. Furthermore, they reveal themselves in therapy as *key factors* that allow the *refiguration* of the narrative created by patients about themselves and of which they are prisoners. In what follows, I would like to demonstrate how it is possible to make use of dreams in working with patients.

10.4 The Case of Mrs. P

When I first met Mrs. P, she had just come from a psychiatric hospital, where she had been sent after a mental breakdown following years of depression. Bravely, she tried to find her way back into life but was exhausted and hopeless. She was 43 years old, still married at that time, with three small children. Mrs. P is of mixed heritage, half Asian, half European. Her Asian mother left her father upon learning he had a love affair with another woman. In rejecting him, she told her daughter for her first 13 years that he was dead. And then, at the age of 13, the young girl was told that her father was *not* dead, that he was alive, and that he "had left us." This led to a complete breakdown of the image she had had of him up to that point.

Mrs. P spent her first 5 years with her grandmother in the countryside. It was an innocent and serene world. She speaks of sacred times, of the convincing peace and tranquility that radiated from her grandmother. At the age of 6, Mrs. P moved to the city to live with her mother, who worked in a hospital as a laboratory aide. The mother was oppressive and depressed and accused her daughter constantly of wrongdoing. At any moment, things could turn for the worse: Mrs. P was frequently and unpredictably beaten as part of her mother's irrational explosions. At the same time, the mother cared affectionately for her daughter; the child was aware of this as well.

At the hospital where she lived with her mother, the child saw many horrifying things. In particular, the overpowering smell of the morgue stays with her. "But all of this was life for me," she says, "In Vietnam, I knew physical death, not the psychic death I would later experience in France." In the street she was in her true element, fully herself, in union with the world surrounding her, however tragic it was. When someone insulted her, she answered with her fists or by grabbing their collar. When she came home, she had to completely change and adapt to the unpredictable nature of her mother. In the street, however, she could restore her balance day by day, despite the constraints at home.

This balance was broken when her mother revealed the true story about her father. The idealized image on which she had constructed herself was taken away. She speaks of real depression that she could never overcome. Over the years, however, she succeeded to live on her reserves; she was a good student and tried to pull herself up, as she always would. At 18, she came to France and worked as a secretary, trying to adapt to this new world. Her mother joined her 3 years later, and things turned sour immediately. Her mother was deeply depressed and was eventually placed in the psychiatric ward. At 23, Mrs. P met her husband. Sexually, she couldn't open up to him and felt absent in her body when he touched her. Even with the mutual respect and love they shared, she felt a kind of permanent sexual harassment. For many years, the tension between love and rejection led her to depression and the eventual contemplation of suicide due to the overriding feeling that there was no way out. Mrs. P had always been a loving mother, but, in this state, she was no longer able to take care of her children. As a result, the depression grew ultimately into a breakdown.

Throughout the therapy, she remembered many dreams, two of which merit special attention. In one of our first sessions, she told me about a recurrent childhood dream: She was in a frame, much like the frame of a picture, and a tiny ball faced her. The ball swelled up progressively, pushing her back against the wall until she was flattened against it, her body reduced to a simple surface. The feeling of oppression in the dream is associated with the oppression felt during her mother's fits. This recurrent dream became an equally recurrent theme in therapy, symbolizing the experience of oppression throughout her life.

A dream she had close to the end of her therapy reveals itself to be centrally important: She wore a Vietnamese-style shirt and ankle boots; apart from this, she was naked. Looking down, she saw herself with a penis. She was quite troubled and wondered about the strangeness of it all. When she awoke from the dream, she thought immediately, "This is my father." It was a very strong perception, and she was surprised that this was so evident to her. She felt nothing repulsive, none of the kind of repulsion she felt toward her husband. Upon having this dream, she experienced inner peace, a perception of wholeness. She felt secure and without fear.

The dream, as it unfolds in its manifest content, and what she says about it should not be dissociated; it makes a whole. What matters is Mrs. P's convincing statement and not any interpretation of the therapist. "This is my father" is the unconditional truth. The real content of this dream is the narrative—its appearance and the specific affects linked to it. When she proclaims with such absolute certainty that "This is my father," no further doubt should be permitted. How a dream like this comes to be and of which life fragments it is composed remain unknown. What it might hide or intend to hide should not matter. In such a case, the therapist must restrain him- or herself and accept the patient's absolute truth. Here, the self affirms its existence, erasing any doubt or restraint, and proclaims *ergo sum*: "This is my father, so I am." A penis coming from nowhere, placed on her body, is the surrealistic narrative of the dream, followed by the no less surrealistic affirmation: "Me, this woman with the penis, is my father." Representing the unrepresentable, she thus poses without any doubt her true existence: "It's me, I am myself."

After this dream, the father dramatically resurfaced in therapy. Of her father, she would say: "He oppresses me and empties me," adding, "How could I possibly find a way to myself, how could I possibly be myself, how could I recover my lost childhood, with a story like this?" She calls the story of her father "[a] confusion placed in myself, like an inerasable mark." In the states of confusion that Mrs. P continues to sporadically experience, she misses this father, from whom she would like to hear, "Don't be afraid, go ahead." To learn that he was alive and that he had left the family made her feel "[l]ike an empty shell." Calling her true self "the empty self," she relates this emptiness to her missing father. In this feeling of abandonment, she had progressively filled herself through eating, and she could not control this bulimia despite her efforts.

Recently, she lost her excess weight, almost spontaneously, as though she no longer needed to fill herself by eating. She herself made the connection between her eating and the story of her father. In the next therapy session, she spoke about writing: "I have to write lines in myself, inside my body." Writing lines within oneself could equally mean either giving form to the formless or creating a new kind of inner space. In the dream of the father, the nonrepresentable had been represented; however strange the dream may have been, it had powerful consequences. The regular shifting between depression and bulimia came to an end. She reconnected with her true being as it had been experienced in childhood and later in the street, facing life in a head-on fight, renewing the capacity to project herself into the future.

The first related dream gave Mrs. P clear insight into her life story and helped to refigurate the narrative about herself. The second dream, which I would like to call "The Epiphany of the Father," happened to be the turning point in her therapy—the fundamental shift in her narrative. Narrative identity, as Ricoeur understands it, is a dynamic process that means not so much *knowing* oneself, but rather *producing* this very self.

10.5 The Case of Mrs. B

A 55-year-old woman, who has survived colon cancer and liver metastasis and who had at the time a 40% chance of surviving, comes to therapy seeking help in coming to terms with her illness as well as with difficulties she faces in other aspects of her life. She is aware that she has dreams but cannot remember any of them; at times, she has just a vanishing impression that she had dreamed. When asked whether she could remember previous ones, maybe only small fragments or those from childhood, she could recall the following two recurrent dreams from when she was about 10 years old. The first dream:

> *She is alone on a beach; a huge ship, very close, dangerously inclined and menacing to crush her; the feeling that she can't escape; she is terrified.*

The second dream:

> *She tries to fly; working hard with her arms she succeeds in doing so; she flies over the woods, very close to the canopy; there is a wall amidst the trees; she passes easily what could otherwise have been an impassable obstacle; it is a highly positive experience.*

The first dream could be considered as figuring an *impasse situation*, that is, a life-threatening situation with no way out. The second dream is almost antipodal to the first: She experiences the power of flying, the feeling of liberty, and the ability to transcend adversity; the opposite of the impasse situation of the first dream.

The therapy work, which I won't mention here, could establish almost term for term how these dreams recalled in the first session mirrored the essential life events of her childhood, as well as the later existential impasses. She could find a way out of all those actual problems, first through understanding the impasse situation in which she was trapped and second by using her own power of resilience and capacity of action to break the walls of her own prison.

She had a "conclusive" dream the night before the final session: A man was chasing her. Then she remembers that she was flying in the dream; it was a strong experience. Her final words concluding the therapy: "I now know that I am able to fly." Like Mrs. P, Mrs. B *refigurated* the narrative about herself.

10.6 Some General Remarks on Dreaming

In 1900, Freud stated that the dream carries the function of protecting sleep; he also believed that the dream was the disguised realization of unconscious desires. It follows that dreams had to be systematically interpreted to discover the hidden meaning. In contrast, Allan Hobson, Director of the Laboratory of Neurophysiology at the Massachusetts Mental Health Center, correlates dreams with quantifiable brain events due to random energy signals. The cortex is attempting subsequently to make sense of them by combining them into coherent stories. Thus he dismisses the notion of unconscious meanings and states that his research entirely invalidates Freud's beliefs. Nevertheless, even putting random signals together into coherent stories supposes a constructive activity that is not entirely random. Hobson's theory is thus self-contradictory and implies, in spite of itself, the intervention of the subject, as does Freud's.

Dreams are fictional productions freed from the repression of the superego and the barriers of reason. Space and time are the projections of the dreamer (Sami-Ali,

1997, 1999, 2011), and ultimately it is always the subject who *creates* the narrative. This has to be fully integrated through therapy. When Mrs. P says, "This is my father," she profoundly changes her horizon of anticipation. "This is my father" is no neutral statement. She immediately feels projected into the future, into life's "immanent purposiveness" (Thompson, 2007). As such, the dream must be looked at as a work of fiction. To show the fundamental role that it plays in therapy, we must take the detour of Ricoeur's writings on literary fiction: "[T]he text is the medium through which we understand ourselves" (Ricoeur, 1986, p. 86–87):

> *In contrast to the tradition of the cogito and to the pretention of the subject to know itself by immediate intuition, it must be said that we understand ourselves only by the long detour of the signs of humanity deposited in cultural works. What would we know of love and hate, of moral feelings, and, in general, of all that we call the self if these had not been brought to language and articulated by literature? ... [W]hat must be interpreted in a text is a* proposed world *that I could inhabit and wherein I could project ... my ownmost possibilities.*

Shouldn't we consider *The Epiphany of the Father* in Mrs. P's dream as the "proposed world" in her case, a world that she could for the first time inhabit and wherein she could finally project her "ownmost possibilities"? Her father coming from nowhere is the representation of the unrepresentable, "discordant concordance," as Ricoeur puts it, "characteristic of all narrative composition" and defined by him as "the synthesis of the heterogeneous" (Ricoeur, 1992, p. 141).

> *The world of the text is therefore not the world of everyday language. [The same could be said of the dream.] In this sense, it constitutes a new sort of distanciation that could be called a distanciation of the real from itself. It is this distanciation that fiction introduces into our apprehension of reality. ... Through fiction and poetry, new possibilities of being-in-the-world are opened up within everyday reality. Fiction and poetry intend being, not under the modality of being-given, but under the modality of power-to-be.*
>
> Ricoeur, (1986, p. 86)

The power-to-be could be considered the very essence of narrative identity; it could be thought of as the very essence of the dream, as well. When we are dreaming, we easily have the feeling of watching a story independent of ourselves, without noticing that the train passing on the horizon and the cows in the field are but our creation. We are this train and these cows, in a sense, as we are all that exists and happens in the dream. The power-to-fly in the last dream of Mrs. B is the power-to-be that Mrs. B gives to herself.

In their most prospective aspect, dreams figure the unthinkable. It is essential to a subject's physical and mental balance that he or she is prepared to be set in motion by the imagination within. Beyond dreams, this includes all that can be considered the equivalent of dreams: all imaginary production, literature, poetry, music, fine art, as well as day dreaming, fantasy, affect in general. All of these contribute to the vivid self-understanding that he or she experiences, that which we will ultimately call narrative identity.

In Tolstoy's novella *The Death of Ivan Ilyich*, we find the narrative shift par excellence. The dying Ivan Illych, brought face-to-face with his mortality, cannot make sense of his successful but useless life and experiences the very meaning of authentic life thanks to the compassion of his peasant servant Gerasim, a simple soul. In the midst of his atrocious suffering, Ilyich suddenly sees a light, and "it grew clear to him that what had been oppressing him... was all dropping away... 'And death... where is it?' He sought his former accustomed fear of death and did not find it. Where is it? 'What death?' There was no fear because there was no death. In the place of death there was light." And just before dying: "Death is finished, he said to himself. It is no more!"

References

Ricoeur, P.(1983, 1984, 1985). *Time and narrative (Temps et Récit)*, 3 Vols. (K. McLaughlin & D. Pellauer, Trans.). Chicago, IL: University of Chicago Press (1984, 1985, 1988).

Ricoeur, P. (1986). *From text to action: Essays in hermeneutics II* (K. Blamey & J. B. Thompson, Trans.). Evanston, IL: Northwestern University Press (1991).

Ricoeur, P. (1991). Narrative identity. *Philosophy Today*, 35(1), 73–81.

Ricoeur, P. (1992). *Oneself as another (Soi-même comme un autre)* (K. Blamey, Trans.). Chicago, IL: University of Chicago Press.

Sami-Ali, (1997). *Le rêve et l'affect. Une théorie du somatique*. Paris: Dunod.

Sami-Ali, (1999). *Le corps, l'espace et le temps*. Paris: Dunod.

Sami-Ali, (2011). *Penser l'Unité*. Paris: L'esprit du Temps.

Somers, M. R. (1994). The narrative constitution of identity: A relational and network approach. *Theory and society*, 23, 605–649.

Thompson, E. (2007). *Mind in life*. Cambridge, MA: Harvard University Press.

Tolstoy, L. (1886). *The death of IvanIlyich* (L. A. Maude, Trans). (in Russian). <http://www.ccel.org/ccel/tolstoy/ivan.txt>. Accessed August 27, 2012.

Part Two

Clinical Aspects

11 Implicit Memories and the Structure of the Values System After the Experience of Trauma in Childhood or Adulthood

Krzysztof Rutkowski, Edyta Dembińska
Department of Psychotherapy, Jagiellonian University Medical College, Kraków, Poland

11.1 Introduction

It is difficult to demonstrate evidence of memory other than verbal (declarative) memory. One of the first works on this subject was Jung's galvanic phenomenon (galvanopsychophysical reflex), which draws out the presence of unconscious associations (Jung, 1995). For this reason, it is important to seek manifestations of memory in all aspects of functioning, not just in what we say and want to remember. One way of gaining access to extraverbal memory is through evaluation of the value hierarchy that is created through the influence of environmental circumstances, upbringing, and other factors affecting development, such as extreme stress. In this chapter, we will demonstrate the link between trauma stress, memory, and expression of the trauma through the individual value hierarchy.

Identification of personal values is currently the subject of studies in areas of scientific interest as diverse as consumer behaviors, prosocietal behaviors, workplace and organization behaviors, political elections, behaviors connected with teaching and parenting, psychotherapy research, and studies of cultural differences (Domurat, 2009). Values are also being addressed in clinical trials in response to the belief that they are a significant element of the personality.

For a long time, values remained the domain of philosophy and religion, a question intrinsically linked to morality. They were treated by many scientists with suspicion, as too subjective and difficult to define in scientific research. The reversal of this approach to research into values came in the first half of the twentieth century, when psychologists endowed them with more prosaic significance by linking them with everyday actions such as reading the newspapers, watching films, and voting.

The pioneer in research into values was the German philosopher and psychologist Eduard Spranger, who in the early twentieth century formulated a conception to describe six personality types based on their preferred dominant values (Spranger & Pigors, 1928). Spranger's work was continued by his students Allport, Vernon, and Lindzey (Allport, Vernon, & Lindzey, 1951; Vernon & Allport, 1931), who distinguished between six types of value attitudes: theoretical, economic, esthetic, social, political, and religious. They also created the first tool for studying values, known as the Study of Values (Vernon & Allport, 1931).

Gradually, theories stating that values were autonomous elements dictating behavior evolved into theories according to which people develop their own hierarchy from the values accessible in a given culture (Rokeach, 1973, 1979; Schwartz, 2006). This change in the thinking about human values was initiated by the works of Milton Rokeach (Rokeach, 1973, 1979), who proposed the next tool for gauging values: the Rokeach Value Survey (Rokeach, 1973). Rokeach based his definition of a value—"an enduring belief that a specific mode of conduct or end-state of existence is personally or socially preferable to an opposite or converse mode of conduct or end-state of existence"—on cognitive theories. According to his theory, the various values do not constitute separate components of the psyche, as Spranger and his successors had proposed, but combine to form a system defined as "an enduring organization of beliefs concerning preferable modes of conduct or end-states of existence along a continuum of relative importance" (Rokeach, 1973). The value system forms the core of the personality and the foundation for the self-concept. Rokeach distinguishes two types of values: terminal and instrumental. *Terminal values* represent desirable end-states or accomplishments, which include personal values (e.g., happiness and inner harmony) and social values (e.g., national security and the safety of the family). *Instrumental values* are processes or ways of achieving terminal values that incorporate moral values (e.g., honesty and forgiveness) and competencies (e.g., imagination and initiative).

Spranger's and Rokeach's were the first of many varied psychological theories of values and tools for assessing them. Contemporary conceptions employed in research are based above all on the works of Kohn (Kohn, 1969; Kohn & Schooler, 1983), Rokeach (Rokeach, 1973, 1979), Kluckhohn (Kluckhohn, 1951), and Schwartz (Bilsky & Schwartz, 1994; Schwartz, 1992, 2006; Schwartz & Boehnke, 2004), and they have their roots in cognitive theory. A summary of the state of knowledge in the area of values might encompass six statements: (1) Values are convictions, cognitive structures that are closely linked to affective structures. (2) Values are relative to desirable end-states. (3) Values go beyond specific behaviors and situations. (4) Values serve as standards or criteria. (5) Values are ordered relative to each other depending on their importance (they constitute a hierarchy). (6) The relative importance of a group of significant values influences behavior.

Values may be examined at the individual and social levels. At the individual level, they are internalized convictions on life goals and ways to attain them. At the social level, they are convictions upheld by members of a given social group that serve to distinguish certain social systems from others. As such, values may be understood as instrumental to both individual and social development.

Individuals' value hierarchy develops as a product of their individual needs, character traits, temperament, culture, socialization process, and personal experiences. There is an element of choice in the way it—unlike needs—is built up. People are conscious of their system of values, though they are not always aware of the role of those values in driving their behavior.

The fundamental sources in the creation of value hierarchies are an individual's biologically conditioned needs and temperament, which constitute restrictions on the socialization process. The personal hierarchy of values is shaped by the confrontation of needs and temperament with capabilities and difficulties, with what is permissible, and with what is prohibited in a given social milieu.

The other source shaping an individual's personal hierarchy of values is social experience. In many cases, this experience is common to people from the same social class (in terms of education, age, gender, or profession), but it may also be individual (relations with parents, emigration, illnesses, or traumatic events suffered). A comparison of group and individual value hierarchies shows the influence on the value priorities of subpopulations of social changes (e.g., changes in the business, economic, or political situation) and individual experiences (e.g., emigration and traumas) to which they have been exposed.

Because values develop and evolve in the social context, they may be understood as a link between the self and the social environment. Values that are a central element of the self are less vulnerable to change than attitudes or needs, but the individual value hierarchy is nevertheless a flexible structure, and the circumstances of a given life govern which values are activated at any one time. Such changes are usually connected with a given stage of life, aging, and the impact of individual or group experiences (e.g., war and economic crisis). With age, the values of security, tradition, and conformity become increasingly important, while the significance of stimulation, hedonism, and achievement decreases. The stable economic and political situation in Western Europe in recent decades and the resultant reduction in existential fears have increased the importance to young people of values such as hedonism, stimulation, and self-determination and have caused them to attach less significance to security, tradition, and conformity. Change can also be caused to the system of values as a result of psychotherapeutic intervention. It is furthermore important to note that the influence of circumstances on the value hierarchy is not unidirectional; high-priority values also exert a certain influence on the circumstances that a person encounters in life. For instance, the decision to become involved in conspiratorial activity or a demanding job is linked to preferred values.

11.2 Aim of the Study

This chapter presents the results of a study carried out in a group of people with experience of trauma and describes observations concerning the chronic consequences of that trauma. The purpose of the study was to assess the influence of painful early childhood experience on subsequent personality development. The importance of emotional situations experienced in childhood has been known to psychiatry for years, but there are few publications on it and few opportunities to compile data statistically and to draw conclusions from the observed facts.

The research was conducted in the Centre for Victims of Political Persecutions at the Jagiellonian University Medical College among people persecuted for political reasons in Poland in the years 1939–1956. Among the subjects were concentration camp prisoners, people deported by the Soviet authorities to Siberia, and political prisoners serving sentences for action in the anticommunist underground. Only individuals who had never received psychiatric treatment or suffered any other form of trauma were included in the study.

The group was divided into two subgroups: people who suffered trauma before the age of five and those who experienced it at a later age or in adult life. This was done to differentiate between verbal memory and specific relations as well as social needs. Trauma experienced after 5 years of age is more easily remembered and is associated with behavior later on; also, in the development period, this is a time of greater autonomy. The earlier years are characterized by significant dependence on the care received and usually by a lack of memories from that time. Even if memories do appear, they are fragmentary and hesitant, and there still is a lack of proper self-defense mechanisms to manage the experience of the trauma.

11.3 Subjects

A total of 327 people underwent the examination. The average age at the moment of the examination was 68 years, with the age ranging from 44 to 88 years. The subjects were divided into two groups: Group 1 comprised of people who had suffered trauma before the age of 5 (130 people) and Group 2 of those who had suffered it at a later age or in adult life (197 people). The mean age in Group 1 was 62.9, and in Group 2 it was 71.2.

There was a noticeable difference between the groups in the distribution of the sexes. In Group 1, the difference was not so big, though there were more women (55%) than men (45%). In Group 2, there were considerably more men (65%) than women (35%). The differences result from the social structure of the groups: In Group 2, more people had been directly involved in conspiratorial activity and in guerrilla squads; hence, there was a higher number of men in this group. Deportations and imprisonments in concentration camps, however, took place irrespective of the sex (especially in the case of children); hence the gender composition of Group 1 is different.

Concluding the description of trauma in both research groups, it is clear that Group 1, in which people were exposed to the trauma in early childhood, comprises mostly deportees (90%). In Group 2, prison sentences and exile account for about 40%, shared evenly, whereas the remainder of the group had suffered other types of trauma. The duration of the trauma was on average 54.8 months: 59 months in Group 1 and 52.1 months in Group 2. This is about 4.5 years on average.

Comparison of the average age of the people examined and the first year of their marriage reveals that most people got married at about 20–25 years of age. This corresponds with the cultural norms of the times. The percentages of married people are almost identical in both groups at 88%. A majority of people (more than one-third) had two children. However, almost the same number of people did not have children at all, and one in six of the subjects had one or three children. In conclusion, family functioning in both groups is very similar, and the differences are not statistically valid.

All the people undergoing examination had been diagnosed with posttraumatic disorders of the posttraumatic stress disorder (PTSD) type, according to DSM-IV-TR (F43.1 or F62.0 according to ICD-10).

11.4 Methods

The primary tool used in the study was the Value Survey compiled by Milton Rokeach in 1973 (Rokeach, 1973) and adapted for use in Poland in the early 1980s (Brzozowski, 1989). The survey is based on the author's personality theory, which refers to a system of convictions. Although personality theory itself is not sufficient, it is very pertinent to the research and provides considerable possibilities for statistical analyzes. It was also chosen in view of the influence of traumatic experience on the values in question. The survey includes two groups of values: 18 terminal values and 18 instrumental values. The task of the subject is to rank each value from 1 (the most important) to 18 (the least important) within each group according to its importance.

The fundamental aim of using the Value Survey was to assess the values as declared by the subjects. Values here are interpreted as a way of expressing one's personality. They are stable features and undergo slow dynamic changes in the course of time, along with the changing and growing personality. However, they are stable and not susceptible to changes such as those influenced by temporary fear. This makes declared values good research data for comparing personality features, and they were used accordingly.

11.5 Results: Terminal Values

The three most highly rated terminal values are the following: family security, national security, and wisdom (Table 11.1). However, analysis of the averages indicates considerable differences in the ranking of these values. Family security is markedly more important than the other values; it is followed by national security and wisdom, and the remaining values are ranked less distinguishably between one another. The last value is an exciting life, and it also stands apart from other values at the bottom of the list.

The two groups being compared differ significantly in the position of three values: family security, a comfortable life, and happiness.

Variation comparison (Figure 11.1) indicates that the views of people exposed to trauma in early childhood are more differentiated in terms of the range of family security, pleasure, and an exciting life than those of people exposed to trauma in later

Table 11.1 Comparative Statistics: Terminal Values

Variable	Trauma in Childhood	Trauma in Adulthood	Difference
National security	2	2	0
Family security	1	1	0
Mature love	12	11	1
A comfortable life	8	13	−5
Wisdom	3	4	−1
A sense of accomplishment	14	14	0
Self-respect	5	5	0
A world at peace	4	3	1
True friendship	10	9	1
Pleasure	17	17	0
Inner harmony	7	6	1
Equality	13	12	1
Happiness	6	10	−4
A world of beauty	16	16	0
Social recognition	15	15	0
Freedom	9	7	2
Salvation	11	8	3
An exciting life	18	18	0

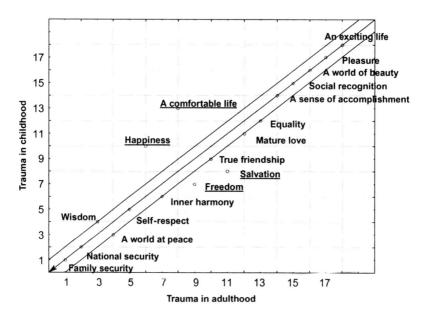

Figure 11.1 Terminal values hierarchy: Comparative presentation.

life. This is particularly visible in the case of family security. This absence of variation uniformity poses problems in interpreting the averages. People in Group 1 rank a comfortable life and happiness higher.

The order of the values shows a difference between the subjects in the two groups regarding the ranking of four values. People in Group 1 value happiness and a comfortable life more highly, and people in Group 2 value their freedom and salvation. Other values remain within the same range, assuming a difference of ±1.

This vividly brings us to the interpretation that people who in adult life experienced a loss of freedom and doubts concerning the choices they made (e.g., whether to engage in the fight for independence) place a greater value on their freedom and salvation, understood not only from the religious or moral perspective. People traumatized in childhood have a higher regard for happiness and a comfortable life. These are values experienced in a passive way, which is dependent on the environment, and typical of childhood experiences. Happiness is something that is lived and experienced; freedom is a value that one takes advantage of actively. It is noticeable that the ability to make use of freedom is acquired in adolescence, at which point it also becomes a value. In both cases, these values (above all freedom and a comfortable and happy life) are the situations that were lost with the experience of the trauma. This explains why the moment of trauma experience differentiates the groups with regard to declared values.

The visible grouping of values different from the average can easily be explained by means of the theory of complexes. This indicates a certain similarity of these data with those gathered in the word association experiment, for example, in which these contents appear subconsciously and are associated with one another (Jung, 1995). Here, the binding content is the trauma. A *complex*, which is created around the trauma, includes values. As has been mentioned, for people who were exposed to the trauma in early childhood, these values are their happiness and a comfortable life, whereas for those exposed to the trauma in later life, they are freedom and salvation (morality).

11.6 Results: Instrumental Values

Instrumental values are a system of moral and competence values, that is, the convictions that concern functioning in society, for example, following the code of law and competition. For these reasons, the system of instrumental values will take shape mainly in relationships and in the reflections of one's own activities.

Similarly, in this case, it is clear that extreme values stand out. The most important value is honesty, and after that comes responsibility (Table 11.2). The others are grouped in a less distinguishable structure, in which the most outstanding is obedient.

Statistical analysis and comparison of both groups by means of the Mann–Whitney test indicate considerable statistical differences in the values loving, cheerful, and self-controlled.

Table 11.2 Comparative Statistics: Instrumental Values

Variable	Trauma in Childhood	Trauma in Adulthood	Difference
Ambitious	4	3	1
Clean	12	13	−1
Intellectual	10	10	0
Loving	3	5	−2
Logical	7	6	1
Independent	15	12	3
Imaginative	14	16	−2
Responsible	2	2	0
Courageous	9	7	2
Self-controlled	5	8	−3
Broad-minded	17	14	3
Cheerful	13	17	−4
Helpful	6	4	2
Obedient	18	18	0
Honest	1	1	0
Polite	8	9	−1
Capable	16	16	1
Forgiving	11	11	0

Variation analysis shows that the views of people who were exposed to the trauma in early childhood are more differentiated than those who were exposed to the trauma in later life; this is in accordance with the terminal values analysis (Figure 11.2).

The order of the values reveals differences between the subjects in the two groups regarding the ranking of eight values, with the condition of ±1. People exposed to trauma in early childhood value the following more: independent, courageous, broad-minded, and helpful. People exposed to trauma in later life set greater store for the following: loving, imaginative, self-controlled, and cheerful.

The instrumental values that rank higher in Group 1 are the features that undergo the biggest disturbances in personality disorders. Symptoms like difficulties in building stable relationships with a proper feeling of independence, foreseeing activities, and freedom are responsible for the clinical picture of personality disorders. Instrumental values in Group 2 may be more closely connected with active symptoms of PTSD, such as hypervigilance and irritability.

This points to the interpretation that experiencing trauma, which can be accompanied by a sense of loss (e.g., the loss of one's current life), may result in giving higher priority to the instrumental values required in self-functioning. This indicates also that more desirable and expected forms of behavior that are more handicapped by disorder symptoms are ranked higher.

However, it seems worth drawing attention to the fact that the experience of trauma sometimes results in visible consequences that manifest in a completely unconscious way (i.e., consequences that develop before the emergence of the ability to remember and recall verbal memories). People with such symptoms obviously

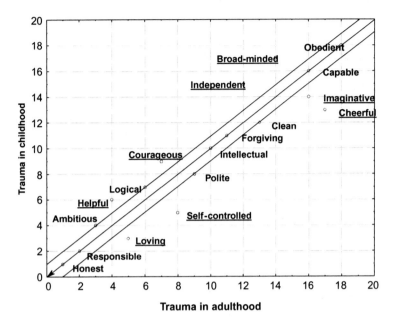

Figure 11.2 Instrumental values hierarchy: Comparative presentation.

function socially and make choices, such as when voting, under the influence of complexes focused around the trauma and concerning the related values (and also based on these values). Such situations reveal the importance of the consequences of the trauma and also of not working them through or letting them remain unconscious. They influence whole societies because the results of, for example, polls in one country influence the policies of others in many ways.

11.7 Conclusions

In 1939, well-known child development researchers (Bowlby, Miller, and Winnicott) wrote an open letter to the *British Medical Journal* in which they warned against the dramatic consequences of evacuating children under 5 years of age and pointed out the risk connected with separation, which would lead to psychological disorders (Winnicott, Miller, & Bowlby, 1939). At the same time, attention was focused on the fact that evacuation and the loss of their home caused less suffering to children older than 5 years (Winnicott, 2000).

The same cutoff age was adopted for this research. However, the adoption of this age was based on the development of verbal memory and the ability to recall events. The lack of this sort of memory and the lack of full memories (or fragmentary memories) indicate that a given experience cannot have a conscious influence on a person. It is also possible that the importance of the age limit of 5 years is connected with the unconscious (nonverbal) way that a child lives and the different mechanisms it uses in relationships up to that age.

For the people around, a child's consciousness of its life begins only when it can reflect on itself and understand the notion of I (Jung, 1991). However, this does not mean that earlier experience has no influence. What is more, other observations and the results of this research indicate that this influence is significant.

The results unequivocally confirmed the assumed thesis. The statistical value of the data surmounted expectations of the research; the analysis showed the very high statistical validity of the results. This practically proves undeniably that early life experience has a huge impact on the further consolidation of the personality structure.

The study was conducted on people who had experienced extreme stressors; nevertheless, the confirmation of such an impact shows the overall influence of the early years on later choices, emotions, relations, and so on. It seems significant that the period under study has a bearing on the whole of a person's later life and hence also that the trauma is experienced in its beginning, when the verbal memory is not yet developed and the experience cannot be remembered and then recollected. This was a considerable methodological challenge, but, when compared with the results obtained from people who experienced similar trauma in later life, the results gathered in this study made it possible to estimate the influence of the traumatic experience, on the one hand, and also the influence of the early years, on the other.

The study has a certain uniqueness: the fact that it compares people who were exposed to severe stress in their early childhood with those who suffered similarly in later years. Both groups had never been treated, and they lived in similar conditions after the trauma. They had never consulted a specialist, which precludes the possibility of their personality being influenced by a therapeutic experience. Both groups were gathered at random. All this contributes to the uniqueness of the research. It is impossible to imagine nowadays how one could repeat the study on a group of people who are known to have experienced trauma, especially in early childhood, and would not have undergone any therapy. The data gathered are statistically representative and can be transferred to other groups, such as casualties of accidents or people abused in childhood. By confirming the influence of the traumatic experience in the early period of childhood, we are also confirming its importance for the rest of life.

References

Allport, G. W., Vernon, P. E., & Lindzey, G. (1951). *Study of values*. Boston, MA: Houghton Mifflin Co..

Bilsky, W., & Schwartz, S. H. (1994). Values and personality. *European Journal of Personality*, 8, 163–181.

Brzozowski, P. (1989). *Skala Wartości (SW). Polska adaptacja value survey m. Rokeacha*. Warszawa: Polskie Towarzystwo Psychologiczne.

Domurat, A. (2009). Identyfikacja wartości osobistych w badaniach psychologicznych: *Wartości jako cele działań i wyborów*. Warszawa: Wydawnictwo Uniwersytetu Warszawskiego.

Jung, C. G. (1991). *The development of personality* (Vol. 17). London: Routledge.
Jung, C. G. (1995). Über die psychphysischen begleitercheinungen im assoziationsexperiment. In C. G. (1995). Jung (Ed.), *Experimentaelle untersuchungen* (Vol. 2). Walter-Verlag: Solothurn und Düsseldorf.
Kluckhohn, C. (1951). Values and value-orientations in the theory of action: An exploration in definition and classification. In T. Parsons & E. Shils (Eds.), *Toward a general theory of action (pp. 388–433)*. Cambridge, MA: Harvard University Press.
Kohn, M. L. (1969). Class and conformity: *Homewood, IL.* Dorsey Press.
Kohn, M. L., & Schooler, C. (1983). *Work and personality.* Norwood, NJ: Ablex.
Rokeach, M. (1973). *The nature of human values.* New York, NY: The Free Press.
Rokeach, M. (1979). *Understanding human values.* New York, NY: The Free Press.
Schwartz, S. H. (1992). Universals in the content and structure of values: Theory and empirical tests in 20 countries. In M. (1992). Zanna (Ed.), *Advances in experimental social psychology* (Vol. 25, pp. 1–65). New York, NY: Academic Press.
Schwartz, S. H. (2006). Basic human values: Theory, measurement, and applications. *Revue française de sociologie, 47*(4), 249–288.
Schwartz, S. H., & Boehnke, K. (2004). Evaluating the structure of human values with confirmatory factor analysis. *Journal of Research in Personality, 38,* 230–255.
Spranger, E., & Pigors, P. J. (1928). *Types of men: The psychology and ethics of personality.* Halle: M. Niemeyer.
Vernon, P., & Allport, G. W. (1931). A test for personal values. *Journal of Abnormal and Social Psychology, 26,* 231–248.
Winnicott, D. W. (2000). *Deprivation and deliquency.* London: Routledge.
Winnicott, D. W., Miller, E., & Bowlby, J. (1939). Letter. *British Medical Journal, 16,* 1202–1203.

12 Moving Beyond Childhood Adversity: Association Between Salutogenic Factors and Subjective Well-Being Among Adult Survivors of Trauma[*]

Shanta R. Dube[1], Vincent J. Felitti[2], Shobhana Rishi[3]

[1]National Center for Chronic Disease Prevention and Health Promotion, Centers for Disease Control and Prevention, Atlanta, GA, USA
[2]Department of Preventive Medicine, Southern California Permanente Medical Group (Kaiser Permanente), San Diego, CA, USA
[3]California Department of Education, Sacramento, CA, USA

12.1 Introduction

Medical and public health advances in recent times have contributed significantly to reducing morbidity and mortality throughout the life span, including the most notable, the reduction in childhood mortality due to infectious diseases (Centers for Disease Control and Prevention, 1999a, 1999b). Despite the overall efforts to improve health and well-being, the period of childhood and adolescence is still a precarious time when multiple types of experiences and exposures can impact development. To date, much research has been conducted to examine how early childhood adversity impacts early development and health later in life. The Adverse Childhood Experiences (ACE) Study is a large-scale epidemiological investigation of the long-term health impact of childhood trauma on adult health outcomes (Felitti et al., 1998).

Multiple reports from the ACE Study have demonstrated that childhood stressors in the form of abuse, neglect, and household dysfunction are related to physical and mental health problems that emerge in adolescence and persist into adulthood (Anda et al., 1999; Chapman et al., 2004; Dube, Cook, & Edwards, 2010; Dube et al., 2003, 2006, 2009; Felitti et al., 1998). Moreover, we now know that various types of abuse, neglect, and family dysfunction are common and highly interrelated. Biological plausibility of the ACE Study findings is documented in studies that have

---

[*] The findings and conclusions in this chapter are those of the authors and do not represent the views of the Centers for Disease Control and Prevention or the California Department of Education.

shown that exposure to childhood abuse and other forms of trauma in the childhood family environment are likely to activate the stress response, potentially disrupting the developing nervous, immune, and metabolic systems of children (DeBellis et al., 1999; Lehman, Taylor, Keife, & Seeman, 2005; Stein, Koverola, Hanna, Torchia, & McClarty, 1997; Teicher, Ito, Glod, Andersen, Dumont, & Ackerman, 1997). Thus, evidence from the ACE Study and other studies alike has provided insights into the childhood determinants of adverse health outcomes throughout the life span and the need for the primary prevention of these exposures.

12.2 Trauma Survivors and Salutogenesis

Despite what is now known about the negative health consequences associated with childhood trauma, it is well recognized that individuals who experience traumatic events in childhood go on to survive the experiences (Cortez et al., 2011), even when faced with the health sequelae. The salutogenic (health-promoting) paradigm suggests that humans possess an innate capacity to move toward health and well-being (Antonvsky, 1972, 1979, 1987, 1993, 1996). Within this paradigm, a salient distinction between health promotion and curative and preventive medicine can be made (Antonovsky, 1996). Salutogenesis is a stress resource–orientated concept, which focuses on assets, strengths, and motivation as a way to maintain and improve the movement toward health. Using this paradigm, a shift from the risk factor–disease (pathogenic) model permits the examination of health-promoting factors that accentuate a *positive* capability to identify problems and to activate *healthy* solutions that may help individuals overcome adversity and stress (Antonvsky, 1972, 1979, 1987, 1993, 1996).

Salutogenesis may encompass both modifiable behaviors and personal resources. For example, the uptake of physical activity and abstinence from smoking are well-established examples of health-promoting behaviors that have significant health benefits. Physical activity has been shown to have a number of salient positive health benefits, including reducing the risk of cardiovascular disease (United States Department of Health and Human Services, 2008). Smoking, which continues to be a leading cause of disease and death, is clearly a health risk behavior where never starting or quitting is key to promoting health and preventing disease (Department of Health and Human Services, 2004, 2012; Morita et al., 2007). Personal resources, such as intellectual capacity, emotional regulation, and social support, can be defined as assets (Glanz, 2002). Epidemiologic evidence has shown for years the positive impact of socioeconomic factors, such as educational level; persons with a high level of education have a lower probability of morbidity and mortality compared with those with lower levels of education (Koh, Piotrowski, Kumanyika, & Fielding, 2011). Social support has also gained significant attention in health promotion literature as an important factor in sustaining positive health outcomes, including longevity (Fiori, Antonucci, & Cortina, 2006).

Examining health-promoting factors in relation to subjective well-being, in particular health-related quality of life, is an important emerging area within the salutogenic paradigm. Self-reported subjective health appraisals reflect individuals' experience, internal processing, and feeling as they relate to multiple dimensions of health and well-being: biological, physical, social, emotional, mental, and intellectual. For example, in chronic disease prevention and health promotion, subjective health appraisals may provide a depth to understanding how individuals move toward positive and healthy ways of living, even when adversity or negative health outcomes are at large. The single-item measure of self-rated health (SRH), which is holistic and multidimensional, is one of the most widely used and simplest measure for health status. Researchers have consistently reported SRH to be a strong predictor of morbidity and mortality even after controlling for demographics, measures of health, and risk factors (Barsky, Cleary, & Klerman, 1992; Benyamini, Blumstein, Lusky, & Modan, 2003; Benyamini & Idler, 1999). However, most research in the area of SRH has focused on the association of risk factors with the lower end of the scale (poor/fair) at the expense of neglecting research into the association of salutary factors with the upper end of the scale (excellent/very good).

Given the increased recognition that childhood traumatic stress is widespread (Copeland, Keeler, Angold, & Costello, 2007), there is need to better understand the salutogenic model among adult survivors of trauma. Therefore, we sought to examine whether there is an association between four types of health-promoting factors (smoking abstinence, physical activity, social support, and educational attainment) with subjective well-being (good or excellent self-reported health), mean mental health component score (MCS), and physical health component score (PCS) from the Standard Form-36 (SF-36) among adult survivors of ACE. In addition, we examine protective associations between these factors and depressed affect because previous findings from the ACE Study found that persons with ACE are more likely to report depressed affect compared with persons with no ACE (Dube et al., 2001). We tested the hypothesis that, among adult survivors of childhood trauma, the health-promoting factors will be positively associated with good or excellent self-reported health and that there would be lower odds (protective) of depressed affect.

12.3 Methods

The data used for the present chapter are based on the ACE Study. The ACE Study is a collaboration between Kaiser Permanente's Health Appraisal Center (HAC) in San Diego, California, and the National Center for Chronic Disease Prevention and Health Promotion, Centers for Disease Control and Prevention, in Atlanta, Georgia. The objective of this study is to assess the impact of interrelated forms of childhood abuse, neglect, and family dysfunction on adult health status. The ACE Study was approved by the Institutional Review Boards of the Southern California Permanente Medical Group (Kaiser Permanente) and the Office of Human Research Protection, Department of Health and Human Services.

Methods of the study have been described in detail elsewhere (Felitti et al., 1998). Briefly, the study population included adult members of the health maintenance organization, Kaiser Health Plan in San Diego, California, and they received a standardized medical and biopsychosocial examination at Kaiser's HAC to obtain complete health assessments, rather than for symptom- or illness-based care, which were conducted in two waves. Wave 2 of the ACE Study was conducted between June and October 1997. The ACE Questionnaire was mailed 2 weeks after participants visited the HAC and included detailed information about childhood exposure to abuse (emotional, physical, or sexual), neglect (physical or emotional), and household dysfunction (parental separation or divorce, witnessing domestic violence, family substance abuse, incarcerated family members, or family mental illness). This information was then related to health outcomes and behaviors in adulthood.

12.3.1 Definitions of ACE and ACE Score

All questions about ACE (Table 12.1) pertained to the respondents' first 18 years of life. Questions adapted from the Conflict Tactics Scale (Straus & Gelles, 1990) had five response categories: never, once or twice, sometimes, often, or very often. The three types of childhood abuse measured included emotional, physical, or contact sexual abuse (Wyatt, 1985). Emotional and physical neglect was assessed using the Conflict Tactics Scale (Bernstein et al., 1994). In addition, the questionnaire dealt with five types of exposure to household dysfunction during childhood: exposure to substance abuse (Schoenborn, 1995), mental illness, violent treatment of mother or stepmother (Straus & Gelles, 1990), criminal behavior in the household, and parental separation/divorce. Respondents were defined as exposed to a category if they responded yes to the dichotomously coded question. The ACE were summed to create the ACE Score (range: 0–10). Operationalization of adult trauma survivors was based on reporting at least one category of ACE.

Of the 8667 respondents in Wave 2, a total of 7641 returned the SF-36. Of the 7641, 28 were excluded due to missing information about race and educational attainment, leaving a sample size of 7613. Because the aim of our study was to examine health-promoting factors among survivors of trauma, we subset our sample to those who reported at least one ACE ($n = 5069$). Because of missing information on items from SF-36 for the MCS and PCS used to examine mental and physical functioning, 165 were deleted. Therefore, the analysis examining MCS and PCS utilized a sample of 4904.

12.3.2 Health-Promoting Factors

Four variables were operationalized as health-promoting factors: physical activity, smoking abstinence, social support, and educational attainment. Physical activity was defined as engaging in any exercise for recreation or to keep in shape at least 1 day per week during the past 30 days for 20 min or more. Smoking abstinence included two groups: never smokers and former smokers, with current smokers as the referent. Never smokers were defined as respondents who reported no to the question, "Have you ever smoked 100 cigarettes in your life?" Former smokers were defined as respondents who reported smoking 100 cigarettes but currently did not smoke; current smokers were defined as respondents who reported smoking 100 cigarettes and currently smoking. Never smokers or former smokers were defined as not currently smoking. Social support was defined with the following question: "How many

Table 12.1 Definition and Prevalence (%) of Each Category of ACE Among Survivors

ACE	n = 5069
Abuse	%
Emotional	15.1
(Did a parent or other adult in the household …)	
1. Often or very often swear at you, insult you, or put you down?	
2. Sometimes, often, or very often act in a way that made you afraid that you might be physically hurt?	
Physical	39.3
(Did a parent or other adult in the household …)	
1. Sometimes, often, or very often push, grab, slap, or throw something at you?	
2. Ever hit you so hard that you had marks or were injured?	
Sexual	30.8
(Did an adult or person at least 5 years older ever …)	
1. Touch or fondle you in a sexual way?	
2. Have you touch their body in a sexual way?	
3. Attempt oral, anal, or vaginal intercourse with you?	
4. Actually have oral, anal, or vaginal intercourse with you?	
Neglect (Childhood Trauma Questionnaire (CTQ))	
Emotional	21.7
1. There was someone in my family who helped me feel important or special.	
2. I felt loved.	
3. People in my family looked out for each other.	
4. People in my family felt close to each other.	
5. My family was a source of strength and support.	
Physical	14.4
1. I didn't have enough to eat.	
2. I knew there was someone there to take care of me and protect me.	
3. My parents were too drunk or too high to take care of me.	
4. I had to wear dirty clothes.	
5. There was someone to take me to the doctor if I needed it.	
Household dysfunction	
Battered mother	19.1
(Was your mother (or stepmother) …)	
1. Sometimes, often, or very often pushed, grabbed, slapped, or had something thrown at her?	
2. Sometimes, often, or very often kicked, bitten, hit with a fist, or hit with something hard?	
3. Ever repeatedly hit over at least a few minutes?	
4. Ever threatened with or hurt by a knife or gun?	
Parental discord/divorce	35.9
1. Were your parents ever separated or divorced?	
Mental illness in household	30.1
1. Was a household member depressed or mentally ill? Or …	
2. Did a household member attempt suicide?	
Household substance abuse	41.6
1. Live with anyone who was a problem drinker or alcoholic? Or …	
2. Live with anyone who used street drugs?	
Incarcerated household member	8.9
Did a household member go to prison?	

close friends or relatives would help you with your emotional problems or feelings if you needed it?" Respondents who reported three or more family members or friends were defined as having social support. Educational attainment was defined as having a high school diploma or General Educational Diploma (GED), having some college or technical school, or being a college graduate; having no high school diploma was the referent. The total number of health-promoting factors was then developed into a score from 0 to 4, where 0–1 health-promoting factor was the referent.

12.3.3 Subjective Well-Being

Subjective well-being was examined using one item on self-reported general health (SRH). We dichotomized SRH to persons reporting good or excellent health with persons reporting fair or poor health as the referent. In addition, we use the SF-36 to examine the relationship between MCS and PCS with total number of health-promoting factors. The summary scores were calculated using questions for eight scales of the survey: physical functioning, role-physical, bodily pain, general health, vitality, social functioning, role-emotional, and mental health (Ware & Kosinski, 2001). The MCS and PCS can provide a better precision, smaller confidence intervals (CIs), and simpler analysis and interpretation (Ware & Kosinski, 2001).

12.3.4 Depressed Affect

Depressed affect was defined as a yes response to the question, "Have you had or do you now have depression or feel down in the dumps?" This measure was compared to a validated screening tool developed by the Rand Corporation for lifetime prevalence of major depression and dysthymia and was included in the ACE Study (Dube et al., 2001).

12.3.5 Statistical Analyzes

Adjusted odds ratios (ORs) and 95% CIs were obtained using logistic regression models. All logistic regression models included demographic variables (race, age, and sex) as covariates; reports of any disease at baseline (diabetes, cardiovascular disease, chronic obstructive pulmonary disease, hypertension, asthma) were also included in the models. All analyzes were conducted using SAS v9.2. In addition, we used General Linear Models to test for relationship between the MCS and the PCS with the total number of health-promoting factors.

12.4 Results

12.4.1 Demographics

The study population ($n = 5069$) included 55% women; the racial/ethnic distribution was nearly three-quarters (73%) White, 12% Hispanic, 7% Asian, 5% Black, and 0.4% Native American, with the remaining classified as Other. The mean age was

54.2 years (±14.9) with 78% reporting being either college graduates, technical school graduates, or having attended some college; 7% reported not completing high school.

Among adult survivors of childhood trauma, 41% reported growing up with household substance abuse, and 39% reported physical abuse. Emotional neglect was reported by 22% of adult survivors of childhood trauma (Table 12.1).

Fifty percent of adult trauma survivors engaged in physical activity in the past month, 90% reported not currently smoking, and 60% reported having three or more friends or family for support. For the health-promoting factors score, 5.1% reported factor 0–1, 23.3% reported factor 2, 43.8% reported factor 3, and 27.9% reported all four factors. Close to one-third (34.5%) reported depressed affect, and 78.3% reported having good or excellent health.

12.4.2 Health-Promoting Factors and Subjective Well-Being

Among adult survivors of childhood trauma, smoking abstinence, physical activity in the past month, educational level, and social support as individual factors as well as the total number of these health-promoting factors were associated positively with reporting good or excellent health. Persons were 30% more likely to report good or excellent health if they reported having three or more family or friends to support with emotional problems ($p < 0.05$). Persons were almost two times (OR: 1.8, 95% CI: 1.6–2.1) likely to report good or excellent health if they engaged in any physical activity in the past month. Persons not currently smoking also were more likely to report good or excellent health ($p < 0.05$). Educational attainment had a positive graded relationship to reporting good or excellent health; compared with persons with no high school diploma, those who completed high school or attained a GED were 50% more likely to report good or excellent health; those with some college were 60% more likely to report good or excellent health, and those with college degree were two times more likely to report good or excellent health ($p < 0.05$) (Table 12.2). In addition, as the total number of health-promoting factors increased, the odds of reporting good or excellent health also increased.

We found significant linear relationships with the health promotion factor score for both the MCS ($p < 0.001$) and PCS ($p < 0.001$). The mean MCS for 0–1 health-promoting factor was 47.9 (SD ± 10) compared with a mean MCS of 52.2 (SD ± 8) for all four health-promoting factors. Similarly for PCS, the mean was 46.4 (SD ± 10) for 0–1 health-promoting factor compared with a mean of 53.0 (SD ± 8) for all four health-promoting factors. A protective association of the health-promoting factors against depressed affect was observed for physical activity, smoking abstinence, and social support. As the total number of health-promoting factors increased, the odds of reporting depressed affect decreased.

12.5 Discussion

In public health, we strive for primary prevention of risk factors associated with disease and death using a model of pathogenesis. The approach uses the presence or absence of disease or health outcomes in relation to the presence or absence of an

Table 12.2 Adjusted[a,b] ORs for the Relationship Between Health-Promoting Factors with Self-Reported Health and Depressed Affect Among Adult Trauma Survivors ($n = 5069$)

Health-Promoting Factors	Adjusted ORs (95% CI)	
	Good or Excellent Self-Rated Health	Depressed Affect
Physical activity[a]		
No physical activity	1.0 (referent)	1.0 (referent)
Physical activity	1.8 (1.6–2.1)	0.82 (0.73–0.93)
Smoking status[a]		
Currently smokes	1.0 (referent)	1.0 (referent)
Does not currently smoke	1.6 (1.3–1.9)	0.67 (0.54–0.82)
Social support[a]		
Zero to two family or friends	1.0 (referent)	1.0 (referent)
Three or more family members or friends	1.3 (1.2–1.5)	0.78 (0.68–0.88)
Education[a]		
No high school diploma	1.0 (referent)	1.0 (referent)
High school diploma or GED	1.5 (1.2–2.0)	1.0 (0.77–1.3)
Some college	1.6 (1.3–2.1)	1.1 (0.84–1.4)
College graduate	2.1 (1.6–2.7)	1.2 (0.91–1.5)
Health-promoting factor score[b]		
0–1	1.0 (referent)	1.0 (referent)
2	1.5 (1.2–2.0)	0.83 (0.62–1.1)
3	2.4 (1.8–3.2)	0.66 (0.50–0.86)
4	4.3 (3.2–5.8)	0.55 (0.41–0.73)

[a]Models include sex, age at baseline, race, physical activity, smoking abstinence, social support resources, educational attainment, and reports of any disease.
[b]Model includes sex, age at baseline, race, and reports of any disease.

exposure. Although this approach is meritorious in its own right and has led to many major public health successes (Centers for Disease Control and Prevention, 1999a, 1999b), some limitations exist. In particular, it is based on an infectious disease model, which strives to prevent the presence of an infectious agent and subsequently the related disease. However, the model may not be as applicable to chronic diseases or in instances when psychosocial issues are in play because in many instances health may be considered a biopsychosocial continuum and does not merely represent the absence or presence of a disease (Antonovsky, 1996). The salutogenic approach utilizes an alternative model and can be used to promote health whether or not disease is present. For trauma survivors, a salutogenic paradigm (Figure 12.1) would permit a method to examining the factors that may move individuals toward healing, recovery, and well-being even in the presence of disease.

Beyond the immediate impact of witnessing or experiencing trauma among children, many long-term health sequelae are associated with ACE that span into adulthood. Once experienced, the trauma cannot be prevented or removed, and the health sequelae must be addressed. The data presented here on trauma survivors suggest that certain health-promoting factors may be beneficial to positive subjective

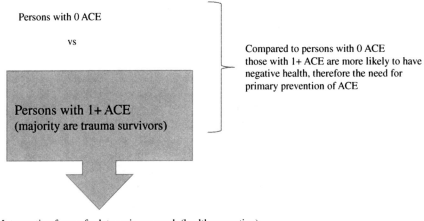

Figure 12.1 Model of salutogenesis for trauma survivors.

well-being. Given that a large proportion of the population may go through life with unresolved childhood traumatic experiences (Cortez et al., 2011), factors associated with subjective well-being may inform current programs that address both trauma and sequelae associated with trauma.

Both the promotive and protective association of modifiable behaviors, such as smoking abstinence and physical activity, and personal resources, such as education and social support, are critical to overall well-being among trauma survivors. In the present study, never smoking or quitting smoking and engaging in past-month physical activity were positively associated with good/excellent health and protective of reporting depressed affect. This is not surprising because smoking continues to be the leading cause of death, disease, and disability, and the mechanism by which tobacco smoke causes disease is now better understood (United States Department of Health and Human Services, 2010). Therefore, continued efforts to prevent smoking and to help trauma survivors quit smoking are needed. Physical activity also has both a promotive and a protective association with the outcomes examined in the study, as has been shown. The findings are supported by reviews of studies showing the physiological and psychological benefits of exercise, including the release of endorphins that may help to regulate negative affect (Biddle & Asare, 2011; Fox, 1999).

Social support was associated with good/excellent health and protective of depressed affect among trauma survivors. This finding is not surprising and is supported by a separate study of trauma survivors that reported that social networks are critical in the healing and recovery process (Cortez et al., 2011). In that study, findings further suggested that the quality of the support is also an important consideration (Cortez et al., 2011). For example, listening, being validated, and the need to have contact with others who have shared similar experiences may be critical elements in seeking and attaining social support (Cortez et al., 2011). Based on our findings, further research on both the number and quality of the social and emotional support is needed to fully understand the benefits of social networks for trauma survivors.

Education is one of the leading social determinants of health (Koh et al., 2011), and the impact of education level on health and well-being is underscored by numerous epidemiological studies. A clear positive relationship between high levels of education and positive health, social, and behavioral outcomes (Cohen, Doyle, & Baum, 2006) has been established. Building the capacity for problem-solving, critical thinking, and being resourceful begins early in the life span. In the present study, we found promotive elements of educational level on good or excellent SRH. It is possible that the economic benefits of education may support the resources needed for coping with adversity (Schuller et al., 2004).

In addition to examining the four health-promoting factors separately, a health-promoting score was utilized to assess the association between the total number of salutogenic factors with positive well-being. The data indicate a strong association between the total number of health-promoting factors and positive health outcomes, including mental and physical functioning, and the health-promoting score appears to be protective of reporting depressed affect; the strength of the associations increase as the health-promoting score increases. Although the present study cannot provide in-depth information on how and why trauma survivors may have to quit smoking, the extent and quality of physical activity, or the quality of the social support, it does help in understanding what personal resources and modifiable health behaviors are important in positive well-being.

There are several limitations of the study findings. First, current findings suggest simply that there are correlations between health-promoting factors and the outcomes examined among trauma survivors and cannot provide any temporal relationship. Further research studies to examine the benefits of these and other health-promoting factors among trauma survivors are needed, particularly in a longitudinal design. Second, the findings are based on self-reported data and are subject to some recall and reporting bias. Third, other health-promoting factors were not measured in the ACE Study; dietary assessments, the use of complementary and alternative therapies, and other lifestyle and self-management resources may be salient to examine.

Despite these limitations, the present study suggests that utilizing a model of salutogenesis may be informative for trauma survivors because it provides an opportunity to address all levels of prevention. The best possible scenario is completely preventing childhood trauma from occurring because, once it has occurred, childhood trauma cannot be removed. Given that a large proportion of individuals experience some form of childhood trauma, taking a holistic approach to facilitate a state of health and a process of well-being is useful. In the present study, among trauma survivors, we were able to identify four health-promoting factors that have been identified previously in the literature: physical activity, smoking abstinence, education attainment, and social support. Although we do not know to what extent these factors assisted in the healing and recovery of the ACE Study cohort, epidemiologically, we did observe that these particular health-promoting factors were associated with positive subjective well-being. Our findings may also inform health promotion integration into clinical practice (Jonas, 2000). Thus, expanded research in the area of salutogenesis among trauma survivors is needed in order to identify other key health-promoting and resiliency factors associated with healing and recovery.

References

Anda, R. F., Croft, J. B., Felitti, V. J., Nordenberg, D., Giles, W. H., Williamson, D. F., et al. (1999). Adverse childhood experiences and smoking during adolescence and adulthood. *Journal of the American Medical Association, 282*, 1652–1658.

Antonovsky, A. (1972). Breakdown: A needed fourth step in the armamentarium of modern medicine. *Social Science and Medicine, 6*, 537–544.

Antonovsky, A. (1979). *Health, stress and coping*. San Francisco, CA: Jossey-Bass.

Antonovsky, A. (1987). *Unraveling the mystery of health*. San Francisco, CA: Jossey-Bass.

Antonovsky, A. (1993). The structure and properties of the sense of coherence scale. *Social Science and Medicine, 36*, 725–733.

Antonovsky, A. (1996). The salutogenic model as a theory to guide health promotion. *Health Promotion International, 11*, 11–18.

Barsky, A. J., Cleary, P. D., & Klerman, G. L. (1992). Determinants of perceived health status of medical outpatients. *Social Science and Medicine, 34*, 1147–1154.

Benyamini, Y., Blumstein, T., Lusky, A., & Modan, B. (2003). Gender differences in the self-rated health—mortality association: Is it poor self-rated health that predicts mortality or excellent self-rated health that predicts survival? *The Gerontologist, 43*, 396–405.

Benyamini, Y., & Idler, E. L. (1999). Community studies reporting association between self-rated health and mortality: Additional studies, 1995–1998. *Research on Aging, 21*, 392–401.

Bernstein, D. P., Fink, L., Handelsman, L., Foote, J., Lovejoy, M., Wenzel, K., et al. (1994). Initial reliability and validity of a new retrospective measure of child abuse and neglect. *American Journal of Psychiatry, 151*, 1132–1136.

Biddle,, S. J., & Asare, M. (2011). Physical activity and mental health in children and adolescents: A review of reviews. *Public Health Nutrition, 2*, 411–418.

Centers for Disease Control and Prevention, (1999a). Ten great public health achievements— United States, 1900–1999. *Morbidity and Mortality Weekly Report, 48*(12), 241–243.

Centers for Disease Control and Prevention, (1999b). Achievements in public health, 1900–1999: Changes in the public health system. *Morbidity and Mortality Weekly Report, 48*(50), 1141–1147.

Chapman, D. P., Whitfield, C. L., Felitti, V. J., Dube, S. R., Edwards, V. J., & Anda, R. F. (2004). Adverse childhood experiences and the risk of depressive disorders in adulthood. *Journal of Affect Disorders, 82*, 217–225.

Cohen, S., Doyle, W. J., & Baum, A. (2006). Socioeconomic status is associated with stress hormones. *Psychosomatic Medicine, 68*, 414–420.

Copeland, W. E., Keeler, G., Angold, A., & Costello, E. J. (2007). Traumatic events and post-traumatic stress in childhood. *Archives of General Psychiatry, 64*, 577–584.

Cortez, P., Dumas, T., Joyce, J., Olson, D., Peters, S., Todahl, J., et al. (2011). Survivor voices: Co-learning, re-connection, and healing through community action research and engagement (CARE). *Progress in community health partnerships: Research, education and action, 2011*, 133–142.

DeBellis, M. D., Keshavan, M. S., Clark, D. B., Casey, B. J., Giedd, J. N., Boring, A. M., et al. (1999). Developmental traumatology. Part II: Brain development. *Biological Psychiatry, 45,* 1271–1284.

Dube, S. R., Anda, R. F., Felitti, V. J., Chapman, D., Williamson, D. F., & Giles, W. H. (2001). Childhood abuse, household dysfunction and the risk of attempted suicide throughout the life span: Findings from adverse childhood experiences study. *Journal of the American Medical Association, 286,* 3089–3096.

Dube, S. R., Cook, M. L., & Edwards, V. J. (2010). Health related outcomes of adverse childhood experiences in Texas, 2002. *Preventing Chronic Diseases, 7*(3), A52. <http://www.cdc.gov/pcd/issues/2010/may/09_0158.htm> Accessed 6.03.2012.

Dube, S. R., Fairweather, D., Pearson, W. S., Felitti, V. J., Anda, R. F., & Croft, J. B. (2009). Cumulative childhood stress and autoimmune diseases in adults. *Psychosomatic Medicine, 71,* 243–250.

Dube, S. R., Felitti, V. J., Dong, M, Chapman, D. P., Giles, W. H., & Anda, R. F. (2003). Childhood abuse, neglect, and household dysfunction and the risk of illicit drug use: The adverse childhood experiences study. *Pediatrics, 111,* 564–572.

Dube, S. R., Miller, J. W., Brown, D. W., Giles, W. H., Felitti, V. J., Dong, M., et al. (2006). Adverse childhood experiences and the association with ever using alcohol and initiating alcohol use during adolescence. *Journal of Adolescent Health, 38,* 444.e1–444.e10.

Felitti, V. J., Anda, R. F., Nordenberg, D., Williamson, D. F., Spitz, A. M., & Edwards, V. (1998). Relationship of childhood abuse and household dysfunction to many of the leading causes of death in adults. *American Journal of Preventive Medicine, 14,* 245–258.

Fiori, K. L., Antonucci, T. C., & Cortina, K. S. (2006). Social network typologies and mental health among older adults. *The Journals of Gerontology Series B: Psychological Sciences and Social Sciences, 61B,* 25–32.

Fox, K. R. (1999). The influence of physical activity on mental well-being. *British Journal of Sports Medicine, 45,* 886–895.

Glanz, K., Rimer, B. K., & Lewis, F. M. (2002). *Health behavior and health education: theory, research, and practice.* 3rd Edition. Jossey, San Francisco: John Wiley & Sons.

Jonas, S. (2000). *Talking about health and wellness with patients: Integrating health promotion and disease prevention into your practice.* New York, NY: Springer.

Koh, H. K., Piotrowski, J. J., Kumanyika, S., & Fielding, J. E. (2011). Healthy people: A 2020 vision for the social determinants approach. *Health Education and Behavior, 38,* 551–557.

Lehman, B. J., Taylor, S. E., Keife, C. I., & Seeman, T. E. (2005). Relation of childhood socioeconomic status and family environment to adult metabolic functioning in the CARDIA Study. *Psychosomatic Medicine, 67,* 846–854.

Morita, I., Nakagaki, H., Kato, K., Murakami, T., Tsuboi, S., Hayashizaki, J., et al. (2007). Salutogenic factors that may enhance lifelong oral health in an elderly Japanese population. *Gerodontology, 24,* 47–51.

Schuller, T., Preston, J., Hammond, C., Brassett-Grundy, A., & Bynner, J. (2004). *The benefits of learning: The impact of education on health, family life, and social capital.* New York, NY: RoutledgeFalmer.

Shoenborn, C.A. (1995). Exposure to alcoholism in the family: United States, 1998. Advance data no. 205. Hyattsville, MD: National Center for Health Statistics, 1995. *Vital Health Stat,* 16(21). DHHS Publication No. (PHS)95-1880.

Stein, M. B., Koverola, C., Hanna, C., Torchia, M. G., & McClarty, B. (1997). Hippocampal volume in women victimized by childhood sexual abuse. *Psychological Medicine, 27,* 951–959.

Straus, M., & Gelles, R. J. (1990). *Physical violence in American families: Risk factors and adaptations to violence in 8,145 families*. New Brunswick, NJ: Transaction Press.

Teicher, M. H., Ito, Y., Glod, C. A., Andersen, S. L., Dumont, N., & Ackerman, E. (1997). Preliminary evidence for abnormal cortical development in physically and sexually abused children using EEG coherence and MRI. *Annals of the New York Academy of Sciences, 821*, 160–175.

United States Department of Health and Human Services, (2008). *Physical activity guidelines for Americans* Available at: <http://www.health.gov/paguidelines/pdf/paguide.pdf> Accessed 07.06.12.

United States Department of Health and Human Services, (2010). *How tobacco smoke causes disease: The biology and behavioral basis for smoking-attributable disease*. Atlanta, GA: Centers for Disease Control and Prevention. Available at: <http://www.cdc.gov/tobacco/data_statistics/sgr/2010/index.htm> Accessed June 03.06.12.

United States Department of Health and Human Services, Office of the Surgeon General, (2004). *The health consequences of smoking: A report of the surgeon general*. Atlanta, GA: U.S. Department of Health and Human Services, CDC.

United States Department of Health and Human Services, Office of the Surgeon General, (2012). *Preventing tobacco use among youth and young adults: A report of the surgeon general*. Atlanta, GA: U.S. Department of Health and Human Services, CDC.

Ware, J. E., & Kosinski, M. (2001). Interpreting SF-36 summary health measures: A response. *Quality of Life Research, 10*, 405–413.

Wyatt, G. E. (1985). The sexual abuse of Afro-American and white American women in childhood. *Child Abuse and Neglect, 9*, 507–519.

13 Working with Unconscious and Explicit Memories in Psychodynamic Psychotherapy in Patients with Chronic Depression

Svenja Taubner

Institute for Psychology, University of Kassel, Kassel and International Psychoanalytic University Berlin, Berlin, Germany

13.1 Introduction

Psychoanalytic theory understands psychopathology within a developmental framework. Mental disorders like depression are seen as rooted in the individual past of a patient, that is, either as a residuum of early experience or as the expression of primitive modes of psychic functioning (Fonagy & Target, 2003). Within this framework, psychoanalytic concepts focus on the consequences of early interactions with significant others. These are thought to not only influence the development of psychic functioning but also build up the content of the individual self. The self as the subjectively experienced part of a psyche is seen as an integration of representations. These representations are memories of past interactions with others that shape how we experience ourselves and others in the present. Being part of the implicit memory, representations function as schemas that operate below consciousness. Whenever an individual takes part in a social interaction, representations serve as knowledge base and form expectations. Different terms have been used in psychoanalytic theory to name psychic representations: Kernberg (1984) focused on the dissociation of positive and negative self-object-affect triads in the borderline personality organization. Stern (2000) described the normal process of storing repeated infant–caregiver experiences in the episodic memory as "representations of interactions that have been generalized" (RIGs). In Stern's view, RIGs create an unconscious expectation of the other ("mother will behave in a way as she has behaved before"), but new experiences with significant others can change RIGs. The older an individual becomes, the more interactions will contribute to the formation of RIGs, which in turn will lead to a decreased changeability of the representations. The unique contribution of Sandler and Sandler's (1998) concept of inner self-object relations such as fantasies, thoughts, and the like that serve as pattern or template for any psychic activity, is how internalized representations form behavior. Internal objects push an individual unconsciously to repeat past interactions by forcing others in the roles of their internal objects and thus creating perception identity with the inner and the outer worlds.

In the present paper, the representational theory of inner working models (IWMs) of attachment will be applied because it is empirically well validated. After a brief introduction to attachment theory, this chapter focuses on the question of how depression can be understood from the perspective of attachment theory. Furthermore, I shall address if and how psychic representations in depressed patients can be changed in psychoanalytic psychotherapy from a recent psychotherapy study.

13.2 Representations of Early Attachment Experiences

Attachment theory describes a biological system with a survival function that is activated under pressure, separation, and danger (Bowlby, 1969). An activated attachment system elicits attachment behavior in children (approaching, seeking contact, and maintaining contact), which in turn leads to caregiving behavior by adults. Repeated sequences of attachment signals and corresponding caregiving behavior are internalized and later on become mentally accessible. Internalized attachment experiences called IWMs of attachment serve as generalized expectations and organizing intrapsychic structures. If caregivers provide security and protection, this paternal behavior will be complemented and later replaced on a representational level by an inner feeling of security and self-worth (Bretherton, 1999; Bretherton & Munholland, 2008; Main, 1995a). Therefore, attachment experiences develop into psychic structures with lifelong consequences. Thereby, the internalized expectancies mirror strategies that used to enable the best way to satisfy the attachment needs (Grossmann & Grossmann, 2006). If caregivers primarily act sensitively with responsive availability, the child will most likely internalize the experience that his or her need for protection and comfort has been adequately satisfied (secure IWM). Some children experience that their attachment signals are not or not adequately answered by their caregivers. This can lead to a reduced attachment signal (insecure–avoidant IWM) or attachment behavior that is ambivalent (insecure–ambivalent IWM) due to an insecurity about the availability of the caregiver (Bowlby, 2002). Furthermore, a secure IWM entails (unconscious) beliefs that, in principle, the individual is capable to create a feeling of safety in different social contexts, either intrapsychic or interpersonal. Therefore, securely attached individuals have a high flexibility in social interactions, whereas insecure IWMs lead to rigid interpersonal behavior. If strategies to deal with attachment-related stress fail because the attachment figure itself acts as the source of fear (e.g., in the context of abuse), this leads to states of helplessness and disorientation. A breakdown of regulation strategies can be observed in infants and has been described as disorganized attachment or unresolved trauma in adults, respectively. Main (1995a) described the observations of disorganized infants as "look of fear with nowhere to go." Thus, attachment theory provides a framework to understand why the lack of care, the separation from the attachment figure, and abuse can have lifelong consequences. Indeed, longitudinal and resilience research could demonstrate that secure attachment serves as a protective factor, whereas insecure attachment is regarded as a risk factor for psychological development (Egle, Hoffmann, & Steffens, 1997). Attachment security mediates the relationship between abuse and later psychopathology in children and can therefore be regarded as a "risk buffer" (Alink, Cicchetti, Kim, & Rogosch, 2009). But, of course, insecure attachment does not automatically lead to psychopathology, and secure attachment is not a guarantee of mental health (Sroufe, Carlson, Levy, & Egeland, 1999).

13.3 Insecure Attachment, Loss, and Depression

Severe psychopathology like depression has been linked to early disturbances in the caregiver–child interaction. Thus, attachment theory may be highly relevant in the understanding of the etiology of depression (Bowlby, 1980). Adopting a diathesis-stress perspective, Bowlby (1980) claimed that increases in depressive symptoms should most likely occur when vulnerable individuals (those with certain insecure attachment orientations) experience stressors that test and strain their relationships. Such experiences can increase depressive symptoms by enhancing negative beliefs about the self (as being someone unworthy of love and support) or by accentuating negative beliefs about others (as being unloving and unsupportive partners). The experiences of early loss, separation, and rejection by the parent or caregiver (conveying the message that the child is unlovable) may all lead to insecure IWMs (Dozier, Stovall-Mcclough, & Albus, 2008).

Empirically, the association between attachment and depression has been mainly assessed in retrospect. The gold standard for assessing adult attachment is based on narrative assessment. This tradition uses interview assessments and classifies attachment through the examination of the person's state of mind with respect to attachment as expressed in linguistic qualities of the narratives (Main, 1995b). Classification falls into two main attachment groups: organized/resolved and disorganized/unresolved. Disorganized/unresolved individuals are flooded with painful affect, often evidenced through verbal descriptions of intense fear or linguistic disorientation (Main, 1995a). Studies using the Adult Attachment Interview (AAI) (George, Kaplan, & Main, 1984), which have examined both adults and adolescents, have yielded inconsistent results concerning depression (Dozier et al., 2008). However, small sample sizes and different diagnostic, inclusion and exclusion criteria have probably contributed to the contradictory findings. Adult depression has been related to insecure–avoidant (Patrick et al., 1994), insecure–ambivalent attachment representation (Cole-Detke and Kobak, 1996) or both (Mcmahon et al., 2006), and unresolved trauma (Fonagy et al., 1996). Dozier and colleagues (2008) suggest that internalizing and externalizing dimensions in depression account for these differences. Harris, Brown, and Bifulco (1990) could demonstrate that timing is critical with regard to possible consequences of early losses of the mother: 42% of the girls who had lost their mothers before the age of 11 developed a depression, whereas only 14% of the girls who had lost their mothers after the age of 11 suffered from depression. More severe depressive symptoms have also been reported in animal experiments for early childhood trauma in comparison to trauma in adolescence (Zalsman, 2010).

IWMs, as described, are likely to reflect repeated associations between the proximity of attachment figures and both internal needs and external signs of threat, mediated through amygdala, nucleus accumbens, prefrontal cortex, and hippocampus (Hofer, 2006). Animal studies suggest that limbic structures are involved in attachment deprivation (Insel, 1997). Maternal grooming in rodents effects glucocorticol receptor gene expression underlying hippocampal and hypothalamic-pituitary-adrenocortical axis (Weaver et al., 2004). This result has recently been replicated for human survivors of childhood abuse (Mcgowan et al., 2009). Structural neuroimaging studies show reduced hippocampus and amygdala volumes in patients reporting traumatic attachment histories (Tebartz van Elst et al., 2003; Wignall et al., 2004). In sum, IWMs of attachment are most probably encoded in nonsymbolic procedural parts of the brain, making them difficult or requiring more time to change.

13.4 Psychodynamic Treatment of Pathological Grief and Depression

Although stable changes after short-term psychotherapy are not expected for disorders with recurring episodes like major depressive illnesses (Westen, Novotny, & Thompson-Brenner, 2004), long-term psychodynamic treatments have been effective in changing these more severe psychopathologies (Leichsenring & Rabung, 2008) and have even demonstrated to change IWMs (Levy et al., 2006). From a psychoanalytic point of view, relationship representations linked with childhood experience are thought to influence any interpersonal social expectation and therefore reemerge in the course of psychodynamic treatment (i.e., in a transference relationship) (Westen & Gabbard, 2002). The objectives of psychodynamic psychotherapy with depressed patients are to work toward a stable modification of social expectations and affect regulation strategies related to the depressive pathology by reactivating IWMs within the therapeutic relationship. The distinctive features of psychodynamic therapies, in contrast to other psychotherapies, include the following (Shedler, 2010): (1) focus on affect and the expression of emotion, (2) exploration of attempts to avoid the aspects of experience, (3) identification of recurring themes, (4) discussion of past experiences, (5) focus on interpersonal relations and on the therapeutic relationship, and (6) explorations of wishes, dreams, and fantasies. Psychoanalytic interaction can be characterized by three domains (Castonguay & Beutler, 2006; Kernberg, 1984): First, the therapist reacts mainly to the patient's initiative and serves as a secure base for patients to explore their mental world; second, the main task is to create meaning for difficult to understand behavior or symptoms; and third, therapeutic change is achieved by enabling the patient to think about mental states of self and others instead of using defense mechanisms (e.g., the mourning of loss and trauma).

The third domain has recently been addressed mostly within the concept of mentalization, that is, the capacity to perceive and understand oneself and others' behavior in terms of mental states such as feelings, beliefs, intentions, and desires (Fonagy, Target, Steele, & Steele, 1998). Mentalizing involves two modes: (1) an implicit or nonconscious process that is mainly procedural, enabling the individual to interpret nonverbal body language or emotional expressions and (2) an explicit or conscious one, which is closely related to the individual's verbal ability (Allen, 2003). Furthermore, mentalization also links a cognitive activity such as attributing mental states (as in theory-of-mind assessments) with an affective, empathizing activity that helps to connect mental states and emotions to behavior. It therefore makes one's own behavior and emotional experiences and that of others meaningful and predictable (Bateman & Fonagy, 2004). According to Fonagy and Target (2003), mentalization develops in the context of early attachment relationships. In normal development, infants begin to understand the self as a psychological agent by experiencing that their momentary affective states are adequately and markedly mirrored by the caregiver. Hence, through the process of exploring their own minds through the mind of the attachment figure, infants begin to develop a mental representation of their own emotional state as a feeling that facilitates emotional awareness and affect regulation (Allen, Fonagy, & Bateman, 2008). Fonagy and colleagues (Fonagy, Gergely, & Target, 2007; Sharp & Fonagy, 2008) postulate that secure attachment facilitates emotional attunement between caregiver and child and allows the development of the child's reflectiveness. Mentalization can "mature" and develop (e.g., through the secure base of a therapeutic alliance), and it can be undermined by adverse experiences such as early attachment trauma that may lead to deficits or distortions of mentalization (Levinson & Fonagy, 2004; Sharp, 2006). Regarding the dynamic interaction between psychopathology and mentalization, Fonagy et al. (1998) showed empirically that patients who suffered from early attachment trauma were more likely to develop a borderline personality disorder if moderated by low mentalization (Fonagy, 2000; Fonagy, Target, Gergely, Allen, & Bateman, 2003). Impaired mentalization in patients who suffered trauma may be the result of a defensive withdrawal from the mental world that in turn makes it more difficult for the individual to cope with the traumatic experience.

The capacity to think about mental states of self and others as a metacognitive ability is considered to be a key factor for therapeutic change (Fonagy and Bateman, 2006). In some patients, it has to be fostered first in order to allow psychotherapeutic change to happen eventually, such as in personality disorders (Fonagy, Gergely, Jurist, & Target, 2002). In less-disturbed patients, who are able to mentalize, more work may be needed on the content of their representations (Fonagy, Moran, Edgcumbe, Kennedy, & Target, 1993). This is most likely the case with patients with depressive disorders.

13.5 Changes of Reflective Abilities and Attachment Disorganization in Depressed Patients After Long-Term Psychoanalytic Psychotherapy

The Hanse-Neuro-Psychoanalysis-Study investigated psychic and neural changes of 20 chronically depressed patients in comparison to a healthy control group

(Buchheim et al., 2008). Patients had a history of an average of 5.5 major depression episodes, the age of onset of depression ranged from 8 to 50 years ($m = 20$, SD $= 9.5$). Fifty percent of the patients also fulfilled the criteria for anxiety disorders, and 65% had comorbid personality disorder. Sixteen state-licensed psychoanalysts, working in private offices, participated in the study. This group can be considered as highly experienced with a mean of 22.4 years (SD $= 7.9$) practicing as psychoanalysts. The psychoanalysts offered psychoanalytic therapy using the couch setting. The number of sessions per week varied from two (nine cases), through three (nine cases), and to four (two cases) per week.

In this study, psychoanalytic concepts about the causes and maintenance of depression were assessed and used to create individualized stimuli for brain research. Experiments focused either on dysfunctional repetitive relationship patterns (as conceptualized with the operationalized psychodynamic diagnosis) or on attachment disorders (Kessler, Wiswede, & Taubner, 2012).

In this study, it could be demonstrated that neural functioning in response to individualized stimuli referring to social expectancies and attachment experiences differed in patients and controls (Kessler et al., 2011) and changed or normalized after long-term psychodynamic treatment (Buchheim, George, & Taubner, 2012). In this chapter, attachment experiences of loss and mentalizing abilities are the focus of attention. The capacity to mentalize was measured according to the Reflective-Functioning (RF) Scale (Fonagy et al., 1998) from AAI transcripts. The AAI consists of 20 questions asked in a set order with standardized probes. Individuals are asked to describe their childhood relationship with their parents, choosing five adjectives to characterize each relationship and supporting these descriptors with specific memories. To elicit attachment-related information, they are asked how their parents responded to them when they were in physical or emotional distress (e.g., during times when they were upset, injured, and sick as children). They are also asked about memories of separation, loss, experiences of rejection, and times when they might have felt threatened, including, but not limited to, those involving physical and sexual abuse. The interview requires the participants to reflect on their parents' styles of parenting and then they consider how childhood experiences with their parents may have influenced their personality. The RF Scale assesses whether participants understand attachment-related experiences in terms of mental states (Fonagy et al., 1998). Statements are coded on an 11-point scale from antireflective (-1) to exceptionally reflective (Brethewrton & Munholland, 2008). Qualitative markers of RF are the acknowledgment of opacity of mental states, separateness of minds, developmental aspects, and efforts to understand the behavior in terms of mental states. RF coding was done by two trained and reliable coders; one was blinded. Interrater reliability in 75% of transcripts was high (Cronbach's alpha, $r = 0.86$). Before starting therapy, the general level of RF was not impaired in comparison to the control group: Mean RF scores were 4.0 (SD $= 1.0$) for patients and 3.6 (SD $= 1.5$) for controls, but patients showed significantly lower reflective skills when thinking about depression-related topics, especially when dealing with loss (Taubner, Buchheim, Kächele, Kessler, & Staun, 2011). When being asked to describe their individual thoughts and feelings concerning the loss of a significant other, many patients were unable to maintain their basic reflective abilities (Staun, Kessler, Buchheim, Kachele, & Taubner, 2010). One patient, for example, reacted with disavowal ("I do not want to talk about this anymore"), presumably because his affects became too strong to continue to reflect on his loss. Another patient attributed mental states that appeared inappropriate when talking about the loss of her grandmother: "I came an hour too late to say goodbye to her and there was a lot of hostility from my family but I just felt happy." In the third example, a patient reacted with hostility toward the interviewer when being asked about her feelings when her father died. Inappropriate attributions and hostile behavior during the interview are coded as antireflective and refer to a breakdown of reflective capacities. After 20 months of psychoanalytic psychotherapy, patients improved their global RF significantly to $M = 4.4$ (SD = 0.9), but they still had lower RF scores for loss in relation to their global RF scores $[t(17) = 2.76, p = 0.014]$ (Taubner, Buchheim et al., 2011; Taubner, Kessler, Buchheim, & Staun, 2011).

Attachment representations or IWMs were assessed with the Adult Attachment Projective (AAP) Picture System (George, West, & Pettem, 1999). This projective test is designed to gradually activate the attachment system by using eight pictures with attachment-related contents. Participants are asked to tell stories about each picture. This procedure is meant to allow assessing the content of their IWM. The AAP was validated on the AAI but allows for a more time-effective assessment (Buchheim et al., 2003). Pictures consist of line drawings of different valence: Monadic pictures mirror scenes where no attachment figure is available, such as loneliness, breakdown, loss, and threat, whereas dyadic pictures address themes like separation, comfort, and illness. Narrations were audiotaped and transcribed. In the patient sample, the majority of transcripts were coded with unresolved attachment trauma or disorganized attachment ($n = 11$). Nine patients showed organized strategies to cope with attachment-related stress in their narratives; those were mainly insecure avoidant, and only one patient was securely attached. Qualitative markers for attachment trauma are so-called segregated systems markers that mirror a mental breakdown or disregulation of affect. To code a trauma marker, the hypothetical character in the patient's narrative must be trapped in an unsolvable and potentially dangerous situation with no capacity to act, to seek for help, to protect him or her, or to think about the situation. In our sample, trauma markers occurred most pronouncedly in stories about the picture "cemetery" relating to loss (Buchehim et al., 2012). In the following narrative, the trauma marker is underlined; most strikingly, the protagonist is trapped in pathological grief:

> A man stands in front of a grave. It is the grave of his wife and he is very miserable. He had lived with her for 50 years and realizes that he will spend the rest of his life without her. He feels desperately alone, incapable to move on without his wife. He is not in contact with his inner strength to cope with the situation. And he feels rage because she died before him. Who will care for him? The next 10 years he will suffer from depression, finding no meaning in his life. Fate has struck him hard and everyone else is to blame!

After 20 months of psychoanalytic psychotherapy, seven patients changed their attachment representation from disorganized to organized, and patients who had organized IWM remained organized (Buchheim et al., 2012). This result showed that patients had changed the content of their IWMs, enabling them to create narratives with resolution or containment strategies for difficult attachment-related emotions.

13.6 Conclusions

In the presented sample, chronically depressed patients had difficulties mentalizing about personal losses in comparison to their overall reflective abilities. Therefore, it can be assumed that this topic lead to a breakdown of normal reflective abilities due to strong affects in this sample. Results from the AAP test showed that IWMs of chronically depressed patients concerning loss narratives are more often disorganized than concerning other themes. The memory or fear of losing an attachment figure activates disorganized IWMs that cannot be reflected upon. After 20 months of psychoanalytic therapy, seven patients had changed from disorganized to organized attachment representations. This means that IWMs were indeed changed in content. Furthermore, the average RF had improved, but for dealing with loss, RF scores were still significantly lower. It could be argued that, for patients reflecting on their personal loss, there remained a difficulty and that this may represent a continuous vulnerability. It is unclear whether higher RF is the basis for reshaping the content of representations or vice versa. Assumedly, both happened at the same time because reshaping the content of rigid representations may be accompanied by improved metacognitive thinking about representations.

In sum, the results support the assumption that the implicit and explicit contents of representations as well as the ability to mentalize IWMs are impaired in chronically depressed patients. Psychoanalytic theory, therapy, and our results lead to the conclusion that simply remembering stressful life events will not change IWMs because they operate below consciousness and are the result of numerous interactions with significant others. Thus, from the psychoanalytic viewpoint, to change the content and increase reflection on IWMs (e.g., "I am a lovable person though I sometimes doubt it"), it is necessary and possible to reshape IWMs within an affective, intense, and meaningful therapeutic relationship.

References

Alink, L. R., Cicchetti, D., Kim, J., & Rogosch, F. A. (2009). Mediating and moderating processes in the relation between maltreatment and psychopathology: Mother–child relationship quality and emotion regulation. *Journal of Abnormal Child Psychology, 37*, 831–843.

Allen, J. G. (2003). Mentalizing. *Bulletin of the Menninger Clinic, 67*, 91–112.

Allen, J. G., Fonagy, P., & Bateman, A. W. (2008). *Mentalizing in clinical practice.* Washington, DC: American Psychiatric Publishing.

Bateman, A., & Fonagy, P. (2004). *Psychotherapy for borderline personality disorder. Mentalisation-based treatment.* Oxford: University Press.

Bowlby, J. (1969). *Attachment and loss.* New York, NY: Basic Books. Dt. (1975). Bindung. München: Kindler.

Bowlby, J. (1980). *Attachment and loss.* London: Pimlico.

Bowlby, J. (2002). Bindung: Historische Wurzeln. In G. Spangler & P. Zimmermann (Eds.), *Die Bindungstheorie: Grundlagen, Forschung und Anwendung.* Stuttgart: Klett-Cotta.

Bretherton, I. (1999). Internal working model in attachment relationships: A construct revisited. In J. Cassidy & P. Shaver (Eds.), *Handbook of attachment* (pp. 89–111). New York, London: Guilford.

Bretherton, I., & Munholland, K. A. (2008). Internal working models in attachment relationships: Elaborating a central construct in attachment theory. In J. Cassidy & P. Shaver (Eds.), *Handbook of attachment* (pp. 103–129). New York, London: Guilford.

Buchheim, A., George, C., & Taubner, S. (2012). Bindung, Psychotherapie und Bildgebung: Einblick in eine neurowissenschaftliche Studie zur psychoanalytischen Psychotherapie bei chronisch depressiven Patienten. In H. Böker & E. Seifritz (Eds.), *Psychotherapie und Neurowissenschaften: Integration - Kritik - Zukunftsaussichten* (pp. 388–413). Bern: Hans Huber Verlag.

Buchheim, A., George, C., & West, M. (2003). Das Adult Attachment Projective (AAP)—Gütekriterien und neue Forschungsergebnisse. *Psychotherapie, Psychosomatik, Medizinische Psychologie, 53*, 419–426.

Buchheim, A., Kachele, H., Cierpka, M., Munte, T. F., Kessler, H., Wiswede, D., et al. (2008). Psychoanalysis and neuroscience: Neurobiological changes during psychoanalytic treatment in patients with depressive disorders. *Nervenheilkunde, 27*, 441–445.

Buchheim, A., Viviani, R., Kessler, H., Kachele, H., Cierpka, M., Roth, G., et al. (2012). Changes in prefrontal-limbic function in major depression after 15 months of long-term psychotherapy. *Plos One, 7*, e33745.

Castonguay, L., & Beutler, L. (2006). *Principles of therapeutic change that work*. Oxford: University Press.

Cole-Detke, H., & Kobak, R. (1996). Attachment processes in eating disorder and depression. *Journal of Consulting and Clinical Psychology, 64*, 282–290.

Dozier, M., Stovall-Mcclough, K. C., & Albus, K. E. (2008). Attachment and psychopathalogy in adulthood. In J. Cassidy & P. Shaver (Eds.), *Handbook of attachment. Theory, research, and clinical applications* (pp. 718–744). New York, NY: The Guilford Press.

Egle, U. T., Hoffmann, S. O., & Steffens, M. (1997). Psychosocial risk and protective factors in childhood and adolescence as predisposition for psychiatric disorders in adulthood. Current status of research. *Nervenarzt, 68*, 683–695.

Fonagy, P. (2000). Attachment and borderline personality disorder. *Journal of the American Psychoanalytic Association, 48*, 1129–1146.

Fonagy, P., & Bateman, A. W. (2006). Mechanisms of change in mentalization-based treatment of BPD. *Journal of Clinical Psychology, 62*, 411–430.

Fonagy, P., Gergely, G., Jurist, E., & Target, M. (2002). *Affect regulation, mentalization and the development of self*. New York, NY: Other Press.

Fonagy, P., Gergely, G., & Target, M. (2007). The parent–infant dyad and the construction of the subjective self. *Journal of Child Psychology & Psychiatry, 48*, 288–328.

Fonagy, P., Leigh, T., Steele, M., Steele, H., Kennedy, R., Mattoon, G., et al. (1996). The relation of attachment status, psychiatric classification, and response to psychotherapy. *Journal of Consulting and Clinical Psychology, 64*, 22–31.

Fonagy, P., Moran, G. S., Edgcumbe, R., Kennedy, H., & Target, M. (1993). The roles of mental representations and mental processes in therapeutic action. *The Psychoanalytic Study of the Child, 48*, 9–48.

Fonagy, P., & Target, M. (2003). *Psychoanalytic theories: Perspectives from developmental psychopathology*. New York, NY: Wiley.

Fonagy, P., Target, M., Gergely, G., Allen, J. G., & Bateman, A. W. (2003). The developmental roots of borderline personality disorder in early attachment relationships. *Psychoanalytic Inquiry, 23*, 412–459.

Fonagy, P., Target, M., Steele, H., & Steele, M. (1998). Reflective functioning scale manual. In: London. (this is an unpublished manuscript)

George, C., Kaplan, N., & Main, M. (1984, 1985, 1996). The Berkeley adult attachment interview. In: Berkeley. (unpublished manuscript)

George, C., West, M., & Pettem, O. (1999). The adult attachment projective: Disorganization of adult attachment at the level of representation. In J. Solomon & C. George (Eds.), *Attachment disorganization* (pp. 462–507). New York, NY: The Guilford Press.

Grossmann, K., & Grossmann, K. E. (2006). Bindungen - das Gefüge psychischer Sicherheit. Stuttgart: Klett Cotta.

Harris, T. O., Brown, G. W., & Bifulco, A. T. (1990). Depression and situational helplessness/mastery in a sample selected to study childhood parental loss. *Journal of Affective Disorders, 20*, 27–41.

Hofer, M. A. (2006). Psychobiological roots of early attachment. *Current Directions in Psychological Science, 15*, 84–88.

Insel, T. R. (1997). A neurobiological basis of social attachment. *The American Journal of Psychiatry, 154*, 726–735.

Kernberg, O. (1984). *Severe personality disorders*. New Haven, CT: Yale University Press.

Kessler, H., Taubner, S., Buchheim, A., Munte, T. F., Stasch, M., Kachele, H., et al. (2011). Individualized and clinically derived stimuli activate limbic structures in depression: An fMRI study. *Plos One, 6*, e15712.

Kessler, H., Wiswede, D., & Taubner, S. (2012). Individualisierte Stimuli aktivieren limbische Strukturen bei depressiv Erkrankten—eine fMRI-Verlaufsstudie. In H. Böker & E. Seifritz (Eds.), *Psychotherapie und Neurowissenschaften: Integration - Kritik - Zukunftsaussichten* (pp. 581–592). Bern: Hans Huber Verlag.

Leichsenring, F., & Rabung, S. (2008). Effectiveness of long-term psychodynamic psychotherapy: A meta-analysis. *Journal of the American Medical Association, 300*, 1551–1565.

Levinson, A., & Fonagy, P. (2004). Offending and attachment. The relationship between interpersonal awareness and offending in a prison population with psychiatric order. *Canadian Journal of Psychoanalysis, 12*, 225–251.

Levy, K. N., Clarkin, J. F., Yeomans, F. E., Scott, L. N., Wasserman, R. H., & Kernberg, O. F. (2006). The mechanisms of change in the treatment of borderline personality disorder with transference focused psychotherapy. *Journal of Clinical Psychology, 62*, 481–501.

Main, M. (1995a). Desorganisation im Bindungsverhalten. In G. Spangler, & P. Zimmermann (Eds.) *Die Bindungstheorie*. Stuttgart. Klett-Cotta.

Main, M. (1995b). A move to the level of representation in the study of attachment organisation: Implications for psychoanalysis. In *Annual research lecture to the British psychoanalytical society*. London.

Mcgowan, P. O., Sasaki, A., D'alessio, A. C., Dymov, S., Labonte, B., Szyf, M., et al. (2009). Epigenetic regulation of the glucocorticoid receptor in human brain associates with childhood abuse. *Nature Neuroscience, 12*, 342–348.

Mcmahon, C. A., Barnett, B., Kowalenko, N. M., & Tennant, C. C. (2006). Maternal attachment state of mind moderates the impact of postnatal depression on infant attachment. *Journal of Child Psychology and Psychiatry, and Allied Disciplines, 47*, 660–669.

Patrick, M., Hobson, R., Castle, D., Howard, R., & Maugham, B. (1994). Personality disorder and the mental representation of early social experience. *Development and Psychopathology, 6*, 375–388.

Sandler, J., & Sandler, A. M. (1998). *Internal objects revisited*. London: Karnac.

Sharp, C. (2006). Mentalizing problems in childhood disorders. In J. G. Allen & P. Fonagy (Eds.), *Handbook of mentalization-based treatment* (pp. 101–121). New York, NY: Wiley.

Sharp, C., & Fonagy, P. (2008). The parent's capacity to treat the child as a psychological agent: Constructs, measures and implications for developmental psychopathology. *Social Development, 17*(3), 737–754.

Shedler, J. (2010). The efficacy of psychodynamic psychotherapy. *The American Psychologist, 65,* 98–109.

Sroufe, L., Carlson, E., Levy, A., & Egeland, B. (1999). Implications of attachment theory for developmental psychopathology. *Development and Psychopathology, 11,* 1–13.

Staun, L., Kessler, H., Buchheim, A., Kachele, H., & Taubner, S. (2010). Mentalization and chronic depression. *Psychotherapeut, 55,* 299–305.

Stern, D. (2000). *The interpersonal world of the infant: A view from psychoanalysis and developmental psychology.* New York, NY: Basic Books.

Taubner, S., Buchheim, A., Kächele, H., Kessler, H., & Staun, L. (2011). The role of mentalization in the psychoanalytic treatment of chronic depression. *Psychiatry: Interpersonal and Biological Process, 74,* 51–59.

Taubner, S., Kessler, H., Buchheim, A., & Staun, L. (2011). Structural and symptomatic changes one year after termination of long-term psychoanalytic therapies with chronically depressed patients. In: *Annual international meeting of the society for psychotherapy research.* Bern. Annual Meeting of the Society for Psychotherapy Research (SPR) Bern, Switzerland, 30.6.2011.

Tebartz van Elst, L., Hesslinger, B., Thiel, T., Geiger, E., Haegele, K., Lemieux, L., et al. (2003). Frontolimbic brain abnormalities in patients with borderline personality disorder: A volumetric magnetic resonance imaging study. *Biological Psychiatry, 15*(54), 163–171.

Weaver, I. C., Cervoni, N., Champagne, F. A., D'alessio, A. C., Sharma, S., Seckl, J. R., et al. (2004). Epigenetic programming by maternal behavior. *Nature Neuroscience, 7,* 847–854.

Westen, D., & Gabbard, G. (2002). Developments in cognitive neuroscience: II. Implications for theories of transference. *Journal of the American Psychoanalytic Association, 50,* 99–134.

Westen, D., Novotny, C., & Thompson-Brenner, H. (2004). The empirical status of empirically supported psychotherapies: Assumptions, findings, and reporting in controlled clinical trials. *Psychological Bulletin, 130,* 631–663.

Wignall, E. L., Dickson, J. M., Vaughan, P., Farrow, T. F., Wilkinson, I. D., Hunter, M. D., et al. (2004). Smaller hippocampal volume in patients with recent-onset posttraumatic stress disorder. *Biological Psychiatry, 56,* 832–836.

Zalsman, G. (2010). Timing is critical: Gene, environment and timing interactions in genetics of suicide in children and adolescents. *European Psychiatry, 25,* 284–286.

14 Overcoming Hurting Memories by Wisdom and Wisdom Psychotherapy

Barbara Lieberei, Michael Linden

Research Group Psychosomatic Rehabilitation at the Charité University Medicine Berlin and Department of Behavioral and Psychosomatic Medicine, Rehabilitation Center Seehof, Teltow/Berlin, Germany

14.1 Vulnerability and Resilience to Negative Life Events

Negative life events are known to everybody. It is normal to have conflicts with others, to fail, to be let down, to lose beloved ones by death or separation. Mankind has lived forever under conditions of war, hunger, illness, or poverty. People are well equipped to cope with such burdens and to go on. In times of war or hunger, people still marry and have children, have festivities, and are nevertheless joyful. The capacity to overcome negative experiences, to go on, and to look forward is called *resilience* (Herrman et al., 2011; Johnson & Baker, 2004; Kalra et al., 2012; Pejušković, Lečić-Toševski, Priebe, and Tošković, 2011). Persons with good resilience are not forced to look back, and, if they do so, it is typically in the form of tales that are presented for the sake of education or entertainment: "Once upon a time…, in those days…, when that happened…, you do not believe how times have been.…" Negative experiences can even lead to learning and personal growth, such as in the form of better appreciation of life, intensification of personal relations, appreciation of personal strength, or development of new perspectives in life (Glück, 2010; Tedeschi & Calhoun, 2008). Burdens that can be mastered are called *eustress*.

There is an abundant body of research on potential negative consequences of burdens, in life and psychological trauma (Dohrenwend & Dohrenwendt, 1974; Filipp, 1995; Reck, 2001). But longitudinal prospective studies on subjects undergoing a specific negative life event, such as the death of a loved one, the loss of employment, or severe illness, showed that such events could not predict the future reaction of persons (Chen et al., 1999; Kasl, Gore, & Gore, 1975; Leino-Arjas, Liira, Mutanen, Malmivaara, & Matikainen, 1999; Lichtenstein, Gatz, & Berg, 1998; Maguire et al., 1978). In summary, there is a general consensus that the consequences of a special negative life event cannot be foreseen. Environmental stress is mediated by a predisposing diathesis (diathesis-stress model or transactional stress model). *Diathesis* is the individual preparedness to react in a certain way to certain environmental circumstances.

It has physiological as well as psychological aspects. An essential feature of the diathesis-stress model is the assumption that the diathesis, be it resilience or vulnerability, has no bearing as long as no stressful event occurs (Abela & Allessandro, 2002; Brown & Harris, 1978). Examples for such a diathesis are cognitive schemata (Beck, 1967), which decide how persons react differently to the very same life event and which may be functional or dysfunctional, depending on the context. Further examples for resilience factors are ego strength, prior mastery of similar events, gender, age, sense of coherence, hardiness, self-efficacy, or optimism (Antonovsky, 1979; Bandura, 1977; Ben-Zur & Zeidner, 1991; Cohen, 1981; Cwikel & Rozovski, 1998; Kobasa, 1979; Muthny, Gramus, Dutton, & Stegie, 1987; Norris, Perris, Ibañez, & Murphy, 2001; Scheier & Carver, 1992; Toukmanian, Jadaa, & Lawless, 2000). In addition to individual parameters, there are also social factor that influence the response to burdens. They include societal structures, cultural or religious norms, or social support (Ben-Zur & Zeidner, 1991; Cohen, 1981; Karanci, Alkan, Balta, Sucuoglu, & Aksit, 1999; Schwarzer & Leppin, 1991; Schwarzer & Schulze, 2002).

Because such personal, social, and context factors are so manifold and heterogeneous, it is evident that they cannot be comprehensively assessed and that therefore the prediction of consequences of burdens is almost impossible. This also makes it impossible to define in a general way what must be called a burden or how to measure severity of a stressor (Filipp, 1995; Schwarzer & Schulz, 2002). It also makes obvious that coping with burdens in life needs complex and multidimensional capacities and that there are no effective cookbook recipes, which is one reason to turn to wisdom psychology.

14.2 Memories of Negative and Traumatic Life Events

An important aspect in suffering from or overcoming of negative life events is how they are kept in memory. The events, such as a car crash, last sometimes only seconds, but the memory persists and makes the problem. Not only "exceptional and life-threatening" events, as required for the diagnosis of posttraumatic stress syndrome (PTSD), but also "normal" negative life events like divorce, loss of job, conflicts at the workplace, death of a relative, or illness can be followed by psychological impairment (Amiel-Lebigre, Kovess, Labarte, & Chevalier, 1998; Fischer & Riedesser, 1999; O'Brian, 1998; Paykel, 2001). It is in many cases not the change in the real world that causes the problem but that it is impossible to forget. Many adjustment, reactive, or posttraumatic disorders must therefore be seen as disorders of haunting and hurting memories.

Psychological research on memory and emotion has well documented that negative events are remembered more often and more vividly than positive events (Christianson, 1992; Laposa & Rector, 2012; Michael, Ehlers, Halligan, & Clark, 2005; Weymar, Löw, Melzig, & Hamm, 2009). The stronger and more negative the emotion is that is associated with an event, the better it will be remembered or the more often it will come to mind (Banich et al., 2009). Also, emotional memories are in general long lasting. Evidence suggests that the emotional loading of an event slows the process of forgetting, so that emotional episodes are forgotten in a slower rate than neutral ones (Reisberg, 2006).

The question is whether forgetting is possible at all? How could one ever forget the name of one's spouse, especially after a divorce and ugly fights? Forgetting needs at least three steps: (1) the willingness to forget, (2) no further training of memories, and (3) dealing with memories in a relaxed manner.

Although memories of negative life events are typically associated with negative emotions and are therefore painful and hurting for the person, it is still not so that there is always a willingness to forget. This is true for individuals and societies. So an interesting question is why there is the urge to keep in mind what is hurting. One aspect is revenge. Many political memorials serve as signs to show aggressors what they did and to keep them suffering. There are almost no public memorials of reconciliation but most express reproachfulness. Memorials are most of the time aggressive acts, pointing a finger to somebody else. There are numerous examples, such as in Northern Ireland or the Balkans, showing that memorials can provoke counter-aggression. So it would not be convincing if a spouse would declare that he or she forgives the infidelity of the partner but would at the same time initiate a memorial day and erect a monument of infidelity, in order not to forget. This is aggression, and aggression is self-rewarding even if it hurts. Forgiveness psychology (Wade, Post, & Cornish, 2011; Worthington, 2001), therefore, has pointed out that forgiveness first of all means a willingness to forgive and forget, along with a decision that one wants to come to an end and no longer wants neither to retaliate nor to remember.

Even if one wants to forget, it is not easy to do so. One can learn to ride a bicycle in 10 min but not forget how to do it for a life time. One is introduced to an important person and will remember this event forever. One had a shocking experience and will never forget it. Apart from this difficulty with forgetting as such, memories can become better by training and repetition. This is the basis of learning and school education. The more often one remembers an event, the better one will remember and the easier memories will be reactivated. That this can be a problem has been shown by side effects of early debriefing after catastrophic experiences (Bisson, Jenkins, Alexander, & Binnister, 1997; Mayou, Ehlers, & Hobbs, 2000). Under the good intention of helping survivors of traumatic events to overcome their negative experience, helpers talked with the victims about what happened. The result was that treated persons developed PTSD more often than controls (Bradley, Greene, & Russ, 2005; NICE Guidelines, 2005; Rose, Bisson, Churchill, & Wessely, 2002; Van Emmerik, Kamphuis, Hulsbosch, & Emmelkamp, 2002). The mechanism of this side effect is easy to understand. Instead of helping to forget, debriefing served to improve memories of the trauma. A cup of tea would have had better results than "working through" the event. When one wants to forget, it is not helpful to indulge oneself in memories or work through memories because this will increase the vividness of the memories, images, and emotions.

Not to engage in memories does not mean that memories can be fully avoided. They will come up whenever there is a reminder. This can be in similar situations, through signs, smells, stories, or just free-floating thoughts. If it is impossible to forget painful life events, the question is how to remember without being hurt and upset? This is even more so if nothing can be done about what has happened. The death of a beloved one that could have been prevented or humiliation in front of colleagues can never be undone. The infidelity of one's partner will be remembered forever and can easily revive emotions in similar situations. The advice to forget, let it be, and look forward to the future is easily given but difficult to follow. Even less helpful would be to say that nothing serious happened and that it therefore is useless to think about it. This would in essence be an additional insult. The question now is how to remember without the reenactment of hurting emotions. There are two ingredients: first, the event must be reattributed, so that it loses its present relevance; and secondly, the unavoidable emotions must be accepted as they are and tolerated without additional emotional arousal.

All three of these steps on the road to forgetting or remembering without arousal need different actions and solutions. One approach is given by wisdom psychology or, in cases of illness, by wisdom psychotherapy.

14.3 Wisdom in Reconciliation with Hurting Memories

Wisdom is a psychological capacity, similar to assertiveness or social competency, that can help someone cope with past negative life events that cannot be undone and leave behind what cannot be changed. There is a large body of scientific work on wisdom psychology, which arose from life span psychology (Baltes & Smith, 1990; Baumann & Linden, 2008; Böhmig-Krumhaar, Staudinger, & Baltes, 2002; Kramer, 2000; Meeks & Jeste, 2009; Staudinger & Glück, 2011; Sternberg, 1998). Wisdom has been defined as an expert knowledge system in the fundamental life pragmatics or, more generally, as the "capacity to solve unsolvable problems" (Baumann & Linden, 2008). This capacity is given to everybody and needed on a daily basis. Many things in life are disappointing, hurting, and regrettable; many things one would have better done otherwise, are shameful, or have hurt others, but that cannot be undone. Even more, some daily situations are ambivalent by their very nature so that there is no simple solution. Insecurity, regret, or pain is unavoidable, such as deciding whether to go to work or stay with the sick child, to marry a certain person or not, spending money for goods or saving it for the future. Empirical studies have shown that a high degree of wisdom allows individuals to act in spite of ambiguities, to go on instead of being hung up in ambivalence, to find compromises and solutions that are acceptable for all, instead of rigidity and stubbornness, and to look forward instead of being stuck in the past (Staudinger & Glück, 2011).

Similar to assertiveness or social competency, wisdom is a multidimensional construct including cognitive, reflective, and affective components (Linden, Rotter, Baumann, & Lieberei, 2007). Core dimensions are (1) factual and procedural knowledge, (2) long-term perspective, (3) contextualism, (4) value relativism, (5) change of perspective, (6) empathy, (7) recognition and acceptance of one's own emotions, (8) emotional serenity, (9) distance from oneself, (10) uncertainty tolerance, and (11) control over one's own levels of aspiration. Detailed definitions are given in Box 14.1.

Wisdom can, first of all, help with the decision that one wants to forget. Knowledge about the world teaches which actions will have positive results or that justice and legality are not the same. Long-term perspective teaches that it does not help with the future to be stuck in the past. Contextualism and value relativism allow

> **Box 14.1 Dimensions of Wisdom (Baumann & Linden, 2008; Linden, 2008)**
>
> 1. *Factual and procedural knowledge:* General and specific knowledge on how the world or specific situations are set up and functioning
> 2. *Long-term perspective:* Knowledge about positive and negative consequences in the short term and the long term, and the ability to act according to the optimal outcome
> 3. *Contextualism:* Ability to see that present problems are relative to the context, be it time, situation, or persons
> 4. *Value relativism:* Ability to accept that there are different and possibly contradictory values, which does mean to hold on to one's own values and not to fight and belittle other values
> 5. *Change of perspective:* Ability to look at problems from different sides and to take on the perspective of other persons
> 6. *Empathy:* Ability to feel how other persons feel
> 7. *Recognition and acceptance of one's own emotions:* Ability to see, accept, and endure how one feels
> 8. *Emotional serenity:* Ability to control one's own emotions and not allow them to overflow oneself
> 9. *Distance from oneself:* Ability to see oneself through the eyes of others and to accept that one is not the center of the world
> 10. *Uncertainty tolerance:* Ability to tolerate that nothing is for sure in life and that everything can have unexpected courses and outcomes, while this does not hinder from acting
> 11. *Control over one's own levels of aspiration:* Ability to control one's own aspirations and not make judgments relative to what others have, or what one had or desires.

the reframing of what happened by accepting the situational condition. Change of perspective, empathy, and distance from oneself help in not taking events personally. Recognition and acceptance of one's own emotions and emotional serenity help to accept things as they are and to act in an intelligent way in spite of the fact that it hurts emotionally. Uncertainty tolerance allows to go forward without knowing for sure that the way taken is optimal. Control over one's own levels of aspiration allows to accept things as they are in humility. In summary, wisdom allows to do what forseeably will have positive outcomes under a long-term perspective and under consideration of what is best to all involved and not only for oneself. It will further allow individuals to come to an end where things cannot be changed, even if it may be regrettable that things are as they are. Therefore, one can forget, and, because one wants to forget, there is no need to actively go on with rumination, reenactment of memories about what happened, and cognitive rehearsal about what should have been done or should be done.

Of special importance is the ability to recognize, accept, and control one's own emotions. There is typically a mixture of emotions when life events cannot be mastered, like feelings of humiliation, insufficiency, anger, enviousness, revenge, and the like. Many of these emotions are inacceptable if not vilifying to the person oneself. Nobody would like to openly accept that one is mean, sneaky, backstabbing, malicious, or injust. But such emotions are nevertheless there; they are also hurting and humiliating, and there is the urge to suppress them. To recognize and accept that oneself has also dire thoughts, wishes, and emotions and that one is therefore to some degree of the same manner and species as the offender helps in not becoming overwhelmed by such emotions but rather enduring them when they pop up involuntarily and in bringing them under control.

14.4 Wisdom Psychotherapy

When persons are overwhelmed by negative life events and unable to cope with what happened, and when they become victims of persisting hurting memories, professional psychotherapeutic help is needed. One approach can be wisdom psychotherapy, which has been derived from concepts of wisdom psychology and theories about the etiology of adjustment disorders and posttraumatic embitterment disorder (PTED) (Baumann & Linden, 2008; Baumann, Linden, and Rotter 2009; Linden, 2006, 2008; Linden, Baumann, & Schippan, 2006; Linden et al., 2007; Schippan, Baumann, & Linden, 2004). It is embedded in cognitive behavior therapy and is related to psychotherapeutic reattribution and reframing interventions. The core of this approach is to teach or stimulate wisdom competencies. This form of therapy can be applied as individual or group psychotherapy and offers special interventions for the treatment of patients with adjustment disorders, especially PTED. It does not aim to solve patient's problems but to foster problem-solving skills and to increase competencies that allow them to accept unchangeable situations. The goal of wisdom therapy is not to change the validation of the hurting experience but to get more emotional distance, so that hurting memories and intrusions can decrease and patients can learn to remember without being hurt.

14.4.1 Initial Steps

The treatment of patients who suffer from reactive disorders is difficult because they come with the idea that the cause of their problem is the environment or some negative life event and that, therefore, not they themselves have to change but others. In their view, the world must change, not the patient. Furthermore, patients who have been confronted with unjust and humiliating life experiences and who have developed embitterment often even bluntly reject help because they want "the world to see what it did to me." Furthermore, therapy is often complicated by a fatalistic-aggressive attitude of the patient, which inhibits the development of new life perspectives or new perspectives on what has happened.

Therefore the first and difficult therapeutic task in the treatment of patients with reactive and posttraumatic disorders is, independently of any specific treatment focus, to establish a working relationship between therapist and patient. Because these patients are distrustful and do not always accept help, therapists have to convey with empathy and unconditional acceptance that they appreciate the patient's suffering, are clearly on the side of the patient, understand what has occurred, and look for some kind of revenge or reversal of what happened.

The next step is to analyze what the critical event and concomitant emotions have done to the patient, what is the role of intrusive thoughts, and how these lead to bad emotions. Avoidance behavior is assessed, such as why patients no longer go to particular shops or sometimes avoid whole areas of the city. It is analyzed, with the patient, how and why he or she retreats from friends and even the family and no longer attends social or cultural events. Patients learn that they are not only being punished by the critical event but even more by the consequences of their present mental status, which is a double punishment. The question is whether patients want to allow the aggressor to punish them twice, first by the critical event and now by social withdrawal and a bad mood. With empathy and sympathy, it is possible to communicate that patients do not deserve this, and that they have suffered enough. A paradoxical intervention can be used. The aggressor is given a message or even "punished" by not allowing him or her to influence the patient's life and by showing that the patient can stand up.

14.4.2 Wisdom Strategies to Cope with Hurting Memories and Emotions

An important goal of wisdom therapy is to change hurting memories and intrusions concerning the critical event into normal memories (learning to remember without being aroused and hurt). The hurting experience does not have to be changed, but the emotional distance has to be increased. Therefore, strategies are helpful that activate wisdom competencies to cope with the individual problem and get more inner distance from what has happened.

Patients often feel overwhelmed by their emotions when reminded of the negative life event and try to suppress hurting memories. This is one reason for avoidance behavior. The therapeutic answer is exposure in sensu and in vivo. This means to describe in detail one's emotions and to learn to accept them. Patients are asked to reactivate all facets about the critical event through cognitive rehearsal. They are stimulated to report not only their cognitive evaluations but also feelings and emotions. Patients tend to disclaim negative, undesirable, or "unacceptable" emotions like anger, humiliation, and thoughts of revenge. A first step is to accept the presence of the full blend of emotions and especially "unacceptable" emotions. The therapeutic method is to summarize emotions of the patient as emotions that are held also by the therapist (e.g., "If I hear what happened to you, thoughts of revenge come to my mind, I would damage his car"). Patients can learn to look at their emotions and hurting memories from a metaperspective in order to gain control and inner emotional distance. Also strategies of distraction can be helpful. Another cognitive strategy is to build up a rivalry over the control of the patient's emotions between the patient and the offender. This can be established by asking patients how much power over their feelings and emotions they want to give to their offenders.

One way to change negative and nagging memories and emotions is to reevaluate and reframe what has happened. It is natural that somebody who was let down takes a personal and one-sided view of the event, but this often is attended by an increasevof humiliation and embitterment. Therefore, it is helpful to look at what happened from other perspectives, such as that of the aggressor or other involved persons. This does not mean that patients have to recognize that there may be other sights on the experienced injustice, but rather to see the world and especially the critical event and its development with the eyes and the feelings of the offender. What made offender act as he did? What circumstances influenced him? Would I have acted differently if I had been in his position? This guided change of perspective opens the opportunity to recognize that the offender may have acted in reaction to practical constraints or other legitimate origins and not with the intention of a personal attack or devaluation. It also can lead to a better sense of empathy. It is helpful to discuss with patients that understanding the perspective, feelings, and motives of the offender does not mean that they have to accept or forgive his attitude.

Many patients firmly adhere to their ideas of justice, honor, personal strength, innocence, and guilt. Therefore, an indispensible goal of treatment is the modification of cognitions and attitudes. An important therapeutic question is, "What hurts you most? What makes you really mad?" This helps to understand what caused the turmoil of emotions and what basic beliefs and values were violated. A strategy to reconcile with what has happened is the modification of dysfunctional cognitions. For this, cognitive therapy has many established treatments like reframing, internal dialogue, or reality testing (Linden & Hautzinger, 2011). Therapeutic methods like role change can help to accept that negative life events, strokes of fate, justice, and guilt can mean different things to different persons and depend on the special context or situation. This stimulation of value relativism and contextualism helps to put one's own evaluations in a larger context and find more objective frames of reference in judging what is right and wrong.

Another approach is to change the focus of attention from short-term considerations to a life span perspective. Patients tend to see short-term consequences and harm; they are focusing on what they lost. This hinders them in seeing what they have and what still can be done. Attention must be directed to remaining options and long-term development. The blockade of old goals is always a chance for a new beginning. Even negative life events can have intellectual or emotional gains. Patients can be asked what the experience can teach them. The critical event can be seen as a test (by God, fate, or life) that needs to be accomplished. The notion that people who overcome difficult life problems have a high social reputation can be helpful. Patients can be motivated by the idea that coping with such a severe crisis might be the greatest and most important challenge in their life. This change of focus helps to quiet the mind and leads to an increasing inner distance. So patients can learn to look back to what has happened with different emotions and validations, what helps to change hurting memories into touching but normal memories.

To cope with feelings of uncertainty and unbearable helplessness, patients have to learn that fighting is good when you can win and get control over events but that acceptance of the inevitable is also a very important and valuable human capacity. Another idea can be helpful for the patient; the awareness that adverse situations and circumstances like severe illness, death, war, hunger, disaster, damage, and conflicts are all part of human life in general. The major question in life is not to avoid burdens but to cope with challenges in a decent and successful way.

14.4.3 The Method of Unsolvable Problems

A specific and newly developed intervention in wisdom therapy is the method of unsolvable problems (Baumann & Linden, 2008; Linden, 2008; Linden et al., 2007; Schippan et al., 2004). Fictitious unsolvable life problems, combined with special questions, are used to activate wisdom-related knowledge and teach wisdom-related strategies to the patient. The use of fictitious problems reduces the risk of reactance by the patients because they are not personally concerned. It is well-known that it is much easier to see solutions for the problems of others than for one's own.

Patients are given the description of some severe negative life event that has been unjust, blameful, irreversible, without a clear solution, and not related to the present problem of the patient. Three persons are involved: the victim (or aggrieved person), the offender (or acting person), and some third party (bystander or innocent beneficiary). The descriptions leave room for speculation and interpretation (Box 14.2).

Box 14.2 Example of Fictitious Negative Life Events

Ms. Miller, 28 years old, is asked by her sick mother to visit her on Christmas. She cannot come because her boyfriend has booked a skiing trip and wants her to come with him. Ms. Miller decides to go skiing. Soon after Christmas, her mother dies, and Ms. Miller does not see her again.

Mr. Smith has worked for many years as manager in a company and invested everything in his work. When one of his projects threatens to fail because of a wrong decision by his superior, his boss calls him in and tells him that he is fired because they need a "real" manager.

The scenario allows for problem-solving training. To support a structured learning process, the patient can be asked the following questions in relation to the fictitious life problems:

- Please describe your feelings and thoughts when thinking about this life problem. How does the problem affect you?
- Please put yourself into the place of the aggrieved person/victim. How would you feel? What would you think? What would you do?
- Please put yourself into the place of the acting person/offender. How would you feel? What would you think? What would you do?
- Please put yourself into the place of the third involved person. What would you think? What would you do?
- Please put yourself into the place of the aggrieved person/victim. What reactions would you consider as harmful? Which "solutions" could add insult to injury?
- What reactions to solve the problem would you consider reasonable and appropriate for the current situation? Which reactions would be reasonable and appropriate in the long run?
- Could you imagine that the presented life problem could have, besides all adversities, any positive outcomes for the aggrieved person?

- Please imagine the further development of the aggrieved person/victim. How could her/his life look like in 5 years from now? How will she/he reconsider the problem?
- Imagine, you are a psychologist (manager, priest, grandmother with much life experience, etc.). What could be a typical approach to difficult life problems for such a person? What would such a person advise?
- Please imagine, years from now, you are writing your biography with all the ups and downs of your life. How would you describe and evaluate the current difficult period of life? Is it possible to describe it with more humor and calmness from a distance?

These questions first assess the subjective relevance of the presented life problem. Patients are asked to describe and differentiate their own negative and positive emotions. This facilitates the perception and acceptance of emotions. The patient is stimulated to practice a change of perspective and empathy toward the other involved persons (especially toward the offenders and their possible motives). Moreover, general knowledge about problem solving is activated. This also facilitates value relativism (different values, motives, and life goals of the involved persons can be distinguished, resulting in different perspectives and behaviors), as well as contextualism (the temporal and situational embedding of the problem may be reflected). In particular, the behavior of the offender can be discussed and reattributed (specific situational requirements and the enforcement of specific interests can explain specific behavior). Furthermore, the contribution of the aggrieved person to the development of the problem can be brought up. In addition, it may be elaborated that, under certain circumstances, the patient would have done the same thing as the offender. The identification of dysfunctional strategies (e.g., self-harm by suicide or alcohol, acts of revenge, long-lasting social and occupational adversities caused by despair or embitterment) and, in contrast, functional strategies help to clarify goals and can activate a reorientation and the development of new perspectives. By contrasting short- and long-term consequences, the patient shall become aware that complex life problems always have negative as well as positive consequences and that it is important to accept these ambiguities.

Of importance is that there is no "correct" solution, or any solution at all, but rather a more or less functional or dysfunctional coping. The goal of treatment is not to find solutions to the problem of the patient but to teach basic knowledge and skills about coping with unsolvable problems. This can later be applied to the personal problems of the patients to foster emotional distance to the problem and also decrease the intensity of hurting memories.

Empirical evidence supports that this approach can help to overcome negative life events (Linden, 2008; Linden, Baumann, Lieberei, Lorenz, & Rotter, 2011). It does not aim to solve life problems but to teach basic problem-solving skills, which help to get emotional distance to the critical life events and to change hurting memories into normal memories. This results in a reduction not only of general symptoms but also of intrusive memories. Figure 14.1 shows results from the Impact of Event Scale. PTED patients who were treated with wisdom therapy reported a significant decrease of intrusions after 6 weeks of wisdom therapy.

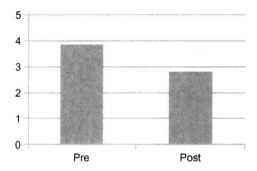

Figure 14.1 Intensity of intrusions according to the Impact of Event Scale in PTED patients, pre- and post-wisdom therapy ($n = 28$).

14.5 Conclusions

It has long been known that some people show persisting and impairing reactions in the aftermath of negative life events. This depends not so much on the event as such but much more (1) on the meaning of the event to the person (i.e., attributions, cognitions, or so-called judgment dispositions) and (2) on the match between the event and the capacities of the individual to cope with the event (Filipp, 1995; Lazarus, 1995, 1999; Paykel, 2001). Any treatment approach will therefore have to deal with the cognitive frame of reference and value system of the patient (Eid & Larson, 2008).

Wisdom is a psychological capacity that helps to put one's own experience in a greater context and not be overwhelmed by adverse experiences. Wisdom psychology has been developed independently of any clinical context by developmental and life span psychologists. Because wisdom is an indispensible human capacity that helps individuals master daily life, it is natural to refer to wisdom when the mastery of negative life events is insufficient. The task is to teach and to activate wisdom capacities in order to equip the person with the capacities needed to cope with what happened. Wisdom does not provide solutions. The goal is not to solve the problem or to say what and who are right or wrong. Instead, the person has to learn the skills needed to solve an unsolvable problem by factual knowledge, change of perspective, empathy, acceptance of one's own emotions, serenity, contextualism, value relativism, control of aspirations, distance from oneself, uncertainty tolerance, or long-term perspective.

Wisdom psychotherapy provides an arsenal of interventions to teach wisdom strategies, especially the method of unsolvable problems in life. With respect to hurting memories, wisdom encourages the decision to leave behind what happened, gives a new meaning and a sense of coherence to negative life experiences, helps individuals accept and master undesirable emotions, and stimulates them to look forward. This stops the persistent reactivation of memories, reduces their emotional strain, and stimulates internal dialogues that allow a better mastery of unwanted and automatic negative thoughts.

References

Abela, J. R. Z., & D'Allessandro, D. U. (2002). Beck's cognitive theory of depression: A test of the diathesis-stress and causal mediation components. *British Journal of Clinical Psychology, 41*, 111–128.

Amiel-Lebigre, F., Kovess, V., Labarte, S., & Chevalier, A. (1998). Symptom distress and frequency of life events. *Social Psychiatry and Psychiatric Epidemiology, 33*, 263–268.

Antonovsky, A. (1979). *Health, stress, and coping.* San Francisco, CA: Jossey-Bass.

Baltes, P. B., & Smith, J. (1990). Weisheit und weisheitsentwicklung: Prolegomena zu einer psychologischen Weisheitstheorie. *Zeitschrift für Entwicklungspsychologie und Pädagogische Psychologie, 22*, 95–135.

Bandura, A. (1977). Self-efficacy: Toward a unifying theory of behavioral change. *Psychological Review, 84*, 191–215.

Banich, M. T., Mackiewicz, K. L., Depue, B. E., Whitmer, A., Miller, G. A., & Heller, W. (2009). Cognitive control mechanisms, emotion, and memory: A neural perspective with implications for psychopathology. *Neuroscience and Biobehavioral Reviews, 33*, 613–630.

Baumann, K., & Linden, M. (2008). *Weisheitskompetenzen und weisheitstherapie.* Verlag, Lengerich: Pabst.

Baumann, K., Linden, M., & Rotter, M. (2009). Kompetenzen zur bewältigung belastender lebensereignisse und der schutz vor anpassungsstörungen. *Journal für Neurologie, Neurochirurgie und Psychiatrie, 10*, 82–86.

Beck, A. T. (1967). *Depression: Clinical, experimental, and theoretical aspects.* New York, NY: Harper & Row.

Ben-Zur, H., & Zeidner, M. (1991). Anxiety and bodily symptoms under the threat of missile attacks: The Israeli scene. *Anxiety Research, 4*, 79–95.

Bisson, J. H., Jenkins, P. L., Alexander, J., & Binnister, C. (1997). Randomised controlled trial of psychological debriefing for victims of acute burn trauma. *British Journal of Psychiatry, 171*, 78–81.

Böhmig-Krumhaar, S. A., Staudinger, U. M., & Baltes, P. B. (2002). Mehr toleranz tut not: Lässt sich wert-relativierendes wissen und urteilen mit hilfe einer wissensaktivierenden gedächtnisstrategie verbessern? *Zeitschrift für Entwicklungspsychologie und Pädagogische Psychologie, 34*, 30–43.

Bradley, R., Greene, J., Russ, E., et al. (2005). A multidimensional meta-analysis of psychotherapy for PTSD. *The American Journal of Psychiatry, 162*, 214–227.

Brown, G. W., & Harris, T. O. (1978). *Social origins of depression: A study of psychiatric disorder in women.* New York, NY: Free Press.

Chen, H., Bierhals, A. J., Prigerson, H. G., Kasl, S. V., Mazure, C. M., & Jacobs, S. (1999). Gender differences in the effects of bereavement-related psychological distress in health outcomes. *Psychological Medicine, 29*, 369–380.

Christianson, S. A. (1992). *The handbook of emotion and memory: Research and theory.* Hillsdale, NJ: Lawrence Erlbaum.

Cohen, F. (1981). Stress and bodily illness. *Psychiatric clinics of north America, 4*, 269–286.

Cwikel, J., & Rosovski, U. (1998). Coping with the stress of immigration among new immigrants to Israel from Commonwealth of Independent States (CIS) who were exposed to Chernobyl: The effect of age. *International Journal of Aging and Human Development, 46*, 305–318.

Dohrenwend, B. S., & Dohrenwendt, B. P. (Eds.). (1974). *Stressful life events: Their nature and effects.* New York, NY: John Wiley & Sons.

Eid, M., & Larsen, R. J. (Eds.). (2008). *The science of subjective well-being.* New York: Guilford.

Filipp, G. (1995). Ein allgemeines modell für die analyse kritischer lebensereignisse. In G. Filipp (Ed.), *Kritische lebensereignisse* (pp. 3–52). München: Beltz.

Fischer, G., & Riedesser, P. (1999). *Lehrbuch der psychotraumatologie*. München: Reinhardt.

Glück, J. (2010). She looks back with bitterness: Wisdom as a developmental opposite of embitterment?. In M. Linden & A. Maercker (Eds.), *Embitterment*. Vienna: Springer.

Herrman, H., Stewart, D. E., Diaz-Granados, N., Berger, E. L., Jackson, B., & Yuen, T. (2011). What is resilience? *Canadian Journal of Psychiatry, 56*, 258–265.

Johnson, M. P., & Baker, S. R. (2004). Implications of coping repertoire as predictors of men's stress, anxiety and depression following pregnancy, childbirth and miscarriage: A longitudinal study. *Journal of Psychosomatic Obstetrics and Gynaecology, 25*, 87–98.

Kalra, G., Christodoulou, G., Jenkins, R., Tsipas, V., Christodoulou, N., Lecic-Tosevski, D., et al. (2012). Mental health promotion: Guidance and strategies. *European Psychiatry, 27*, 81–86.

Karanci, N. A., Alkan, N., Balta, E., Sucuoglu, H., & Aksit, B. (1999). Gender differences in psychological distress, coping, social support and related variables following the 1995 Dinal (Turkey) earthquake. *North American Journal of Psychology, 1*, 189–204.

Kasl, S. V., Gore, S., & Gore, S. (1975). The experience of losing a job: Reported changes in health, symptoms and illness behaviour. *Psychosomatic Medicine, 37*, 106–122.

Kobasa, S. C. (1979). Stressful life events, personality, and health: An inquiry into hardiness. *Journal of Personality and Social Psychology, 37*, 1–11.

Kramer, D. A. (2000). Wisdom as a classical source of human strength: Conceptualization and empirical inquiry. *Journal of Social and Clinical Psychology, 19*, 83–101.

Laposa, J. M., & Rector, N. A. (2012). The prediction of intrusions following an analogue traumatic event: Peritraumatic cognitive processes and anxiety-focused rumination versus rumination in response to intrusions. *Journal of Behavior Therapy and Experimental Psychiatry, 43*, 877–883.

Lazarus, R. S. (1999). *Stress and emotion: A new synthesis*. London: Free Association Books.

Leino-Arjas, P., Liira, J., Mutanen, P., Malmivaara, A., & Matikainen, E. (1999). Predictors and consequences of unemployment among construction workers: Prospective cohort study. *British Medical Journal, 319*, 600–605.

Lichtenstein, P., Gatz, M., & Berg, S. (1998). A twin study of mortality after spouse bereavement. *Psychological Medicine, 28*, 635–643.

Linden, M. (2006). Reaktionen auf belastende lebensereignisse und anpassungstörungen. In F. Hohagen & T. Nesseler (Hrsg.), *Wenn geist und seele streiken. Handbuch seelische gesundheit*. München: Südwest Verlag.

Linden, M. (2008). Posttraumatic embitterment disorder and wisdom therapy. *Journal of Cognitive Psychotherapy, 22*, 4–14.

Linden, M., & Hautzinger, M. (2011). *Verhaltenstherapie*. Berlin: Springer.

Linden, M., Baumann, K., Lieberei, B., Lorenz, C., & Rotter, M. (2011). Treatment of posttraumatic embitterment disorder with cognitive behaviour therapy based on wisdom psychology and hedonia strategies. *Psychotherapy and Psychosomatics, 80*, 199–205.

Linden, M., Baumann, K., & Schippan, B. (2006). Weisheitstherapie. Kognitive therapie der posttraumatischen verbitterungsstörung. In A. Maercker & R. Rosner (Eds.), *Psychotherapie der posttraumatischen belastungsstörungen* (pp. S208–S227). Thieme.

Linden, M., Rotter, M., Baumann, K., & Lieberei, B. (2007). *Posttraumatic embitterment disorder*. Bern: Huber.

Maguire, G. P., Lee, E. G., Bevington, D. J., Kuchemann, C. S., Crabtree, R. J., & Cornell, C. E. (1978). Psychiatric problems in the first year after mastectomy. *British Medical Journal, 319*, 600–605.

Mayou, R. A., Ehlers, A., & Hobbs, M. (2000). Psychological debriefing for road traffic accident victims: Three-year follow-up of a randomised controlled trial. *British Journal of Psychiatry, 176*, 589–593.

Meeks, T. W., & Jeste, D. V. (2009). Neurobiology of wisdom: A literature overview. *Archives of General Psychiatry, 66*, 355–365.

Michael, T., Ehlers, A., Halligan, S., & Clark, D. (2005). Unwanted memories of assault: What intrusion characteristics are associated with PTSD? *Behaviour Research and Therapy, 43*, 613–628.

Monroe, S. M., & Simons, A. D. (1991). Diathesis-stress theories in the context of life stress research: Implications for the depressive disorders. *Psychological Bulletin, 110*, 406–425.

Muthny, F. A., Gramus, B., Dutton, M., & Stegie, R. (1987). *Tschernobyl-erlebte belastung und erste verarbeitungsversuche*. Weinheim: Studienverlag.

NICE, (2005). *Posttraumatic stress disorder—the management of PTSD in adults and children in primary and secondary care*. London: National Institute for Clinical Excellence: NICE Guidelines. <www.nice.org.uk>.

Norris, F. H., Perris, J. L., Ibañez, G. E., & Murphy, A. D. (2001). Sex differences in symptoms of posttraumatic stress: Does culture play a role? *Journal of Traumatic Stress, 14*, 7–28.

O'Brien, L. S. (1998). *Traumatic events and mental health*. Cambridge: Cambridge University Press.

Paykel, E. S. (2001). Stress and affective disorders in humans. *Seminars in Clinical Neuropsychiatry, 6*, 4–11.

Pejušković, B., Lečić-Toševski, D., Priebe, S., & Tošković, O. (2011). Burnout syndrome among physicians—the role of personality dimensions and coping strategies. *Psychiatria Danubina, 23*, 389–395.

Reck, C. (2001). *Kritische lebensereignisse und depression*. Berlin: Lengerich.

Reisberg, D. (2006). Memory for emotional episodes: The strengths and limits of arousal-based accounts. In B. Uttl, N. Ohta, & A. Siegenthaler (Eds.), *Memory and emotion: Interdisciplinary perspectives* (pp. 15–36). New York, NY: Blackwell.

Rose, S., Bisson, J., Churchill, R., & Wessely, S. (2002). Psychological debriefing for preventing post traumatic stress disorder (PTSD). *Cochrane Database of Systematic Reviews* (2: CD000560).

Scheier, M. F., & Carver, C. S. (1992). Effects of optimism on psychological and physical well-being: Theoretical overview and empirical update. *Cognitive Therapy & Research, 16*, 201–228.

Schippan, B., Baumann, K., & Linden, M. (2004). Weisheitstherapie—kognitive therapie der posttraumatischen verbitterungsstörung. *Verhaltenstherapie, 14*, 284–293.

Schwarzer, R., & Leppin, A. (1991). Social support and health: A theoretical and empirical overview. *Journal of Social and Personal Relationships, 8*, 99–127.

Schwarzer, R., & Schulz, U. (2002). The role of stressful life events. In A. M. Nezu, C. M. Nezu, & P. A. Geller (Eds.), *Comprehensive handbook of psychology* (Vol. 9). New York, NY: Wiley.

Staudinger, U. M., & Glück, J. (2011). Psychological wisdom research: Commonalities and differences in a growing field. *Annual Review of Psychology, 62*, 215–241.

Sternberg, R. J. (1998). A balance theory of wisdom. *Review of General Psychology, 2*, 347–365.

Tedeschi, R. G., & Calhoun, L. G. (2008). Beyond the concept of recovery: growth and the experience of loss. *Death Stud, 32*, 27–39.

Toukmanian, S. G., Jadaa, D., & Lawless, D. (2000). A cross-cultural study of depression in the aftermath of a natural disaster. *Anxiety, Stress, and Coping, 13*, 289–307.

Van Emmerik, A. A., Kamphuis, J. H., Hulsbosch, A. M., & Emmelkamp, P. M. (2002). Single session debriefing after psychological trauma: A meta-analysis. *Lancet, 360*, 766.

Wade, N. G., Post, B. C., & Cornish, M. A. (2011). Forgiveness therapy to treat embitterment: A review of relevant research. In M. Linden & A. Maercker (Eds.), *Embitterment*. Wien: Springer.

Weymar, M., Löw, A., Melzig, C. A., & Hamm, A. O. (2009). Enhanced long-term recollection for emotional pictures: Evidence from high-density ERPs. *Psychophysiology, 46*, 1200–1207.

Worthington, E. L. (2001). *Five steps to forgiveness: The art and science of forgiving*. New York, NY: Crown House Publishing.

Part Three

Societal Aspects

15 Healing of Psychological Trauma from Military Operations by Transformation of Memories

Andreas Gewandt[1], Peter L. Zimmermann[2]

[1]Salus gGmbH, Fachkrankenhaus Uchtspringe, Klinik für Psychiatrie und Psychotherapie, Emil-Kraepelin-Strasse 6, 39576 Stendal
[2]Bundeswehrkrankenhaus Berlin, Klinik für Psychiatrie, Psychotherapie und Psychotraumatologie, Scharnhorststrasse 13, 10115 Berlin

15.1 Historical Background

Although the scenarios of violent military conflicts have always been accompanied by impairment to soldiers' health and illness, no connection with intrapsychic processes has been directly established for long periods of warfare. We know, for example, of case reports from military hospitals in the American Civil War (1861–1865) containing descriptions of such symptoms as shortness of breath, dizziness, chest tightness, and heart complaints, which were initially attributed to structural changes to soldiers' hearts and lungs due to their involvement in hostilities (soldier's heart) (da Costa & Medes, 1871).

In World War I (1914–1918), the clinical picture, especially of the soldiers who fought from trenches where they endured long-term exposure to shelling and gunfire, was referred to as that of *Kriegszitterer*, whereas the English-speaking world used terms like *bomb shell disease* and *shell shock*. Symptoms included the persistent trembling of limbs or of the whole body that did not improve even after the soldiers suffering from them had been evacuated from combat. The cause of this was initially assumed to be direct cerebral damage due to blast injuries (Zimmermann, Hahne, Biesold, & Lanczik, 2005), before a possible psychogenesis of such diseases was found later on (Nonne, 1934).

In World War II (1939–1945), the main symptoms that developed were somatoform syndromes that occurred after soldiers had been involved in fighting, especially gastrointestinal disorders, which due to their high prevalence finally resulted in the establishment of *Magenbataillone* (literally, "stomach battalions"), whose members continued to perform military service but were put under considerably less strain (Zimmermann et al., 2005).

It was not until the psychological effects of the Vietnam War (1957–1975) that it became evident, in particular to the American public, that more thorough psychiatric research into such diseases was needed. As a result, the diagnosis of posttraumatic stress disorder (PTSD) was included in DSM-III in 1980.

Symptoms such as troubled sleep, difficulty in concentrating, vegetative liability, depression, as well as joint and muscle pain were subsumed under the Gulf War syndrome, the causes of which remained unclear for a long time. Here, too, a psychological genesis has been identified as one of the most probable causes (Lee & Jones, 2007).

15.2 Symptoms and Epidemiology of Military-Related Psychiatric Illnesses

Military service in a war zone may involve special circumstances and strains, such as extreme physical stress in an adverse environment, prolonged sleep deprivation, physical injuries, exposure to life-threatening events and threats such as (suicide) attacks, snipers, ambushes, and indirect rocket and mortar fire, and exposure to various noxious substances. Certain events, such as having to injure or kill others or seeing a friend killed in action, can have psychological consequences that are often accompanied by feelings of guilt or shame (Litz et al., 2009; Siegel & Zimmermann, 2010).

All these experiences show additive effects on health through psychophysiological mechanisms of the neuroendocrine and autonomic nervous systems. Added to these are significant social effects, in particular on partnership, parenthood, educational objectives, and military and civilian employment. Moreover, the stress of military service in war regions has increased the suicide rate in the U.S. forces (not, however, in the Bundeswehr), in those branches of service most often engaged in hostilities (e.g., combat troops as the U.S. Marine Corps) (Zimmermann, Masuhr, & Hoge, 2012).

This trend is reflected in the growing use of psychiatric services at Bundeswehr hospitals, in particular since Germany's commitment in Afghanistan. For example, although in 2008, 245 outpatient and inpatient cases of PTSD were recorded in the Bundeswehr, this number increased to 466 by 2009, to 729 by 2010, and to 922 by 2011 (Kowalski, 2012).

15.2.1 Military-Related PTSD

Military-related PTSD is a psychological disorder that frequently develops in soldiers after they have served in war and crisis zones. In the conflicts in Iraq and Afghanistan, U.S. studies have identified prevalence rates of 2–6% (similar to that of the general population) before soldiers went out on deployment and 6–20% after their return, with the prevalence rate largely being a function of the frequency with which the soldiers were involved in fighting and the intensity of the combat (Hoge, 2004). Added to this are a considerable number of soldiers suffering from a subclinical PTSD that is also referred to as posttraumatic stress or combat stress. These subclinical symptoms may well have severe pathological dimensions, though they do not amount to full-blown PTSD. For the Bundeswehr, the 12-month prevalence rate in a representative controlled study was about 3% of the personnel who served in the Afghanistan mission (Wittchen et al., 2012).

The symptoms of PTSD and of organic and psychological comorbid diseases are described in other chapters of this book and the pertinent literature in detail (Zimmermann et al., 2012). PTSD is difficult to diagnose especially in members of forces such as police forces, firefighters, and other first responders, not only military forces. The personnel are normally well trained in how to respond to traumatic stress so that they tend to suffer less frequently from anxiety, helplessness, or horror, which are typical reactions of civilian trauma victims (Zimmermann et al., 2012). Moreover, symptoms of PTSD ultimately represent a soldier's adaptive survival response in a combat situation and therefore are not necessarily of a primarily pathological nature. Instead, excess physiological excitation, aggressiveness, and the ability to suppress other emotions may—in combat—prove to be useful qualities that soldiers may have developed in realistic training they have undergone before experiencing traumatic events. Such responses only become symptoms if they adversely affect the soldiers' reintegration into everyday civilian life after they return to their home country (Zimmermann et al., 2012).

15.3 How Deployment-Related Mental Disorders Are Dealt With in the Bundeswehr

Upon their completion of operational deployments, soldiers undergo a number of measures that have been established for the purposes of screening and secondary prevention of secondary deployment-related mental disorders (Zimmermann, 2010). Each soldier is asked by their primary care providers (unit physicians or general practitioners) whether they suffer from mental symptoms, with the posttraumatic stress scale 10 (PTSS-10) being used as the basis for evaluation (Maercker, 2003). Soldiers in whom abnormal test results are found and/or who report psychiatric symptomatology are urged to undergo an examination in a psychiatric department of a Bundeswehr hospital, with outpatient or inpatient therapeutic measures being initiated as required. The Bundeswehr attaches great importance to its personnel being treated as early as possible because some of the soldiers concerned are employed for no more than 2–4 years, and this time limit can hinder the implementation and completion of suitable therapies. It can well be that soldiers develop mental problems long after retiring from active service. To close the gap, veterans are contacted (by the Medical Service and/or at the expense of the Bundeswehr) about 6 months after discharge and informed about the follow-up psychosocial care that can be provided to them.

Mental stress may also become evident in the so-called postdeployment seminars: Within 3 months of redeployment, all the soldiers concerned are required to attend a 3-day seminar where they talk in groups in a structured and manualized manner and under the supervision of trained moderators, psychologists, social workers, or chaplains about the mission and their subsequent reintegration. At this point, anyone suspected of suffering from a deployment-related mental disorder is advised to undergo a psychiatric examination.

Anyone showing symptoms of the onset of psychovegetative exhaustion, though not yet having a manifest mental illness, can quickly and unbureaucratically apply for a 3-week strengthening treatment (preventive treatment program) at a contracted civilian rehabilitation hospital. This option is being used by a growing number of military personnel, with more than 4000 soldiers participating in 2011 (Bundeswehr Medical Office, Munich).

Moreover, to facilitate the early detection of psychological effects of military operations as well as to improve cooperation among the professional groups concerned, so-called psychosocial networks have been established since 2005. They have been broadly established with the help of psychiatrists, unit physicians, psychologists, military chaplains, and social workers who meet at regular intervals to exchange experience or to hold interdisciplinary case conferences. The basic specialist knowledge and skills needed by the psychosocial care providers engaged in these networks can be acquired in Bundeswehr in-house training courses. Moreover, several Internet counseling and information services have been established to facilitate low-threshold access to the support systems (www.angriff-auf-die-seele.de and www.ptbs.hilfe.de).

Treatment of deployment-related psychological illnesses is mainly carried out at Bundeswehr hospitals because one of the several important preconditions of successful treatment is a profound understanding of experiences made in the operational environment and of their implications, with the therapists ideally having acquired their own. What is also needed is knowledge of overarching pathodynamic connections and of aspects of individual ways of grappling and identifying with being a member of a military hierarchical system and associated social norms (sense of duty, loyalty, etc.). Trauma therapy methods applied in the Bundeswehr comply with recommendations given by scientific associations, summarized in and adopted as the S3 medical guideline by the Working Committee of Medical-Scientific Societies Arbeitsgemeinschaft Wissenschaftlich Medizinischer Fachgesellschaften (AWMF). Accordingly, the emphasis of the inpatient psychotherapeutic settings is on Shapiro's EMDR technique (Eye Movement Desensitization and Reprocessing) (Shapiro, 1998) as well as on cognitive behavioral methods. Recommended adjuvant therapies such as stabilization groups, ergotherapy, art therapy, music therapy, exercise therapy, acupuncture, and physiotherapy are being applied in varying degrees as part of comprehensive treatment programs at Bundeswehr hospitals. A recent retrospective evaluation of an inpatient treatment setting provided information on the effectiveness of EMDR in the long-term catamnesis of Bundeswehr soldiers (Zimmermann, Biesold, Barre, & Lanczik, 2007). After treatment, however, patients on average still showed signs of clinically relevant trauma-related residual stress; there seemed to be a correlation between the therapeutic prognosis and the severity and quality of trauma (Zimmermann et al., 2007). The primary therapeutic objective is to restore or at least clearly improve patient health. Normally, soldiers consider operational deployments an integral part of their profession and therefore often explicitly identify the restoration of their medical fitness for deployment as one of their therapeutic concerns.

Sometimes, treatment of military-related mental illness remains without success. In such cases, the individual concerned may file an application for the recognition of a service-incurred disability, which is then assessed by psychiatrists on the basis of guidelines that are also applied in the civilian sector (in accordance with Sozialverband VdK as revised in 2009). If the deployment-related cause of the disability is accepted, the individual concerned receives benefits and pensions according to the severity of the disability. In addition, the term of enlistment with the

Bundeswehr can be extended to ensure that the patient has social security coverage and receives adequate treatment [Act on the Continued Employment of Personnel Injured on Operations (Einsatz-Weiterverwendungsgesetz)]. If a chronified mental disorder of a Bundeswehr soldier is accompanied by severe restrictions in his ability to do his job and/or adapt, he can apply for the initiation of a disability procedure. Before that, all the inpatient and/or outpatient therapeutic options must have been exploited, and the patient's unfavorable prognosis must have been identified by means of an internal psychiatric assessment. A disability procedure for temporary-career volunteers results in their premature discharge from military service; regular soldiers, who are comparable to civil servants, go into early retirement.

Although this preventive, therapeutic, and follow-up support system of the Bundeswehr offers a host of measures, catamnestic studies of PTSDs in the Bundeswehr and other armed forces have identified risks of chronification and unfavorable prognosis (Zimmermann et al., 2007). This made it necessary for the Bundeswehr to increase its research work to prevent such trends by further developing preventive and therapeutic concepts. This is why the Bundeswehr Research and Treatment Centre for Psychotraumatology (Psychotrauma Centre) was established at the Berlin Bundeswehr Hospital in 2009.

15.4 Case Report

15.4.1 History

The 35-year-old career soldier (NCO) was admitted to the Bundeswehr hospital Berlin for suffering from chronic pain of the rows of teeth of both his upper and lower jaw and adjacent osseous areas for 3 years. On account of this pain, he had undergone extensive dental and orthodontic treatment, but there had been no improvement in the symptoms. Treatment included apicectomies and the subsequent extraction of nine teeth, all of which turned out to be healthy. The patient also reported that, over the same period, he had been suffering from low spirits, irritability up to open aggressiveness, brooding, social withdrawal, difficulties in falling asleep, and bitterness. Certain, faintly sweet smells brought back scenic memories from his deployment to Kosovo in 1999, in connection with a distinct feeling of disgust. These memories also included the sight of dead bodies, although the patient was not initially able to describe the scenes in detail. He went on to say that, because of his irritability, he had had trouble with his peers, including, in April 2010, under the influence of alcohol, a physical fight with police officers for a trivial reason. The patient said that he found it impossible to establish a long-term partnership due to his state of tension and pain.

15.4.2 Treatment

The patient was treated on an inpatient basis for 36 days. He underwent an inpatient trauma therapy based on the three-phase model, which included two 90-min EMDR sessions (Shapiro, 1998). During the first phase of the therapy, resource stabilization was carried out, including a special imaginative stabilization technique referred to as inner safe place, trauma-related psychoeducation, resumption of sports activity, and an attempt to improve his relationships with his mother and sister. During the confrontation phase, the first EMDR session, which was conducted on the basis of the priorities established by the client, focused on dealing with an incident of personal insult that the patient had experienced at work in 2005 and that, according to the patient, had involved unjustified accusations. The patient reported that he had been especially disappointed by the lack of support and the derogatory comments from his superiors and peers. During the session, odontalgia was able to be reduced from 9 points (maximum of 10 points) to 3 points but worsened in the following few days and went back up to 5–6.

The second EMDR session focused on a violent incident that the patient had experienced during his deployment to Kosovo in 1999. This particular incident was only one on a trauma map that featured a multitude of similar incidents. The patient had been unexpectedly confronted with the sight of a murdered old woman whose face had been severely mutilated. The patient's task had been to document her injuries. He had known the woman from meeting her on several occasions when she was still alive. When the session began, the patient's subjective units of disturbance (SUD) were assessed between 8 and 9 on a 10-point scale. The initial memory was accompanied by feelings of shock and horror but also by being angry with the people who had committed the crime, whom he suspected to be among the crowd of smirking onlookers. During the session, he also noted physical reactions, including muscular tension in his head, trunk, and back. To deal with this, he developed a vision of cure, in this case a vision of being rid of his pain and of no longer being so grim.

During the processing phase, the patient experienced mostly aggressive but also sad abreactions as well as distinctly heightened tension. Toward the end of the processing phase, the feeling of aggression disappeared completely (SUD 0–1). The muscular tension remitted as well. For the patient, this phenomenon was most noticeable in his face, leaving him free from dental pain and feeling comfortably warm.

The integration phase, which was continued during the outpatient follow-up treatment, focused on analyzing the very high demands the patient placed on himself and his low frustration threshold. These issues were also well verbalized in a complementary supportive group therapy for traumatized patients of the ward, where the patient felt that his peers understood and supported him. The patient agreed that, after being discharged, he would take part in an outpatient psychotherapeutic follow-up program conducted by the trauma therapist who had been in charge of the patient's therapy at the hospital. The catamnesis revealed stable pain remission.

15.5 Discussion

As the case vignette shows, psychological trauma involves considerable changes in psychological and physical processes, primarily the memories, thoughts, and cognitions of the individual concerned. The military setting plays a certain part with regard to both the traumatogenic mechanisms concerned and the differences in the way soldiers and other groups of traumatized patients process the events.

- "I must do everything my employer demands of me"
- "My employer / my superiors have failed"
- "My superiors do not acknowledge my achievements"
- "I have failed as a soldier"
- "I have let my mates down"
- "As a soldier, I must be strong and invulnerable"
- "I must not be a wimp / weakling"
- "I must not show any feelings or that I have got any problems"

Figure 15.1 Maladaptive cognitions of Bundeswehr soldiers suffering from PTSD.

Hurting memories (hurting and hurt memories after traumatic stress) may have effects in different areas of personality and daily life, which are summarized once again here. Posttraumatic memories in a military population are subject to qualitative differences in comparison to civil patients, including specific cognitions and related affective reactions. Figure 15.1 shows a list of potentially destructive cognitions that play an important role in the clinical therapy of traumatized Bundeswehr soldiers and should be addressed in psychotherapeutic sessions (Zimmermann, 2011; Zimmermann, Jacobs, & Kowalski, 2011). Another consequence might be the repression and dissociation encouraged by aspirations of a particular social desirability and focus on duty. As a result of such cognitions, a good many soldiers suffer from moral feelings of guilt and/or shame. When they feel guilt, the underlying memory is associated with incident-related self-blame, such as for something they perceive as a mistake, which results in intentions to compensate. Shame, on the other hand, refers to a situation where previously chronified feelings of guilt are included in one's self-esteem and subsequently might lead to the development of autodestructive mechanisms (e.g., autodestructive behavior, addiction) (Siegel & Zimmermann, 2010).

The healing process induced by applying these trauma therapy techniques does not erase trauma-related memories, although this is what clients often hope for, at least at the beginning of the therapy. In psychotraumatology, healing is connected with a transformation of memories. *Transformation* means that the individual concerned gains control over intrusive memories and is more able to put them into the overall context not only of the traumatic situation but also of his or her personal history. Equally, however, transformation means that concomitant destructive feelings and thoughts are understood and put into perspective and hence that hurting memories are transformed into neutral or even constructive memories. Ideally, such a transformation may even stimulate mental growth and maturing processes—developments also known as posttraumatic growth—which have lasting positive effects not only on trauma-related memories but also on the entire personality of an individual (Zimmermann, 2011; Zimmermann et al., 2011).

References

da Costa, T., & Medes, J. (1871). On irritable heart: A clinical study of a form of functional cardiac disorder and its consequences. *The American Journal of the Medical Sciences, 61*, 18–52.

Hoge, C. W., Castro, C. A., Messer, S. C., McGurk, D., Cotting, D. I., & Koffman, R. L. (2004). Combat duty in Iraq and Afghanistan, mental health problems, and barriers to care. *The New England Journal of Medicine, 351*, 13–22.

Kowalski, J. T., Hauffa, R., Jacobs, H., Höllmer, H., Gerber, H., & Zimmermann, P. (2012). Inanspruchnahme psychiatrisch-psychotherapeutischer leistungen nach einsatzbedingten belastungen bei soldaten der Bundeswehr. *Ärzteblatt, 418*, 11.

Lee, H. & Jones, E. (2007). Introduction. In H. Lee, & E. Jones (Hrsg.), *War and health. Lessons from the Gulf War* (pp. 1–4). Chichester: Wiley.

Litz, B. T., Stein, N., Delanay, E., Lebowitz, L., Nash, W. P., Silve, C., et al. (2009). Moral injury and moral repair in war veterans: A preliminary model and intervention strategy. *Clinical Psychology Review, 29*, 695–706.

Maercker, A. (2003). Posttraumatische-Stress-Skala-10 (PTSS-10). In J. Hoyer, & J. Margraf (Hrsg.), *Angstdiagnostik—grundlagen und testverfahren* (pp. 401–403). Berlin: Springer.

Nonne, M. (1934). Therapeutische Erfahrungen an den Kriegsneurosen in den Jahren 1914–1918. In O. V. Schjerning, & V. K. Bonhoeffer (Hrsg.), *Handbuch der ärztlichen erfahrungen im weltkriege 1914–1918. Bd. IV: Geistes- und nerven-krankheiten* (pp. 102–120). Leipzig: Barth.

Shapiro, F. (1998). *EMDR—grundlagen und praxis*. Paderborn: Junfermann.

Siegel, S., & Zimmermann, P. (2010). Moralische verletzungen von soldaten im auslandseinsatz. *Wehrmedizinische Monatsschrift, 54*(6–7), 1–4.

Wittchen, H. U., Schönfeld, S., Kirschbaum, K., Thurau, C., Trautmann, S., Steudte, S., et al. (2012). Traumatic experiences and posttraumatic stress disorder in soldiers following deployment abroad: how big is the hidden problem? *Deutsches Ärzteblatt International, 109*(35-36), 559–568. doi:10.3238/arztebl.2012.0559.

Zimmermann, P. (2011). Traumatisierungen nach militärischen Einsätzen. In G. H. Seidler, H. J. Freyberger, & A. Maercker (Eds.), *Handbuch der psychotraumatologie* (pp. 356–361). Stuttgart: Klett-Cotta.

Zimmermann, P., Biesold, K. H., Barre, K., & Lanczik, M. H. (2007). Long-term course of posttraumatic stress disorder (PTSD) in German soldiers: Effects of inpatient eye movement desensitization and reprocessing therapy and specific trauma characteristics in patients with non-combat related PTSD. *Military Medicine, 172*(5), 456–460.

Zimmermann, P., Hahne, H. H., Biesold, K. H., & Lanczik, M. (2005). Psychogene Störungen bei deutschen soldaten des ersten und zweiten weltkrieges. *Fortschritte der Neurologie/Psychiatrie, 73*(2), 91–102.

Zimmermann, P., Jacobs, H., & Kowalski, J. T. (2011). ISAF und die seele. Zwischen schädigung und wachstum. In A. Seiffert (Eds.), *Sozialwissenschaftliches institut der Bundeswehr. Jahresbericht* (pp. 143–152). Strausberg: SOWI-Verlag.

Zimmermann, P., Masuhr, F., Hoge C. W. (2012). Neuropsychiatrische erkrankungen in zusammenhang mit militärischen auslandseinsätzen. In M. Dietel, N. Suttorp, & M. Zeitz *Harrisons innere medizin* (pp. 1–7). Berlin: ABW Wissenschaftsverlag.

Zimmermann, P., Biesold, K. H., Hahne, H. H., & Lanczik, M. (2010) Die psychiatrie der bundeswehr im wandel – standortbestimmung und perspektiven. *Trauma und Gewalt* 4(3), 2–11.

16 The Creation and Development of Social Memories of Traumatic Events: The Oudewater Massacre of 1575

Erika Kuijpers

Institute for History, Leiden University, Leiden, The Netherlands

16.1 Culture and Memories

Every culture has its own memory practices, that is, ways of encoding and transmitting of memories in narratives, images, rituals, display of emotions, or coping strategies after traumatic events. Cultural concepts and conventions determine the behavior of individuals and the cultural group as a whole. Coping strategies after traumatic events are also culturally determined. Medical staff working in war zones all over the world find that cultural and social conditions very much affect the diagnosis, treatment, and resilience of war victims (North et al., 2005). Diagnosis by Western counselors is sometimes hindered by the unfamiliarity with the way people experience, express, and evaluate stress in non-Western societies (Knipscheer & Kleber, 2008; Shiraev, 2007). History offers an opportunity to study the development of memory practices over a longer period and across cultures. Although memory studies of the twentieth century are booming since the 1990s, only recently have historians of the premodern era (i.e., the period before 1800) taken an interest in the study of memory and, more specifically, in the way individuals and societies remembered war experiences (Fox, 1999; Ford, 2001; Harari, 2004; Pollmann, 2009; Walsham, 2011).

Europeans who lived in the sixteenth and seventeenth centuries, especially in the countryside, had a fair chance of becoming victims of plundering armies. The Reformation provided one of the main sources of political conflict. In the Holy Roman Empire, territorial rulers waged war over religion. France suffered from bloody religious conflicts between Protestants and Catholics. In the Netherlands, the Habsburg regime executed thousands of people for their dissident ideas. Thousands of people must have had to cope with the distressing memories of these experiences. How did they cope with the memory of violence, humiliation, and loss?

The distance in time offers historians the advantage of a long-term perspective and the possibility of comparing societies, cultures, and historical situations. However, they also have to deal with the important drawback that the objects of study are no longer alive and have never been diagnosed according to modern criteria. Moreover, in retrospect, it is impossible to know whether war victims developed disorders. Their memories, as well as the descriptions of their symptoms, if mentioned at all, are preserved in images and texts that speak in their own cultural idiom and that tell a story that must have made sense to their contemporaries but that is not necessarily understandable to us.

Still, there is something to be learned from the way past societies dealt with memories of war and atrocities. Reading studies on memories or memory practices in premodern Europe, we observe both continuity with and striking differences from modern memory practices. The differences, basically, concern the way people think about the relation between body, mind, and soul, about what memory is and can do to a person, and about the task and destiny of the individual in earthly life. The suffering of the soul is usually not medicalized, unless it is ascribed to physical causes, such as 'melancholia' (Gowland, 2006; Haskell, 2009; Lund, 2010; Schmidt, 2007). Secondly, one's past is not evaluated in terms of personal development through experience but rather as a temporal road to eternal salvation, a road that is meant to be hard in order to test the true believers. Finally, the role of individuals in events like war is usually seen as part of a collective experience or as destined by a divine plan. Of course, these different premises have consequences for the way people make sense of their memories and for the coping strategies they develop.

From the therapeutic practices in modern postwar societies, we have learned that a number of preconditions seem necessary for the resilience of traumatized war victims: (1) safety, the socio-economic perspective of recovery, reconstruction, and future welfare; (2) recognition of victimhood, justice, solidarity, and social bonding, and (3) the production of a comprehensible narrative of what happened that gives meaning to the memory, that can be shared with others, and that creates a distance between the traumatic event and the actual situation that is no longer threatening.

The twentieth century offers many examples of postwar situations in which one or more of these preconditions were not in place. Some areas were in a state of war for more than a generation; children grew up in refugee camps or in shattered families or communities, without any perspective of a normal life in the nearby future. The lack of solidarity and recognition was one of the main problems that hindered the recovery and caused embitterment of both Holocaust survivors and practically all war veterans of the past century (Assmann, 2006; Hunt, 2010; Winter, 1999). The creation of a narrative has often been delayed or obstructed by the politics of forgetting, feelings of guilt or shame, conflicts about who is to blame for what happened, or the disintegration of the community that should have formed the audience. In preindustrial Europe, this was often the case as well. Elsewhere, we described under what conditions the massacres of the Dutch Revolt were publicly remembered (Kuijpers and Pollmann, 2013). In many cases, the political regime or the economic situation did not allow for the emergence of public memory practices. Local societies that were politically or religiously divided would not agree on a shared narrative of the past, and in the Habsburg Netherlands, various towns had to sign a treaty of *oubliance*, which stated that it was no longer permitted to talk about what had happened. In the Northern Netherlands, towns immediately started to remember their victories, while the commemoration of atrocities, although generally acknowledged, would not start until much later.

Oudewater, a small town in Holland, halfway between Utrecht and The Hague, will serve as an example of how and why a violent past could be publicly remembered across the centuries. This case shows that, even when the conditions for mental recovery are optimal, the creation of a narrative that frames victimhood in a satisfactory way is not self-evident and takes more than one generation.

16.2 The Destruction and Massacre of Oudewater in 1575

In the summer of 1566, a wave of iconoclasm by Protestants spread through the Netherlands. The Habsburg regime, headed by Philip II of Spain, responded with severe persecution combined with a centralistic policy that undermined the autonomy and privileges of both towns and nobility. By 1568, the Low Countries had plunged into a civil war that would last 80 years until peace was signed at last in Munster, 1648. In April 1572, a growing number of cities in Holland, Brabant, and Flanders openly rejected the Habsburg regime and declared their support for the rebel prince William of Orange. The Spanish regime began a violent military campaign to force the rebel cities to surrender. The cities that had themselves invited the rebels in or that had refused to take in a Spanish garrison were punished by putting them to the sack. In the towns of Mechelen, Zutphen, and Naarden, hundreds—of men, women, and children were murdered or died when trying to escape. Many others were tortured in order to get as much money from them as possible.

The small Holland town of Oudewater had sided with the rebels since June 1572. On August 6, 1575, the Spanish commander Hierges besieged it and subsequently captured, sacked, and burned down the town on August 8. Hundreds of the approximately 3000 inhabitants—men, women, and children—were killed; the exact numbers are unknown. One of the Protestant ministers was hanged outside the town walls. There are eyewitness accounts by survivors who fled, wounded, half naked, and barefoot, to other towns in the area. Many people lost their possessions and loved ones. It is hard to say how badly Oudewater was destroyed. One source states that only the church and eight houses were left standing. Probably many survivors went to live elsewhere. By the end of 1576, Oudewater was recaptured by the rebel army of the Prince of Orange. At that point, the town was still in ruins, and it would take a while for the town to be fully restored. An Amsterdam diarist mentioned the burial of a former inhabitant of the town of Oudewater. This man went back to his hometown in 1578 and, seeing its desolate condition, got ill and died of grief a few days after his return to Amsterdam (Jacobsz, 1959, II, p. 724). Yet local research shows that the restoration and economical recovery of the town took place more quickly than one would expect. Oudewater was exempted from land taxes for a long time, and the States of Holland invested in the restoration of the fortifications and gates because the town was strategically important. In the accounts, we find wages for the transport of debris and rubble until 1579. The number of new citizens rose every year in the 1580s. By 1588, the renovation of the town hall was also completed (Boon, 1975).

Figure 16.1 Frans Hogenberg, news print of the Oudewater Massacre. Cologne, s.i., Leiden University Library, collection of Bodel Nijenhuis.

16.3 The Production of Collective Memory

While the survivors in Oudewater were rebuilding their town, the event became canonical in the history of the Dutch Revolt. Various actors were involved in the production of the collective memory of this event. At that time, Hogenberg, a printer in Cologne, produced news accounts immediately after each political or military event (Mielke & Luijten, 2009). These broadsheets found their way all over Europe to a public that was longing for information, news, and excitement (Figure 16.1). The news about the massacre of Oudewater thus spread rapidly. The Hogenberg image shows the plundering and burning of the town of Oudewater and says in its caption: "Here you can see what tyranny and cruelty took place in Oudewater by God and infamous felons. They killed, spoiled and violated, both virgins and married women. One of which they hanged naked, tore the fruit from her womb, and threw it away like filth."[1] The hanging of a pregnant woman in her doorway in

---

[1] "Hie ist zu sehen in was Gestalt, Gross tyranni und Gross gewalt, Zu Oudewater wird angerichtt, Durch Gott und eherlose boswicht, Die morden, plundern unzucht treiben, Schenden vill jungfrawn und weiber, Deren seie ein nackt auff gehenckt, Gar iemerlich haben gerissen, Die frucht auss irm leib gerissen, Und schenlich die hinweg geschmissen."

The Creation and Development of Social Memories of Traumatic Events

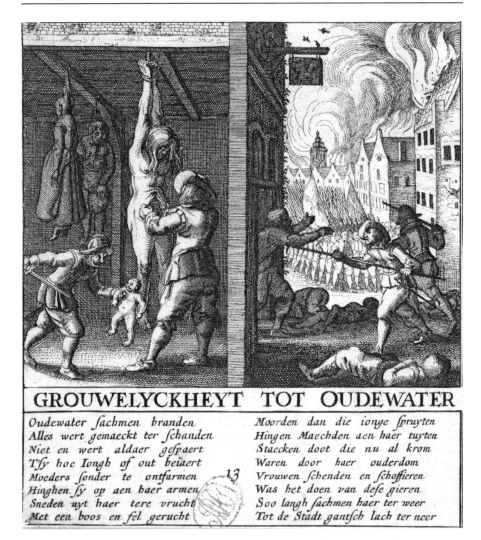

Figure 16.2 Anonymous broadsheet, 1618–1624, "Horrific events in Oudewater 1575," Rijksmuseum, Amsterdam.

Oudewater, as depicted by Hogenberg, became an icon of the so-called black legend of Spanish cruelty in the Netherlands and was used as war propaganda by the protestant party (Figure 16.2). The theme underlines the innocence of the victims on the one hand—with the unborn baby as the epitome of innocence—and the devilish cruelty of the soldiers on the other hand. In the early seventeenth century, both in popular pamphlets and history books, this theme must have become widely known and connected to the Oudewater case. However, comparison with earlier prints about Spanish behavior in the Americas and of Catholic violence against Protestants in France has shown that the killing babies and women formed an iconographical theme that probably preexisted, a reference as well to the massacre of the innocents in Bethlehem, and that does not need to reflect what actually happened in Oudewater (Cilleßen, 2006). In any case, these images were circulating throughout Europe long before any of the personal stories of victims appeared in print.

The first seriously documented histories of the events were quite factual about the military aspects, the numbers of soldiers on both sides, the number of shots fired at the city on August 7, the condition of the fortifications, and other details. In his 1599 history of the Revolt, the London-based author Van Meteren mentions he heard that Protestant citizens had staged a mock procession on the town walls in order to provoke the Spaniards, thus knowingly signing their death sentence. According to his account, no more than 20 men survived the massacre (Van Meteren, 1599, Fol. LXXXV). More detailed information and eyewitness accounts came from the military and from prominent citizens who survived and reported to the Prince. They were first cited by the well-informed historian Peter Bor, whose voluminous 1621 edition of the history of the war contained the first extensive description of the taking of Oudewater. One of the few eyewitness accounts Bor cited was the local bailiff named Crayestein, who managed to escape by pretending to be one of the plundering soldiers and hiding in a ditch overnight. He arrived in Gouda naked, was dressed by friends, and was brought to the Prince of Orange where he reported on the sack (Bor, 1621, VIII, p. 121v). During the rest of the seventeenth century, most authors copied Bor's history. Others just name Oudewater as a gruesome example of Spanish cruelty, without adding any historical detail.

The question is what happened with the personal memories of the victims of the sack. Did they identify with the story as it was published? Did they talk at all about what happened to them? The fact that the Oudewater massacre had become a well-known event in the history of the Dutch Revolt had some practical advantages. For example, little had to be explained if one needed help. This was certainly the case for Anna Jansdochter, widow of the Reformed minister of Oudewater who had been hanged 2 days after the sack in 1575. In 1582 she solicited a pension from the States of Holland. Her request was accompanied by an attestation by the burgomaster of Gouda on the condition in which the corpse had been found when the rebel army reconquered Oudewater 16 months later. According to him, the body was still fully intact, the color normal, the face not yet hollow, the eyes fresh and bright as if the corpse had been hanging there for only 4 days, this "being a divine miracle." The States of Holland were impressed and granted Anna's request in view of "her husband's perseverance and the miraculous ways of the Lord with him" (National Archive, The Hague, Arch. 3.01.04.01).

At some point—it is unclear when exactly—the States of Holland also decided to give a pension to all survivors who were still alive. From 1615 onward, we possess the lists on which the Oudewater magistrates annually recorded the names of survivors. The 1615 list still contained 321 names while the last list, dating from 1664, mentions two old women as the last living survivors of the sack (Old town archive Oudewater, Inv. Nr. 165). This is the first and only instance we know of where no distinction was made among the survivors; they were all considered to have suffered equally by virtue of having been in Oudewater at the time. One woman who was still in her mother's womb during the sack, even made a successful claim for compensation.

16.4 Time for Commemoration

It was more than 30 years before the survivors in Oudewater started a public commemoration. In 1608, we find the first notice on an annual memorial service and sermon held on the first Sunday after August 8 or on the eighth itself, the day of the massacre. Another 30 years later, the next generation decided that this was not enough. Around the time when the Peace of Westphalia was signed in 1648, the Oudewater burgomasters commissioned an immense artwork to commemorate the massacre. The painting, by the relatively unknown painter Dirk Stoop, is 5 m wide and still hangs in the town hall today (Stoppelenburg, 2005). From 1650 onward, the annual memorial service in church was followed by a visit to the painting in the town hall. This tradition is carried on until today.

It thus seems that around 1650 there was a renewed interest in the 1575 massacre. The list of survivors applying for the States' pension in 1650 shows that there were no more than 32 of them left, all of very old age, because 75 years had now passed. The names on these lists have short marginal comments, such as "she lay under corpses" or "lost his father and mother." Possibly, the annual compiling of the list facilitated the appearance and transmission of individual stories in the public domain in Oudewater. In 1669, almost a century after the massacre and after the last survivors had died, Arnoldus Duin, a local grocer, took an interest in them and wrote a very detailed history of the events. In his introduction, Duin emphasized that Oudewater, now prospering again, should forever remember the tales of ancestral suffering. To this effect, he included a great number of completely "new" eyewitness accounts and personal stories, "from old people who heard these stories many times from their ancestors" and "from people who I have known and who I have spoken to myself, who have a good knowledge of the event and who were already 17 years old" (Duin, 1669).

Some of these again focused on spectacular escapes, the bravery of the citizens, and the demonic cruelty of their assailants. It is interesting to see how individuals framed their own experience in the preexisting narratives. In the course of the seventeenth century, a number of eyewitnesses came forward, to testify to the hanging of a pregnant woman in Oudewater, for instance. In 1624, Judith Adriaensdochter testified for a notary in Utrecht that Anna van Danswijck, mother of Marrichgen and Trijntge Thonisdochter, was hanged in her doorway (Stoppelenburg, 2005). In the list of survivors of 1650, Anna Pelgrums, at the age of 82, attests that "two" children were cut from her aunt's body (Old town archive Oudewater, Inv. Nr. 165). Duin mentions one Aeltgen Pieters and notes that she was pregnant, this time with triplets (Duin, 1669, p. 18). Typically, witnesses to the death of fellow citizens attest that they died either heroically or devoutly like martyrs. "A certain citizen named Pieter

Willemsz, hearing the crying and moaning of his wife and children, bid farewell as he did not think he would return, walked out of his house with an axe in his hand right into the arms of his enemy. He slashed around furiously, thus ending his life in battle" (Duin, 1669, pp. 11–12).

There is also praise for a mother who forbids her children to kneel and implore Spanish soldiers to save their lives: She "pulled the child out of the Spanish hands with courage and steadfastness, and exhorted her children that they should not beg the soldiers, but pray to God who gave them their lives and who was the only one who could save them" (Duin, 1669, pp. 17–18). Throughout Duin's story, the working of divine providence can be discerned. Before the sack, some women assisting a woman in childbirth had seen prodigious signs in the sky. They saw an army, heard the noise of weapons and gunfire, and saw blood dripping down on the earth, followed by a fire. Three children survived although they had been fully covered with molten lead, pitch, and tar, and a baby remained silent for 3 days under a heap of straw, without anything to eat or drink. Another mother was taken to her child by a fair young man without being seen, although they passed through streets where soldiers were plundering and killing. Some people thought he must have been an angel (Duin, 1669, pp. 23–24).

The account also tells of indignation, anger, and blame, mostly about the lack of solidarity and compassion of the neighboring towns. To begin with, the town of Gouda, also siding with the Revolt, nonetheless refused to pierce the dike in order to inundate the fields around Oudewater; Their harvest came first. In need, you get to know your friends, Duin comments. People from Montfoort, a nearby town still loyal to the king, came over to Oudewater to look for goods in the burnt houses after the sack. They fished corpses out of the harbor, in order to steal the clothes. There are two stories of women who fled to Montfoort with their children in a deplorable state and were refused shelter, scolded as heretics, and chased away. One of them was even sent away by her own sister (Duin, 1669, p. 23).

Duin also included tales that are less loaded with moral portent. To modern readers, the stories seem very authentic because they are unspectacular and focus on minor details and sensory experience. One is the tale of Japikje Pieters, who was a young girl in 1575 and who had lived until the 1650s. Japikje herself was severely injured in the sack. She survived because she was hidden under a pile of corpses before she was eventually found by a Spanish soldier, who took her with him through the city and into the Spanish encampment from which she was redeemed by someone from Utrecht who felt compassion for her. Her mother survived as well, though she gave birth to a misshapen baby. Spanish women gave her clothes "to cover her shame." In Oudewater, she lost 14 sons and two daughters whose clothes she later recognized in a second-hand store in Utrecht (Duin, 1669, p. 14).

There are also the memories of one Jan Dirksz van Dam, who also was still a child in 1575. He was taken by a Spaniard who made him carry goods to the military camp. Tradeswomen bandaged him in the Spanish camp. He witnessed how people had to undress before they were killed in order to keep the clothes clean. He saw German soldiers on a cemetery dividing animals that were burned by the fire and how they carried the burnt meat to their camp. He saw Spaniards bathing in the river

IJssel moaning because lead had been poured over them. The Spaniard who kept little Jan seemed about to kill him several times, taking him away to hidden places and forcing him to undress. He also had to walk barefoot through the streets, burning his feet on the hot stones and smouldering wood (Duin, 1669, pp. 14–15).

16.5 Conclusion

We shall never know what happened in Oudewater on August 8, 1575, nor will we be able to assess the psychological damage done to individuals on that day. We can observe, however, the rise and persistence of public memory practices until today.

The emergence of public memories of victimhood is not self-evident, yet in Oudewater the necessary preconditions were present: The town recovered rapidly after the sack and lived in wealth and peace from the seventeenth century onward. Moreover, the victimhood of the survivors was acknowledged by both political authorities, by the public media, and by the community itself. Finally, a comprehensible narrative of what happened was produced that gave meaning to individual memories. This offered individuals the opportunity to share their memories with others.

The creation of a narrative of victimhood is complicated. Victims often feel shame. Important elements in the successful creation of a shared narrative of the Oudewater victimhood were striving for unity and a unifying history by way of blaming the enemy on one hand and by highlighting their own innocence, heroism, and endurance on the other. Contemporary religious beliefs offered the semantic categories to do so; because God tests his chosen people, suffering made sense.

One important condition for the collective commemoration of violence is the existence of what Aleida Asmann has called a *Solidargemeinschaft*, a community of solidarity (Assmann, 2006, p. 75). Victims share their experiences with their peers, with their community, and ultimately with the world at large only if these are prepared to listen and acknowledge their experiences. This does not always happen in postwar situations, let alone when war continues and there is a threat of further violence or when people are set adrift or are completely preoccupied with survival. Yet in the Northern Netherlands, the Revolt succeeded and Oudewater became part of the new Dutch Republic and was completely restored in about 10–20 years. By 1600, the local economy must have been flourishing as never before. Moreover, the fate of its citizens was acknowledged as part of the founding history of the new Protestant state. This history was marked by collective suffering under a tyrannical regime, heroic struggle, divine mercy, and faith. The memory of the internal division of the citizenry in the 1570s and issues of political blame and shame had to be buried. Oudewater, too, had been divided. Catholic survivors blamed their fellow citizens for having provoked Spanish fury, if not punishment from above (Jacobsz, 1559). Whereas Arnoldus Duin had remained silent on the mock procession on the walls, in 1712 Catholic priest Ignatius Walvis suggests that the massacre was not forgotten easily. He knew "a reputable person who had heard a very old woman in Oudewater tell repeatedly" of the mock procession with saints' images and a dog with a chalice, which had incited the Spanish to even greater fury and trashed the last chance of clemency (Walvis, 1999, p. 143). Instead of focusing on internal divisions, Duin, instead, scapegoats neighboring towns and anonymous outsiders.

It is possible that victims did not talk much about their memories until at least 30 or 40 years after the massacre, when the annual commemoration had been started and lists of survivors were compiled for the first time. Initially, only the stories of martyrdom and heroism were highlighted, a process that was facilitated by the existence of templates for such narratives in the media. Telling others of one's memories is a way to recovery, yet to be able to talk about painful or terrifying memories requires one to find a semantic category in which to do so. Victimhood was nothing to be proud of unless you endured it as a martyr, which implies moral victory. In the sixteenth- and seventeenth-century accounts of the sacks and massacres, we therefore find two general categories of narratives: the one emphasizing the innocence of the victim (such as the unborn baby) and the inhumane cruelty of the aggressor, and the other stressing individual or collective heroism (or martyrdom). The stories of Japikje Pieters and Jan Dirksz van Dam did not need to be heroic or very devout because they were still children at the time and thus innocent.

The historical material suggests that the victims of the massacre of Oudewater were offered quite optimal opportunities for coping. The religious and social environment provided for narrative schemata that made perfect sense of what happened. One's fate in earthly life is of secondary importance to those who believe that suffering is a test and that redemption will follow hereafter. Moreover, cross-cultural medical research suggests that, of all coping strategies, the solidarity of victims and witnesses, as well as the rebuilding of the social world, is most crucial. This is what the Oudewater community did. They restored social order, went back to work, and provided solidarity to the victims. Moreover, good had overcome evil, the true church had triumphed, and suffering had led to a better world."God has always been an avenger of the blood of his elect," Duin writes. History serves to remind mortal souls that they will stand before his throne at the last day.

References

Assmann, A. (2006). *Der lange Schatten der Vergangenheit: Erinnerungskultur und Geschichtspolitik*. München: C.H. Beck Verlag.
Boon, J. G. M. (1975). *Oudewater, 1570-1580: Vrijheid en gezag*. Oudewater: Gemeentebestuur van Oudewater.
Bor, P. C. (1621). *Nederlantsche oorloghen, beroerten, ende borgerlijcke oneenicheyden*. Leiden: Govert Basson.
Cilleßen, W. (2006). Massaker in der niederländischen Erinnerungskultur: Die Bildwerdung der schwarzen Legende. In C. Vogel (Ed.), *Bilder des Schreckens: Die mediale Inszenierung von Massakern seit dem 16. Jahrhundert* (pp. 93–135). Frankfurt am Main: Campus.
Duin A. (1669). *Oudewaters moord: Of waerachtig verhael van d'oudheid, belegering, innemen en verwoesten der geseide stad*. Oudewater.
Ford, A. (2001). Martyrdom, history and memory in early modern Ireland. In I. McBride (Ed.), *History and memory in modern Ireland* (pp. 43–66). Cambridge: Cambridge University Press.

Fox, A. (1999). Remembering the past in early modern England; oral and written tradition. *Transactions of the Royal Historical Society*, 9, 233–256.

Gowland, A. (2006). The problem of early modern melancholy. *Past & Present, 191*, 77–120.

Harari, Y. N. (2004). *Renaissance military memoirs: War, history, and identity, 1450–1600*. Woodbridge: Boydell Press.

Haskell, Y. (2009). The languages of melancholy in early modern England. *The British Journal for the History of Science*, 42(2), 275–280.

Hunt, N. C. (2010). *Memory, war and trauma*. Cambridge: Cambridge University Press.

Jacobsz, W. (1959). *Dagboek van broeder wouter jacobsz (gualtherus jacobi masius) prior van stein: Amsterdam 1572–1578 en Montfoort 1578–1579*.

Knipscheer, J., & Kleber, R. (2008). *Psychologie en de multiculturele samenleving*. Den Haag: Boom Lemma Uitgevers.

Kuijpers E., & Pollmann J. (2013). Why remember terror? Memories of violence in the Dutch revolt. In J. Ohlmeyer & M. O'Siochrú (Eds.), *Ireland 1641: Contexts and reactions* (pp. 176–196). Manchester: Manchester University Press.

Lund, M. A. (2010). *Melancholy, medicine and religion in early modern England: Reading "The anatomy of melancholy"*. Cambridge: Cambridge University Press.

Meteren, E. (1599). *Belgische ofte Nederlantsche historie, van onsen tijden.: Inhoudende hoe de Nederlanden aenden anderen ghehecht, ende aen Spaengien ghecomen zijn... Meest onder de regeeringhe van Philippus de II. coninc van Spaengien, tot synen doot, ende den vvtgaenden iare 1598. Eensdeels int Latijn ende Hoochduytsche stuckwijs in druck wtghegaen, maer nuby den autheur selve oversien, verbetert ende vermeerdert, wtghegeuen*. Delft: Vennecool, Jacob Cornelissz Delft, 1596–1605.

Mielke, U., & Luijten, G. (Eds.). (2009). *Frans hogenberg: Broadsheets*. Amsterdam: Rijksmuseum.

National Archive, The Hague, Archive 3.01.04.01, States of Holland, Inv. Nr. 333, folio 519v–520.

North, C. S., Pfefferbaum, B., Narayanan, P., Thielmans, S., McCoy, G., & Dumont, C. (2005). Comparison of post-disaster psychiatric disorders after terrorist bombings in Nairobi and Oklahoma city. *The British Journal of Psychiatry*, 186(6), 487–493.

Old Town Archive Oudewater, Inv. Nr. 165, Lists of survivors of the Oudewater massacre, 1615–1664.

Pollmann, J. (2009). Burying the dead, reliving the past. Ritual, resentment and sacred space in the Dutch Republic. In B. Kaplan, B. Moore, & H. van Nierop (Eds.), *Catholic communities in protestant states. Britain and the Netherlands, 1580–1700*. Manchester: Manchester University Press.

Schmidt, J. (2007). *Melancholy and the care of the soul: Religion, moral philosophy and madness in early modern England*. Aldershot: Ashgate Publishing.

Shiraev, E. (2007). *Cross-cultural psychology: Critical thinking and contemporary applications*. Boston, MA: Pearson Education.

Stoppelenburg, N. (2005). *De Oudewaterse moord. [S.l.]: Stichting cultureel sociaal fonds mooyman-martens*.

Walsham, A. (2011). The reformation of the landscape: Religion: *Identity, and memory in early modern Britain and Ireland*. Oxford: Oxford University Press.

Walvis, I. (1999). *Het goudsche aarts priesterdom*. Delft.

Winter, J. (1999). *War and remembrance in the twentieth century*. Cambridge: Cambridge University Press.

17 Conflict Avoidance, Forgetting, and Distorted Memories by Media Influence on Family Memories: Grandpa Was No Nazi and No Communist

Klaus Bachmann
Warsaw School of Social Sciences and Humanities, Warsaw, Poland

17.1 Distorted Memories of the Political Activities of Family Members

In 2002, Harald Welzer's research revealed some of the mechanisms that govern the development of family memory in Germany (Welzer, 2007; Welzer, Moller, & Tschuggnall, 2005). Welzer and others had conducted a number of loosely structured qualitative interviews in small family groups comprising members of several generations.[1] The interviewers inclined the family members to talk about the past, with a focus on World War II, the Third Reich, and the Holocaust. Most of the interviews showed that families communicate in a very rudimentary, enigmatic way about the difficult past of family members (Keppler, 1994). Mainly two elements of this research evoked discussion because of their counterintuitive and surprising character. First, the interviews showed a tendency that ran contrary to the official "historical policy" of the Federal Republic of Germany. Whereas in the official discourse of politicians, intellectuals, and the media, the construction of the Third Reich had become more and more exclusive and self-critical, family memory tended to become more and more inclusive and uncritical. Welzer and Keppler's interviews revealed how members of the later generations whitewashed their fathers and grandfathers in retrospect, even when compromising information about their past actions was easily obtainable and had not been hidden by the older generation. These findings inspired the title of Welzer's book, *Opa war kein Nazi* ("Grandpa was no Nazi"; Welzer et al., 2005). Even when children and grandchildren of a former party member knew about

---

[1] It is worth mentioning that trauma was no issue in Welzer's research and is none in this study. The families should be regarded as a random sample, and our interviewers had no knowledge about possible traumas in those families before they started the interviews.

Hurting Memories and Beneficial Forgetting.
DOI: http://dx.doi.org/10.1016/B978-0-12-398393-0.00017-1
© 2013 Elsevier Inc. All rights reserved.

the past, they strongly tended to excuse him with phrases pointing to the pressure that he had allegedly been exposed to. In such cases, respondents retrospectively put their ancestors on the good side of the historical barricades and "the Nazis" on the bad side. Grandpa had not been a real Nazi because he had been forced to become member of the National Socialist German Workers Party (NSDAP), whereas "the Nazis"—all other members of that party who remained anonymous in these accounts—were regarded as bad guys.

The second surprise concerned the frequent inclusion of media frames into family and personal memory. Welzer et al. (2005) found numerous examples when family members structured their personal experiences and stories about their ancestors in the same way as in popular films, in literary fiction, or on television. In some cases, even frames from *Schindler's List* or the German film *Das Boot* ("The Submarine") were being retold as personal experience. In a later volume, Welzer (2007) and some other authors tried to extend their research to other societies and create something like a transnational approach in family memory research. These attempts included West European countries or Croatia and Serbia.

17.2 Study of Family Memories in Poland

In a similar study in Poland,[2] in the framework of an MA sociology course, we elaborated a guideline for family interviews. The students were trained to address every issue of the questionnaire without revealing their own position about the topic. If possible, they should carry out the interviews in the presence of members of at least two generations of a family and, when possible, in a three-generational setting. In some cases, this proved difficult either because the members of the oldest generation were too old or too ill to be interviewed or, in other cases, because, although the grandpa generation was responsive and able to answer in a meaningful way, the members of the youngest generation did not yet have any knowledge of or interest in the past (e.g., when a grandchild was only 8 years old). We obtained 26 interviews with 61 different respondents, that is, 23 interviews with members of two different generations and 5 interviews in a three-generational setting. Some of the interviews were carried out with several respondents at the same time, when they were available together. The interviews were recorded and then written down by the students. All respondents were informed about the complete anonymity of the interviews, and the interviewers were instructed not to reveal the names of their respondents in the transcripts. They also were asked to give general assessments about the reaction of

---

[2] I am grateful to the following students who took part in the project conducting and documenting the interviews: Natalia Żukowska, Agnieszka Sojczyńska, Renata Salamończyk, Hubert Remiszewski, Tomasz Pilitkowski, Łukasz Paradowski, Natalia Napiórkowska, Dominika Małkowska, Joanna Karbowiak, Piotr Luterek, Marta Mierzejewska, Marta Kowalska, Damian Mikszto, Anna Anczarska, Aleksandra Domosławska, Elżbieta Jaszczyk, Magdalena Kahl, Anna Wdowia, Ewa Bender, Marcin Hyndle, Liliana Korczyńska, Agnieszka Karbowiecka, Wojciech Kocięcki, Marek Zubacz, Zuzanna Krawczyk, and Wojciech Iwaszczuk.

their respondents during the interview and the conditions under which the interviews were carried out. As an additional test for the emergence of media frames in personal and family memory of the respondents, each respondent was asked to fill in an (also anonymous) questionnaire, which enumerated the most popular Polish films (from Polish TV and from Polish and international cinema) and books dealing with the issues mentioned in the main questionnaire. We used a five-item scale for detecting the level of our respondents' familiarity with these films, ranging from "I saw it and remember details" to "I never heard about it," including one evasive answer ("I don't know, I can't say").

All respondents came from Warsaw and the immediate environment, which does not mean that these people had always lived in Warsaw. During World War II, the city was destroyed, and in 1944 only about 800 people were still living in the ruins (Borodziej, 2006). After that, Warsaw attracted immigrants from all over the country.

The main points of the interview were

- the relationship of respondents and their ancestors to Jews,
- their collaboration with either the Soviets or the Germans during World War II,
- whether they had taken part in official activities under communism (like elections and the First of May parades),
- their relationship to Jaruzelski or Walesa, and the imposition of martial law by General Jaruzelski in 1981, and
- their attitude during the first competitive elections following the Round Table talks in 1989.

All these questions aimed at inclining respondents to take a side. Most interviewers were either friends or acquaintances of their respondents' families or were even related to them, which enhanced trust and contributed to a relaxed atmosphere between interviewers and respondents. No interviewers reported tensions between them and some or all of their respondents.

Among the 26 interviews, 11 revealed elements of an intergenerational conflict about differing normative approaches to the past, mostly about the membership of a family member in the Polish United Workers Party (PUWP), the Union of the Socialist Youth, or the cleavage between Solidarity members and PUWP members during the eighties. In some cases, the cause of conflict was the past attitude of family members to Jews. Also, some media frames were identified, one of which was highly amazing. Not all media frames could be identified; in one case, a younger respondent even admitted (without being asked) that she probably "remembered nothing from own experience, but all from films."

Very often, older respondents revealed feelings of intensive stress, which in some cases interviewers also mentioned in their general assessment. In a few cases—and uniquely with regard to events related to World War II—the interview had to be interrupted and continued after respondents had recovered. The stress was not only due to a limelight effect, whose origin was the mere fact of being formally interviewed, but also to the specific questions asked by the interviewers. Some of the latter felt this tension to an extent that inclined them either to avoid some questions from the questionnaire or to put them off to the end of the interview (which was in accordance with the instructions) or to drop the question immediately and switch to other issues, once they became aware of their respondents' feelings. In a few cases, interviewers anticipated the presumed stress of their respondents and changed the direction of their questions (asking, e.g., about "Jews saved by family members" instead of asking about anti-Semitism and denunciation of family members).

The Jewish question seems to be the biggest taboo case in Polish family memory. Most respondents either used evasive answers to address it or denied any knowledge about Polish–Jewish relations in their immediate environment. One respondent told us, when asked about war experiences, "We rather tried to erase that from our memory." The silence about the past in some families went so far that some of the interviews revealed hardly any information about the past. This was linked not only to potentially hurting memories (like the deportation of several members of the family to concentration camps and to Siberia) but also to the past as such. Whereas the interview with the 70-year-old grandmother proved almost totally inconclusive, the interview with her daughter revealed a possible reason for the prevalent silence in the family. Asked whether a family member had collaborated with the Germans during the occupation, the 48-year-old woman said, "That is possible, but we don't talk about that." Asked about the reason for that suspicion, she responded, "From family gossip I know that something like that could have happened, but no one ever talked about that. I don't want to talk about it either because that would mean to denigrate someone after death. However, such doubts are there, at least I have heard about them."

The second issue, which dominated respondents' accounts about their past, was a complete absence of political engagement or even interest for politics. When asked about their role in past conflicts (like Poland's postwar crucial events in 1956, 1968, 1970, 1981, or 1989), the overwhelming majority declared passivity. One respondent told us, "We inherited lack of political interest in our blood" ("*Apolityczność mamy we krwi*").

17.3 Intergenerational Conflict About the Past

Throughout the recent past, Polish society has been divided along political lines on several occasions. During World War II, the country was occupied first by Germany and the Soviet Union (between 1939 and 1941), then by Germany (1941–1944), and then again by the Soviet Union, which installed a minority regime loyal to the Soviet leadership in Moscow (Jatrzebski, 2010). During the war, Poles fought for Germany (which had annexed the western parts of prewar Poland and recruited Silesians into the Wehrmacht), for the Soviet Union (after being recruited in the territories annexed in 1939 by the Soviet Union), and for Great Britain (after a number of Polish soldiers had been transferred from the Soviet Union through the near East to the Western Front). In the country, the nationalist and anti-Communist Home Army (Armia Krajowa, AK) was the strongest resistance force against the German occupation, whereas Communist and pro-Soviet units were weaker. After the war, the country was politically divided into pro-Western supporters of Polish independence and pro-Soviet forces, which were strongly supported by the Soviet Union. In

1956, after violently crushed workers' protests, all political forces, the church, and the overwhelming majority of the population rallied behind the renewed PUWP leadership, fearing that the rapid de-Stalinization of the party and the reinstitution of a new national Communist leadership could trigger a similar military intervention by the USSR as in Hungary. In 1967–1968, the government responded to massive protests of intellectuals and a large part of the youth with a police crackdown on protesters and a fiercely nationalist and anti-Semitic campaign, which led to the emigration of tens of thousands of Polish Communists of Jewish origin, who had worked in the state administration, the Army, and the security sector.

The next historical watershed took place in 1970, when the Army cracked down on worker protests at the Polish coast, causing several casualties and a reshuffling of the party leadership. Finally, in 1980, huge strikes all over the country forced the government to legalize Solidarity, the first labor union in a Warsaw Pact member, which was independent from the Communist party. After several waves of strikes and increasing tension between Solidarity, on the one hand, and the party leadership and the government, on the other hand, a junta of generals under the leadership of General Wojciech Jaruzelski imposed martial law, forbade and dissolved Solidarity, and weakened the civil PUWP leadership, introducing military rule. Unable to reform the economy and paralyzed by a yearlong stalemate between Solidarity (which controlled the factories) and the military leadership (which controlled the security sector and the state administration), both sides agreed to Round Table talks and partly free and competitive elections, which ended the PUWP's rule forever.

From the perspective of family memory, all these events happened far away from everyday life and were hardly ever the subject of discussions in the families who agreed to answer our questions. This shows a huge divide between the official patriotic discourse, which emphasizes and promotes pride about these events (mostly presenting them as the courageous fight of "the nation" against "the Communists" or "for freedom"), and family memory, which emphasizes the passivity, opportunism, or pragmatism of ordinary citizens. Whereas textbooks paint a picture of a resistant and heroic society fighting against foreign oppressors, family memory reveals a society in which people stay away from conflicts and political engagement and wait for the result of a struggle that is staged by others. "We don't talk about the past," one respondent, a 79-year-old grandmother, told one of our interviewers bluntly. A 62-year-old daughter, when asked whether her parents ever were party members or were engaged in the opposition, responded, "It's difficult to answer because I never talked to my parents about that and they also never spoke about it." In one case, respondents mentioned that their grandfather had been a camp inmate in Germany during World War II, but they were unable to give any details because he had never spoken about it. The context made it apparent that the other family members had kept silent about it in order to avoid anticipated stress for the grandfather, who obviously seemed to prefer to bury his difficult memories rather than to share them. But in some other cases, families had kept quiet even about quite heroic episodes of family members. During one interview, a 41-year-old son learned from his father about his uncle's participation in the first battle of World War II on Westerplatte (a Polish island close to what was then the Free City of Danzig, which was the first

Polish position attacked by the German navy in 1939), an event that to this today is shrouded in myth. In another family, an interviewer started his three separate interviews with an 85-year-old grandmother, who told him about her deportation to Siberia, incidentally mentioning that she probably survived "because someone had to survive in order to weep for the whole family that perished." Subsequently, the interviewer asked the members of the other generations about their knowledge of the family fate in World War II. They were much more detailed in their account. Apparently, everybody knew that "the whole family had been killed," but no one was able to give any further details, let alone the causes of the death and the conflict side (the Germans, the Soviets) responsible for their death.

Interviewer: Ludka, do you know anything about the fate of your family during World War II?

Ludka (63): As far as I know, a part of my family lived in Georgia [in the former Soviet Union, KB] and they sent them to the front. My father, a famous specialist in bridge construction ended up on the Arctic Circle, so he missed the whole massacre, but all the others lived in Georgia; they were busy with their things and the Germans never arrived there, but the part of family here went to the East, the rest stayed here, and unfortunately the whole family was totally extinguished. Probably they were killed during the first period because otherwise they would have sent some sign of life. When father got the proposition to go to Poland after the war, there were all the time searches and it was impossible to find out anything.

After the 63-year-old mother, the interviewer asked her 45-year-old daughter about the same events. The following dialogue took place:

Interviewer: Justyna, do you know the fate of your family during World War II?

Justyna (45): More or less, just as much as grandma spoke about it. From her, I know that the whole family was killed either by the Germans or the Russians. Grandma's father and the part of the family which was in Warsaw had already died at the beginning of the war in 1939, and about the others no one knows where and when they died. I know that the brother of my mama with his wife and children died in Warsaw. They just were all killed.

The youngest among the respondents seemed to know more about the events than the oldest, reducing the "whole family" to two adults with their children. The fragment also indicates that despite the strongly affirmative approach, which prevails in Poland with regard to the recent past, family memory is transmitted from generation to generation in more or less the same fragmentary and scattered way as in Germany. In no single family did we encounter any information about structured and systematic talks about history. Family history is passed from generation to generation in the form of enigmatic utterances, which are difficult to understand for outsiders and mostly avoid normative loading. They are strongly mixed up with elements from outside, fragments of books, information retrieved from the media, and general knowledge, whose origin is impossible to detect. During one interview, a respondent praised the allegedly "perfect order and tidiness" in occupied Warsaw, which he could not have witnessed personally because he was born in 1956.

Just as in the German studies quoted at the beginning of the chapter, Polish family memory is strongly inclusive. When asked about party members in the family or even members of the Communist secret police, respondents either denied any knowledge about the issue or, when mentioning such cases, symbolically included them, justifying their comportment, mostly by claiming that they were "forced" or "compelled" to adhere.

17.4 The Inclusiveness of Polish Family Memory

In the majority of cases when respondents admitted behavior that, from their own retrospective assessment, was regarded as a potential source of shame, they immediately justified it by referring to duress. In one case, participation in the strongly ritualized mass rallies on May 1 was described as "funny" ("*to byla frajda*") and at the same time as something done under coercion. There were only a few families whose members described their participation in those rallies as a source of fun and happiness. These families showed a strong affiliation to the Polish post-Communist left and strong ties with the *nomenklatura* during the eighties. Almost always, when family members told their stories about May 1 (not all respondents did), they highlighted weaker or stronger degrees of state pressure as the main reason for participation. This ranged from the fear of reprisals at the workplace to more general allegations, such as "We were forced to go," "One had to participate," or "That's what we had to do."

In the same way, families justified party membership or membership in state-sponsored mass organizations. Family members who had become PUWP members at a certain time in their career were exculpated with arguments involving external pressure. In a few cases, family members of later generations explained the adherence of their ancestors to ideologically driven organizations by referring to their idealism. In one case, even a member of the Democratic Party (*Stronnictwo Demokratyczne*) was excused as an incurable idealist. The respondent even reinforced this claim by suggesting that other family members had taken advantage of his relative's idealism and his position in order to garner privileges for themselves. In another case, a respondent explained his father's membership in the PUWP as "stupidity" (*z glupoty*) and his own membership in the Socialist Youth as the result of "calculation" (*z wyrachowania*). Hardly ever did family members taking different sides during the critical junctures of Polish history become a source of lasting tension within a family. Families avoided lasting conflicts by resorting to silence. No one would confront family members with their work for the secret police or the police during the eighties—for the sake of peace in the household. The moral dilemmas of potentially hurting memories were avoided by avoiding questions about issues that could reveal uncomfortable knowledge. In a very tense and sometimes even angry dispute between a 56-year-old mother and her 22-year-old son, the latter attacked her for the silence about history in the family: "They avoided this issue [World War II] like fire."

> Interviewer: So you did not learn anything from them?
> Son: They never wanted to say anything about the war—the only interesting topic about which they could talk, but they sat silent.

Interviewer: Did you try to get something out of them?
Son: I asked.
Interviewer: So what did they tell you?
Son: Nothing.
Interviewer: What did they say?
Son: lalalala.
Mother: One had to keep silent because otherwise one could get a bullet in the head during the war.

In this family, a strong intergenerational conflict between a pro-Communist mother (who had adhered to the PUWP and voluntarily taken part in the May 1 parades) and her apparently anti-Communist son became visible, which even led to a dialogue during which the son accused the mother of denouncing others to the secret police. However, this interview constitutes an absolute exception among the other interviews. If there was a conflict among members of two generations, it usually developed as in the following dialogue between a 53-year-old mother and her 28-year-old daughter. Apparently, there had been a conflict between the family of the mother's husband and her own parents. During the first meeting, she claimed, her father-in-law had claimed to be a former AK member, who had "executed verdicts" during the occupation. Between 1939 and 1944, AK had issued about 3500 such verdicts mostly against low-ranking members of the German administration and informers who had passed information about the resistance movement and Jews who had fled the ghetto and gone into hiding to the German authorities. About 2500 of these verdicts had been carried out. In another time and other circumstances, this would have been a reason of pride. But the respondent's husband had, for unknown reason, been beaten up by people who were associated with AK. When both interlocutors tried to explain this to the interviewer in a scattered and disrupted dialogue, it turned out that the issue was still a source of tension in the family.

Interviewer: Why did they beat him?
Mother: They were living together very closely then. Yes, I know, maybe they didn't like something, but it's good they did not kill him.
Interviewer: So would you say that someone of the family was persecuted?
Mother: Rather no.
Interviewer: And those who beat the father?
Daughter: That's what I wanted to say.
Mother: Well, yes, that would mean, my grandfather was beaten up by gangs. [Respondent uses the expression bandy, which was frequently used in Communist propaganda to emphasize the nonpolitical and allegedly criminal character of the armed anti-Communist opposition: KB.]
Interviewer: No one wanted anything from you?
Mother: Mom says they were gangs. No, they didn't want anything from me.
Daughter: So they were gangs of AK fighters?
Mother: No, they never said it was AK, just gangs.
Daughter: Those from AK were gangs, right?
Mother: For them they were gangs, but I don't know whether this was actually the same or not, I don't know today.
Daughter: So not AK, but gangs.

Mostly, it was not the wartime that aroused tensions in the families during the interviews but the differing attitudes of family members toward PUWP membership and the imposition of martial law in 1981. During an interview between a 59-year-old father and his 26-year-old son, such a clash emerged. Before, the son had mentioned his mother's story about the soldiers who had accompanied her home during martial law when she was pregnant with the respondent's sister. He used this as a proof that these soldiers had been polite and helpful.

Father: So why should they not be polite, they were human being, though.
Son: Such a ZOMO was not polite at all. [ZOMO was a popular abbreviation for antiriot police, which, heavily armed, was used against oppositional demonstrators during and after martial law: KB.]
Father: What do you know about that? You weren't born yet.
Son: I read books, I have internet, TV.
Father: The point of view depends on the point of where you sit [A Polish proverb: KB.]. Nobody was hit without a reason.
Son: And Popieluszko? [Jerzy Populuszko was an anti-Communist priest, close to the political opposition, who in 1984 was killed by a death squad of the secret police, KB.]
Father: Who knows, how this really happened.

17.5 The Impact of Media Frames

In many more cases than initially expected, we were able to detect traces or whole frames from modern media, which were integrated into family members' memory (and sometimes into the intergenerational memory). Sometimes, these frames appeared only as scattered fragments of larger frames used in literature, for example, when a respondent (a 90-year-old grandmother whose family had fled at the beginning of World War II from Kraśnik near Lublin to Krzemieniec Podolski, which is now in the western part of Ukraine) told the interviewer about the "fights between Poles and Ukrainians" and "whole villages burning in the night"[3] (Polska–Ukraina, 2006; Torzecki, 1993). The latter fragment is part of a larger frame, coming from popular accounts about the Polish–Ukrainian conflicts in Wolynia, which has

---

[3] In the eastern parts of prewar Poland and in the provinces of Wolynia and Eastern Galicia (in Polish Małopolska Wschodnia), a nationalist partisan movement, the so-called Ukrainian Insurgent Army (Українська Повстанська Армія, UPA), launched a major offensive in 1943–1944 against the presence of the Polish administration, strongholds of the Polish partisan movement, and predominantly Polish villages in the ethnically mixed borderland. According to moderate calculations, accepted by Polish and Ukrainian mainstream historians, about 80,000 Poles fell prey to these actions, which best can be described as ethnic cleansing, and caused violent vengeance from Polish partisans. Victim organizations in Poland usually refer to much higher numbers of victims. See the special issue on Polish–Ukrainian relations during World War II (Polska–Ukraina, trudne pytania, Materiały międzynarodowego seminarium historycznego, Stosunki polsko-ukraińskie w latach II wojny światowe. Toruń, 11–12. października 2006, vol. 11, Warszawa 2006, pp. 15–112 and also Torzecki, Ryszard: Polacy i Ukraińcy. Sprawa ukraińska w czasie II wojny światowej na terenie II Rzeczypospolitej. Warszawa 1993, passim).

become a kind of national narrative and today often shows up even in narrations of people who were born after the war and who have never been in the territories where these conflicts took place. The frame about the "burning villages," which is often accompanied by much more cruel accounts about the behavior of "Ukrainian nationalists" or "the Ukrainians," is part of a narrative that was shaped by popular historical accounts, many of which were to a large part invented. They emerged during the sixties and often had a strong ideological bias. Nevertheless, they remained popular even long after 1989 and were taken as truthful by many because they fit into their personal experiences. In many cases, these accounts show up in personal stories about the past in the form of specific phrases, like the ones about "burning villages" (*paliły się wioski*), "massacres" (*rzezi*, a word that is almost entirely reserved for the description of Ukrainian atrocities against Poles), and "fiery glow" (*łuny*, another word almost entirely reserved for the Polish–Ukrainian context, due to a famous best seller, titled *Fiery Glows in the Carpathian Mountains* (Łuny w Bieszczadach).[4] In the case of the 90-year-old lady from Krzemieniec Podolski, the burning-village frame lost its attraction in the subsequent generations, whose members did not mention any conflicts with Ukrainians, when they told their stories about the family's past. No Ukrainian frames showed up then, although the member of the second generation was interviewed together with the old lady. The old lady seemed to remember Gerhard's story about the Polish–Ukrainian fights in the Carpathian Mountains much better than her daughter. In the questionnaire, the latter indicated only that she had "watched the movie but did not much remember about it," whereas the grandmother told the interviewer to mention in the questionnaire that she "remembered the book much better than the film."

Similar frames were detected when one of our interviewers monitored the talk between a mother and her son. She was recounting about her husband's relatives fighting east of Warsaw during the final days of World War II: "On my side of the family, almost everyone fought." At that moment, her son interrupted her, saying, "Even Uncle Edek, who had this pseudonym 'parasol'? 'Watch'? I don't know, but that is how it was supposed to be. His grave is on the Powązki cemetery and there it is written on the tombstone." In Polish, the word *parasol* is the same whereas the Polish equivalent of *watch* (the word he actually used during the interview) is *zegar*, which starts with the same letter as *Zośka* (a maiden name). *Zośka i Parasol* are the names of two AK battalions that fought during the Warsaw Uprising and were immortalized by writer Aleksander Kamiński in a famous novel *Zośka i Parasol*. After the comment from her son, the mother did not return to this issue. She mentioned only that the respective uncle was a chief accountant and then went on with her story.

In a similar way, a frame from a famous Polish film, the first postwar comedy, emerged in the narration of a grandmother, interviewed together with her daughter and granddaughter. The plot of the film takes place in a crowded flat, where different

---

[4] Jan Gerhard's book, *Łuny w Bieszczadach*, also became the basis of a popular film titled *Ogniomistrz Kaleń*, which appeared on Polish cinema screens in 1961 and later on TV.

people are waiting for their own apartment in postwar Warsaw. During her monologue, the grandmother even mentioned the film from which stems her account, *The Treasure (Skarb)*. Her aunt had to leave Warsaw during the war.

> *And then, my aunt told me, "that since we, the people from Warsaw, were not always well treated by the people we met on our way, so I will accommodate everyone who needs help." And that's what she did. There was, as I remember, when we once came to her during vacation, in the evening; I don't know whether you know the film The Treasure?*
> *Interviewer: A long time ago, I did.*
> *Grandmother: So there was the same: People came, not at all related to my aunt and nothing, everyone could pop up his cot, a mattress on the soil and so on ... [The door bell rings.]*
> *Granddaughter: I am going to open.*
> *Grandmother: ... and just like this, she accommodated foreign people. They stayed for the night, in the morning, they left, and then in the evening again, until they found their own flat.*

These were only fragmentary elements of popular media frames. They were too scrappy to shape the whole story and even too fragmentary to attribute meaning or interpretation to the narrated facts. Respondents used expressions from popular books and films while telling their own stories, but—opposite to some examples from the German interviews—they did not integrate whole narratives from the media and present them as own experiences. Frame elements were used as a kind of cliché, a shortcut that appeals to the pictures that other interlocutors most likely have stored in their memory. In one interview with a 75-year-old father and his 41-year-old son, the latter answers the interviewer's question about how he experienced the introduction of martial law in 1981 Poland. The response contains a popular description that may come from personal experience as well as from documentary films, popular accounts, and the literature: "I remember, the winter was harsh and the Army was at roadblocks; there were coke ovens and Topas vehicles." The "harsh winter," the "Army at roadblocks," and the "coke ovens" serve as shortcuts by which almost any interlocutor in Poland would be able to identify that the story told is related to martial law, just as the term *tuny* suggests a link with Ukrainians and the Eastern territories.

But some cases indicated the inclusion of more than just shortcuts into their stories that they regarded as their personal experience. This became apparent during an interview with a 59-year-old mother and her 23-year-old daughter, who were talking about the war experience of the latter's grandmother, who had died 12 years before the interview. The dialogue went like this:

> *Interviewer: You don't remember the wartime, but certainly you have some memories from the stories of your parents.*
> *Mother: To say the truth, my parents were not very much harmed by the war. My mother lived in Polesie, which today belongs to Ukraine; my grandfather, her father, ran a distillery, which means that he lived in peace with the Germans and the Russians, and they did not need to hide, they did not have reason to be scared.*

Daughter: But grandma spoke about some concentration camp which was nearby and that she saw people there who went mad from hunger and threw themselves at the electric fence and they died of course. Am I wrong?
Mother: Maybe she said something like that, probably about Sobibor, but I never harassed her with questions like you did, so I don't know how it was.

In this case, there are two possibilities about how this frame entered family memory: We can assume that the grandmother integrated it into her story and then told the story about "mad prisoners jumping at the electric wire" to her granddaughter, or we can assume that the granddaughter enriched the memory of her grandmother retrospectively by adding a frame from popular culture. It is quite clear that the frame could not have originated in the personal experience of the grandmother because there never was an electric fence in Sobibór. (There was, however, a barbed wire fence, and the soil outside the fence was mined.) Electric fences were used in other camps, from Sachsenhausen to Auschwitz and Stutthof, and that is most probably where the frame comes from.

Another frame is more evident but also much more puzzling because it contains elements that are not at all popular or even known in Poland but that are quite widespread among the generation of Germans who were expelled from Poland's prewar western parts at the end of the war. It was extremely surprising to find such a frame in the story of a very pro-Communist family who had migrated from northern Poland to the border town of Bydgoszcz before the outbreak of World War II. In Bydgoszcz, which is better known in Germany as Bromberg, there was a vibrant and numerous German minority, who had come under Polish rule after Germany had lost World War I and Bromberg had become a Polish town. When in the first days of September 1939, the Wehrmacht invaded Poland and the Polish troops had to withdraw quickly and often in huge disarray, a number of German citizens in the town were accused of treason and collaboration with the enemy and were killed by Polish soldiers and civilians. According to different sources, between 103 and 379 Germans were killed in Bydgoszcz. Subsequently, the German propaganda inflated the number of victims to several thousand and finally to the horrendous number of over 50,000 German casualties in western Poland. These claims about "Polish atrocities" (which actually had taken place but had caused far fewer victims than claimed) were used to justify retaliation mostly against the Polish intelligentsia in the territories that the Third Reich later annexed. In West German postwar historiography, as well as in many popular accounts written and read by *Vertriebenen*, this has become known as the Bloody Sunday of Bromberg (*der Bromberger Blutsonntag*), a term that was initially invented by the Third Reich's propaganda office (Schubert, 1989). In Polish, the corresponding term "*Krwawa Bydgoska Niedziela*" was used only in quotation marks in order to demonstrate the reservations that Polish historians had about German claims of Polish atrocities. It never became a popular topic of Polish historiography, and only a handful of historians dedicated their work to the elucidation of the events during the first days of September 1939. The whole notion can therefore be regarded only as a frame, whose origin and recent use are German in the sense that it is used within a specific (and quite narrow) German audience, the audience of readers of and contributors to *Vertriebenenliteratur*. One would never expect the notion of the Bloody Sunday of Bromberg to be included in the stories of a pro-Communist Polish family. But this is what happened when one interviewer carried out two subsequent interviews with, first, an 81-year-old lady and (at another time and in another place) her 54-year-old son. First, the following dialogue took place:

> *The lady: We were in Kościerzyna [a small town in the Kashubian part of Poland: KB] until my sixth year, which means I was born in 1929, until I was 35 years old. Then we went to Bydgoszcz because my father was offered work in the middle school there, and we moved to Bydgoszcz and lived there until World War II broke out. In Bydgoszcz, the famous "Bloody Sunday" took place; there, Germans attacked the Polish intelligence and not only the Germans that arrived, but also the ones who were living permanently in Bydgoszcz, because in Pomerania a lot of Germans used to live and they gathered and attacked the Poles. My father managed to escape, because if he had stayed, he would have been killed. A day earlier he managed to get through the border from Bydgoszcz. We stayed and Dad went to Krakow, where his family was at that time, Dad's brother. We stayed in Bydgoszcz until January 1940.*

In this fascinating fragment of the interview, the respondent not only integrated the Bloody Sunday frame into her own experience but also inverted it into the opposite. Whereas the classical frame, known from German historical literature, deals with Poles attacking the German minority in Bromberg, here the frame is about Germans who attack a Polish minority—not even invading German soldiers but local Germans from the town. One of the basic frames of German *Vertriebenenliteratur* was incorporated into the narrative of a Polish family. It would be to no avail to speculate how and why this happened. It may be a trace of *hegemonic discourse* in Pierre Bourdieu's (1991) sense. Besides, the story does not end there. The same topic showed up in the talk that the interviewer conducted with the lady's 54-year-old son. The frame appeared again, but this time it was not an inverted version of the original German one. It now described the persecutions of Polish intelligentsia in Bydgoszcz after the town had fallen prey to the German troops, those of large-scale arrests having started together with fake trials against alleged members of the Polish mob, who were (often falsely) accused of having killed the German civilians.

> *Interviewer: During World War II, where was the family, and what was its fate?*
> *Respondent: In September 1939, when the Germans invaded Bydgoszcz, it was during September 6 or 8, as far as I remember, the so-called Bloody Sunday happened, where the Polish intelligentsia[5] was eliminated, which means they shot the Polish intelligentsia, and my grandfather managed to escape because he was a biology professor and therefore a member of the intelligentsia and at the same time a painter; he managed to escape to Krakow.*

---

[5] Polish word "inteligencja" means both "intelligence" and "intelligentsia".

17.6 Conclusions

Just like the German interviews, Polish family talk about the past is predominantly inclusive and runs contrary to the countrywide debate. There seems to be a deep divide between an official, patriotic, and heroic discourse, on the one hand, which posits "the nation" against the evils of Communism and German occupation and, on the other hand, family memory, which highlights passivity, opportunism, and pragmatism. Whereas public discourse makes sharp normative distinctions between those who did good and bad in the past, family memory is much less normative and mainly refers to rational notions of behavior, like aspirations of a better life or the wish to protect the family against external threats or to avert harm and poverty. Just as in Germany, family memory in Poland is strongly inclusive. We found no single case in which a family would have ousted a member (even symbolically, e.g., by stating that "he is no member of the family any more") for being on the wrong side of the historical barricades. If families were divided in the past, they usually manage to deal with the tension that arises from the division by keeping silent about the past or by exculpating their potential black sheep. Tension between older and younger generations was noticed, but it was the exception to the rule. Heroic attitudes, like the participation in the Warsaw Uprising, in the war resistance, or in Solidarity, are important issues in the public sphere; they are hardly ever a topic for family discussions. Families tend to include media frames into their personal and family histories, but they do it in an unstructured, scattered way, which almost never enhances the meaningfulness of their stories. These frames and frame elements are used as tools that facilitate mutual agreement with an interlocutor rather than as a means to structure one's own stories and attribute meaning to them.

References

Borodziej, W. (2006). *The Warsaw uprising 1944*. Madison: University of Wisconsin Press.
Bourdieu, P. (1991). *Language and symbolic power*. Cambridge: Polity Press.
Jatrzebski, W. (2010). *Mniejszość niemiecka w Polsce we wrześniu 1939 roku*. Adam Marszałek: Toruń.
Keppler, A. (1994). *Tischgespräche. Über Formen kommunikativer Vergemeinschaftung am Beispiel der Konversation in Familien*. Frankfurt/Main: Suhrkamp Verlag.
Polska–Ukraina, *trudne pytania, Materiały międzynarodowego seminarium historycznego "Stosunki polsko-ukraińskie w latach II wojny światowej"* (2006). Torun, 11–12. października 2006, vol. 11. Warszawa: Instytut Studiów Politycznych Polskiej Akademii Nauk.
Schubert, G. (1989). *Das Unternehmen "Bromberger Blutsonntag". Tod einer Legende*. Köln: Bund Verlag.
Torzecki, R. (1993). *Polacy i Ukraińcy. Sprawa Ukraińska w czasie II wojny światowej na terenie II rzeczypospolitej*. Warszawa: PWN.
Welzer, H. (Ed.). (2007). *Kollaboration und Widerstand im europäischen Gedächtnis*. Frankfurt/Main: Fischer Verlag.
Welzer, H., Moller, S., & Tschuggnall, K. (2005). *"Opa war kein Nazi." Nationalsozialismus und Holocaust im Familiengedächtnis*. Frankfurt/Main: Fischer Verlag.

18 Acting Out and Working Through Traumatic Memory: Confronting the Past in the South African Context

Pumla Gobodo-Madikizela

Post-graduate School, University of the Free State, Bloemfontein, South Africa

18.1 When Memory Kills: Acting Out Traumas

The so-called necklace murders were an extreme form of violence that was associated with the antiapartheid struggle and that spread throughout South African Black townships in the mid-1980s during the height of apartheid's violent repression. *Necklacing* was a method of killing people suspected of collaborating with the apartheid government police. A tire doused with petrol was placed around the neck of a person suspected of being a police collaborator. The person was then set alight and circled by a group of people dancing around the burning body until the victim collapsed and died. Research conducted on narratives of young people who were involved in these murders suggested a link between the violence of the necklace and the experiences of collective trauma suffered by the young people interviewed and by their communities (for a comprehensive study of necklace murders, see Gobodo-Madikizela, 1999). In this sense, then, necklace murders can be seen as the reenactment of events from the past, an acting out of the memory of trauma and the interaction of this traumatic memory with the tragic continuities of the trauma in the present. Significantly, the reenactment of trauma in a social context involves collective action because the cumulative effect of the trauma of oppression and subjugation, the loss of dignity, and the losses by violent death, as well as the everyday injustices, link individuals' experiences to those of the group and community. It is a shared memory of trauma and suffering, playing itself out through acts of collective violence.

18.2 Reenactment of Trauma

18.2.1 Perspective from Social Psychology

The field of social psychology is dominated by tension between two opposing theoretical viewpoints regarding collective violence. One of these viewpoints maintains that people participating in collective violence become disinhibited and *lose* their self-awareness in a group. What this perspective describes is a mental state that is similar to what is commonly referred to as mob behavior, which is inspired by feelings of anonymity in a crowd, suggestibility, conformity under influence of a group, and the like. The conceptual framework that underpins these ideas is referred to as *deindividuation* (Diener, 1980; Zimbardo, 1969, 1974).

The alternative to this theoretical perspective suggests that the behavior of individuals engaged in collective action derives from the emotional significance that group membership holds for them at a given moment. In other words, the issue is not one of the loss of sense of self. Rather, instead of losing self-awareness, the individual experiences a transition into a collective and less personal identity. The best way to think about this situation is to imagine an individual group member aligning the self with the beliefs, views, and actions of the group within which the collective action is taking place in relation to another group (or its individual members). The theoretical concept that explains this process is social identity theory (Tajfel, 1979). The theory suggests that the core of collective group action is that self-perception as a group member takes on greater prominence than self-perception as an individual; this includes identifying with the groups' belief system and rules of engagement in relation to others perceived as outsiders.

18.2.2 Psychoanalytic Perspective

The theories of social psychology fall short of providing adequate explanatory models for the brutal inhumanity of the necklace murders. A psychoanalytic perspective offers another useful perspective to understand the problem of necklace violence that erupted during the antiapartheid struggle. The psychoanalytic perspective can also contribute meaningfully to understanding the reasons for the reemergence of the necklace murders in Black townships in contemporary South Africa. For the sake of brevity, mainly two elements that were striking about the narratives of the young people interviewed about their participation in necklace brutality will be highlighted.

First, each of the narratives involved layers on layers of memories of repression, humiliation, and degradation, which they experienced as Blacks under the rule of the apartheid government. They described some of the most destructive acts of violence to the human soul, which were experienced as daily acts of humiliation, exclusion, and assault on their dignity and the dignity of their parents and communities. These experiences of "insidious trauma" are very subtle, systematic acts of violence perpetrated by the apartheid government, and they were aimed at undermining the dignity of Black people and their sense of worth and destroying their psychological and spiritual integrity.

Second, some of the young people interviewed about their role in the necklace murders reported confronting the reality of what they had done only the day after the incident. At the time of their involvement in the singing and dancing around the burning body of the victim of their necklacing, their participation was as if they were part of a surreal event, as if the murderous drama of the necklace were not real. This element of the surreal suggests dissociation, a complex psychological mechanism that operates as the mind's strategy to split off the link between anxiety-provoking experience and its consciousness. What this means is that, far from the conscious intention of group members aligning themselves with the group's social identity, as suggested by the social identity explanation of collective violence described earlier, the dissociation points to an intrapsychic dimension that requires some elaboration.

Extreme forms of trauma lead to psychic rupture and a fragmentation of traumatic memories, often dominating the mental life of many victims of trauma. There is sufficient evidence to show that these traumatic memories, along with difficulties in their assimilation, may return as behavioral reenactment, both at the interpersonal level and within societies (Laub & Lee, 2003; McFarlane & van der Kolk, 1996). The reenactment of trauma, scholars in this field inform us, is a major cause of violence in society. The reenactment of trauma may occur in contexts that may be far removed from or have no relationship with the original trauma. In other words, the link between the original trauma and its reenactment is hidden from conscious awareness.

In experiences of collective trauma, a group shares the disruptive effects of trauma. The traumatic events are engraved, becoming part of the group's identity, along with the disruptive and humiliating effects of the trauma in the group's sense of identity. Therefore, at the core of reenactment behavior at group level is a desire to restore the group's sense of dignity, to strengthen the group's identity, and to reclaim a sense of pride in the context of the humiliating effects of trauma and its recurring memory. Vamik Volkan, a psychoanalyst, political psychiatrist, and specialist on large-group identity, describes traumatic reenactments at a group level as "chosen traumas." Volkan explains that, when a group has suffered victimization and shares humiliating injury, the narrative of this victimization establishes an imprint in the group's identity that becomes a theme in group members' violently acting out of this traumatic memory.

Another widely accepted theory of violent reenactment suggests that reenactment is a way of dealing with the sense of powerlessness, shame, and humiliation experienced at the time of the original trauma. In this view, the goal of repetition is to regain a sense of control and mastery over past trauma (Herman, 1997). Unfortunately, this attempt at mastery may establish the basis for a pattern of violent behavior because being in the position of aggressor does not authentically resolve the feelings of shame and humiliation that lie within, which are the very issues that inspired acting out aggressively in the first place (Gilligan, 1997). This is why the stories of violence reported across the country in South Africa almost daily are becoming more gruesome, graphic, and inexplicable. Violence does not confer the honor it promises, and what promises to be a moment of control reclaimed might draw itself out into a pattern of bondage to aggression as the humiliated group or its individual members move from one short-lived feeling of control to another. Each subsequent act lowers the threshold for committing the next by desensitizing them, liberating them even further from society's taboos against violence.

18.3 Transgenerational Transmission of Traumatic Memory

Another gloomy detail of this story of traumatic repetition is that these traumatic reenactments are known to be passed on from one generation to the next, playing out cycles of violence that so often repeat themselves historically. An example of this transgenerational repetition of the past, albeit in symbolic form, is an observation of a group of young girls playing the necklace game in one of the townships in the Eastern Cape of South Africa. A group of girls who were about 8 years old were playing in the middle of one of the streets of the Black township of Mlungisi in the Eastern Cape region of South Africa. They were gathering around one girl who appeared to be their leader, calling the other girls to join her in playing the necklace game. The leader among the girls pushed the others aside as if to open up the stage. Rotating through the role of victim, then killers, then onlookers, she seemed to recall virtually everything that actually happened in a real necklace murder, even though she had not been born when the last necklace killing occurred in her township. Nervously, she put an imaginary tire around her neck and made a gesture simulating the striking of a match, as if her friends—now a crowd of executors—had forced her to light herself up. As imaginary flames engulfed her, she threw her arms wildly into the air. "Now sing and dance and clap your hands. I'm dying," she said. Her friends started clapping and singing in a discordant rhythm. They formed a circle and went round and round her body. Consumed by the flames, she slowly lowered herself to the ground and died. It was all make-believe.

None of the girls had actually seen a necklace murder. Their action seemed to suggest that the unspoken events of the past—the silence of Mlungisi's lambs—had become imprinted on their minds. What was poignant was not just the outward form of the game. Rather, it was its inner significance for communal life. It seemed that through their memory act, the girls carried the collective fear and horror somewhere deep within them. Reenacting the death dance of a necklace victim may well have been a way of transforming its memory into something more accessible and less fearful for them.

This death dance provides an illuminating metaphor for the way in which trauma is passed on intergenerationally through silence, fear, and unacknowledged psychological scars and pain. Cycles of violence do not occur in a vacuum; they are symbolic of unacknowledged painful events from the past, a reenactment of old scripts that find voice in the present. When these scripts are acted out in the social domain, the consequences can be quite explosive.

The language of violence is etched in the memory of many victims of violent conflict and passed on to the next generation, and to the next, "in ways subtle and not so subtle." The externalized skit of the necklace murder could be seen as an expression of that which cannot be spoken and as a desire to escape the cycle of psychic pain that is part of the young girls' individual and communal lives. This repetition of real events from the past transforms inexpressible traumatic memory into ritual. It is a cathartic way of enacting the struggle to find language to express the frustrations, helplessness, and the disempowerment that comes with the continuing effects of the traumatic past, including dire poverty.

18.4 Working Through the Past

There are, however, other ways of dealing with traumatic memory, and traumatic memory need not find expression through violent ways. The telling of narratives about the traumatic past can mediate traumatic effects and rescue individuals and groups from the humiliating effects of the past. Creating the space for remembering the past by listening to victims and survivors' narratives can restore victims' sense of dignity by opening up the possibility for recognition of their humanity. In essence, narratives about the past confront the past not in order to set it aside as a condition for moving on into the future, but rather to remember the past in order to transcend its traumatic effects. These are precisely the ideas that were embodied within the Truth and Reconciliation Commission (TRC) of South Africa. In the following sections, these insights concerning the role of narrative will be elaborated, and the significance of narrative will be clarified by presenting material from postgraduate seminars on trauma at the University of Cape Town. In these seminars, often video footage, audio recordings, and transcripts of TRC testimonies were presented for class discussion. The TRC archival material has evoked a range of responses from students in the classes over the years. Particularly striking were the nuances and subtleties in the kinds of responses that the material triggered in Black and in White students.

18.4.1 Provocations of Empathy: When Memory Heals

At the core of listeners' responses to testimonies of trauma is what can be called a provocation of empathy, which unfolds because of the reciprocal mutual engagement (Stolorow & Lachmann, 1987) that occurs in the dialogic engagement between victims' trauma testimonies and listeners. Openness in the stance of the listener creates the possibility for meaningful engagement with testimonies of victims. This means that engagement with victims' testimonies may extend beyond the external to touch the listener's own memory of the past, evoking a complex set of emotions that play out in what we have captured metaphorically as *making public spaces intimate* (Gobodo-Madikizela, 2008a, 2008b). The intimate and innerworld memories of the listeners are evoked by a rendering of victims' traumatic narratives into the public space created by the dialogic encounter with victims' testimonies. There is an intrapsychic dynamic at work in the provocation of empathy, particularly in relation to the pivotal turn to perspective taking and gaining an integrated view of both the self and the other. In essence, it is gaining new consciousness—seeing things anew. This provocation of empathy and unfolding of a new consciousness is illustrated in the discussion in the following section.

18.4.2 Working Through Trauma, Working Through Shame and Guilt

Mrs. P's narrative,[1] drawn from the TRC archive, depicts the image of the lifeless body of an 11-year-old Black boy shot by the apartheid government police in the streets of a Black residential area, Mlungisi Township, and Mrs. P wailing over

[1] Narrative adapted from Gobodo-Madikizela (2003).

him, beside herself with anguish at the loss of her only child. "My son was eleven," she began her story to the member of the TRC, who recorded her statement from her home:

He came home during school break at ten o'clock. I was sitting right there where you are sitting, just sitting exactly where you are sitting in that chair. He walked in dressed in his school uniform, and went to the cupboard over there and cut himself a slice of bread. He is doing all of this in a rush. He is like that when he comes home during break. He spread peanut butter on it and then put the rest of the bread back, leaving the crumbs all over the cupboard, and the knife, still smudged with peanut butter. He ran out. He is still chewing his bread and holding it in his hand. It wasn't long—I heard shots outside. Some commotion and shouts. Then I'm hearing, "uLuthando, uLuthando, nank'uLuthando bamdubule!" ["This is Luthando. They have shot Luthando!"] and then someone calling out for me: "mama kaLuthando!" ["Luthando's mother!"] I went flying out of this house. Now I am dazed. I ran, not thinking. My eyes are on the crowd that has gathered (Statement of Mrs. P, recorded May 1996).

Mrs. P recalled the final moment when she arrived at the scene and saw her son's lifeless body: "Here is my son," she said, gesturing with her hand toward her kitchen floor. She continued:

It was just blood all over. My anguish was beyond anything I ever thought I could experience. They have finished him. I threw myself down on him. I can feel the wetness of his blood—I felt his last breath leave him. He was my only child (Mrs. P's statement).

One gets the sense that in recounting her traumatic memory, Mrs. P is searching for coherence and engaging in a process of working through the trauma of the loss of her only child. Indeed, as I prepared to leave her house, she said she wanted to show me something. Then Mrs. P turned the tap on, letting the water run into her kitchen sink: "You see; now I have running water *inside.* No more queuing in line with a bucket at the communal taps." Then she flicked the electrical switch on, then off: "I have lights in the house, no more candles—you see, my son did not die in vain."

Mrs. P seems to be freed, even if only briefly, from the destructive grip of the traumatic past by searching for (perhaps *clutching* at) a reparative vision that she finds in the simple things of life. For a moment, the electricity and water *inside* her house seem to bestow meaning to her son's death. This does not mean that she is miraculously healed from her unspeakable anguish; however, her positive reference to aspects of change in her home symbolizes the healing of her traumatic memory and gestures toward a resolution. It conveys a reparative vision, a desire for the transformation of her story of trauma into one that offers hope and the possibility of reparation. All these are attempts at working through traumatic memory. What remains then is for Mrs. P's story to be heard in order to create the narrative possibilities that are a crucial pivot in these testimonies when secondary witnesses, to borrow Laub's (1992) phrase, are present. This narrative possibility is illustrated by the response of a student who was asked to read the text of Mrs. P's testimony during a master's seminar on trauma. The student broke down in tears in the course of his reading. He later wrote as follows about his reaction:

> *Why did I choke back tears when I was reading the testimony? I did the math for how old her son would be now and I realized that I was exactly his age when the incident happened. If I say my tears were for him or his mother, that would not be the truth. What I felt at the time was an indescribable guilt and shame (and later embarrassment for showing my emotions in class!) because of a memory that popped into my mind just as I realized that the year that her son was killed was the year I turned eleven (White male student).*

The student then went on to describe the memory that Mrs. P's story evoked in him. His birthdays were always a major celebration in his family because he was an only child. He described in detail an incident that occurred when his family was preparing for a weekend trip to celebrate his eleventh birthday. He was in the car with his cousin, and his father was waiting for the last pieces of luggage and for his mother to lock up before their trip. He had to run back to the house to pick up something from his bedroom. As he came closer to the door, the old man who was the gardener suddenly stopped at the door, carrying bags in both hands, and did not immediately give way. "*Loop!*" ("Move!"), the little boy shouted at the old man. The student wrote that it was the memory of that singular moment that suddenly rushed back into his consciousness for the first time since the incident happened. The shame he felt for the power of position and the superiority of Whiteness that allowed him to address the old man in such a derogatory manner caused him to cringe and to choke back tears as he read the testimony of the mother whose 11-year-old son died in a hail of bullets in a dusty township street. The student ended his written response by saying that he wanted to "give back" in whatever way he could. A year later, the student was working as a volunteer at a center for children orphaned after the death of their parents from AIDS in one of the Black townships in Cape Town.

This story and other similar stories from students' reactions to TRC testimonies seem always to contain a reparative element, a desire to give back, even if only in symbolic form. Both Mrs. P's testimony and the student's response to it are infused with hope and point to building a new future. Faced with Mrs. P's testimony in class, the student had to confront the reality of his actions for the first time. His obnoxious behavior toward the elderly man who was the gardener in his home can be understood to have been motivated by the fact of his racial superiority. He became aware of what his actions meant, what they *mean*. This awareness bestowed a new consciousness in him, making him a witness to his own internal brokenness. He was therefore forced to confront his complicity, a crime captured most aptly by Sanders's phrase as "folded-togetherness" (2002, p. 5) with apartheid, which means a crime not by acting, but rather by the inaction of complicity. More importantly, he was also able to go beyond the emotional reaction embodied in his tears and through his HIV/AIDS volunteer work to engage in action that would symbolize some sense of giving back and taking "responsibility for the Other" (Levinas, 1998, p. 148).

18.5 Conclusion

The model of dialogue discussed in the student's encounter with a victim's testimony from the TRC is an illustrative example of the kind of opportunities that can be created as a way of working through traumatic memory in order to transform its destructive effects into empathic dialogue about the past. This framework requires a process of moral imagination, a certain intentional openness to the possibility of reaching *out* beyond the self and toward the Other. The model also offers a very rich context for beginning the process of mourning, in other words, facing the past and its uncomfortable and internally unsettling truths (for more on the discussion of this point, see Gobodo-Madikizela, 2012). Engagement with victims' testimonies then creates opportunity for breaking cycles of repetition, transforming the effects of both traumatic memory and guilt into a much deeper process of engagement with self and Other in ways that can foster reconciliation dialogue and prevent or at least limit the possibility for acting out the past.

References

Diener, E. (1980). Deindividuation: The absence of self-awareness and self-regulation in group members. In P. B. Paulus (Ed.), *Psychology of group influence (pp. 209–242)*. Hillsdale, NJ: Eribaum.
Durham, M. S. (2000). *The therapist encounters with revenge and forgiveness*. Philadelphia, PA: Jessica Kingsley.
Gilligan, J. (1997). *Violence: Reflections on a national epidemic*. New York, NY: Vintage Books.
Gobodo-Madikizela, P. (1999). *Legacies of violence: An in-depth analysis of two case studies based on interviews with perpetrators of a "necklace" murder and with Eugene de Kock*. Unpublished doctoral dissertation, University of Cape Town.
Gobodo-Madikizela, P. (2003). *A human being died that night: A South African story of forgiveness*. Boston, MA: Houghton Mifflin.
Gobodo-Madikizela, P. (2008a). Trauma, forgiveness and the witnessing dance: Making public spaces intimate. *Journal of Analytical Psychology, 53*, 169–188.
Gobodo-Madikizela, P. (2008b). Transforming trauma in the aftermath of gross human rights abuses: Making public spaces intimate. In A. Nadler, J. Fisher, & T. Malloy (Eds.), *Intergroup reconciliation*. London: Oxford University Press.
Gobodo-Madikizela, P. (2012). Remembering the past: Nostalgia, traumatic memory, and the legacy of apartheid. *Peace and Conflict: Journal of Peace Psychology, 18*, 252–267.
Herman, J. (1997). *Trauma and recovery: The aftermath of violence—from domestic abuse to political terror*. New York, NY: Basic Books.
Laub, D. (1992). Bearing witness or the vicissitudes of listening. In S. Felman & D. Laub (Eds.), *Testimony: Crises of witnessing in literature, psychoanalysis, and history* (pp. 57–74). New York, NY: Routledge.
Laub, D., & Lee, S. (2003). Thanatos and massive psychic trauma. *Journal of the American Psychoanalytic Association, 51*, 433–463.
Levinas, E. (1998). *Otherwise than being: Or beyond essence*. Pittsburgh: Duquesne University Press.

McFarlane, A. C., & van der Kolk, B. A. (1996). Trauma and its challenge to society McFarlane van der Kolk (Eds.), *Traumatic stress: The effects of overwhelming experience on mind, body and society (pp. 25–45)*. New York, NY: The Guilford Press.

Sanders, M. (2002). *Complicities: The intellectual and apartheid*. Durham: Duke University Press.

Stolorow, R., & Lachmann, F. (1987). Transference—the organization of experience. In R. Stolorow, B. Brandchaft, & G. Atwood (Eds.), *Psychoanalytic treatment: An intersubjective approach (pp. 28–46)*. Hillsdale, NJ: Analytic Press.

Tajfel, H. (1979). *Differentiation between social groups: Studies in the social psychology of intergroup relation*. New York, NY: Academic Press.

Zimbardo, P. G. (1969). The human choice: Individuation, reason, and order versus deindividuation, impulse, and chaos. In W. D. Arnold & D. Levine (Eds.), *Nebraska symposium on motivation (pp. 237–307)*. Lincoln, NE: University of Nebraska.

Zimbardo, P. G. (1974). On "obedience to authority". *American Psychologist, 29*, 566–567.

19 Empathy, Forgiveness, and Reconciliation: The Truth and Reconciliation Commission in South Africa

Melike M. Fourie[1,2], Pumla Gobodo-Madikizela[1], Dan J. Stein[3]

[1]Postgraduate School, University of the Free State, Bloemfontein, South Africa
[2]Department of Psychology, University of Cape Town, Cape Town, South Africa
[3]Department of Psychiatry, University of Cape Town, Cape Town, South Africa

South Africa may be best known for its apartheid government, which from 1948 to 1994 was responsible for the systematic oppression of and violence against Black South Africans, while White South African supremacy was maintained. Today, South Africans still have vivid recollections of the atrocities committed in the name of racial segregation. Although younger generations were not exposed to the levels of discrimination that existed during the apartheid era, racial discrimination is not left fully in South Africa's past. It appears as if a fingerprint of these racial inequalities remains imprinted on the society, with lasting consequences for interpersonal health and well-being (Charasse-Pouele & Fournier, 2006). Although much attention has been paid to right the wrongs of the past at a sociopolitical level, additional thought is needed as to what is required at a more interpersonal level to restore a sense of security and promote interracial reconciliation. We suggest that empathy and forgiveness are critical components of this process.

Empathy and *forgiveness* are complex constructs, with several questions about their nature unresolved (Stein, 2005; Stein & Kaminer, 2006). Empathy may be defined as "the ability to experience and understand what others feel without confusion between oneself and others" (Decety & Lamm, 2006, p. 1). It is therefore an intersubjective emotional resonance, or empathic connection, whereby the experiences of the other come to be shared with an aim of understanding his or her perspective. Forgiveness, in turn, comes from the Middle English and Anglo-Saxon words *fore*, which means "away," and *give* or "gift." Therefore, the word literally suggests foregoing or letting go of something, on the one hand, and offering an altruistic or undeserved gift, on the other hand (Worthington et al., 2000). These two aspects are also regarded as the first two important attributes of forgiveness. A third attribute is that forgiveness is a process that usually takes time, involving a shift from an initial negative response to a benevolent response (McCullough, Fincham, & Tsang, 2003).

Of interest to our current discussion, however, is the fact that forgiveness has also been described as "empathy toward the perpetrator" (Macaskill, Maltby, & Day, 2002, p. 663). Gobodo-Madikizela (2008a), likewise, suggests that "empathic repair" is a useful concept for understanding the process of interracial forgiveness in the aftermath of gross human rights violations. A better understanding of the psychobiological underpinnings of empathy therefore may shed light on ways to go about overcoming the bidirectional implicit racism that pervades the relationships between Black and White South Africans. What remains unclear, however, are the precise mechanisms that may lead to empathy and to forgiveness.

The South African Truth and Reconciliation Commission (TRC) provides a useful exemplar with which to think about the nature of empathy and of forgiveness. The TRC was instituted immediately after democracy was established in South Africa, in an attempt to engage with and heal the atrocities of the past. The TRC was notable for taking an approach that relied on restorative justice rather than on retributive justice (Boraine, Levy, & Scheffer, 1997), in order to help deconstruct the barriers that had separated South Africans for so long. In this process, testimonies of both victims and perpetrators were explored. Gobodo-Madikizela (2008a, 2008b) has applied the concepts of forgiveness and empathy in a social context in relation to her work on the TRC, arguing that the restorative model of the TRC created the possibility for ethical engagement between former adversaries. The TRC thus provides a particularly useful tool with which to examine the psychosocial aspects of empathy and forgiveness.

This chapter explores the TRC, emphasizing key psychological questions raised by the TRC, including their biological and societal aspects. First, it addresses the question of whether apartheid left enduring psychological scars on the population. Second, it asks the question of how to best provide survivors with psychological care. Third, it explores the nature of perpetrators of societal evil. Finally, it suggests that a better understanding of the psychobiological underpinnings of empathy may shed light on these complex issues and their enduring nature and help to prevent future such abuses.

19.1 Enduring Effects of Discrimination

The apartheid system has often been described as a major cause of mental distress and psychiatric disorder in South Africa (Swartz, 1998); yet few empirical studies have been conducted to verify these claims. Consequently, there are at least two different views of the mental health consequences of apartheid. The first states that apartheid was a major stressor that led to significant mental disorders. A contrasting approach is that the political struggle against apartheid fostered resilience among those who were engaged in it (Basoglu et al., 1994; Stein, 1998).

The adverse effects of unfair treatment on physical and mental health are well documented (Adams, 1965; Krieger, 1990). Williams, Yan, Jackson, and Anderson

(1997), for example, found that perceived discrimination, both economic and noneconomic, plays an incremental role in accounting for racial differences in health status in the United States. That is, African–Americans self-reported higher rates of ill health, lower levels of psychological well-being, and more bed-days compared with Whites. More recently, Williams et al. (2008) conducted a study in South Africa to assess the relationships between perceived discrimination, race, and health in a nationally representative sample. Consistent with expectations, all Black groups in South Africa (African, colored, and Indian) reported significantly higher levels of racial discrimination compared with Whites. Acute and chronic racial discrimination, however, was unrelated to ill health and played no role in accounting for racial differences in self-rated health. Although all Black groups reported higher levels of psychological distress than Whites, this was most strongly associated with perceived chronic nonracial discrimination. Similarly, data from the South African Stress and Health Study have suggested that acute and chronic forms of racial discrimination were associated with an elevated risk of a 12-month psychiatric disorder when adjusted for sociodemographic factors but that, when other sources of social stress were taken into account, this association was no longer significant (Moomal et al., 2009). By comparison, the association between chronic nonracial discrimination and 12-month and lifetime psychiatric disorders was significant across mood, anxiety, and substance use disorders in the fully adjusted models. Current epidemiological data therefore suggest that perceived racial discrimination does not necessarily predict mental health status and that mental disorders are common in all racial groups in South Africa (Herman et al., 2009; Seedat et al., 2009).

Rather than playing down the importance of experiences of racial discrimination in South Africa, however, these findings emphasize the complexity of experiences of discrimination. The finding that racial discrimination is not related to ill health has several possible explanations. First, it is important not to underestimate the resilience of those subjected to such racial discrimination. Many factors, including strong family supports, community cohesion (exemplified by the South African notion of *Ubuntu*), or being part of the political struggle may have contributed to some South Africans enduring racial discrimination with less than expected effects on health. Second, it is important not to underestimate the cumulative impact of multiple types of discrimination (and trauma). Racial discrimination by itself is one thing, but when compounded with multiple other kinds of stressors, including poverty, violence, and nonracial discrimination, an entirely different set of outcomes may be expected.

The subject of posttraumatic stress disorder (PTSD) has been raised a number of times in the TRC hearings. The classical view of PTSD is that it is a normal, albeit exaggerated, emotional response to severe or abnormal stress. Consistent with this view, progressive practitioners have argued that apartheid has resulted in a chronic PTSD in many South Africans (Foster, Davis, & Sandler, 1987). However, this classical view fails to take into account the complex psychobiological nature of PTSD. Evidence about PTSD suggests that this condition is in fact an abnormal response to relatively common life traumas, with specific biological underpinnings that differ from those responsible for other disorders (Yehuda & McFarlane, 1995). Indeed, just as we have argued that discrimination is complex, it can be argued that trauma is complex. Furthermore, the literature on PTSD emphasizes the resilience found in the vast majority of those exposed to major traumas and the complex factors that contribute to the emergence of PTSD in a minority. Those with exposure to multiple traumas certainly deserve a forum that acknowledges their suffering, but those who have PTSD likely deserve additional interventions, including clinical assistance.

One of the key lessons learned from the TRC may be the importance of focusing on resilience rather than on traumatic stress. It has been argued that the revenge of those who survived the Holocaust was not the Nuremberg trials but rather going forward and succeeding with life (Stein, 1998). Similarly, the emphasis of the TRC on the normality of emotional responses to trauma and the expectation that the TRC itself will lead to social normalization are consistent with a view that emphasizes resilience rather than psychopathology. Although it is important for clinicians not to underdiagnose psychopathology, given the valuable advantages that medical and psychiatric approaches to trauma can offer (Stein, Kaminer, Zungu-Dirwayi, & Seedat, 2006), it appears paramount to recognize and encourage the strengths and resilience of individuals exposed to both everyday discrimination and to gross human rights violations.

19.2 Survivors and Psychological Care

An important question in newly democratic countries is how best to deal with the gross human rights violations of previous regimes. In South Africa, the postapartheid government responded by passing the Promotion of National Unity and Reconciliation Act, which in turn established the TRC. As mentioned, the TRC focused on restorative rather than on retributive justice (allowing amnesty of perpetrators) in order to promote national unity and reconciliation in a spirit of understanding (Boraine et al., 1997). Consequently, great importance was placed on bearing witness to the past. This was done by giving victims the opportunity to recall their past traumas in order to obtain reparations and by giving amnesty to perpetrators who fully disclosed politically motivated acts. In this process of truth telling, it was hoped that national reconciliation may be achieved.

During the TRC hearings, however, where witnesses often spoke of the incredible suffering they had endured at the hands of the apartheid government, the question arose in the South African mental health community as to whether testifying at the TRC has in fact therapeutic value. On the one hand, the importance of catharsis in healing and the value of testimony therapy has been emphasized (Agger & Jensen, 1990; Cienfuegos & Monelli, 1983). Many psychotherapeutic treatment models of PTSD, for example, insist that patients verbalize their past traumas. On the other hand, there was the concern that testimony risks the possibility of secondary traumatization. Later psychodynamic models of the mind emphasize the importance of the relationship between the testifying victim and his or her listeners. Relating traumatic experiences to an unsympathetic audience may therefore result in retraumatization. Although the TRC was helpful at a national level, the question of its value for individuals who participated in the process was therefore contentious (Byrne, 2004; Swartz, 1998).

To date, few empirical studies have been conducted to tease apart the relationship between participation in the TRC and subsequent psychiatric status. In 2001, a study conducted by Kaminer and colleagues found that PTSD was not predicted by testifying at the TRC, either publicly or by way of a closed statement (Kaminer, Stein, Mbanga, & Zungu-Dirwayi, 2001). Instead, there was a higher incidence of PTSD among participants with low forgiveness scores compared with those with high forgiveness scores. Interestingly, a gender effect emerged among the public testifiers, with women significantly less forgiving compared with men. Of significance, however, is the fact that there was no correlation between participating in the TRC and improvement in either individual psychological symptoms or forgiveness. The authors concluded that testifying at the TRC may be qualitatively different from sharing experiences in a clinical setting (i.e., testimony therapy).

More recently, Stein et al. (2008) assessed the impact of bearing witness to the TRC on psychological distress and forgiveness in a large, nationally representative sample of the South African population. Significant relationships between increased distress and anger, having a TRC-relevant experience to share, and negative perceptions of the TRC led the authors to conclude that bearing testimony was not necessarily helpful to survivors. Similar to the findings of Kaminer, Stein, Mbanga, and Zungu-Dirwayi (2001), forgiveness was inversely related to distress and anger.

These findings are consistent with those of the previous section, which emphasize the complexity of experiences of discrimination and of severe trauma. Those suffering from psychopathology as a result of such experiences likely require an individualized response that can address the multiple relevant underlying mechanisms. From the little empirical evidence available, it seems reasonable to argue that testifying at the TRC was unlikely to have helped those with disorders like PTSD. Individuals exposed to gross human rights violations may well require additional forms of social support or psychological intervention. However, Stein et al. (2008) report that, in the population as a whole, perceptions of the TRC were moderately positive irrespective of many sociodemographic variables. Some witnesses have also stated that the process of relaying their past hurts before the commission has allowed them to move forward with their lives (Orr, 1998). Moreover, it could be argued that the TRC facilitated the process of forgiveness for many (Allan, Allan, Kaminer, & Stein, 2006), with extensive evidence suggesting that forgiveness is associated with improved mental health (Coyle & Enright, 1997; Freedman & Enright, 1996). The TRC therefore provides an important exemplar of social approaches to justice and acknowledgment of past injustices. Despite its criticisms, the fact that so many appeared willing to accept the TRC process as a valid way of making sense of past struggles seems significant.

19.3 Perpetrators of Evil

We have argued that discrimination and trauma are complex phenomena, where overly simplistic approaches are unlikely to work. A similar argument can be made about the nature of those who inflict trauma on others. One view of perpetration is that humans are innately aggressive and that, under certain circumstances, all of us have the capacity to inflict harm on others with minimal compassion. The classic studies of Milgram (1963) and Zimbardo (Haney, Banks, & Zimbardo, 1973) come to mind. A contrasting view is that only a minority of individuals have the capacity, perhaps innate, to inflict gross trauma on others. For example, there is the phenomenon whereby some humans use empathic processes precisely in order to inflict maximal harm on others (Stein, 2005). Whereas studies of intergroup conflict suggest that such processes may be more common than we would like to admit, it would also seem that only a minority of individuals are able to regularly use empathic processes to inflict harm on others (Kaminer & Stein, 2001; Stein, 2000).

When dealing with gross human rights violations of the past in countries going through political transition, an important question is raised: How were perpetrators able to silence their conscience when they returned, again and again, to murder those identified as enemies of the state? How does conscience get suppressed to the point that people can allow themselves to commit systematic acts of murder? It has often been said that most people who commit gross human rights abuses are not psychopaths—a psychological diagnosis that is accompanied by an inability to feel empathy or guilt. Explaining the behavior of a person who has a working conscience yet who does extremely bad things even though his conscience tells him that what he is doing is wrong is therefore complex. In his book, *The Roots of Evil* (1989), political psychologist Ervin Staub explores the question of how conscience gets suppressed to the point that people can allow themselves to commit horrible acts against others. He explains how a climate of genocidal ideology is set in motion that enables a society and its members to suppress their voice of conscience. But are perpetrators then simply caught up in their governments' or political organizations' plans of corruption and dehumanization of others? Perhaps a closer look at the different perspectives on the evolution of evil may shed light on this question.

The first view concerning the development of evil suggests that perpetrators are predisposed to violence because of childhood experiences of trauma (Gilligan, 1997). The second view is that evil is not a result of a predisposition because most who have suffered unspeakable trauma do not turn out as monsters. By this second partly philosophical, partly empirical view, people have free choice. The sovereignty of the heart is essentially inviolable, and although the decision to pursue what is right may on occasion be horrendously difficult, people can choose not only not to commit evil but also to make the kinds of choices that make it easier to avoid committing evil.

Our own position is that the evolution of evil is more complex than either of these views. Those who have been traumatized *are* vulnerable to falling into a mode of psychological repetition of the trauma they suffered. But whether individuals turn out this way or that depends on a complex set of factors, one being whether they are "violently coached" (Rhodes, 1999) and another being whether they are exposed to positive experiences that can help mend the humiliation they suffered and restore their sense of identity. Those who do turn out to be violent are more likely to have had direct or indirect encouragement to be violent. In her book based on her experiences on the TRC, Gobodo-Madikizela (2003) discusses the complexity of the issue of evil. In discussing the role of one of the apartheid government's chief assassins,

Eugene de Kock, she shows how, in addition to his history of trauma, de Kock's role as "apartheid's crusader" had his future of violence carved out for him by his political leaders. Therefore, when, in addition to the presence of vulnerability, an individual is plunged into a system in which his career is defined by violence, the issue of choice may not be as easy as it seems. Violent abuse damages and even corrupts the individual's psyche. It intrudes upon and invades the victim's unconsciousness so that, in an environment that rewards evil, there are few resources on which the person can draw to resist it.

This position on evil raises at least three sets of issues: Does abuse only *damage* a person's psyche so that he is like a person with an illness (e.g., someone who deserves society's sympathy)? Or can abuse also *corrupt* a person's psyche, which implies that the person, although no fault of his own, can grow up predisposed to becoming a *morally* evil person? If the latter is the case—that abuse can predispose hitherto innocent people to evil—do they deserve our sympathy based on the view that the corruption came from an external source and was imposed on them? Or do they deserve the same judgments we direct toward other evil people because that person has now become a morally evil person, not just a person with a damaged psyche? Our view is that people who commit evil deeds should be held morally responsible for their actions. While the nature of free will remain a contentious philosophical issue, in both clinical and social contexts, it is key to respond to others as free agents. Indeed, this is precisely why understanding the role of empathy is so critical because this helps us understand not only how we are predisposed to have certain thoughts and feelings but also how we can choose alternative pathways, particularly in the context of compassionate human relationships.

19.4 The Role of Empathy

It is perplexing to consider that humans can be effortlessly altruistic under certain circumstances but can participate in the violent oppression of others under different circumstances. Empathy is a complex psychological phenomenon that may lie at the heart of these diverging human interactions. It has been described as a process essential for relieving human suffering and for the creation and preservation of social bonds (Watt, 2007). Recent empirical data point to the fact that empathy does not function as a binary construct (i.e., either on or off), however, but is a flexible phenomenon affected by a host of factors that modulate both automatic and controlled cognitive processes (Cheng et al., 2007; Lamm, Meltzoff, & Decety, 2009). Consequently, research into intergroup empathy has attempted to identify some of the interpersonal and cultural factors that influence cross-racial attitudes, in an attempt to break down the invisible barriers that divide "us" and "them."

To explain more clearly what we mean when we allude to implicit racial biases that may remain present in our society, despite attempts to do away with past injustices, we refer to Allport's work on the dehumanization of others and racial prejudice. In his book, *The Nature of Prejudice* (1954), Allport describes what he terms a "state of conflict" experienced by many White Americans in their relationships with

Black Americans. Being in a state of conflict suggests that, ideologically, White people may be opposed to racial prejudice, on the one hand, but may harbor underlying racial bias, on the other hand. Other scholars have elaborated on Allport's research and found that, while people may identify with an egalitarian outlook, they may simultaneously possess implicit racial associations that operate at a deeply unconscious level (Baron & Banaji, 2006; Devine, 1989; Devine, Monteith, Zuwerink, & Elliot, 1991; Monteith & Voils, 1998; Wilson, Lindsey, & Schooler, 2000). In other words, the mental processes that influence their behavior and beliefs operate automatically but out of awareness.

Following Allport's early studies, social psychology research has continued to illuminate the nature of prejudice and to build our understanding of racially biased attitudes. Most of these studies, however, have relied on self-reports and therefore lack the scientific basis for establishing the existence of implicit attitudes that influence an individual's responses to racially charged situations. In contrast, the new field of social neuroscience, which seeks to demonstrate the neural regions involved in these implicit attitudes when people encounter others from historically prejudiced groups, is an important counterexample to this criticism of these social psychology studies. Various neuroscience studies employing physiological measures, for example, have demonstrated that prejudice reactions frequently manifest at a neural level, despite the fact that individuals report egalitarian attitudes on self-reported measures of prejudice (Amodio et al., 2004; Phelps et al., 2000).

In a similar vein, a new wave of research into the neuroscience of empathy is focused on the important role of culture in shaping the nature of (automatic) empathic responses to another's suffering, particularly in intergroup contexts (Chiao, 2011). Recent studies investigating the neural basis of intergroup empathy have demonstrated that neural responses in regions associated with the component processes of empathy are heightened when one perceives the pain of an in-group member versus an out-group member (Chiao & Mathur, 2010; Xu, Zuo, Wang, & Han, 2009). The underlying premise of these investigations is that empathic resonance is automatically increased when the observer and target belong to the same social category (Hornstein, 1978). Critically important, however, is the view that empathic response differences across social categories are not inevitable. Rather, they appear to be modulated by factors such as the neural circuitry and neurochemistry (Montoya, Terburg, Bos, & van Honk, 2012; van Honk et al., 2011) and the particular environment of the individual (Cheon et al., 2011; Chiao, 2011). Such empathic differences may thus result from culturally acquired prejudices, rather than from inherent social group preferences.

A notable case in point is a recent study that demonstrates compellingly the effect of cultural prejudice on empathic responding (Avenanti, Sirigu, & Aglioti, 2010). Black and White participants' empathic sensorimotor contagion was measured using transmagnetic stimulation (TMS) when observing a needle penetrate a muscle in either a Black, White, or Violet hand. Results indicated that Black and White participants responded with significant sensorimotor contagion (i.e., empathic resonance) not only when witnessing same-race targets in pain but also when witnessing culturally unfamiliar (i.e., purple-skinned) targets in pain. Sensorimotor contagion was impaired, however, when witnessing culturally marked out-group members in pain. In-group biases in empathic responses therefore appeared to occur as a function of culturally acquired racial prejudice.

From these findings, it is evident that significant cross-racial attitudes may interfere with an individual's empathic response to an out-group member in pain and that this may be true more in countries where culturally acquired prejudices prevail. Since "empathic repair," as suggested by Gobodo-Madikizela (2008a), seems to be what is needed in South Africa in order to promote interracial reconciliation, the question then arises as to what can or must be done to promote cross-racial empathy.

One important argument in response to this question is that rehumanization of the other must occur. The notion of "rehumanization of the other" has been conceptualized by Gobodo-Madikizela (2002) as central in encounters aimed at promoting cross-racial empathy. She argues that rehumanization is a two-way process and that, when perpetrators are remorseful in their apologies and victims/survivors respond by reaching out with forgiveness, the encounter rehumanizes both victim and perpetrator.

Halpern and Weinstein have applied the notion of rehumanization to intergroup contexts and argue that "healthy psychological and physical functioning requires overcoming the hatred that pervades the relationships between ethnic groups, and that, in turn, this depends upon seeing their recent enemies in human terms" (2004, p. 562). Furthermore, they stress that the reparation of the social fabric of societies should be the central public health task for countries emerging from periods of turmoil, rather than establishing processes at the level of the state (e.g., the creation of institutions, legal reform, and economic development). Reform should therefore concern the rebuilding of individual relationships. Critical to their argument regarding the necessity of rehumanization for cross-racial reconciliation to occur, however, is the development of empathy between former enemies. Because social identity theory suggests that individuals instinctively classify themselves within some social framework (Turner & Onorato, 1999), the dilemma of rehumanization therefore is how to remove this categorization from individuals and return humanity to the out-group who has become dehumanized. Halpern and Weinstein argue that empathy, described as a "fundamentally individualizing view of another," is fundamental to this process. An empathic connection must therefore occur if the desired outcome of a country is reconciliation, rather than mere coexistence.

Because different definitions of empathy prevail, it is important to grasp exactly what Halpern and Weinstein denote with an empathic connection. Whereas sympathy is about experiencing shared emotions, empathy, in addition, involves imagining and seeking to understand the particular perspective of another person (Halpern, 2001). Such perceptual shifts, which occur when one becomes interested in the distinct subjective reality of another person, presume a sense of the other as a distinct individual and are central to rehumanizing the enemy. The major function of empathy is therefore to individualize and to seek another person's distinct perspective, rather than to stereotype and to generalize.

These views on empathy between victim and perpetrator are echoed in Gobodo-Madikizela's paper, "Empathetic repair after mass trauma: When vengeance is arrested" (2008a). She argues that the circumstances that might invite the emergence of empathy with another are within the relational, intersubjective realm of the victim–perpetrator encounter. Moreover, she concludes that the empathic connection shared by victims and perpetrators is a result of a "pivotal turn to perspective taking and gaining an integrated view of the other" (Gobodo-Madikizela, 2008a, p. 343). It is this empathic movement toward the other, then, that opens up the possibility of forgiveness. And insofar as forgiveness recognizes the unconscious motivation of the other's crime, it presents an opportunity for new relationships and a new beginning (Kristeva, 1987).

Empathy may therefore play a crucial role in restorative processes such as the TRC, at both the individual and national levels. It seems that when survivors of different races gave their testimony, the nation as a whole identified with them (Stein et al., 2008). Experiencing empathy toward the other may also be regarded as an important facilitator of social change and reform. The potential of prosocial emotions to transform advantaged groups' apathy into action strategies with an aim of social cohesion or equality may well be underrecognized (Thomas, McGarty, & Mavor, 2009). In the words of Jung (1938, p. 32), "There can be no transforming of darkness into light and of apathy into movement without emotion."

Empathy is also important in therapeutic approaches to survivors and indeed of any psychotherapy. It has been argued to have several key advantages in the clinical context: It may encourage patients to provide better histories and so improve diagnosis; it may increase patients' self-efficacy and so lead to increased participation in treatment; and it may lead to therapeutic interactions that directly improve symptoms (Halpern, 2001). Perpetration, however, remains poorly understood. Yet empathy also provides a potential window into understanding the nature of cruelty and dehumanization. Various psychopathies, for example, are marked by impaired empathy. One of the key features that distinguish psychopaths from other criminals is their marked lack of concern or empathy for their victims (Decety, 2011). Moreover, a recent imaging study has demonstrated that normal and psychopathic individuals recruit significantly different brain areas while perceiving others in distress (Cheng, Hung, & Decety, 2012). A deeper understanding of the mechanisms that mediate empathy may therefore also shed light on the motivations of those individuals who are apparently impaired at this most vital of human emotions.

19.5 Conclusion

In conclusion, the TRC provides an important exemplar with which to think about the nature of empathy and of forgiveness in the wake of gross human rights violations. We have discussed the importance of forgiveness and empathy in facilitating interracial reconciliation, with a focus on "empathic repair" (Gobodo-Madikizela, 2008a) as the first step in this process. First, we argued that discrimination and more severe traumas are complex phenomena, so that South Africans are not simply traumatized or heroic but rather that multiple underlying mechanisms need to be further delineated in order to allow a full understanding of the range of responses to trauma. Second, we showed that the TRC does not appear to have clear psychotherapeutic value for the individual with PTSD but may have facilitated the process of forgiveness for many, and it may well have had a positive effect in the population as a whole. Third, the perpetration of trauma is also not simply a dichotomous construct, where some are born with an innate capacity for violence and others not. Humans are able to demonstrate a broad range of harmful behavior, which may be critically influenced by early traumatic experiences as well as by subsequent positive experiences or encouragement of violent behavior. Finally, we unpacked the concept of intergroup empathy and offered at least one comprehensive perspective of what must be done to promote cross-racial empathy, namely, the rehumanization of former adversaries.

References

Adams, J. S. (1965). Inequity in social exchange. In L. (1965). Berkowitz (Ed.), *Advances in experimental social psychology* (Vol. 2, pp. 267–299). New York, NY: Academic Press.

Agger, I., & Jensen, J. B. (1990). Testimony as ritual and evidence in psychotherapy for political refugees. *Journal of Traumatic Stress, 3,* 115–130.

Allan, A., Allan, M. M., Kaminer, D., & Stein, D. J. (2006). Exploration of the association between apology and forgiveness amongst victims of human rights violations. *Behavioral Sciences and The Law, 24*(1), 87–102.

Allport, G. W. (1954). *The nature of prejudice.* Reading, MA: Addison-Wesley.

Amodio, D. M., Harmon-Jones, E., Devine, P. G., Curtin, J. J., Hartley, S. L., & Covert, A. E. (2004). Neural signals for the detection of unintentional race bias. *Psychological Science, 15*(2), 88–93.

Avenanti, A., Sirigu, A., & Aglioti, S. M. (2010). Racial bias reduces empathic sensorimotor resonance with other-race pain. *Current Biology, 20*(11), 1018–1022.

Baron, A. S., & Banaji, M. R. (2006). The development of implicit attitudes. Evidence of race evaluations from ages 6 and 10 and adulthood. *Psychological Science, 17*(1), 53–58.

Basoglu, M., Paker, M., Paker, O., Ozmen, E., Marks, I., Incesu, C., et al. (1994). Psychological effects of torture: A comparison of tortured with nontortured political activists in Turkey. *The American Journal of Psychiatry, 151*(1), 76–81.

Boraine, A., Levy, J., & Scheffer, R. (1997). *Dealing with the past: Truth and reconciliation in South Africa* (2nd ed.). Cape Town: IDASA.

Byrne, C. C. (2004). Benefit or burden: Victims' reflections on TRC participation. *Journal of Peace Psychology, 10,* 237–256.

Charasse-Pouele, C., & Fournier, M. (2006). Health disparities between racial groups in South Africa: A decomposition analysis. *Social Science and Medicine, 62*(11), 2897–2914.

Cheng, Y., Hung, A., & Decety, J. (2012). Dissociation between affective sharing and emotion understanding in juvenile psychopaths. *Development and Psychopathology, 24,* 623–636.

Cheng, Y., Lin, C. P., Liu, H. L., Hsu, Y. Y., Lim, K. E., Hung, D., et al. (2007). Expertise modulates the perception of pain in others. *Current Biology, 17*(19), 1708–1713.

Cheon, B. K., Im, D. M., Harada, T., Kim, J. S., Mathur, V. A., Scimeca, J. M., et al. (2011). Cultural influences on neural basis of intergroup empathy. *NeuroImage, 57*(2), 642–650.

Chiao, J. Y. (2011). Towards a cultural neuroscience of empathy and prosociality. *Emotion Review, 3*(1), 111–112.

Chiao, J. Y., & Mathur, V. A. (2010). Intergroup empathy: How does race affect empathic neural responses? *Current Biology, 20*(11), R478–R480.

Cienfuegos, A. J., & Monelli, C. (1983). The testimony of political repression as a therapeutic instrument. *The American Journal of Orthopsychiatry, 53*(1), 43–51.

Coyle, C. T., & Enright, R. D. (1997). Forgiveness intervention with postabortion men. *Journal of Consulting and Clinical Psychology, 65*(6), 1042–1046.

Decety, J. (2011). Dissecting the neural mechanisms mediating empathy. *Emotion Review, 3*(1), 92–108.

Decety, J., & Lamm, C. (2006). Human empathy through the lens of social neuroscience. *The Scientific World Journal, 6,* 1146–1163.

Devine, P. G. (1989). Stereotypes and prejudice: Their automatic and controlled components. *Journal of Personality and Social Psychology, 56*(1), 5–18.

Devine, P. G., Monteith, M. J., Zuwerink, J. R., & Elliot, A. J. (1991). Prejudice with and without compunction. *Journal of Personality and Social Psychology, 60*(6), 817–830.

Foster, D., Davis, D., & Sandler, D. (1987). *Detention and torture in South Africa.* Cape Town: David Philip.

Freedman, S. R., & Enright, R. D. (1996). Forgiveness as an intervention goal with incest survivors. *Journal of Consulting and Clinical Psychology, 64*(5), 983–992.

Gilligan, J. (1997). *Violence: Reflections on a national epidemic.* New York, NY: Random House, Inc.

Gobodo-Madikizela, P. (2002). Remorse, forgiveness, and rehumanization: Stories from South Africa. *Journal of Humanistic Psychology, 42*(1), 7–32.

Gobodo-Madikizela, P. (2003). *A human being died that night: A South African story of forgiveness: Boston, MA.* Houghton Mifflin.

Gobodo-Madikizela, P. (2008a). Empathetic repair after mass trauma. When vengeance is arrested. *European Journal of Social Theory, 11*(3), 331–350.

Gobodo-Madikizela, P. (2008b). Trauma, forgiveness and the witnessing dance: Making public spaces intimate. *Journal of Analytical Psychology, 53*(2), 169–188.

Halpern, J. (2001). *From detached concern to empathy: Humanizing medical practice.* Oxford: Oxford University Press.

Halpern, J., & Weinstein, H. M. (2004). Rehumanizing the other: Empathy and reconciliation. *Human Rigths Quarterly, 26*(3), 561–583.

Haney, C., Banks, W., & Zimbardo, C. (1973). Interpersonal dynamics in a simulated prison. *International Journal of Criminology and Penology, 9*(1–69–97)

Herman, A. A., Stein, D. J., Seedat, S., Heeringa, S. G., Moomal, H., & Williams, D. R. (2009). The South African Stress and Health (SASH) study: 12-month and lifetime prevalence of common mental disorders. *South African Medical Journal, 99*(5 Pt 2), 339–344.

Hornstein, H. A. (1978). Promotive tension and prosocial behavior: A Lewinian analysis. In L. Wispe (Ed.), *Altruism, sympathy, and helping: Psychological and sociological principles (pp. 177–207).* New York, NY: Academic.

Jung, C. G. (1938). Psychological reflections: A Jung anthology. *Psychological Aspects of the Mother Archetype, 9*

Kaminer, D., & Stein, D. J. (2001). Sadistic personality disorder in perpetrators of human rights abuses: A South African case study. *Journal of Personality Disorders, 15*(6), 475–486.

Kaminer, D., Stein, D. J., Mbanga, I., & Zungu-Dirwayi, N. (2001). The Truth and Reconciliation Commission in South Africa: Relation to psychiatric status and forgiveness among survivors of human rights abuses. *British Journal of Psychiatry, 178,* 373–377.

Krieger, N. (1990). Racial and gender discrimination: Risk factors for high blood pressure? *Social Science and Medicine, 30*(12), 1273–1281.

Kristeva, J. (1987). *Black sun.* New York, NY: Columbia University Press.

Lamm, C., Meltzoff, A. N., & Decety, J. (2009). How do we empathize with someone who is not like us? A functional magnetic resonance imaging study. *Journal of Cognitive Neuroscience, 22*(2), 362–376.

Macaskill, A., Maltby, J., & Day, L. (2002). Forgiveness of self and others and emotional empathy. *Journal of Social Psychology, 142*(5), 663–665.

McCullough, M. E., Fincham, F. D., & Tsang, J. A. (2003). Forgiveness, forbearance, and time: The temporal unfolding of transgression-related interpersonal motivations. *Journal of Personality and Social Psychology, 84*(3), 540–557.

Milgram, S. (1963). Behavioral study of obedience. *Journal of Abnormal and Social Psychology, 67*, 371–378.

Monteith, M. J., & Voils, C. I. (1998). Proneness to prejudiced responses: Toward understanding the authenticity of self-reported discrepancies. *Journal of Personality and Social Psychology, 75*(4), 901–916.

Montoya, E. R., Terburg, D., Bos, P. A., & van Honk, J. (2012). Testosterone, cortisol, and serotonin as key regulators of social aggression: A review and theoretical perspective. *Motivation and Emotion, 36*(1), 65–73.

Moomal, H., Jackson, P. B., Stein, D. J., Herman, A., Myer, L., Seedat, S., et al. (2009). Perceived discrimination and mental health disorders: The South African Stress and Health study. *South African Medical Journal, 99*(5 Pt 2), 383–389.

Orr, W. (1998). The Truth and Reconciliation Commission. *Continuing Medical Education (Medical Association of South Africa), 16*, 142–143.

Phelps, E. A., O'Connor, K. J., Cunningham, W. A., Funayama, E. S., Gatenby, J. C., Gore, J. C., et al. (2000). Performance on indirect measures of race evaluation predicts amygdala activation. *Journal of Cognitive Neuroscience, 12*(5), 729–738.

Rhodes, R. (1999). *Why they kill: The discoveries of a Maverick Criminologist*. New York, NY: Random House, Inc.

Seedat, S., Stein, D. J., Jackson, P. B., Heeringa, S. G., Williams, D. R., & Myer, L. (2009). Life stress and mental disorders in the South African stress and health study. *South African Medical Journal, 99*(5 Pt 2), 375–382.

Staub, E. (1989). *The roots of evil: The origins of genocide and other group violence*. New York, NY: Cambridge University Press.

Stein, D. J. (1998). Psychiatric aspects of the truth and reconciliation commission in South Africa. *British Journal of Psychiatry, 173*, 455–457.

Stein, D. J. (2000). The neurobiology of evil: Psychiatric perspectives on perpetrators. *Ethnicity and Health, 5*(3–4), 303–315.

Stein, D. J. (2005). Empathy: At the heart of the mind. *CNS Spectrums, 10*(10), 780–783.

Stein, D. J., & Kaminer, D. (2006). Forgiveness and psychopathology: Psychobiological and evolutionary underpinnings. *CNS Spectrums, 11*(2), 87–89.

Stein, D. J., Kaminer, D., Zungu-Dirwayi, N., & Seedat, S. (2006). Pros and cons of medicalization: The example of trauma. *The World Journal of Biological Psychiatry, 7*(1), 2–4.

Stein, D. J., Seedat, S., Kaminer, D., Moomal, H., Herman, A., Sonnega, J., et al. (2008). The impact of the Truth and Reconciliation Commission on psychological distress and forgiveness in South Africa. *Social Psychiatry and Psychiatric Epidemiology, 43*(6), 462–468.

Swartz, L. (1998). *Thinking about culture and mental health: A Southern African view*. Cape Town: Oxford University Press.

Thomas, E. F., McGarty, C., & Mavor, K. I. (2009). Transforming "apathy into movement": The role of prosocial emotions in motivating action for social change. *Personality and Social Psychology Review, 13*(4), 310–333.

Turner, J., & Onorato, R. S. (1999). Social identity, personality, and the self-concept: A self-categorization perspective. In T. R. Tyler, R. M. Kramer, & O. P. John (Eds.), *The psychology of the social self (pp. 11–46)*. Mahwah, NJ: Lawrence Erlbaum Associates.

van Honk, J., Schutter, D. J., Bos, P. A., Kruijt, A. W., Lentjes, E. G., & Baron-Cohen, S. (2011). Testosterone administration impairs cognitive empathy in women depending on second-to-fourth digit ratio. *Proceedings of the National Academy of Sciences of the United States of America, 108*(8), 3448–3452.

Watt, D. (2007). *Toward a neuroscience of empathy: Integrating affective and cognitive perspectives, 9*(2), 119–140.

Williams, D. R., Gonzalez, H. M., Williams, S., Mohammed, S. A., Moomal, H., & Stein, D. J. (2008). Perceived discrimination, race and health in South Africa. *Social Science and Medicine, 67*(3), 441–452.

Williams, D. R., Yan, Y., Jackson, J. S., & Anderson, N. B. (1997). Racial differences in physical and mental health: Socio-economic status, stress and discrimination. *Journal of Health Psychology, 2*(3), 335–351.

Wilson, T. D., Lindsey, S., & Schooler, T. Y. (2000). A model of dual attitudes. *Psychological Review, 107*(1), 101–126.

Worthington, E. L., Kurusu, T. A., Collins, W., Berry, J. W., Ripley, J. S., & Baier, S. N. (2000). Forgiveness usually takes time. *Journal of Psychology and Theology, 28*, 3–20.

Xu, X., Zuo, X., Wang, X., & Han, S. (2009). Do you feel my pain? Racial group membership modulates empathic neural responses. *Journal of Neuroscience, 29*(26), 8525–8529.

Yehuda, R., & McFarlane, A. C. (1995). Conflict between current knowledge about posttraumatic stress disorder and its original conceptual basis. *American Journal of Psychiatry, 152*(12), 1705–1713.

CPSIA information can be obtained at www.ICGtesting.com
Printed in the USA
BVOW08*0103060813

327718BV00008B/96/P